Bare-Faced Messiah

Also by Russell Miller

BUNNY, THE REAL STORY OF PLAYBOY

THE HOUSE OF GETTY

BARE-FACED MESSIAH

The True Story of
L. Ron Hubbard

RUSSELL MILLER

HENRY HOLT AND COMPANY
New York

Copyright © 1987 by Russell Miller
All rights reserved, including the right to reproduce
this book or portions thereof in any form.
First published in the United States in 1988 by
Henry Holt and Company, Inc., 115 West 18th Street,
New York, New York 10011.

Library of Congress Cataloging–in–Publication Data
Miller, Russell.
Bare-faced Messiah.
Bibliography: p.
Includes index.
1. Hubbard, L. Ron (La Fayette Ron), 1911–
2. Scientologists—Biography. I. Title.
BP605.S2M55   1988   299′.936′0924   (B)   88-2005
ISBN 0-8050-0654-0

First American Edition

Printed in the United States of America
1 3 5 7 9 10 8 6 4 2

ISBN 0-8050-0654-0

*This book is dedicated to all those
Scientologists who had the courage
to face the truth and speak out*

Contents

Eight pages of photographs follow page 182.

Author's Note

I would like to be able to thank the officials of the Church of Scientology for their help in compiling this biography, but I am unable to do so because the price of their co-operation was effective control of the manuscript and it was a price I was unwilling to pay. Thereafter the Church did its best to dissuade people who knew Hubbard from speaking to me and constantly threatened litigation. Scientology lawyers in New York and Los Angeles made it clear in frequent letters that they expected me to libel and defame L. Ron Hubbard. When I protested that in thirty years as a journalist and writer I had never been accused of libel, I was apparently investigated and a letter was written to my publishers in New York alleging that my claim was 'simply not accurate'. It was, and is.

This book could not have been written without the assistance of the many former Scientologists who were prepared to give freely of their time to talk about their experiences, notwithstanding considerable risks. Some of them are named in the narrative, but there were many others who provided background information and to them all I pay tribute. I was deeply impressed by their integrity, intelligence and courage.

This book could also not have been written without the existence of the Freedom of Information Act in the United States, which may give pause for thought to those who care about the truth yet are opposing the introduction of similar legislation in Britain.

A special word of thanks is due to Jon Atack, a former Scientologist resident in East Grinstead, who has assembled one of the most comprehensive archives about Scientology and its founder and generously made his files available to me. I would also like to thank George Hay and John Symonds in London; Lydia and Jimmy Hicks in Washington DC; David and Milo Weaver in San Francisco; Connie and Phil Winberry in Seattle; Skip Davis in Newport, Rhode Island; Diane Lewis in Wichita; Arthur Jean Cox, Lawrence Kristiansen and Boris de Sidis in Los Angeles; Ron Newman in Woodside, California; Ron Howard of George Washington University; Sue Lindsay of the *Rocky Mountain News*, Denver; Dave Walters of the Montana

Historical Society; and the ever-helpful staff of the Library of Congress. Too many people to name patiently replied to queries by mail and searched their records for the answers to innumerable obscure questions. Their contribution to the whole picture was invaluable.

My editor, Jennie Davies, polished the manuscript with her usual skill and diligence, despite the demands of her newly-born twins. My wife, Renate, read every chapter as it was written and always offered constructive advice. She had to put up with my long absences abroad while I was tracking down the truth about L. Ron Hubbard and then endure the misery of living with an obsessive author through the long months of writing. I could never thank her enough for her patience, love and support.

Russell Miller
Buckinghamshire
England

Introduction

For more than thirty years, the Church of Scientology has vigorously promoted an image of its founder, L. Ron Hubbard, as a romantic adventurer and philosopher whose early life fortuitously prepared him, in the manner of Jesus Christ, for his declared mission to save the world. The glorification of 'Ron', superman and saviour, required a cavalier disregard for facts: thus it is that almost every biography of Hubbard published by the church is interwoven with lies, half-truths and ludicrous embellishments. The wondrous irony of this deception is that the true story of L. Ron Hubbard is much more bizarre, much more improbable, than any of the lies.

The Revelation of Ron

It was a scene that could have been ripped from the yellowing pages of the pulp science fiction that L. Ron Hubbard wrote in the Thirties . . .

A strangely alien group of young people who believe they are immortal set up a secret base in an abandoned health spa in the desert in southern California. Fearful of outsiders, they suspect they have been discovered by the FBI. In a panic, they begin to destroy any documents that might incriminate their leader. It is essential they protect him, for they believe he alone can save the world.

Searching through the top floor of a derelict hotel, one of their number discovers a stack of battered cardboard boxes and begins pulling out faded photographs, dog-eared manuscripts, diaries written in a childish scrawl and school reports. There are twenty-one boxes in all, each stuffed with memorabilia, even baby clothes.

The young man rummaging through the boxes is ecstatic. He is certain he has made a discovery of profound significance, for all the material documents the early life of his leader. At last, he thinks, it will be possible to refute all the lies spread by their enemies. At last it will be possible to prove to the world, beyond doubt, that his leader really is a genius and miracle worker . . .

Thus was the stage set for the inexorable unmasking of L. Ron Hubbard, the saviour who never was.

* * * * *

Gerry Armstrong, the man kneeling in the dust on the top floor of the old Del Sol Hotel at Gilman Hot Springs that afternoon in January 1980, had been a dedicated member of the Church of Scientology for more than a decade. He was logging in Canada when a friend introduced him to Scientology in 1969 and he was immediately swept away by its heady promise of superhuman powers and immortality. During his years as a Scientologist, he had twice been sentenced to long periods in the Rehabilitation Project Force, the cult's own Orwellian prison; he had been constantly humiliated and his marriage had been destroyed, yet he remained totally convinced that L. Ron Hubbard was the greatest man who ever lived.

The dauntless loyalty Hubbard inspired among his followers was tantamount to a form of mind control. Scientology flourished in the post-war era of protest and uncertainty when young people were searching for a sense of belonging or meaning to their lives. Hubbard offered both, promised answers and nurtured an inner-group feeling of exclusiveness which separated Scientologists from the real world. Comforted by a sense of esoteric knowledge, of exaltation and self-absorption, they were ready to follow Ron through the very gates of Hell if need be.

At the time Armstrong discovered the treasure trove of memorabilia at Gilman Hot Springs, Hubbard had been in hiding for years. His location was known only as 'X', but Armstrong knew that it was possible to get a message to him and he petitioned for permission to begin researching an official biography, forcefully arguing that it would prepare the ground for 'universal acceptance' of Scientology. He saw it as the forerunner of a major motion picture based on Hubbard's life and the eventual establishment of an archive in an L. Ron Hubbard Museum.

By then Hubbard was nearly seventy years old and had lived so long in a world of phantasmagoria that he was unable to distinguish between fact and his own fantastic fiction. He believed he was the teenage explorer, swashbuckling hero, sage and philosopher his biographies said he was. It was perhaps too late for him to comprehend that his life, in reality, far outstripped the fabricated version. He made the leap from penniless science-fiction writer to millionaire guru and prophet in a single, effortless bound; he led a private navy across the oceans of the world for nearly a decade; he came close to taking over control of several countries; he was worshipped by thousands of his followers around the world and was detested and feared by most governments. He was a story-spinning maverick whose singular life eclipsed even his own far-fetched stories. Yet he clung tenaciously to the fiction and when Armstrong's petition to research his biography arrived at his hide-out that January in 1980, he unhesitatingly gave his approval.

Armstrong had no experience as an archivist or researcher, but he was intelligent, industrious, honest and enthusiastic. He moved all the relevant documentation from Gilman Hot Springs to the Scientology headquarters in Los Angeles, where it filled six filing cabinets, and began cataloguing and indexing the material, making copies of everything and reverently preserving the originals in plastic envelopes, acutely aware of their historical importance.

Not long after he had started work, posters appeared in Scientology offices announcing the private screening of a 1940 Warner Brothers movie, *The Dive Bomber*, for which Hubbard had written the screenplay. Every Scientologist knew that Ron had been a successful

Hollywood screenwriter before the war and the screening was to raise funds for the defence of the eleven Scientologists, including Hubbard's wife, who had been indicted in Washington on conspiracy charges. Armstrong decided to help by finding out a little more about Ron's contribution to the film, but at the library of the Academy of Motion Picture Arts and Sciences in Los Angeles he was puzzled to discover that two other writers had been credited with the screenplay of *The Dive Bomber*.

Armstrong remonstrated with the librarian, then sent a memo to Ron to tell him about the mistake in the Academy records. Hubbard replied with a cheery note explaining that Warner Brothers had been in such a hurry to distribute the movie that it was already in the can before it was realized that his name had been left off the credits. He was busy at that time, closing up his posh apartment on Riverside Drive in New York and getting ready to go to war, so he just told the studio to mail the cheque to him at the Explorers Club. After the war, he used the money to take a holiday in the Caribbean.

It was an explanation with which Armstrong was perfectly satisfied except for one niggling worry: like all Scientologists, he had been told that Ron was blind and crippled at the end of the war and that he had only been able to make a recovery because of the power of his mind. Clearly, Armstrong mused, he would not have taken the holiday until after his recovery. In an attempt to fit together the chronology of events, Armstrong made an application under the Freedom of Information Act for Hubbard's US Navy records.

Scientologists were enormously proud of the fact that the founder of their church was a much-decorated war hero who had served in all five theaters and was wounded several times; indeed he was the first US casualty of the war in the Pacific. It was then, with a sense of mounting disbelief and dismay, that Armstrong leafed through Hubbard's records after they had arrived from Washington. He went from one document to another, searching in vain for an explanation, still refusing to believe the evidence of his own eyes: the record seemed to indicate that Hubbard, far from being a hero, was an incompetent, malingering coward who had done his best to avoid seeing action.

Armstrong would not believe it. He set the documents aside and resolved to start his research at the beginning, in Montana, where Hubbard had grown up on his grandfather's huge cattle ranch. But he could find no trace of any property owned by the family, except a little house in the middle of Helena. Neither could he discover any documentation covering Hubbard's teenage wanderings through China. In Washington DC, where Hubbard was supposed to have graduated in mathematics and engineering from George Washington University, the record showed he dropped out after two years because of poor grades. And of Hubbard's fabled expeditions as an explorer there was similarly no sign.

'I was finding contradiction after contradiction,' Armstrong said. 'I kept trying to justify them, kept thinking that I would find another document that would explain everything. But I didn't. I slowly came to realize that the guy had consistently lied about himself.'

By the summer of 1981, Armstrong had assembled more than 250,000 pages of documentation about the founder of the Church of Scientology, but despite the gaping holes appearing in Hubbard's credibility, he remained intensely loyal. 'My approach was, OK, now we know he's human and tells lies. What we've got to do is clear up the lies so that all the good he has done for the world will be accepted. I thought the only way we could exist as an organisation was to let the truth stand. After all, the truth was equally as fascinating as the lies.'

Armstrong's pleas to clear up the lies fell on deaf ears. Since Hubbard had gone into seclusion, the Church of Scientology had been taken over by young militants known as 'messengers'. When Hubbard was the commodore of his own navy, the messengers were little nymphets in hot pants and halter tops who ran errands for him and competed with each other to find ways of pleasing him. Eventually they helped him dress and undress, performed little domestic tasks like washing his hair and smearing rejuvenating cream on his fleshy features, and even followed him around with an ashtray to catch the falling ash from his cigarettes. As the commodore became more and more paranoid, beset by imagined traitors and enemies, the messengers became more and more powerful.

In November 1981 Armstrong presented a written report to the messengers, listing the false claims made about Hubbard and putting forward a powerful argument as to why they should be corrected. 'If we present inaccuracies, hyperbole or downright lies as fact or truth,' he wrote, 'it doesn't matter what slant we give them; if disproved, the man will look, to outsiders at least, like a charlatan . . .'

The messengers' response was to order Armstrong to be 'security checked' – interrogated as a potential traitor. Armstrong refused. In the spring of 1982, Gerald Armstrong was accused of eighteen different 'crimes' and 'high crimes' against the Church of Scientology, including theft, false pretences and promulgating false information about the church and its founder. He was declared to be a 'suppressive person' and 'fair game', which meant he could be 'tricked, cheated, lied to, sued or destroyed' by his former friends in Scientology.

'By then the whole thing for me had crumbled,' he said. 'I realized I had been drawn into Scientology by a web of lies, by Machiavellian mental control techniques and by fear. The betrayal of trust began with Hubbard's lies about himself. His life was a continuing pattern of fraudulent business practices, tax evasion, flight from creditors and hiding from the law.

'He was a mixture of Adolf Hitler, Charlie Chaplin and Baron Münchhausen. In short, he was a con man.'

Chapter 1

A Dubious Prodigy

According to the colourful yarn spun for the benefit of his followers, L. Ron Hubbard was descended on his mother's side from a French nobleman, one Count de Loupe, who took part in the Norman invasion of England in 1066; on his father's side, the Hubbards were English settlers who had arrived in America in the nineteenth century. It was altogether a distinguished naval family: both his maternal great-grandfather, 'Captain' I. C. DeWolfe, and his grandfather, 'Captain' Lafayette Waterbury, 'helped make American naval history'[1], while his father was 'Commander' Harry Ross Hubbard, US Navy.

As his father was away at sea for lengthy periods, the story goes, little Ron grew up on his wealthy grandfather's enormous cattle ranch in Montana, said to cover a quarter of the state [approximately 35,000 square miles!]. His picturesque friends were frontiersmen, cowboys and an Indian medicine man. 'L. Ron Hubbard found the life of a young rancher very enjoyable. Long days were spent riding, breaking broncos, hunting coyote and taking his first steps as an explorer. For it was in Montana that he had his first encounter with another culture – the Blackfoot [Pikuni] Indians. He became a blood brother of the Pikuni and was later to write about them in his first published novel, *Buckskin Brigades*. When he was ten years old, in 1921, he rejoined his family. His father, alarmed at his apparent lack of formal learning, immediately put him under intense instruction to make up for the time he had "lost" in the wilds of Montana. So it was that by the time he was twelve years old, L. Ron Hubbard had already read a goodly number of the world's greatest classics – and his interest in religion and philosophy was born.'[2]

* * * * *

Virtually none of this is true. The real story of L. Ron Hubbard's early life is considerably more prosaic and begins not on a cattle ranch but in a succession of rented apartments necessarily modest since his father was a struggling white-collar clerk drifting from job to job. His grandfather was neither a distinguished sea captain nor a wealthy

rancher but a small-time veterinarian who supplemented his income
renting out horses and buggies from a livery barn. It is true, however,
that his name was Lafayette O. Waterbury.

As far as anyone knew, the Waterburys came from the Catskills, the
dark-forested mountain range in New York State celebrated in the
early nineteenth century as the setting for Washington Irving's
popular short story about Rip Van Winkle – a character only
marginally more fantastic than the Waterburys' most famous scion.

Shortly before the turmoil of the Civil War divided the nation,
Abram Waterbury and his young wife, Margaret, left the Catskills to
join the thousands of hopeful settlers trekking west in covered wagons
to seek a better future. By 1863 he had set up in business as a
veterinarian in Grand Rapids, Michigan, and on 25 July 1864,
Margaret gave birth to a son whom they named Lafayette, perhaps
after the town in Indiana at which they had stopped on their journey
before turning north to Grand Rapids.

Lafayette, undoubtedly thankful to be known to his friends as Lafe,
learned the veterinary trade from his father and married before he was
twenty. His bride was twenty-one-year-old Ida Corinne DeWolfe,
from Hampshire, Illinois. Diminutive in stature, Ida was a gentle,
intelligent, strong-willed young woman whose mother had died in
childbirth, with her eighth child, when Ida was sixteen. John
DeWolfe, her father, was a wealthy banker who clung to a fanciful
family legend about the origins of the DeWolfes in Europe. Details
and dates were vague, but the essence of the story was that a courtier
accompanying a prince on a hunting expedition in France had
somehow saved his master from an attack by a wolf; in gratitude the
prince had ennobled the faithful courtier, bestowing upon him the
title of Count de Loupe, a name that was eventually anglicized to
DeWolfe. [No records exist to support this story, either in Britain or
France; Vice-Admiral Harry De Wolf, twelfth-generation descendant
of Balthazar De Wolf, the first De Wolf in America, says he has never
heard of Count de Loupe.[3]]

DeWolfe offered the young couple the use of a farm he owned in
Nebraska on condition that Lafe would maintain and improve the
property. It was at Burnett, a settlement on the Elkhorn river, one
hundred miles west of Omaha, which had recently been opened up by
the arrival of the Sioux City and Pacific Railroad.

Burnett was an unremarkable cluster of log cabins, dug-outs and
ramshackle pine huts huddled in a lazy curve of the river and
surrounded by gently rolling prairie. It might never have appeared on
any map had not the homesteaders persuaded the railroad to make a
halt nearby. The first train arrived in 1879 and thereafter the town
developed around the railroad depot rather than the river; within a

few years a general store, saloon and livery stable were in business. The Davis House Hotel, opened in 1884, was considered the finest on the whole Fremont, Elkhorn and Missouri Valley Railroad.

By the time Lafe and Ida Waterbury arrived in Burnett, soon after the opening of the hotel, Ida was heavy with child; a daughter, Ledora May, was born in 1885. During the next twenty years Ida would produce seven more children and selflessly devote herself to the upbringing of a happy, close and high-spirited family.

For a couple of years Lafe worked his father-in-law's farm, but a bitter family row developed when DeWolfe indicated his intention to exclude his other children and leave the property solely to Ida and Lafe. Rather than be the cause of strife in the family, Lafe moved out, opened a livery stable in town on Second Street and established himself as a veterinarian. His business was a success because he was well-liked and respected in the area, particularly after playing a starring role in a local domestic drama which briefly held the town gossips in thrall. Ida's sister, who had also moved to Burnett, woke up one morning to discover that her husband had left her and taken their infant son with him to New York. Lafe immediately packed his bags, set off for New York by train, tracked down the erring husband and returned to Burnett in triumph, his nephew in his arms.

When Ida gave birth to another daughter in 1886, it was a typically warm-hearted gesture that prompted them to name the baby Toilie. A young man who used to hang around the livery stable had been engaged to a girl called Toilie before he became mentally deranged; whenever he felt 'strange' he would always, for some reason, seek out Lafe and find reassurance from his company. When he learned that Ida and Lafe had had another daughter, he shyly asked if they would call her Toilie, after the sweetheart he knew he would never be able to marry. Years later the irreverent Toilie would say 'I'm nuts because I was named by a crazy man' and shriek with laughter.

Toilie was still a baby when hard times hit Burnett. In January 1887 a catastrophic blizzard swept across the plains west of the Mississippi, killing thousands of head of cattle; most of the local ranchers were ruined overnight. The farmers fared no better, for that terrible winter was followed by a succession of blistering summers accompanied by plagues of grasshoppers which devastated the already sparse crops. But at a point when many of the despairing townsfolk were talking about giving up the struggle against the unforgiving elements, the climate suddenly improved and the detested grasshoppers disappeared; unlike many small towns in the Nebraska prairie, Burnett survived the crisis.

By 1899 the local newspaper, the *Burnett Citizen*, was able to report, as evidence of increasing prosperity, that Lafe Waterbury was among those who had built new dwelling houses in the town that year. It was a fine, two-storey, wood-frame house on Elm Street, sheltered at the front by two huge elm trees. At the rear, beyond a stand of willows, it overlooked prairie stretching away into hazy infinity; deer and antelope often ventured within sight of the back yard and at night the howls of coyotes made the children shiver in their beds.

The Waterburys certainly needed the space offered by their new home, for by now May and Toilie had been joined by Ida Irene (called Midgie by the family because she was so small), a brother Ray, and two more sisters, Louise and Hope. Another two girls, Margaret and June, would follow in 1903 and 1905. Lafe and Ida doted on their children, thoroughly enjoyed their company and liked nothing more than when the house was full of noise and laughter. Ida was determined that her children would have a happier upbringing than her own – she never forgot being constantly beaten at school for writing with her left hand – and as a consequence the Waterburys were unusually relaxed parents for their time, encouraging their offspring to attend church on Sundays, for example, but caring little which church they attended. Surprisingly, there was considerable choice. For a small town with a population of less than a thousand people, Burnett was an excessively God-fearing community and supported four thriving churches – Baptist, Lutheran, Methodist and Catholic.

Lafe and Ida always claimed they were too busy to go to church themselves, although Lafe openly declared, to his children, his ambivalence towards religion: 'Some of the finest men I have ever known were preachers,' he liked to say, 'and some of the biggest hypocrites I have ever known were preachers.' He was a large, bluff man with an irrepressible sense of humour, a talent for mimicry and a hint of the showman about him: he often used to announce his intention to put all his children on the stage. In the evenings, when he had had a drink or two, he would sit on the porch and play his fiddle, which had a negro's head carved at the end of the shaft.

Tutored by Lafe, who was considered to be one of the best horsemen in Madison County, all the children learned to ride almost as soon as they could walk and each of them was allocated a pony from the Waterbury livery stable. Also quartered with the horses was the family cow, Star, who obligingly provided them every day with as much milk as they could drink.

In 1902, because of confusion with a similarly-named town nearby, the good folk of Burnett decided to change the name of their town to Tilden, thereby commemorating an unsuccessful presidential candidate, Samuel J. Tilden, who had contested the 1876 election won by Rutherford B. Hayes. May was the first of the Waterbury children to graduate, in 1904, from Tilden High School. Tall, outspoken and independent, she was an unashamed feminist – she was outraged when she read in the newspaper that a policeman in New York had arrested a woman for smoking in the street and thrilled to learn that deaf and blind Helen Keller had graduated from Radcliffe College the same year she graduated from Tilden. It surprised no one in the family when May announced that she wanted a career, declaring her belief that there must be more to life than caring for a husband and bearing children. Accordingly, and with the blessing of her parents, she set off for Omaha to train as a teacher. But by the time she had qualified as a high school and institute teacher, certificate of Nebraska, she was writing letters home about a young sailor she had met called 'Hub'.

Harry Ross Hubbard was not a descendent of a long line of Hubbards but an orphan. Born Henry August Wilson on 31 August 1886 at Fayette, Iowa, his mother had died when he was a baby and he had been adopted by a Mr and Mrs James Hubbard, farmers in Frederiksburg, Iowa, who changed his name to Harry Ross Hubbard.

At school, Harry was not a high flier. He briefly attended a business college at Norma Springs, Iowa, but dropped out when he realized he had little chance of a degree. On 1 September 1904, the day after his eighteenth birthday, he joined the United States Navy as an enlisted man. While serving as a yeoman on the *USS Pennsylvania*, he began writing 'romantic tales' of Navy life for newspapers back home, earning useful extra income. He was posted to the US Navy recruiting office in Omaha in 1906 when he met May Waterbury and it was not long before her plans for an independent career were more or less forgotten. They married on 25 April 1909, and by the summer of 1910 May was pregnant; her husband, now discharged from the Navy, had found work as a commercial teller in the advertising department of the *Omaha World Herald* newspaper.

The Waterburys, meanwhile, had left Tilden and moved to Durant in south-east Oklahoma, close to the border with Texas. Lafe had seen the first Model T. Ford trundle cautiously through the main street of Tilden and realized that his livery stable faced an uncertain future; when a close friend in Durant suggested to him that the warmer climate in the south would be better for all the family, he talked it over with Ida and they decided to go, making the eight hundred-mile trip by railroad. Ray, then sixteen, travelled with Star and the horses and fed and watered the animals during the journey.

Only Toilie stayed behind in Tilden. She was twenty-three and working as a nurse and secretary for Dr Stuart Campbell, who had opened a small hospital in a wood-frame house on Oak Street, just a block away from the Waterbury family home. Toilie was reluctant to give up her job and her parents readily accepted her decision not to go with them to Oklahoma.

Campbell, who had set up a practice in Tilden in 1900, had delivered Ida Waterbury's two youngest children, but it was the fact that Toilie was working for him that persuaded May to return to Tilden to give birth to her first child. With only a little more than a year between them, May and Toilie had always been close, walking to and from school arm in arm, sharing a bedroom and incessantly giggling together over childhood secrets.

Toilie was waiting at the railroad depot in Tilden at the end of February 1911 when May, helped by a solicitous Hub, heaved herself down from the train. Although Tilden was still no more than four dirt streets running north to south, intersected by four more running east–west, May noticed plenty of changes in the short time she had been away – four grain elevators had been built, three saloons and two pool halls had opened, Mrs Mayes was competing with the Botsford sisters in the millinery trade and there was even a new 'opera house' – true, it had yet to stage its first opera, but the road shows were always popular, particularly since Alexander's Ragtime Band had set the nation's feet tapping.

May did not have long to wait for the 'blessed event'. She went into labour during the afternoon of Friday 10 March, and Toilie arranged for her to be admitted immediately to Dr Campbell's hospital. At one minute past two o'clock the following morning, she was delivered of a son. She and Hub had already decided that if it was a boy, he would be named Lafayette Ronald Hubbard.

Ida and Lafe Waterbury did not see their first grandchild until Christmas 1911, when Hub, May and the baby arrived to spend the holiday with them in Durant. Lafe, who had been out treating a neighbour's horse, burst into the house, threw his hat on the floor and leaned over the crib to shake his grandson's hand. Baby Ron smiled obligingly and Lafe whooped with pleasure, trumpeting at his wife: 'Look, the little son of a bitch knows me already.'

The biggest surprise for the family was that Ron had a startling thatch of fluffy orange hair. Hub was dark-haired and the Waterburys had no more than a hint of auburn in their colouring – nothing like the impish little carrot-top who gurgled happily as he was passed from one lap to another. Seven-year-old Margaret, known in the family as Marnie, spoke for everyone when she proclaimed her new nephew to be 'cute as a bug's ear'.

During that Christmas May told her parents that Hub had got a new job on a newspaper in Kalispell, Montana, and that they would be moving there from Omaha in the New Year. She was hopeful that it would prove to be a step up for them.

In the spring of 1912, May began writing long and enthusiastic letters from Kalispell. Perhaps missing the family, she often hinted that they might consider joining her and Hub in Montana. Kalispell was a fine, modern city, she wrote, with paved streets, electric lighting and many fine houses. The surrounding Flathead Valley was famous for its fruit and at blossom time the orchards of apples, peaches, pears, cherries and plums had to be seen to be believed. One Kalispell farmer, Fred Whiteside, was so confident about the quality of his fruit that he boasted he would give $1000 to anyone finding a worm in one of his apples.

May's letters gave her parents much to think about, for they both recognized that the move to Oklahoma had not been a success. When they first arrived in Durant, Lafe bought a livery barn on the outskirts of town and for several months the whole family lived in the hayloft above the animals. They built a cookhouse on the property so they had somewhere to eat their meals and then started on a house.

None of the children minded the privations in the least – indeed, they rather enjoyed thinking of themselves as true pioneers – but Lafe found the humid summers very debilitating. It made May's description of the blossoms in Montana all the more enticing.

Ida had been deeply disturbed by an incident that occurred soon after they moved into their new house. A negro raped a white woman in the town and while a posse was out looking for him, a rumour took hold that there was going to be a negro uprising, causing something approaching panic, particularly in remote outlying areas. At nightfall, Lafe and Ray took guns and went out on horses to protect the approaches to their property, while the girls waited behind barred windows, watching flares bounce through the night and listening to the rattle of cartwheels as farmers shepherded their families into the safety of the town.

Although there was no uprising, both Ida and Lafe were concerned that there might be a 'next time' and they did not want to feel that their safety depended on their willingness to protect themselves with guns. In the fall of 1912, the Waterburys once again sold their house, packed up their belongings and loaded their livestock on to railcars, this time bound for Kalispell, Montana, 1500 miles to the north-west. Long delays at railheads, while waiting with their freight cars to be picked up by north-bound trains, added days to the journey and it was a week before they were hooked on to a Great Northern Railway train labouring across the Rocky Mountains through the spectacular passes that led to Kalispell.

The family reunion was the happiest of occasions and no one received more attention than Ron, who had learned to take his first faltering steps. 'He was very much the love child of the whole family,' said Marnie. 'He was adored by everyone. I can still see that mop of red hair running around.'

Lafe found a small house in Orchard Park, a short walk from May and Hub's home and only a block from the fairground, where he hoped to find work as a veterinarian. With only two bedrooms, it was not nearly big enough for the Waterbury tribe, but it had a barn that would accommodate all the horses and still leave enough room for the long-suffering and widely-travelled Star. Marnie and June, the two youngest children, were given one of the bedrooms and Lafe built a big wood-frame tent in the yard for the other four: inside, it was divided by a canvas screen – Ray slept on a bunk on one side and Midgie, Louise and Hope were on the other. They had a stove to keep them warm in the winter and were perfectly content. On summer evenings, Marnie and June often heard their older sisters whispering and tittering in the tent and sometimes they crept outside to join them and share the cherries they stole almost every night from a neighbouring garden.

The Waterburys were happy in Kalispell: Ida and Lafe made no secret of the pleasure they took in being able to see their grandson every day; Midgie met her future husband, Bob, in the town; and Ray developed an impressive talent for training horses. Under his careful tuition, the family ponies learned tricks like counting by pawing the ground with a hoof and stealing handkerchiefs from his pocket. The Waterbury 'show horses', ridden by the Waterbury children, became a popular feature in the town parades and they always competed in the races at the fairground.

Baby Ron remained the centre of the family's attention and the star of the Waterbury photograph albums – Ron perched in an apple tree, Ron with Liberty Bill, their English bull terrier, on the porch of the Kalispell house, Ron trying to measure the back yard with a tape. Having clearly inherited something of his grandfather's showmanship, Ron thoroughly enjoyed being in the family spotlight.

Lafe was walking down Kalispell's main street one day with Marnie and Ron when he bumped into Samuel Stewart, the governor of Montana, whom he had met several times. 'Hey Sam,' he said, 'I'd like you to meet my little grandson, Ron.' Stewart stooped, solemnly shook hands with the boy and stood chatting to Lafe for a few minutes. After he had gone, Marnie, who had been neither introduced nor acknowledged, turned furiously on her father and snapped, 'Why didn't you introduce me? Don't I matter?' Lafe had the grace to apologize, but Marnie could see by his broad grin that he was not in the least repentant.

As well as being favoured so shamelessly, Ron could always count on the support of his many aunts in any family dispute. While he was learning to talk, he would frequently drive his mother to distraction by running round the house repeating the same, usually meaningless, word over and over again. One afternoon at the Waterbury home, the word was 'eskobiddle'. May, at the end of her patience, finally shouted at him: 'If you say that once more I'm going to go and wash your mouth out with soap.'

Ron looked coolly at her and smiled slowly. 'Eskobiddle!' he yelled at the top of his voice. May immediately dragged him off and carried out her threat. A few minutes later, Ida heard shrieks coming from the back yard and discovered Midgie and Louise holding May down and washing her mouth with soap to avenge their precious nephew.

Less than twelve months after the Waterburys arrived in Kalispell, May broke the news that she and Hub were going to move on; Hub was having problems with his job on the newspaper and had been offered a position as resident manager of the Family Theater in the state capital, Helena. Ida and Lafe were naturally upset but, as May said, Helena was only two hundred miles away and it was also on the Great Northern Railroad, so they would be able to visit each other frequently.

Nevertheless, it would not be the same, both doting grandparents gloomily concluded, as having little Ronald in and out of the house almost every day.

Helena in 1913 was a pleasant city of Victorian brick and stone buildings encircled by the Rocky Mountains, whose snow-dusted peaks stippled with pines provided a scenic backdrop in every direction. The Capital Building, with its massive copper dome and fluted doric columns, eloquently proclaimed its status as the first city of Montana, as did the construction of the neo-Gothic St Helena Cathedral, which was nearing completion on Warren Street. Electric streetcars clanked along the brick-paved main street, once a twisting mountain defile known as Last Chance Gulch in commemoration of the four prospectors who had unexpectedly struck gold there in 1864 and subsequently founded the city.

The Family Theater, at 21 Last Chance Gulch, occupied part of a handsome red-brick terrace with an ornate stone coping, but it suffered somewhat from its position, since it was in the heart of the city's red-light district and could not have been more inappropriately named. Respectable families arriving for the evening performance were required to avert their eyes from the colourful ladies leaning out of the windows of the brothels on each side of the theater, although it was not unknown for the occasional father to slip out after the show had started and return before the final curtain, curiously flushed.

Harry Hubbard's duties were to sell tickets during the day, collect them at the door as patrons arrived, maintain order if necessary during the show and lock up at the end of the evening. Although his title was resident manager, he chose not to live at the theater and rented a rickety little wooden house, not much better than a shack, on Henry Street, on the far side of the railroad track. May hated it and soon found a small apartment on the top floor of a house at 15 Rodney Street, closer to the theater and in a better part of town.

Travelling road shows, sometimes comprising not much more than a singer, pianist and a comedian, were the staple fare of the Family Theater. Ron was often allowed to see the show and he would sit with his mother in the darkened auditorium completely enthralled, no matter what the act. Years later he would recall sitting in a box at the age of two wearing his father's hat and applauding with such enthusiasm that the audience began cheering him rather than the cast. He claimed the players took twelve curtain calls before they realized what was happening.[4]

When the Waterburys paid a visit to Helena, Hub arranged for them to see the show, made sure they had the best seats in the house and solemnly stood at the door of the theater to collect their tickets as they filed in. Not long after their return to Kalispell, May heard that her father had slipped on a banana skin, fallen and broken his arm. She did not worry overmuch at first, even when her mother wrote to say that the arm had not been set properly and had had to be re-broken. Indeed, her worries were rather closer to home, for Harry had been told by the owner of the Family Theater that unless the audiences improved the theater might have to close.

The news from abroad was also giving cause for concern, despite Woodrow Wilson's promise to keep America out of the war threatening to engulf Europe. On Sunday 2 August 1914, headlines in the *Helena Independent* announced that Germany had declared war on Russia and a despatch from London confirmed: 'The die is cast . . . Europe is to be plunged into a general war.' Closer to home, rival unions in the copper mines at Butte, only sixty miles from Helena, were also at war. When the Miners' Union Hall was dynamited, Governor Stewart declared martial law and sent in the National Guard to keep order.

It was in this turbulent climate that the Family Theater finally closed its doors, for the audiences did not pick up. Harry Hubbard was once again obliged to look for work, but once again he was lucky – he was taken on as a book-keeper for the Ives-Smith Coal Company, 'dealers in Original Bear Creek, Roundup, Acme and Belt Coal', at 41 West Sixth Avenue. May, meanwhile, found a cheaper apartment for the family on the first floor of a shingled wood-frame house at 1109 Fifth Avenue.

Back in Kalispell, Lafe Waterbury was still having trouble with his arm. He was not the kind of man to complain about bad luck, but no one could have blamed him had he done so. His arm had to be set a third time and just when it seemed it was beginning to heal he was thrown to the ground by a horse he was examining. He was never to regain full strength in that arm and although he was only fifty years old he knew he would not be able to continue working as a vet, with all the pulling and pushing it involved. Only the four youngest Waterbury girls were still at home, but Lafe did not think he could afford to retire, even if that had been his ambition. (His taxable assets were listed in the Kalispell City Directory at $1550, which made him comfortably off, but not by any means rich.) No prospects presented themselves immediately in Kalispell and Lafe and Ida began considering another move. It somehow seemed natural, since they had followed May to Kalispell, that they should now think about moving to Helena.

In the summer of 1915, Toilie, back home on a visit from the East, drove her father to Helena in the family's Model T. Ford so that he could take a look around. They stayed, of course, with May and Hub in their cramped apartment on Fifth Avenue and Lafe was delighted to have the company of his four-year-old grandson every time he went for a walk in town.

Hub presumably talked to his father-in-law about his job and the two men almost certainly discussed the ever-increasing demand for coal and the business opportunities available in Helena. As a bookkeeper, Hub knew the figures, knew the profit Ives-Smith was making and knew the strength of the market – it was information that undoubtedly influenced Lafe's decision to move his family to Helena and set up a coal company of his own.

The Waterburys arrived in 1916 and bought a house at 736 Fifth Avenue, on the corner of Raleigh Street, just two blocks from May and Hub's apartment. Lafe considered himself very lucky to get the property, for it was a sturdy two-storey house, built around the turn of the century, with light and airy rooms, fine stained glass windows, a wide covered porch and an unusual conical roof over a curved bay at one corner. It would quickly become known by everyone in the family, with the greatest affection, as 'the old brick'.

The Waterbury girls had wept bitterly on leaving Kalispell, largely because their father had insisted that Bird, the Indian pony on which they had all learned to ride, was too old to make the journey and would have to be left behind. But their spirits soon lifted as they ran excitedly from room to room in their new home and imagined themselves as fashionable young ladies of substance.

Fifth Avenue was not yet a paved road, but it was lined with struggling saplings which offered the promise of respectability and, more importantly, it was straddled to the east by the Capital Building, a monumental edifice of such grandeur that the girls were all deeply awed by its proximity. To the west, Fifth Avenue appeared to plunge directly into the forested green flanks of Mount Helena and just two blocks south of 'the old brick', Raleigh Street ended in grassy hummocks which led up to the mountains and promised limitless opportunities for play. Marnie, then thirteen years old, could hardly imagine a better place to be.

Lafe rented a yard with a stable adjoining the Northern Pacific railroad track where it crossed Montana Avenue and put up a sign announcing that the Capital City Coal Company had opened for business. It was very much a family affair, as listed in the Helena City Directory for 1917: Lafayette O. Waterbury was president, Ray was vice-president and Toilie (recalled from the East by her father – 'It's time to come home,' he told her, 'I need you.') was secretary-treasurer. Harry Ross Hubbard had also joined the fledgling enterprise, but the only vacancy was in the lowly capacity of teamster.

On 2 January 1917 Ron was enrolled at the kindergarten at Central School on Warren Street, just across from the new cathedral which, with its twin spires and grey stone façade, towered reprovingly over the city. Most days he was walked to school by his aunts, Marnie and June, who were at Helena High, opposite Central School.

Ron, who was known to the neighbourhood kids as 'brick' because of his hair, would later claim that while still at kindergarten he used the 'lumberjack fighting' he had learned from his grandfather to deal with a gang of bullies who were terrorizing children on their way to and from the school. But one of Ron's closest childhood friends, Andrew Richardson, has no recollection of him protecting local children from bullies. 'He never protected nobody,' said Richardson. 'It was all bullshit. Old Hubbard was the greatest con artist who ever lived.'[5]

Although the war in Europe, with its unbelievable casualty toll, was filling plenty of columns in the *Independent*, local news, as always, received quite as much prominence as despatches from foreign correspondents. Suffragettes figured prominently in many of the headlines and after the women's suffrage amendment was narrowly approved in the Montana legislature, the victorious women celebrated by electing one of their leaders, Jeannette Rankin, to a seat in the US Congress. Women voters also helped push through a bill to ban the sale of alcohol as the Prohibition lobby gained ground across the nation.

Even the news, in February 1917, that Germany had declared its intention to engage in unrestricted submarine warfare did not fully hit home until the following month when it was learned that German submarines had attacked and sunk three US merchant ships in the Atlantic. On 6 April, the United States declared war on Germany; Congresswoman Rankin was one of only a handful of dissenters voting against the war resolution.

Mobilization began at once in Helena at Fort Harrison, headquarters of the 2nd Regiment, but the wave of patriotic fervour that swept the state brought in its wake a sinister backlash in the form of witch-hunts for 'traitors' and 'subversives'. In August, self-styled vigilantes in Butte dragged labour leader Frank Little from his rooming house and hanged him from a railroad trestle on the edge of town. His 'crime' was that he was leader of the Industrial Workers of the World, a radical group viewed as seditious.

Although selective draft mustered more than seven thousand troops in Montana by the beginning of August, Harry Hubbard felt, as an ex-serviceman, that he should not wait to be drafted. He had served for four years in the US Navy and his country needed trained seamen. Yes, he had family responsibilities, but he was also an American. He knew his duty and May knew she could not, and should not, stop him. On 10 October, Hub kissed her goodbye, hugged his six-year-old son and left Helena for the Navy Recruiting Station at Salt Lake City, Utah, to re-enlist for a four-year term in the US Navy. Two weeks later, little Ron and his mother joined the crowds lining Last Chance Gulch to watch Montana's 163rd Infantry march out of town on their way to join the fighting in Europe. Ron thought they were just 'swell'.

After Hub had gone, May and Ron moved into 'the old brick' with the rest of the family and May found a job as a clerk with the State Bureau of Child and Animal Protection in the Capital Building. If little Ron experienced any sense of loss from the absence of his father, it was certainly alleviated by the intense warmth and sociability of the Waterbury family. He had grandparents who considered he could do no wrong, a loving mother and an assorted array of adoring aunts who liked nothing more than to spend time playing with him.

It was inevitable that he would be spoiled with all the attention, but he was also a rewarding child, exceptionally imaginative and adventurous, always filling his time with original ideas and games. 'He was very quick, always coming up with ideas no one else had thought of,' said Marnie. 'He'd grab a couple of beer bottles and use them as binoculars or he would write little plays and draw the scenery and everything. Whatever he started he finished: when he made up his mind he was going to do something, you could be sure he would see it through.'

Hub wrote home frequently and made it clear that he was enjoying being back in the service, the war notwithstanding. He had been selected for training as an Assistant Paymaster and if he made the grade, he proudly explained in a letter to May, it would mean that he would become an officer. On 13 October 1918 Harry Ross Hubbard was honorably discharged from enlisted service in the US Navy Reserve Force and the following day he was appointed Assistant Paymaster with the rank of Ensign. He was thirty-two years old, positively geriatric for an Ensign – but it was one of the proudest moments of his life.

Eleven days later, the front pages of the *Helena Independent* was dominated by a single word in letters three inches high: PEACE. Underneath, the sub-heading declared, 'Cowardly Kaiser and Son Flee to Holland.' The terms of surrender were to be so severe, the newspaper innocently reported, that Germany would forever 'be absolutely deprived from further military power of action on land and sea and in the air'.

Unlike most wives whose husbands had gone to war, May knew that the Armistice did not mean that Hub would be coming home; he had already told her that he intended to make a career in the Navy. It was a decision she could not sensibly oppose, for she was obliged to admit that he had been incapable of making progress in his varied civilian jobs and he was clearly happier in the Navy. Furthermore, his position with the Capital City Coal Company was far from secure, for she knew that her father was worried about the business – they were having difficulty finding sufficient supplies of coal from Roundup and a third coal company had opened up in town, increasing competition. The Waterbury girls were helping with the company's cash flow problems by knocking on doors round and about Fifth Avenue to collect payment for overdue bills.

Lafe Waterbury never allowed his business worries to cast a shadow over his family life and for the children, Ron included, weeks and months passed with not much to fret about other than whether or not the taffy [toffee] would set. 'Taffy-pulls' were a regular ritual in the Waterbury household: a coat hanger was kept permanently on the back of the door in the basement to loop the sugar and water mix and stretch it repeatedly, filling the taffy with air bubbles so that it would snap satisfactorily when it was set. Liberty Bill would always sit and watch the proceedings with saliva dripping from his jaws. Once he grabbed a mouthful when the taffy looped too close to the floor and disappeared under a bush in the garden for hours while he tried to suck it out of his teeth.

One day Marnie and June were in the basement pulling taffy with Ron when they heard their father laughing out loud in the front room. They ran upstairs to see what was going on and found him standing at the window, both hands clutched to his quivering midriff, tears streaming down his cheeks. Outside, a young lady in a tight hobble skirt – the very latest fashion in Helena – was attempting to step down from the wooden sidewalk to cross the road. To her acute embarrassment, she was discovering that while it was feasible to totter along a level surface, it was almost impossible to negotiate a step of more than a few inches without hoisting her skirt to a level well beyond the bounds of decorum, or jumping with both feet together. Eventually, shuffling to the edge of the sidewalk, she managed to slide first one foot down, then, with a precarious swivel, the other. By this time Lafe was forced to sit down, for he could no longer stand, and the entire family had gathered at the window.

Laughter was an omnipresent feature of life in 'the old brick'. When Toilie brought home a bottle of wine and gave her mother a glass, the unaccustomed alcohol thickened her tongue and the more she struggled with ever-more recalcitrant syllables, the more her daughters howled. Then there was the time when Lafe leaned back in his swivel chair, overbalanced, fell under a shelf piled with magazines and hit his head as he tried to get up – no one would ever forget that. On the other hand almost the worst incident any of the children could remember was the day when their mother's pet canary escaped through an open window into the snow and never returned. Ida had loved that canary – when she was lying in bed she would whistle and it would fly over, perch on the covers and pick her teeth.

In the summer, the children spent every waking hour after school outdoors. May, who had changed her job and now worked as a clerk in the State Department of Agriculture and Publicity, bought a small plot of land in the foothills of the mountains, about two hours' walk from the family home and paid a local carpenter to put up a raw pine shack. It had just two rooms inside, with a long covered porch at the front. They called it 'The Old Homestead' and used it at weekends and holidays, taking enough food and drink with them to last the duration, and drawing water from a well on a nearby property. Most times Lafe would drive them out in the Model T. and drop them on the Butte road at the closest point to the house, from where they walked across the fields. The children loved The Old Homestead for the simple pleasure of being in the mountains, playing endless games under a perfect blue sky, optimistically panning for gold in tumbling streams of crystal clear water, picking great bunches of wild flowers, cooking on a campfire and huddling round an oil lamp at night, telling spooky stories.

When they were not planning a trip to The Old Homestead, Ron pestered his aunts to take him on a hike up to the top of Mount Helena, where they would sit with a picnic, munching sandwiches and silently staring out over the sprawl of the city below and the ring of mountains beyond. One of the trails up the mountain passed a smoky cave said to be haunted by the men who had used it as a hideout while being stalked by Indians in the mid-nineteenth century. Marnie used to take Ron, squirming with thrilled terror, into the cave to look for ghosts.

Marnie and Ron, with only eight years between them, were as close as brother and sister. When she was in a school play at Helena High, taking the part of Marie Antoinette, he sat wide-eyed throughout the performance then ran all the way home to tell his grandma how beautiful Marnie was.

While the children remained blithely unaware of events outside the comforting confines of 'the old brick' and The Old Homestead, few adults in Montana were able to enjoy such a blinkered existence. After years of abundant crops and high wheat prices, postwar depression brought about a collapse in the market – bushel prices halved in the space of three months – and the summer of 1919 saw the first of a cycle of disastrous droughts. Every day brought further ominous tidings of mortgage foreclosures, banks closing, abandoned farms turned into dustbowls and thousands of settlers leaving the state to seek a livelihood elsewhere.

In this gloomy economic climate, Lafe Waterbury was forced to close down the Capital City Coal Company. For a while he tinkered with a small business selling automobile spares and vulcanizing tires, but the depression meant that motorists were laying up their cars rather than repairing them and Lafe decided to retire, thankful that he still had sufficient capital left to support his family.

May helped with the household expenses, although she realized she and Ron would not be able to stay there forever. Hub had been promoted to Lieutenant (Junior Grade) in November 1919, and whenever he could, had been coming home on leave to see his wife and son. He was still intent on a career in the Navy, although he had already suffered some setbacks. He had been obliged to appear before a court of inquiry in May, 1920, while serving as Supply Officer on the *USS Aroostock*, to explain a deficiency in his accounts of $942.25. He also had an unfortunate tendency to overlook personal debts. No less than fourteen creditors in Kalispell claimed he left behind unpaid bills totalling $125; Fred Fisch, high-grade clothier of Vallejo, California, was pursuing him for $10 still owed on a uniform overcoat; and a Dr McPherson of San Diego was owed $30. All of them complained to the Navy Department, casting a shadow over Hubbard's record.[6] He had a long spell of inactive duty at the beginning of 1921 while he was waiting for a new posting and he and May spent a great deal of time discussing their future. Hub expected May to conform, like other Navy wives, and trail around the country with him from posting to posting; when he was at sea, he wanted her to be close to his ship's home port. May obviously wanted to be with Hub, but she was reluctant to move Ron from school to school and loath to leave her family. She had perhaps secretly hoped that Hub would tire of the Navy and return to civilian life in Helena, but the depression wiped out whatever miserable opportunities he might have had of finding work and she realized it would never happen.

In September 1921, Hub was posted to the battleship *USS Oklahoma* as an Assistant Supply Officer. He anticipated serving on board for at least two years, much of that time at sea, and the opportunities for visits home to Helena would be severely curtailed. As a loyal wife, May felt she could no longer justify staying in Helena. She and Ron packed their bags, bade the family a tearful farewell and caught a train for San Diego, the *USS Oklahoma*'s home port.

Although Ron must have missed the convivial domesticity of 'the old brick', he did not appear to mind, in the least, being a 'Navy brat' – the curiously affectionate label applied to all children of servicemen, many of whom needed more than the fingers of both hands to count their schools. He was a gregarious boy, quick to make friends, and starting a new school held no terrors for him. After about a year in San Diego, the Hubbards moved north to Seattle, in Washington State, when the *Oklahoma* was transferred to Puget Sound Navy Shipyard.

In Seattle Ron joined the boy scouts, an event that would figure prominently in a hand-written journal which he scrawled on the pages of an old accounts book, interspersed with short stories, a few years later: 'The year Nineteen Hundred and Twenty-Three rallied round and found me contentedly resting on my laurels, a first class badge. For I was a boy scout then and deaf was my friend that hadn't heard all about it. I considered Seattle the best town on the map as far as scouting was concerned.'

In October 1923, Lieutenant Hubbard completed sea duty on the *USS Oklahoma* and, after brief spells of temporary duty in San Francisco and New York, was assigned for further training to the Bureau of Supply and Accounts School of Application in Washington DC. The US Navy, which clearly despised any form of land transport, saved itself the cost of two long-distance train fares by giving May and Ron berths on the *USS U.S. Grant*, a German warship acquired by the US Navy after the First World War, which was due to sail from Seattle to Hampton Roads, Virginia, via the Panama Canal. It was thus December, and the snow was thick on the ground, before the Hubbards were re-united in Washington after a voyage of some seven thousand miles, three-quarters of the way round the coast of the United States.

It was on this trip, it seems, that Ron met the enigmatic Commander 'Snake' Thompson of the US Navy Medical Corps, a psychoanalyst he would later claim was responsible for awakening his youthful interest in Freud, although he only made the briefest mention of the journey in his journal. His style of writing was fluent, breezy, schoolboyishly cocksure and addressed directly to the reader. 'If obviously pushed upon,' he wrote, 'I supposed I could write a couple of thousands [*sic*] words on that trip . . . But I spare you.'

He usually referred to himself in a gently ironic tone, perhaps to avoid giving an impression of thinking rather too highly of himself. When he arrived in Washington, two troops of local scouts were battling for a prized scouting trophy, the Washington Post Cup. Troop 100, he noted, belonged to the YMCA 'and would therefore probably lose', so he joined the other outfit, Troop 10, 'which must have sighed loudly when it perceived me crossing the threshhold'.

The journal also contained flashes of humour, delivered deadpan: 'Visualize me in a natty scout suit, my red hair tumbling out from under my hat, doing my good turn daily. Once I saved a man's life. I could have pushed him under a streetcar but I didn't.'

Intent on pushing Troop 10 to victory, Ron began acquiring merit badges with extraordinary speed and dedication. In his first two weeks, he was awarded badges for Firemanship and Personal Health, quickly followed by Photography, Life-Saving, Physical Development and Bird Study. He determinedly thrust his way into the front rank of the Washington scouts (it was absolutely not his nature to languish shyly among the pack) and he was chosen to represent them on a delegation to the White House to ask President Calvin Coolidge to accept the honorary chairmanship of National Boys' Week. He noted the invitation in his journal with characteristic cheek: 'One fine day the Scout executive telephoned my house and told me I was to meet the president that afternoon. I told him I thought it pretty swell of the president to come way out to my house . . .'

Brushed and scrubbed ('even the backs of my hands were thoroughly washed') he waited with forty other boys outside the Oval Office until a secretary emerged and said the president was ready to receive them. 'With fear and trembling, we entered and repeated our names a few times as we pumped Cal's listless hand . . . I think I have the distinction of being the only boy scout in America who has made the President wince.' The great man spoke in such lugubrious tones that Ron compared the occasion to being invited to his own hanging.

In the boy scout diary he kept intermittently around this time, Ron was a lot less forthcoming than in the journal, which was clearly written with an intention to entertain. The most frequent entry in his diary was a laconic 'Was bored.' Yet he would claim in later years that the four months he spent in Washington was a crucial period of his life during which he received 'an extensive education in the field of the human mind' under the tutelage of his friend Commander Thompson.[7] He also noted – in his journal – that he became a close friend of President Coolidge's son, Calvin Junior, whose early death accelerated his 'precocious interest in the mind and spirit of man'.[8]

'Snake' Thompson was apparently a friend of Ron's father and a personal student of Sigmund Freud, under whom he had studied in Vienna. His inauspicious nickname was derived from his love of slithery creatures, but it was in his capacity as a student of the founder of psychoanalysis that he took it upon himself to give the twelve-year-old boy a grounding in Freudian theory as well as 'shoving his nose' into books at the Library of Congress.

[Ron would often refer to Thompson in later life, yet the Commander remains an enigma. He cannot be identified from US Navy records, nor can his relationship with Freud be established. Doctor Kurt Eissler, one of the world's leading authorities on Freud, says he has no knowledge of any correspondence or contact of any kind between Freud and Thompson.[9]]

Presumably the hours that Ron and Thompson spent closeted together in the Library of Congress were somehow dovetailed into the time he devoted to scouting, for on 28 March 1924, a few days after his thirteenth birthday, Ron was made an eagle scout.

'Twenty-one merit badges in ninety days,' he recorded triumphantly in his journal. 'I was quite a boy then. Written up in the papers and all that. Take a look at me. You didn't know the wreck in front of you was once the youngest Eagle Scout in the country, did you?'

Neither did Ron. At that time the Boy Scouts of America only kept an alphabetical record of eagle scouts, with no reference to their ages.[10]

Chapter 2

Whither did he Wander?

Fundamental to the image of L. Ron Hubbard as prophet are the tales of his teenage travels. At the age of fourteen, it seems, the inquisitive lad could be found wandering the Orient alone, investigating primitive cultures and learning the secrets of life at the feet of wise men and Lama priests. 'He was up and down the China coast several times in his teens from Ching Wong Tow to Hong Kong and inland to Peking and Manchuria.'[1] In China he met an old magician whose ancestors had served in the court of Kublai Khan and a Hindu who could hypnotize cats. In the high hills of Tibet he lived with bandits who accepted him because of his 'honest interest in them and their way of life'.[2] In the remote reaches of western Manchuria he made friends with the ruling warlords by demonstrating his horsemanship. On an unnamed island in the South Pacific, the fearless boy calmed the natives by exploring a cave that was supposed to be haunted and showing them that the rumbling sound from within was nothing more sinister than an underground river. 'Deep in the jungles' of Polynesia he discovered an ancient burial ground 'steeped in the tradition of heroic warriors and kings . . . Though his native friends were fearful for him, he explored the sacred area – his initiative based on doing all he could to know more'.[3]

There appeared to be no limit to the young man's abilities: 'I remember one time learning Igoroti, an Eastern primitive language, in a single night. I sat up by kerosene lantern and took a list of words that had been made by an old missionary in the hills of Luzon [Philippines]. The Igorot had a very simple language. This missionary phoneticized their language and made a list of their main words and their usage and grammar. And I remember sitting up under a mosquito net with the mosquitoes hungrily chomping their beaks just outside the net, and learning this language – three hundred words – just memorizing these words and what they meant. And the next day I started to get them in line and align them with people, and was speaking Igoroti in a very short time.'[4]

Throughout this period, Ron was said to have been supported by his wealthy, not to say indulgent, grandfather and it was during his travels in the East that he became interested in the 'spiritual destiny' of mankind. 'L. Ron Hubbard learned that there was more to life than science had dreamed of, that Man did not know everything there was to know about life, and that neither East nor West, the spiritual and the material, had any full answer. To L. Ron Hubbard there was a whole field here that was begging for research.'[5]

It would, to be sure, have been an impressive start to any young man's career, if only it had been true.

* * * * *

At the end of March 1924, the Hubbards left Washington DC and moved, once again, from one side of the continent to the other. Having finished his training at the Bureau of Supply and Accounts School, Harry Hubbard was promoted to full Lieutenant and posted back to the Puget Sound Navy Shipyard at Bremerton, in Washington State, as Disbursing Officer.

Bremerton was a nice little town mushroomed around the great naval shipyard, the northern base of the Pacific Fleet, which sprawled along the shore of Puget Sound. Seagulls wheeled and cawed over the quiet high street and the fishing fleet in the harbour and a tangy aroma of salt, tar and oil scented the breeze off the Sound, where bustling white-painted ferries provided the town's main link to Seattle on the opposite shore. The Hubbards found a house two blocks from the shipyard and their son enrolled in the eighth grade at Union High School, on the corner of Fifth and High Avenues.

Ron liked Bremerton on sight, as would any thirteen-year-old with a taste for outdoor activities. After school in the summer he invariably joined a group of boys to swim and fish and canoe in the Sound and at weekends he cadged a ride out to Camp Parsons, the boy scout camp on the north-west shore of Hood Canal. Parsons was a permanent campsite in the heart of the Olympic National Park and was considered by thousands of boys to be paradise. There were oysters, clams, shrimp and crabs to be fished from the canal and cooked over campfires; eagles soared in the thermals high overhead and the dense forest all around the camp was alive with deer, beavers, bobcats and black bears. Like countless fellow scouts, Ron's favourite trek from Camp Parsons was the 'Three Rivers Hike', which started with the 'poop-out drag' – a long climb up a sun-baked southern slope – and ended in the late afternoon at Camp Mystery at the top of the pass, where there were meadows full of wild flowers and thrilling views over the Olympic mountain wilderness.

It was a boyhood idyll that was to last for only two happy years; in the summer of 1926 his parents decided to move across the Sound back to Seattle. It was no trouble for Harry to commute to work at the shipyard by ferry and they felt that Ron ought to complete his high school education in a bigger and more sophisticated school than Union High. So it was that Ron began his sophomore year at Queen Anne High, a majestic seminary built in sparkling white bricks on a hilltop overlooking Seattle.

He was barely into his second semester when his father received his first foreign posting. Lieutenant Hubbard was to take over as Officer in Charge of the Commissary Store at the US Naval Station on Guam, a remote, mountainous tropical island in the Pacific, three thousand miles west of Hawaii. Largest and southernmost of the Mariana Islands, Guam had been ceded to the United States as a prize in the Spanish-American War in 1898 and, as far as the Hubbard family was concerned, was so far away it might as well have been on another planet.

May and Hub talked long into many nights about how they should accommodate their lives to this new upheaval. Guam was a minimum two-year posting and May naturally wanted to accompany her husband, particularly as there was no chance of him returning home on leave. What most worried them was what to do with Ron, who had immediately assumed he would be going too. Then just sixteen years old, he was thrilled at the prospect of exchanging the dreary routine of Queen Anne High for life on a tropical island.

But officers returning from Guam were full of lurid stories about the island and its inhabitants. Many of them concerned the charms of Guam's 'dusky maidens' and the uninhibited enthusiasm with which they pursued young Americans as potential husbands. There was also much gossip about the horrendous strains of venereal disease which were endemic. Time and time again Hub was told by ex-Guam veterans that they would never let a son of theirs set foot in the place.

In the end they made the painful decision to leave Ron behind. May arranged for him to move back into 'the old brick' with her parents and to finish high school in Helena. Ron made no secret of his disgust when his parents broke the news, although he was slightly mollified by his father's promise to try and arrange for him to travel with his mother out to Guam for a short holiday before returning to Helena.

Lieutenant Hubbard sailed to Guam on 5 April 1927; his wife and son followed several weeks later on the passenger steamship, *President Madison*, bound for Honolulu, Yokohama, Shanghai, Hong Kong and Manila, out of San Francisco. Ron took with him his ukulele and saxophone, two instruments he had been struggling to learn, and a headful of yarns, spun by his father's friends, about how anyone with red hair was instantly proclaimed king on arrival in Guam. To his great chagrin, his return passage was already booked for July, to get him back in time for the start of the junior term at Helena High School. May took sufficient books to tutor her son in history and English during the trip, to make up for him not finishing the semester at Queen Anne High School.

Considering he was still only sixteen, Ron's log of his trip to Guam was acutely observed and literate, even if the prose was occasionally artless and self-conscious ('Westward tugged the ship's twelve thousand horses'). It was also packed with information, reflecting the unashamed curiosity of an inquisitive and extrovert young man travelling abroad for the first time.

Watching San Francisco's Golden Gate disappear from view, Ron admitted to a lump in his throat, although he was soon involved in the timeless and time-wasting pursuits that comprised life on board – shuffle board and deck golf, a dance one evening, a movie the next, and obsessive discussion about who was seasick and who was not. Some of the crew tried to turn Ron's stomach by describing revolting meals of salt pork and slippery oysters, but he was pleased to record that neither he nor his mother succumbed.

First stop, six days out, was Honolulu, where the *President Madison* was greeted in the harbour by flotillas of small boats rowed by lithe, brown-skinned urchins who dived for quarters flipped overboard from the deck of the steamship. They used to dive for pennies, Ron noted laconically, 'thus has the Hawaiian developed his commerce'. Friends showed the Hubbards around the island while the ship was docked and Ron managed to get a swim and a ride on a surf-board at Waikiki beach. The waves were much longer than those in California, he wrote, and sometimes attained speeds of sixty miles an hour.

Outward bound from Hawaii, Ron made friends with the second engineer who took him on a conducted tour of the ship, including the galley, 'spotless with shining equipment and Chinese cooks who grinned and displayed blank teeth'.

Fifty miles off the coast of Japan, they caught their first glimpse of the 'celestial beauty' of Mount Fuji rising through the clouds and cloaked in a 'pink robe of snow' suggesting, Ron thought, a 'garment for royalty'. They stayed three days in Japan, first at Yokohama and then at Kobe. Ron made meticulous notes about everything he saw, including detailed descriptions of how the people dressed. Much of the devastation caused by the earthquake four years earlier was still evident – including the ruin of a 'hideously scrambled' fort guarding the harbour entrance in which 1700 men had died when the walls collapsed. Ron was generally unimpressed by Japan and clearly unprepared, as a young American innocent of foreign ways, for the sights and smells of the Orient – the disease and the dirt, the stinking slums and the beggars sleeping in the street. 'It doesn't look the happy land so pictured in stories,' he concluded. 'Only at cherry blossom time or in the romantic novel do I believe there is beauty in Japan.'

He was rather more cheered by Shanghai, the *President Madison*'s next port of call, partly because the first flag to greet them as they entered the Yangtze river was the Stars and Stripes, flying from the stern of a US Navy destroyer. The bustling river traffic – 'millions of fishing boats and junks' – astonished him, as did the fact that the 'ragged and decrepit' coolies who unloaded the ship only earned fifteen cents a day and 'fifteen cents Mex at that!' They lived, he added somewhat unnecessarily, 'worse than anyone in the world'.

He and his mother accompanied the ship's chief officer, who was also from Seattle, on a drive through the town. 'Opening down the main avenue over which our car travelled were hundreds of narrow intriguing streets, teeming with life. Great fish floated here and there and paper banners hung overhead. The stores were stocked with every sort of junk. Dried fish rattled on strings in the wind. Queer looking foods and drygoods were side by side. Sikh policemen were everywhere. They are big dark bearded fellows and in their turbans and short trousers of khaki look picturesque. They carry great rattan sticks and a rifle across the back. Tommy Atkins was very much in evidence and the American marines, as well as Japanese and British marines. On the outside of the British concession I saw a British tommy take a Chinaman by the coat and knock him across the street. On Bubbling Well Road is a beautiful hotel once the home of a Chinese gentleman. The grounds are laid out with pergolas and fountains and the hotel has tapestries and mosaic tile floors.'

It was clear that by the time he reached Shanghai, Ron had adopted some of the more obvious colonial mannerisms, for he casually reported joining the Madison crowd for 'tiffin' at the Palace Hotel later that day and would also soon be referring to the natives as 'gooks'.

From Shanghai they sailed for Hong Kong, a city that was 'very British on the surface and very native underneath'. May and Ron took a tram up to the top of the mountain overlooking the harbour, but they found the heat and humidity very exhausting, not to mention the throngs of coolies 'not caring where they spit', and they were glad to leave on the last leg of their voyage on the *President Madison* to Manila in the Philippines.

In Manila they were to transfer, with fifteen other Navy families, to a US Navy cargo auxiliary, the *USS Gold Star*, which was anchored across the bay at Cavite, waiting to take them to Guam. There was considerable confusion unloading the baggage from the

President Madison, which Ron blamed on the 'lazy, ignorant natives', and it was some time before their trunks were safely on their way and May and Ron could relax with a glass of lemon squeeze at the Manila Hotel.

Next day Ron went sight-seeing with a Lieutenant McCain from the Cavite Navy Yard, an acquaintance of his father. To a boy who loved blood-and-thunder adventure stories, the old Spanish forts in Cavite exercized a compelling fascination. 'All the old guns have been dismantled, but the emplacements remain. Such an awful place in which to fight. The places were traps as it takes four men to even open a door. There are tunnels connecting all of them to an ancient cathedral which is un-used and filled with snakes, bats and trash. Very mysterious. I looked it over well when Mr McCain told me that millions in Spanish gold were buried in those tunnels. Some day I am going back there and dredge [*sic*] the whole place. *Maybe.*'

That evening he was taken to 'Dreamland', one of the more respectable bars in Manila where girls were available for hire, for dancing, at five centums a dance. 'Of course we didn't dance,' Ron was at pains to record, 'because by doing so one loses cast. The Charleston has just hit them, but it's too hot (I mean the weather).'

Two days later, the *USS Gold Star* weighed anchor and set course for Guam, a seven-day voyage across the Philippine Sea which could not have offered a greater contrast to the comparative luxury of a passenger ship like the *President Madison*. The accommodation was spartan, the food was poor and the officers remained haughtily aloof from their luckless passengers, even eating at a separate table in the dining-room. To make matters worse, the weather was terrible and the ship pitched and rolled and wallowed in a grey, relentlessly heaving sea with the constant threat of a typhoon gathering on the horizon. It was, said Ron, a 'gosh-awful trip'.

When a smudge of land appeared in the far distance and word went round that it was Guam, the relief was palpable. The *USS Gold Star* hove to off Guam on Monday 6 June, thirty-six days after the Hubbards had left San Francisco. Hub was on the second tender that came out to the ship and Ron spoke for both himself and his mother when he noted: 'We were sure glad to see him.'

Ron's first impression of Guam, with its thickly forested green hills and little red-roofed houses, was favourable. Even the sickly sweet aroma of copra which filled the air was distinctly preferable to the stench of open drains that had predominated at all their previous ports of call. The poverty, filth and disease which had been so prevalent elsewhere were kept in abeyance in Guam by the overwhelming presence of the United States Navy, which pushed, prodded and paid the local Chamorro natives to keep the streets clean and to observe basic hygiene.

Hub had been allocated a large bungalow surrounded by banana trees in the town of Agana, about five miles from the harbour. It was still not fully furnished when May and Ron arrived, but Ron liked the cool sparse rooms with their highly polished floors of black hardwood, reflecting the light filtering through the bamboo screens. The family had two houseboys and a cook and lived in a style that none of them had ever previously experienced. May, for example, had never had servants in her life and very much enjoyed the novelty.

Ron's father had arranged for him to spend part of the six weeks he was due to stay on the island teaching English to Chamorro children in the local grade school, which was run by the Navy. Ron did not object to undertaking this chore, but found it a more or less impossible task because of his red hair. Although he had not been instantly proclaimed king on arrival, he quickly discovered that his hair caused much excitement and interest, both on the street and in the classroom. The Chamorros, dark-skinned people of Indonesian stock, seemed unable to believe that a human head could sprout such a fiery crine and Ron's students spent their entire lesson staring uncomprehendingly at the top of his head. His parents laughed when he told them what was happening and his mother, drawing on her own teaching experience, softly advised him just to do his best.

When he was not trying to be a teacher, Ron spent a great deal of his time satisfying his natural curiosity by researching the island's history and culture. Some of his notes about Guam and its people bear a strange similarity to stories that would later be incorporated into the L. Ron Hubbard mythology.

The Chamorro dialect, for example, which had originally contained some two thousand words and idioms, had been reduced over the years to around three hundred idioms with an almost non-existent grammatical structure – curiously akin to Igoroti, the primitive language Ron was said to have learned in a single night by the light of a kerosene lamp. And one of the Hubbards' house boys told Ron about a devil ghost called 'Tadamona' which was believed to haunt Missionary Point, where a fast-flowing underground river made eerie moaning noises at night. . .

In Guam, as elsewhere, Ron was particularly intrigued by the forts, which held a special romance and mystery he toiled to convey in his journal: 'An especially interesting one is the fort of San Juan de 'Apra [sic] in Apra harbour. Its doors have been sealed for years and, as if to hide the structure, vines wind themselves about it. The walls were built with remarkable skill, especially the corners. Most of the prison and turret have been eroded and have fallen [sic] into decay, but the powder house and firing steps remain. The walks that once heard the rhythm of the sentry's beat, and the crash of the evening gun are now the running place of lizards. One cannot imagine the solitude and depression that surrounds it. All that beauty and grandeur which surrounded it yesterday has faded as the rose which dies and leaves its thorn.'

Ron was due to leave Guam on Saturday 16 July 1927, on board an ammunition ship, *USS Nitro*, bound for Bremerton. His parents drove him down to the harbour in the early morning and accompanied him out to the ship to help him with his bags, now crammed with souvenirs and presents for the family back home in Helena. The three of them had a quiet breakfast together on board and at eight o'clock May and Hub said goodbye and returned ashore on a tender, hardly daring to look back at the lonely figure of their son standing at the rail. The *USS Nitro* sailed within the hour.

If Ron was sad to be leaving, he made no mention of it in his journal. He 'felt rather lonely' on the first day out, but the two boys with whom he was sharing a cabin, Jerry Curtis and Dick Derickson, were so homesick that both were close to tears. Ron did his best to cheer them up. He particularly liked Dick, who was from Seattle and whom he had met at Camp Parsons. 'Dick and I have been reading up on atheism,' he noted. 'Such a terrible thing to make an issue of. Something is at the bottom of it. I'll find out in the States.'

Four days out, the *USS Nitro* hove to off Wake Island so that the crew could go fishing and swimming. Ron went ashore in a whale boat and discovered that the island was inhabited by many strange and beautiful birds, apparently quite unafraid of the sailors walking round their nests. In the lagoon, he wrote, the multi-coloured tropical fish looked like 'a forth of July parade' and the water was so clear he could see through thirty fathoms to the rocks on the bottom.

Deprived of the recreations offered on board the *President Madison*, Ron found the return voyage, courtesy of the US Navy, to be unremittingly dreary. He liked to watch the stars at night ('never in my life have I seen such beauties') and during the day he enjoyed visiting the engine-room, but much of the time he was bored.

Ironically, Ron had seriously discussed with his father the possibility of a career in the Navy, although he certainly did not seem much enthused by his experience on the *USS Nitro*. 'If this ship is the cream of the naval duty,' he wrote, 'I'll sure stick to milk. The officers work about an hour and then sit around and look bored. The enlisted personnel bear the brunt of the work.' Nevertheless, he could not have been completely deterred, for he noted that he and Dick would be going to Annapolis (home of the Naval Academy) at the same time.

Off Hawaii, one of the officers told Ron he could go up to the lookout in the crow's nest. 'A moment later found me staring up the forward mast which looked ungodly high. I overcame a nervous tremor and climbed a rope up to the steel ladder . . . Nice prospect a fall was. Then I tackled the first fifty feet of ladder. It surely looked and felt insubstantial. About half way up I thought I'd never been so nervous before. After that ladder came an even smaller steel ladder. Up I went all confidence by this time. In a moment I reached the nest and sure enough there was the lookout reading a 'Western Story'. He invited me to climb in. The last in itself is worse than the rest of it put together. One has to dangle with nothing under him and work half way round to the other edge. Over the side of the box I swung and then in. My God what a relief!'

On 6 August, in thick fog, the *USS Nitro* nosed into Bremerton and moored to Pier 4A at the Navy Yard. Ron disembarked without a moment's regret, thankful to be back on dry land and away from the cramped and stultifying atmosphere of the ship. Next day he caught a train for Helena, where he was welcomed by the Waterburys like the prodigal son. In 'the old brick', savouring the heady fragrance of his grandmother's baking, which he remembered so well, he regaled everyone with the tales of his adventures and if he embroidered the account just a little, who could have blamed him?

Even a local newspaper apparently felt his exploits worth reporting in a double-column story under the headline 'Ronald Hubbard Tells of His Trip to Orient and Many Experiences'. The interview closely followed the notes Ron had made in his journal except for the surprising claim, somehow neglected in his diary, that he had witnessed an execution while he was in China. 'Ronald Hubbard has the distinction', the story concluded, 'of being the only boy in the country to secure an eagle scout badge at the age of twelve years.'

[He had, in fact, been thirteen. But this small slip-up and the curious omission of the 'execution' from his journal were not nearly as puzzling as the fact that it has never been possible to trace the newspaper from which the cutting was taken.[6] It appears to exist only as a photostat in the archives of the Church of Scientology labelled 'Clipping from Helena, Montana, newspaper circa 1929'.]

On 6 September 1927, Ron enrolled in the junior year at Helena High School, a forbidding Victorian building of rough-hewn grey stone with castellated gables and turrets, just five minutes' walk from the Waterbury home. A cousin, Gorham Roberts, who was in the same year, introduced Ron to many of his new school-mates, but no one found it easy to settle down to work, for the whole school was distracted by the frustrating knowledge that Charles A. Lindbergh was visiting Helena. He was on a triumphant tour of the country after flying the Atlantic alone in his tiny monoplane *Spirit of St Louis* and returning as a national hero, and there was not a boy or girl in the school who did not fervently wish to catch a glimpse of him.

At first Ron seemed perfectly happy at Helena High, perfectly happy to be back with his grandparents. In October he joined the Montana National Guard, enlisting at the State Armory on North Main Street and claiming he was eighteen to avoid having to wait months for his parents to send consent papers from Guam. As a private in Headquarters Company of 163rd Infantry he felt he cut quite a dash as he strode through the town in his uniform – broad-brimmed hat, khaki shirt and breeches, gloves tucked into the belt – to report for training at the Armory, where twin flagpoles rose from perfectly manicured patches of green grass.

At school, he managed to get himself appointed to the editorial staff of *The Nugget*, Helena High's bi-monthly newspaper. He would naturally have preferred to have been editor-in-chief, but as a newcomer he had to be satisfied with jokes editor, a position he held jointly with Ellen Galusha. He was photographed with the rest of the editorial staff for the year book, standing in the middle of the group on the steps of the school wearing a suit and a bow tie, eschewing the faintly raffish literary style affected by his colleagues. '*The Nugget* is a really good paper . . .' the caption explained. 'The name originates from the large expensive gold nuggets which the prospectors mined in previous years on the main street of Helena.'

Although Ellen Galusha rather upstaged her fellow jokes editor by winning first place in the district finals of the Extemporaneous Speaking Contest, Ron felt he kept his end up by having one of his essays selected to represent Helena High in the State Essay Contest. He had also written a short play which was performed by the junior branch of the Shriners and very well received.

After school on 2 December, Ron and a group of his friends rushed round to the showrooms of Capital Ford hoping to see the sleek new Model A. Fords which were said to have arrived in town that day. They found a crowd of around four thousand people jamming the street outside the Ford agency, all with the same idea. Replacement for the beloved Model T., the Model A. was not only a completely new design but was also available in a number of different *colours*, a development which caused Ron and his friends to gasp with amazement. Later, over sodas at the Weiss Café on North Main Street, the boys hotly debated which of the models – roadster, sports coupé or sedan – was preferable and which colour each of them would be purchasing as soon as they had some money.

That winter was the worst in living memory for the people of Helena. On 8 December, Ron woke to find the overnight temperature had dropped fifty-eight degrees to thirty-five below zero, one of the coldest on record. Outside, a biting blizzard swept down from the mountains, obliterating the town and the surrounding country.

Morning editions of the *Helena Independent* were full of terrible
stories of families marooned and frozen to death, school buses lost in
the storm and entire herds of cattle wiped out.

The snow had still not melted when Ron began preparing for the
annual Vigilante Day Parade, the high spot of the school year, held
on the first Friday in May. Although the theme of the parade always
harked back to the pioneer days, Ron plumped for a more unconventional role and decided he would go as a pirate. He somehow
persuaded five doubting friends, two boys and three girls, to join
him, casually brushing aside any objections based on the rather
obvious absence of pirate involvement in Montana's early history.
Aunt Marnie helped with the costumes by taking down her drapes
and removing the brass rings to provide the pirates with suitable
earrings, as worn on the Spanish Main.

Thus it was that as the Vigilante Day Parade, led by the Helena
High School Band, progressed along Main Street on the afternoon of
Friday 4 May 1928, the settlers, cowboys, cowgirls, miners, trappers,
prospectors, Indians and sheriffs were inexplicably joined by a small
band of ferocious pirates with eyepatches and painted beards, waving
wooden cutlasses. At the dance after the parade, 'Pirates by R.
Hubbard' won one of three prizes in the 'Most Original' category.

The report on the parade in the *Helena Independent* next day
positively glowed with pride: 'The parade was larger, more ingenious, spectacular, striking, imaginative and suggestive of the past this
year than ever before. The high school students once more covered
themselves with glory – besides having a jolly good time and commu-
nicating a lot of fun to the bystanders . . . As a success the Vigilante
parade was complete, and once more advertized to the world that the
Helena High School and Last Chance Gulch puts on a show once a
year unmatched elsewhere on the globe.'

A week later, Ron disappeared. When he did not show up for
school on Monday 14 May, there were excited rumours in the junior
year that he had been expelled. 'Certainly we believed he had left in a
hurry, under something of a cloud,' said Gorham Roberts. 'The story
was that he had got mad at a teacher and put his butt into a
waste-paper basket. Old A. J. Roberts, the principal, was a German
from Heidelberg and a strict disciplinarian. Ron knew that he would
never put up with such behaviour, so he didn't trouble to come
back.'[7]

Aunt Marnie explained it differently: 'He just got itchy feet. He
wanted to see something new. He was an adventurer at heart. The
wanderlust was in him and he couldn't see himself staying in a little
town like Helena when there was adventure ahead. He went off to
Seattle to stay with my sister Midgie and her husband Bob. They

tried to talk him into staying with them, but he went south, hopped a ship and worked his way back to Guam.'[8]

Whatever the truth, Ron never returned to Helena High. Two years later, he wrote two colourful accounts of the events leading up to his departure from Helena. Although they were only separated by a few pages in his journal, many of the details do not match; indeed some passages read suspiciously like the adventure stories he was constantly scribbling in his spare time.

It seemed he was driving his friends home after the Vigilante Day Parade in his 'mighty Ford' (presumably his grandfather's Model T.) when someone threw a baseball at them and hit him on the head. He stopped the car, chastized the offenders and dealt with them so severely that he broke four 'marcarpals' in his right hand.

'That was the beginning and the end. I couldn't wait and school faded from the picture. My hand was reset four times and life lost its joy. I sold the Ford and went West, taking Horace Greeley's [*sic*] advice.'

He announced to his grandfather that he had decided on a 'change of scenery' and caught a train for Seattle, where he stayed with his aunt and uncle for a couple of days. On 7 June, trading on his 'scout prestige', he moved to Camp Parsons for about a week, until it became too crowded and he decided to move on.

'I set out at noon, hiking a swift pace under a heavy pack through the lofty, virgin Olympics. At nine o'clock that night I made camp about two miles down the trail from "Shelter Rock". Twelve hours later I was limp on top of a boulder pile, saved from a broken spine by my pack. I gazed at the blood pumping from my wrist and decided it was high time I went to visit herr Docteur.'

No explanation is offered for this incident or for how he managed, in such a parlous state, to find his way back to Bremerton. It was there, while being treated by a Navy doctor, he was told that a US Navy transport, *USS Henderson*, was due to leave for Guam from San Francisco in a week's time (in the first account), or two weeks (in the second account). That night (first account), eight days later (second account), he was on a Shasta Limited overnight train heading south for California, apparently intent on rejoining his parents in Guam.

By the time he got to the Transport Dock in San Francisco the *Henderson* had already sailed. With only twenty dollars left in his pocket, Ron invested a nickel in a newspaper and read on the shipping page that the liner *President Pierce*, bound for China, was moored at Dock 28. An hour later he was standing in line at the dock, waiting to sign on as an ordinary seaman. While in the queue, smoking to calm his nerves, he suddenly decided it would be worth a call to Twelfth Naval District to find out where the *Henderson* was. Perhaps, he thought, she had not yet sailed for Guam, but had just moved down the coast to another port. His hunch was correct – an officer at Twelfth District told him the *Henderson* was in San Diego. Within half an hour – he appeared remarkably lucky with connections – he was on a bus bound for San Diego, five hundred miles further south.

When he finally caught up with the *Henderson* in San Diego, 'faint from lack of sleep and food', he was told that Washington would need to approve his request for a passage to Guam. Nothing if not bold, Ron called on the Aide to the Commandant, who turned out to be extraordinarily obliging and agreed to telegraph Washington immediately. Satisfied there was nothing more he could do for the moment, Ron rented a cheap room near the naval headquarters and slept for eighteen hours. When he woke, he learned that a signal had been received from Washington saying that his father's permission would be needed before he could join the ship.

'With fear and trembling, I had a radio sent out to Guam . . . I walked the streets of San Diego all that day with Old Man Worry gnawing at my brow. Would Dad reply "No!" or would he say "Yes"? You see, I had reason to be worried. This would be the first intimation he would have of my portending return . . .'

Out in Guam, Lieutenant Hubbard no doubt wondered what the hell was going on when he received a message from Washington informing him that his son was in San Diego requesting passage on a ship to Guam. It was to his credit that he immediately cabled his permission, which arrived in San Diego, according to Ron, only an hour before the *Henderson* was due to sail.

This does not quiet accord with the deck log of the *Henderson*, which records that 'L.R. Hubbard, son of Lieutenant H.R. Hubbard USN, reported on board for transportation to Guam' at 1620 hours on Saturday 30 June. The ship did not sail until 1330 the following day. Neither do the dates match Lieutenant Hubbard's navy record, which indicates that Ron wrote to the Navy Department asking about transports to Guam as early as 10 May; he submitted a formal application for a passage in the *Henderson* on 28 May.[9]

However, Ron never considered that strict regard for the truth should be allowed to spoil a good story and so he described how he was standing with his suitcase in his hand at the bottom of the gangway to the ship when the cable came through. He had lost his trunk, somewhere between San Francisco and San Diego, but he was unconcerned. 'The *Henderson* sailed with me aboard,' he noted triumphantly. 'My possessions were: two handkerchiefs, two suits underwear, one pair shoes, one worn suit, one thin topcoat, one tooth brush, two pair socks and two pennies. No wardrobe, no money . . .'

He ended this part of his journal with a jaunty little postscript addressed to the reader: 'I will tell you the secret of this strange life I had. Sssh! I was born on Friday the thirteenth.'

It was, unfortunately, not quite true. <u>13 March 1911 was a Monday</u>.

Even stranger: Miller (on pg. 12) records Ron's birth as 3/11/1911, Tilden, NB, 2:00 AM! Maybe the "Rouster" was never born at all?!!

Chapter 3

Explorer Manqué

Hubbard's amazing adventures as an explorer are graphically described in *Mission Into Time*, a book published by the Church of Scientology. It seems that Hubbard spent more than four years, from 1925 to 1929, journeying throughout Asia, financed on his travels by his 'wealthy grandfather'. After his grandfather's death, the 'budding and enthusiastic world traveller and adventurer' returned to the United States, where he enrolled at George Washington University as a student in one of the first nuclear physics courses ever taught in an American university. Naturally, he quickly became an associate editor of the university newspaper and a prominent member of many of the university's clubs and societies.

Cruelly deprived of funds from his wealthy grandfather, the young man supported himself by writing and soon established for himself a reputation as an 'essayist in the literary world'. In 1931, between studies and toiling as an essayist, he also found time to become director, at the age of twenty, of the Caribbean Motion Picture Expedition, which apparently provided invaluable research for the University of Michigan and underwater films for the Hydrographic Office.

Yet this was nothing compared to what was to come in 1932, when L. Ron Hubbard demonstrated his true worth as 'an *exceptional* explorer' by carrying out, as leader of the West Indies Mineral Survey, the first complete mineralogical survey of Puerto Rico. 'This was pioneer exploration in the great tradition, opening up a predictable, accurate body of data for the benefit of others. . . .'

* * * * *

The *USS Henderson* arrived off Guam on 25 July 1928 in heavy squalls and lay to on the lee side of the island for five days, waiting for an opportunity to enter the harbour. The weather did not seem to bother Ron. 'That trip was the best I ever took,' he wrote in his journal, 'and the best I ever hope to take. The Navy gave me a kangaroo court martial, there were nine young grass widows aboard, we danced every other night, the movies were good.'

Ron omitted from his journal any mention of how his parents reacted to his return. After more than a year apart, Harry and May were no doubt happy to see their seventeen-year-old son again, but they could not have been too pleased by his impetuous decision to drop out of High School. Since there was no possibility of getting him back to the United States in time for the start of the senior year – even if he would agree to go – it was decided that he should stay on Guam and be tutored by his mother in preparation for the entrance examination to the Naval Academy.

In spite of the limitations of her teaching experience, May seemed undaunted by the task of bringing her wayward son up to a sufficiently high educational standard to get him through the reputedly tough and highly competitive exam. And with servants padding softly about the house, attending unbidden to every household chore, she had plenty of time to devote to her son's studies.

For his part, Ron could not have been happier to substitute the authoritarian regime of old A.J. Roberts at Helena High for what he considered to be the exotic tropical allure of Guam and the gentle coaching of his mother.

In October, the Hubbards had an opportunity to take a recreational trip to China on the *USS Gold Star*, the ship that had brought May and Ron to Guam in the summer of 1927. Neither of them had much liked the ship, but the prospect of ten days' sight-seeing in Peking outweighed any reservations they might have had about another voyage. Hub warned his son that he would only be allowed to accompany them on condition that he continued his studies while the ship was at sea. Ron readily agreed.

On 6 October, thirty families reported on board the *USS Gold Star* for transportation to the China ports and return. Like the other officers on the excursion, Lieutenant Hubbard signed on for 'temporary duty' – he was Assistant to the Supply Officer. As previously, Ron kept a log of the trip, using one of the accounts books that his father could always provide. 'It is a delightful sensation', he scrawled in an early entry, 'to once more experience the pounding of engines below me and to hear the swish of a dark-blue sea outside our port.' At the bottom of the page was a world-weary, elegiac postcript: 'Another boat caught. Is ever thus?'

After a stop in Manila, which he reported as being like 'Guam plus XXX and a few trimmings', they sailed north towards the China coast. Ron was reluctantly confined to a desk in Cabin 9, claiming good progress with his studies.

The *Gold Star* re-fuelled with coal at Tsingtao, a busy port on the

Shantung Peninsula only recently returned to China after being occupied for some years, first by the Germans, then the Japanese. Ron took the trouble to research Tsingtao's history and concluded that the Chinese, with all their corruption, were unworthy heirs to their own territory inasmuch as they had failed to profit from the efforts of Germany and Japan to clean up their country. 'A Chinaman can not live up to a thing,' he wrote, 'he always drags it down.' On 30 October he noted thankfully: 'We have left Tsingtao forever, I hope.'

On the following day the *Gold Star* anchored off T'ang-ku, from where its passengers took a train to Peking.[1] Like American tourists the world over, they made sure they got at least a glimpse of all the sights, which Ron described as 'rubberneck stations'. He was decidedly unimpressed by Peking's historical and religious architectural heritage.

The Temple of Heaven, probably the supreme achievement of traditional Chinese architecture, he considered 'very gaudy and more or less crudely done'. The summer palace was 'very cheap as to workman-ship' and the winter palace was 'not much of a palace in my estimation'.

The Lama temple, closed a few days after their visit by the newly-formed National Government, was 'miserably cold and very shabby . . . The people worshipping have voices like bull-frogs and beat a drum and play a brass horn to accompany their singing (?).'

As for the Imperial palaces in the Forbidden City, one was 'very trashy-looking' and most of the others were 'not worth mentioning'.

Only the Great Wall of China seemed to fire his imagination and that mostly because it was 'the only work of man's hand visible from Mars'. If China turned it into a 'rolly coaster', he added, 'it could make millions of dollars every year.'

Neither did the Chinese people endear themselves to the opinionated young American. He found them shallow, simple-minded, dishonest, lazy and brutal. 'When it comes to the Yellow Races overrunning the world, you may laugh,' he noted. '. . . [The Chinese] have neither the foresight or endurance to overrun any white country in any way except by intermarriage. One American marine could stand off a great many yellowmen without much effort.'

Even the climate failed to please. Winter lasted from October to May, he said, the cold was intense, and it was so dry that dust formed ankle-deep in the roads and caused 'Peking sore throat', a formidable complaint that endured all winter.

'I believe that the most startling thing one can see in northern China', he wrote, 'is the number of camels. These are of a very mean breed but they resist cold and carry burdens which is all the Chinaman requires of them. Every day in Peking one can see many caravans in

the streets. They have a very stately shamble. They carry their head
high; their mean mouths wagging and their humps lolling from side
to side. All my life I have associated camels with Arabs and it strikes
a discordant note with me to see the beasts shepherded by Chinamen.'

The *Gold Star* stopped at Shanghai and Hong Kong before heading back to Guam, but Ron tired of further descriptive writing, apart
from taking a final swipe at the luckless Chinese race. 'They smell',
he concluded, 'of all the baths they didn't take. The trouble with
China is, there are too many chinks here.'

On the final leg of the voyage, Ron's devotion to his studies rather
appeared to falter, for he began filling his journal with one-paragraph
synopses of short stories that he had either written, or perhaps
intended to write, for magazines like *True Confession* and *Adventure*.
It was clear from these entries that he was already thinking of a career
as a writer, the Naval Academy notwithstanding. Indeed, he gave the
impression that he had been grinding away at a typewriter for years,
ending one synopsis, titled 'Armies for Rent', with a nonchalant
addendum that it would include the 'usual plot complications'.

Predictably, the Orient was his favourite setting and the hero was
invariably a white adventurer, as in 'Secret Service': 'Adventure. All
in a day's work. Casual laddie in Hankow. Saves town. Joins Brit SS
to carry out such orders as "Giovinni in Mukden exciting Communists. Use your own judgement. C13".'

None of his efforts, it must be said, were startlingly original: 'Love
story. Goes to France. Meets swell broad in Marseilles. She takes
him to her sink, bedroom and bath where he lives until notable
citoyens object. He stands them off and takes the next boat for
America having received a long expected will donation.'

On page 119 of the accounts book, Ron settled down to write a
complete, though untitled, story which began: 'A lazy sun peeped
over the horizon to throw glittering streamers of light across the
breakers on the surf. The laggoon [*sic*] lay blue and cool. Tropical
birds winged about their daily business and two figures lay stretched
on the white coral sand. Two ragged figures, several feet apart . . .'

Ron's grasp of English grammar was as uncertain as his spelling. It
transpired that these two figures, a boy and a girl, were the sole
survivors of a shipwreck. The girl roused the boy in traditional
fashion ('Bob! Bob! Speak to me!'), whereupon Bob spoke thus:
'"Their [*sic*] gone, all gone, they're dead and the ship is at the
bottom."'

Alone on a desert island paradise, nature takes it course and they
swear undying, though entirely chaste, love. But after being rescued
and returning to the United States they drift apart. The story –

interrupted on page 123 by the scribbled working of some hated algebra equations – ends with a poignant reunion in a San Francisco hotel lobby during which the couple laugh at their earlier foolishness.

Although Ron's narrative writing was still immature, he demonstrated an obvious talent in the craft of short-story writing, structuring the narrative skilfully and compensating for what he lacked in literary skill by sheer productivity.

The *Gold Star* arrived back at Guam on 18 December and in the weeks and months that followed Ron turned out dozens of stories and essays, filling one accounts book after another. His mother took a photograph of him as a budding young writer, sitting at a desk in the bungalow with his fingers poised on the keys of a big upright typewriter, although he actually preferred to write by hand in a large, untidy script, frequently crossing out words or sentences, sometimes even whole pages, as he progressed.

Like all writers, there were some days when it just would not come right:

'The sun was hot, the day was still, the palm trees gaudy green, lined the beach of that tropical isle . . .

'The sun was hot, the day was still and Hospital Corpsman James Thorpe surveyed his tiny domain . . .

'The sun was hot, the day was still . . .

'The sun was hot and except for the monotonous drone of the sea beating the cruel reef the day was still . . .'

At the age of eighteen, Ron was a pink-faced, lanky youth with a cowlick of red hair and a spotty complexion, but he was writing as if he was a well-travelled man of the world, a carefree, two-fisted, knockabout adventurer with a zest for life. It was an image he was able to create by using the slender experience of his brief travels in the East to provide a gloss of verisimilitude on the overheated combustion of his imagination.

In this way, he felt able to philosophize about 'the untrustworthy, lying, cruel, changeable, satirical Lady Luck', as if he had suffered more than once from her capriciousness: 'This humorist of humorists, this demon of demons has dragged men from their places in the sun into the slime of oblivion; has made beggars kings; has, with a whisper, made and crushed thousands; has laughed at the beings who supposed they ruled our destinies; and has killed enough men to patch hell's highway its blistering length.'

Only when dealing, gingerly, with the opposite sex did the pubescent man of the world lose his assurance. The story that began so tortuously with 'The sun is hot . . .' was about a male nurse in the Navy who fell for his native assistant. 'She took the chair with a sly glance at the boy and folded her slim brown hands in her lap. The

Corpsman was suddenly aware that she was beautiful. He swam for a moment in the depths of her clear brown eyes and then seated himself quickly upon the grass. He was somewhat startled by his discovery and told himself fiercely that she was native, native, native.'

When, inevitably, they fell into each other's arms ('Dimly he saw Marie on the porch and in a moment he felt her in his arms . . .') Ron seemed unsure how to proceed with the story. He scored through the next four lines so heavily as to make them illegible, then abandoned it.

As his attention was so diverted by his fantastic excursions into his imagination, it was perhaps no surprise that Ron failed the entrance examination to the Naval Academy at Annapolis. Mathematics, which he detested, let him down.[2] His father was disappointed but still convinced that Ron could get through the examination. Lieutenant Hubbard's tour of duty in Guam was soon coming to an end and he knew that his next posting would be to Washington DC, where he was to be Disbursing Officer at the Naval Hospital. He discovered that Swavely Preparatory School in Manassas, Virginia – which was within the Washington DC metropolitan area – ran a special course for Annapolis candidates and after a lengthy exchange of telegrams between Guam and Manassas, he managed to enroll Ron for the 1929–30 school year.

The Hubbards returned to the United States at the end of August 1929 and went straight to Helena, Montana, for a happy family reunion. (Their return was not prompted by the death of Ron's 'wealthy grandfather', as suggested in 'official' biographies, since Lafayette Waterbury was still very much alive. He died, aged sixty-seven, on 18 August 1931.) May, who had sometimes found the tropical climate in Guam exhausting, was particularly pleased to be home, filling her lungs with the sweet mountain air of Montana, and she decided to stay on for a while when the time came for Hub to take Ron to Washington.

On 30 September Ron started back at school in the leafy environs of Manassas. In Helena, May sat down to write her son a loving, but gently chiding, letter on the family's rickety typewriter:

> Dearest Ronald,
>
> Am thinking a lot about this, your first day at school. Do hope you like it and that you study every lesson thoroughly. Remember you are paying for the information and so do not hesitate to ask a teacher again and again about anything that is not clear. I want you to hold to just this one job – getting through school and passing examinations at the top. Don't write anything outside your school stuff. Don't read anything outside of school requirements. When you are through with lessons, get outdoors for your health. If you stick to this rule you will win through.

I am feeling worlds better in this mountain air. It is a wonderful change from the tropics. It is too bad that dad could not also have had it instead of going so early on the job. He did it for you so when you feel like slacking, I want you to remember dad gave up his hard earned leave to put you where you are. There is only one way you can pay dad and that is by making good. Your success is our biggest goal in life . . .

May went on to tell her son about the weather, a two-day fishing trip and the trout she had caught, and Toilie being mad because he had not written her any letters. He was to let her know if he wanted his hiking boots. 'I am on my toes to hear all about your school . . .' she concluded. 'With love and best wishes. Mother.'

Lieutenant Hubbard's heartfelt hope that his son would follow him into the US Navy through the Naval Academy was soon to be dashed. During his first semester at Swavely, Ron went to a doctor complaining of eye-strain and was sent to the Naval Hospital for tests. These revealed him to be so short-sighted that he stood no chance of passing the medical requirements for entry to Annapolis. May, meanwhile, had arrived from Helena and moved into a small house in Oakcrest, Virginia, which Hub had rented for them. Many evenings she would sit with her husband fretting about Ron: Hub's gloom about what the future held for his son was greatly exacerbated by the Wall Street Crash, which seemed as if it would engulf the country in catastrophe.

Ron himself exhibited little regret that a career in the Navy was no longer an option. At Swavely he was made an associate editor of the school's monthly newspaper, the *Swavely Sentinel*, and he was also busy rehearsing for his part as Anatol in *Episode*, a one-act comedy which was to launch the Swavely Players' season on 13 December. In truth, being an editor or an actor was a sight more alluring to him than being in the Navy, although he would never have admitted it to his father.

While Ron was happily immersed in school life at Swavely, his father was in frequent contact with the Registrar at George Washington University to try and find a way of getting his son accepted as an undergraduate. Lieutenant Hubbard was advised that if Ron could earn sufficient credits at a recognized school – Woodward School for Boys, a YMCA 'crammer' in Washington DC, was mentioned – he would not be required to sit the College Entrance Examination for the university.

Accordingly, Ron was enrolled at Woodward in February 1930. At the beginning of May he took time off from his studies to enlist as a Private in the US Marine Corps Reserve, adding two years to his age and giving his occupation, for some reason, as 'photographer'. It seems he was unconcerned by such piffling mendacity, even on official documents, for his bold signature appears at the bottom of his Service Record, confirming both the errors and his physical description – height 5'10½", weight 165lb, eyes grey, hair red, complexion ruddy. Six weeks later he was inexplicably promoted to First Sergeant, a leap in rank that was astonishing even by his own standards of self-regard.[3]

Ron's lack of concern for literal truth was exemplified by the persistence with which he claimed he had once been the youngest eagle scout. Even when he won the Woodward school finals in the National Oratorical Contest, with a speech on 'The Constitution; a Guarantee of the Liberty of the Individual', the school newspaper did not fail to mention that he was 'at one time the youngest eagle scout in America', although it was not immediately apparent what this had to do with oratory.[4]

To the intense pleasure of his parents, Ron graduated in June. In a letter to another university (Lieutenant Hubbard was clearly determined to keep his son's options open), his father wrote proudly: 'Ronald worked day and night to prepare for the several examinations and was successful in passing all of them. In my own opinion he has covered considerably more ground than is usual in any high school course and the fact that with all the handicaps he has encountered he has succeeded, he is therefore the best possible subject for university and college work.'[5]

On 24 September 1930, Ron was admitted as a freshman to the School of Engineering at George Washington University, with a major in civil engineering – a discipline suggested by his father. He was photographed for *The Cherry Tree*, the university year book, standing in the back row of the student chapter of the American Society of Civil Engineers in a smart suit and spotted tie, staring solemnly at the camera, hair smarmed back and instantly identifiable by his curiously protuberant lips, which often gave him an unfortunately sullen demeanour.

The GW Campus, in the heart of Washington DC, was a lively place to be at the start of the 'thirties, despite Prohibition and the worst depression in American history. Even though the newspapers were full of stories about children scavenging for food in garbage cans and pictures of gaunt faces waiting in bread lines, civil engineering students seemed to face a bright future, for people were already beginning to talk about the new erea of technocracy, the absolute domination of technology, and the 'Great Engineer' – Herbert Hoover – occupied the White House, just a few blocks from the campus. In New York, the Empire State Building, the tallest building in the world, was nearing completion, testimony to the vision, brilliance and the bright prospects of American civil engineers.

Unhappily, it was a future Ron viewed with some jaundice, for his heart was not in engineering and he had no time for worthy folk like civil engineers. While lecturers droned on about the theory of structure and stress analysis, Ron's imagination roamed the world of the adventure comic strips which were just then beginning to make an impact on American mass culture. His lusty fantasies were still peopled by spies and commissars, pirates and warlords, English soldiers of fortune with impeccable credentials and the stiffest of upper lips pitted against Chinamen of barely credible inscrutability.

His mother's advice – 'don't write anything outside your school stuff' – was quickly forgotten as he covered page after page of his notebooks with swashbuckling yarns, usually set in the Orient and always scribbled in obvious haste as if he could never wait to arrive at the dénouement. His literary interests naturally attracted him to the staff of the university's weekly newspaper, the *Hatchet*, but while Ron considered himself well enough qualified to be an editor, all he was offered was the job of reporter, which lowly position he only managed to endure for a few months in the spring of 1931.

However, he had become much enamoured of late with the infant sport of gliding and the idea of learning to fly and he was able to use his influence at the newspaper to stimulate interest in the formation of a university gliding club. On 1 April 1931, the *Hatchet* reported that an initial meeting of the George Washington University Gliding Club was to be held soon. The club had secured the use of a Berliner primary trainer and plans were being made to buy a power glider to train students for power flight. Anyone interested, the report concluded, should contact L. Ron Hubbard at the *Hatchet* office.

Thereafter, Ron made sure that the activities of the gliding club were extensively covered. On 15 April it was reported that 'several GW men who are well versed in the science of aviation and motorless flight' were expected to attend an initial meeting the following day. 22 April: 'Glider Club Begins Training at Congressional Airport.' 13 May: 'Members of Glider Club Try Out Theories In Air.'

Ron adored gliding and spent a great deal of time hanging around at Congressional Airport in Rockville, Maryland, hoping to cadge an extra flight and a tow in the Old Ford that pulled the gliders into the air. He never hesitated to cut classes if it meant 'going up' and he relied on his fellow students to brief him on the content of the classes he missed. It was not an ideal way to qualify as a civil engineer.

Although Ron was elected president of the gliding club, it rather appeared from the reports in the *Hatchet* that he was in danger of being overshadowed by his vice-president, one Ray A. Heimburger. The 13 May story noted, for example, that Heimburger was the first member to release his tow-line in the air, at the height of forty feet, while Ron was still 'trying his hand at the art of making turns in the air'. Einstein's theories were a 'pipe', Ron was quoted as saying, 'compared to the navigation of a motorless ship'. A few weeks later, Heimburger won second place in a spot landing contest at the Curtis Wright Air Show in Baltimore; another GW student took third place, but Ron did not merit a mention.

If there was any jealousy between the president and his deputy, it was forgotten on 13 July when they both passed their tests at Congressional Airport. Ron was rated 85 – average – by the examiner and was awarded Commercial Glider Pilot Licence No 385.[6] By then he had completed 116 flights – evidence of the amount of time he had devoted to the sport in the two months since the gliding club began training.

It was hardly surprising that Ron's success as a glider pilot was not matched by academic achievement and his grades at the end of the second semester were disappointing. He got an A for physical education, B for English, C for mechanical engineering, D for general chemistry and Fs for German and calculus. His overall grade for the year was D average, a result which gave no pleasure at all to his parents. They were convinced that he could do better.

After a stern warning from his father that he would be expected to show a big improvement in his second year, Ron left Washington to spend the summer vacation at Port Huron, Michigan, where he had arranged to help a friend, Philip Browning, run a gliding school. While he was there, Browning taught him to fly a small stunt plane, although Ron never held a licence for powered flight.[7]

Ron was still in Port Huron when he learned in August that his beloved grandfather had died. The entire family gathered in Helena for the funeral – all six Waterbury 'girls' (Hope had died in childbirth in 1928) were there with their husbands and children and Ray came from Canada with his wife. Lafe was buried at Forestvale Cemetery, a quiet patch of prairie mid-way between the town and the mountains. Immediately after the funeral, Ron returned to Washington to report for two weeks' annual training with the 20th Marine Corps Reserve and was rated 'excellent' for military efficiency, obedience and sobriety.[8]

On the morning of Sunday 13 September 1931, the good people of Gratis, Ohio, a small farming community in Preble County, were surprised to see a small biplane swoop out of the sky and land on a field to the east of the town. The pilots, according to an awed report in the *Preble County News*, were Philip Browning and 'L. Ron "Flash" Hubbard, dare-devil speed pilot and parachute artist'.

The newspaper reported that the two flyers were forced down after running short of fuel. George Swisher, on whose farm they landed, must have been a phlegmatic sort of chap, because it was averred that his first words were: 'Anything I can do for you boys?' After the 'dare-devil speed pilot and parachute artist' had explained the problem, an obliging local by the name of Raymond Boomershine volunteered to run into town to get them some gas.

'Meanwhile,' Ron would recall, 'a lot of people were arriving. They wanted to know if we needed any help. And we said the plane had to be turned around and although they were all in their Sunday best they grabbed the tail and turned her around. Then Raymond Boomershine came back with the gas and helped us fill the tank. We tried to pay him and he said "Nope" and my pal said, "We don't know how to thank you." And Raymond said, "Well, if you put it that way, I always wanted to ride in one of them things. How about a short hop?" That started it. Everyone and his kids got a ride.'⁹

According to the *Preble County News*, a total of thirty-six 'daring souls' were given a joy-ride that Sunday, by which time it was too dark for the fliers to leave. They stayed the night with Mr and Mrs Luther Kiracofe and next day 'roared on to St Louis, headed for more adventures'.

On the same day Ron was roaring to St Louis, he was also placed on 'scholastic probation' at George Washington University because of his poor grades. When he eventually returned to Washington he appeared unabashed by this stricture, for he continued to devote much of his energy to the gliding club in the hope of raising sufficient funds to purchase a soaring plane.

A few years later Ron would provide, in his usual jaunty prose, a picturesque description of how he had become disillusioned with civil engineering: 'I have some very poor grade sheets which show that I studied to be a civil engineer in college. Civil engineering seemed very handsome at the time. I met the lads in their Stetsons from Crabtown to Timbuctu and they seemed to lead a very colorful existence squinting into their transits. However, too late, I was sent up to Maine by the Geological Society to find the lost Canadian Border. Much bitten by seven kinds of insects, gummed by the muck of swamps, fed on johnny cake and tarheel, I saw instantly that a civil engineer had to stay far too long in far too few places and so I rapidly forgot my calculus and slip stick . . .'¹⁰

At the end of the next semester, Ron's grades showed no improvement and he remained on probation. He was nevertheless elected a member of Phi Theta XI, the Professional Engineering Fraternity, and was photographed for the year book in formal evening dress, black tie and starched wing collar, as if grimly intent, like his fraternity fellows, on pursuing a career building bridges.

On the evening of 8 January 1932, Ron could be found among the eight hundred revellers at the first Engineering Ball, held in the west ballroom at the Shoreham Hotel in Washington. Music for dancing was provided by Red Anderson and his orchestra – 'Mood Indigo', 'Goodnight Sweetheart', 'Minnie the Moocher' and 'When the Moon comes over the Mountain' were the popular songs of the day – and the cabaret featured The Troubadours, under the directions of one Trimble Sawtelle. The *Hatchet* listed Ron as one of the members of the organizing committee and declared the event to be a 'pronounced success'.

A more important event for Ron that month was the publication of his first article in a magazine. 'Tailwind Willies', in the *Sportsman Pilot*, described his adventures flying across country in the Midwest with his friend Philip 'Flip' Browning. 'We had three weeks' excess time before we had to get back to the college grind,' he wrote. 'Our resources were one Arrow Sport biplane, two toothbrushes and four itchy feet . . . We carefully wrapped our "baggage", threw the fire extinguisher out to save half a horsepower, patched a hole in the upper wing and started off to skim over four or five states with the wind as our only compass . . .'

The forced landing at Gratis was not apparently considered worthy of mention, perhaps because there appeared to be no shortage of spectacular, not to say unlikely, incidents. At Newport, Indiana, for example, they stopped to take on gas but got stuck in a muddy field. 'I crawled out to let Flip take a whirl at it alone. By using up half the field he managed to wish the muddy *Sparrow* into her element, and after building some altitude, wheeled over to the place where I stood and called down that there was another field a short distance away. After pacifying a sheriff, who was about to lock me up for trespassing, by shoving him into a mud puddle, I hopped onto the running board of a Purdue Boy's car and burned road over to Flip's new landing place – if you could call it that. The second field was little better than the first and three attempts were necessary before we willed the *Sparrow* up just in time to see a nine-foot telephone wire at the height of our prop. Flip threw the nose down and the wires were a scant foot above my head . . .'

Any hope of Ron knuckling down to his studies disappeared early in 1932 when the *Hatchet* announced its intention to publish a monthly Literary Review. Nothing could have suited him better, for it provided him with a further excuse to neglect his tedious engineering books while he wrote more short stories, and sifted through the hundreds he had already written, to find something suitable for publication.

It was unthinkable, out of the question as far as Ron was concerned, for the Literary Reveiw to appear without a contribution from L. Ron

Hubbard and the first issue, published on 9 February 1932, carried a short story eponymously titled 'Tah', about a twelve-year-old boy soldier in China on a route march to a gory death at the point of a bayonet. It was clearly a successful debut, for the third issue included 'Grounded', another bloodthirsty Hubbard story, this one a description of a naval engagement on the Yangtze river, swirling with headless corpses, in which the Commanding Officer of *HMS Spitfire* meets a sticky end.

In May, Ron won the Literary Review's drama contest with a one-act play, *The God Smiles*. Set in a café in Tsingtao in Communist China, the plot hovered uncertainly between Chekhov and farce and involved a White Russian officer and his lover hiding behind a curtain to escape arrest by a tyrannical warlord.

Ron was pleased to have his work acknowledged, but he was by then immersed in a new and consuming project that would temporarily take precedence over all his other interests – even gliding. He was making plans to lead an 'expedition' to the Caribbean.

Other, less bombastic, students might have been inclined to describe the venture as a 'summer cruise', but that was not Ron's way. No, it was to be nothing short of a full-fledged expedition and he was to be its leader. He had already decided on a suitably grandiose title—the Caribbean Motion Picture Expedition. Its dubious scientific aim was to explore and film the pirate 'strongholds and bivouacs of the Spanish Main' and to 'collect whatever one collects for exhibits in museums'.[11]

The background to the 'expedition' was that Ron and his friend Ray Heimburger had discovered a big old four-masted schooner, the *Doris Hamlin*, berthed in Baltimore and available for charter through the summer. Two hundred feet long and 1061 gross tons, she had never been fitted with engines and was thus not exactly overwhelmed with business. Ron had a long talk with the skipper, Captain Fred Garfield, and reckoned that if he could get together about fifty other students they could afford to charter the *Doris Hamlin* for the whole of the summer vacation. After all, he reasoned, with unemployment in the Unites States topping thirteen million, no one could entertain much hope of finding a vacation job. It did not take him long to find enough volunteers to join him – a tribute to his enthusiasm, organizational ability and salesmanship.

The first report of the forthcoming expedition in the *Hatchet*, on 24 May 1932, was not by-lined but bore all the hallmarks of L. Ron Hubbard's florid literary style. 'Contrary to popular belief,' it began, 'windjammer days are not over and romance refuses to die the death – at least for fifty young gentleman rovers who will set sail on the schooner *Doris Hamlin* from Baltimore on 20 June for the pirate haunts of the Spanish Main . . .

'According to L. Ron Hubbard, the strongholds and bivouacs of the Spanish Main have lain neglected and forgotten for centuries and there has never been a concerted attempt to tear apart the jungles to find the castles of Teach, Morgan, Bonnet, Bluebeard, Kidd, Sharp . . . Down there where the sun is whipping up heat waves from the palms, this crew of gentleman rovers will re-enact the scenes which struck terror to the hearts of the world only a few hundred years ago – with the difference that this time it will be for the benefit of the fun and the flickering ribbon of celluloid. In their spare time, if they have any, they will scale the heights of belching volcanoes, hunt in the thick jungles, shoot flying fish on the wing . . .'

Apart from exploring and 're-enacting' pirate scenes (a perhaps questionable contribution to science), the 'gentlemen rovers' also planned to collect valuable botanical specimens, write articles for travel magazines and make a number of short movies. 'Scenarios will be written on the spot in accordance with the legends of the particular island and after a thorough research through the ship's library, which is to include many authoritative books on pirates.'

The itinerary was similarly crowded – during the one hundred-day cruise it was planned to stop at sixteen ports on the islands of Martinique, Dominica, Guadeloupe, Nevis, Montserrat, St Croix, Vieques, Puerto Rico, Haiti, Jamaica, Gonave, Tortue and the Bahamas. More experienced expedition leaders might have paused to ponder the feasibility of attempting to sail five thousand miles in one hundred days in an old four-master with no auxiliary power, but Ron was able to draw on all the overweening confidence of his twenty-one years and would not consider anything remotely less ambitious.

The expedition certainly appeared to have impressive backing. There were reports that the University of Michigan was providing technical support, the Carnegie Institute and the Metropolitan Museum were somehow involved, a sea-plane had been shipped on board to take aerial pictures, Fox Movietone and Pathé News were competing for film rights and *The New York Times* had contracted to buy still photographs. Members of the expedition, it was said, would be sharing the profits from these various lucrative deals.

It seemed that young Ron Hubbard had pulled off quite a coup and it was in the spirit of the greatest possible optimism that the *Doris Hamlin* set sail from Baltimore on 23 June, only a few days behind schedule. As the schooner slipped her moorings, spread her four great sails and leaned into Chesapeake Bay, every man on board believed he was on the threshold of a great adventure. Ron, standing in the bows with the wind ruffling his red hair, was grinning as broadly as the rest,

even though ten of the 'gentleman rovers' had entertained last-minute
second thoughts and pulled out, leaving the expedition in what he
would later ominously describe as a 'delicate financial situation'.

In Washington, nothing was heard of the expedition until 5 August,
when the *Hatchet* reported that the schooner had arrived, 'with
everything ship-shape', at Bermuda on 6 July. The story quoted a
letter, presumably from Ron, explaining some of the expedition's early
difficulties: 'We had one H--- of a time getting out of the Chesapeake
Bay with the wind blowing in like the very devil. After that we had a
couple of days of calm. Then a stiff breeze came along and we keeled
over and ran before it nicely. But next it blew into a storm and for two
days we were tossed and rolled about enough to make nearly everyone
sick. After that we got a break and the last three days our bowsprit has
been cutting through the brine at eight or nine knots.'

What was not explained was why, two weeks after leaving Baltimore,
the *Doris Hamlin* was in Bermuda, six hundred miles out in the
Atlantic and almost as far from Martinique, her planned first port of
call, as Baltimore. It was a question that could not be answered until
early in September when the *Doris Hamlin* sailed back into Chesapeake
Bay three weeks before her expected return. In Baltimore, Captain
Garfield, a man of few words but with thirty years' sailing experience,
sourly declared the voyage 'the worst trip I ever made'.

Even Ron, who did his best to put a brave face on it, could hardly
conceal the fact that the Caribbean Motion Picture Expedition had
been a disaster. From the start, nothing had gone right: after leaving
the east coast of the United States, storms had driven the schooner far
off course and Captain Garfield had told Ron they would have to put
into Bermuda to replenish the fresh water tanks, which had sprung a
leak. Ron, who knew there was barely enough money in the kitty to
cover expenses, ordered the Captain to stand off the island to try and
avoid harbour charges. Garfield refused. A heated argument followed
but the veteran skipper was not of a mind to take orders from a
twenty-one-year-old and sailed his ship into Bermuda harbour.

At this first landfall, eleven members of the expedition promptly
announced they had had enough adventure and intended to go home.
They had been disgusted, Ron explained, by the 'somewhat turbulent
seas'. It transpired that the ship's cook also suffered from seasickness
and so Ron fired him and hired two Bermudans to take his place. By the
time he had paid off the cook and settled the bills for fresh water
supplies, mooring and pilotage, the Caribbean Motion Picture Expedition was in danger of running out of money before it even arrived in the
Caribbean.

Two days out from Bermuda, bound for Martinique, Ron discovered that all the fresh water which had been taken on board had

leaked away and his relationship with the Captain became even more acrimonious. It took the *Doris Hamlin* seventeen days to reach Martinique, where she arrived a month to the day after leaving Baltimore.

As soon as the anchor splashed into the blue water of the bay at Fort de France, once notorious for yellow fever, several more 'gentleman rovers' abandoned ship and made their own way home, disinterested in further roving with Ron. After they had gone ashore, Ron decided on a showdown with the increasingly surly Captain Garfield. As a result of the fresh water débâcle, he said, he would not be handing over any more money to the Captain. Garfield stomped off, muttering dark threats.

News of this development instantly reached the ears of the six-man crew, whom Ron had earlier affectionately described as 'old sea dogs'. Faced with a threat to their wages, they instantly turned rabid and demanded Ron pay them in full, in advance. The leader of the rapidly disintegrating expedition tried to placate them and promised to cable home for more money.

Meanwhile, Captain Garfield was sending his own cable home – to the owners of the *Doris Hamlin*, warning them that the charter fees were at risk. Their response was immediate and unequivocal. Garfield was ordered to sail the ship straight back to Baltimore. Ron pleaded for more time, swore there was no shortage of money, threatened dire retribution in the courts, appealed to the Captain's better nature – all to no avail. In desperation, he went ashore to seek advice from the US Consul in Fort de France, but was told there was nothing that could be done.

The *Doris Hamlin* weighed anchor and set a course for home with not a single pirate haunt explored. The 'gentlemen rovers' could do no more than stare moodily from the schooner's rails as the islands they hoped to visit passed by on the horizon and dropped astern. 'When we left Martinique, the whole aspect of the trip had changed,' Ron confessed. 'Morale was down to zero.'

Captain Garfield was obliged to stop at Ponce in Puerto Rico to take on supplies of food and water and Ron went ashore once more to make a final attempt to salvage the expedition. At the Ponce Harbor Board he was told he could take legal action against the owners of the *Doris Hamlin* but that it might take months to resolve. Sadly, he accepted defeat and the remaining 'gentleman rovers' were carried unwillingly back to Baltimore.

After his return to Washington, he wrote an account of the expedition's troubles for the *Washington Daily News*, contriving to cast Captain Garfield in the worst possible light. To head off assumptions that the whole trip had been a flop, he concluded in

typically rhapsodic vein: 'Despite these difficulties, we had a wonderful summer. The lot of us are tanned and healthy and we know what
few men know these speedy days – the thrill of plowing thru blue seas
in a wooden ship with nothing but white wings to drive us over the
horizon.'

By the time Ron and Ray Heimburger got round to preparing a
report for the *Hatchet* on 17 September 1932, the Caribbean Motion
Picture Expedition had been miraculously transformed into something of a triumph. Slow sailing, unforeseen expenses and lack of
experience were blamed for the cutback in the itinerary, but 'although
the expedition was a financial failure, nevertheless the adventures and
scientific ends accomplished well compensated for the financial
deficit.'

Among the scientific accomplishments claimed was the collection of
a great many specimens of flora and fauna for the University of
Michigan, some of them 'very rare', the provision of underwater film
to the Hydrographic Office, and 'much research work in the field of
natural life while at the various islands'. *The New York Times*, it was
reported, had bought some of the photographs taken on the
expedition.

Life on board the *Doris Hamlin* was presented in the rosiest of
lights and there was even a hint of romantic adventures ashore: 'By
way of amusement on board the ship, the boys entertained themselves
with chess, bridge, volley-ball tournaments, etcetera, and on land,
when they weren't out catching sharks or harpooning or visiting some
colourful spot, they were capably entertained by the dark-eye señori-
tas at the various ports.'

All in all, the report concluded that the expedition was nothing
short of a 'glorious adventure'.

Curiously, no trace may be found of the many contributions to
science which Ron claimed on behalf of the Caribbean Motion Picture
Expedition. The Hydrographic Office has no record of receiving the
expedition's underwater films,[12] the University of Michigan can find
none of the specimens brought back by the 'gentleman rovers'[13] and
the archives at *The New York Times* hold no photographs from the
expedition, no evidence that it was ever intended to buy such
photographs, nor indeed any indication that the newspaper was even
aware of the expedition's existence.[14]

Mystery similarly surrounds the West Indies Minerals Survey, that
'pioneer exploration in the great tradition' during which Ron is said to
have completed the first mineralogical survey of Puerto Rico. This
would certainly have been an impressive achievement for a twenty-
one-year-old civil engineering student, but the US Geological Survey
knows nothing about it[15], neither does the Puerto Rican Department

of Natural Resources[16] nor Doctor Howard Meyerhoff, visiting professor in geology at the University of Puerto Rico, 1931–2.[17]

When Ron returned home from the Caribbean, he discovered that his grades for his second year at George Washington University were disastrous: a B for English, but D in calculus and electrical and magnetic physics, and an F for molecular and atomic physics. He was perhaps not surprised and as his expectation of graduating was fast receding he could see no point in wasting a third year studying a subject in which he had no interest. When he adjudged the moment to be appropriate, he announced to his parents that he had had enough of civil engineering and did not intend to return to university.

May and Harry Hubbard were mortified. As they saw it, their son was squandering a fine opportunity to enter a respectable profession and enjoy a successful career; it seemed such a waste. But Ron adamantly refused to listen to their entreaties that he should face up to his responsibilities, return to university, study hard and graduate.

Lieutenant Hubbard, accepting at last that Ron could not be persuaded to change his mind, cast about for something worthwhile to keep his son occupied until he was ready to think again about a proper career; he was determined not to allow Ron to fritter away his time scribbling more stories. At the Naval Hospital where he was still working as Disbursing Officer, he heard that the Red Cross was looking for volunteers to work in Puerto Rico. On 13 October, he wrote to the Navy Department requesting a passage to San Juan for his son, supporting his request with a note: 'The purpose of sending my son to Puerto Rico is to place his services at the disposal of the American Red Cross in their relief work on that island.' Two days later, the request was approved.

On 23 October 1932, Ron reported on board the US Navy transport, *USS Kittery*, at Norfolk, Virginia, for transportation to Puerto Rico. Among his fellow passengers were a number of nurses and the wife of the director of the American Red Cross. While he was still at sea, readers of the November issue of the *Sportsman Pilot* were entertained by a second L. Ron Hubbard article, this time about his escapades as a glider pilot. He described 'the most terrible nightmare I have ever gone through' – how his glider had folded a wing at four hundred feet, how he had battled to prevent it going into a spin and how, as he crashed, 'so many wires wrapped themselves about my neck that I was unable to wear a collar for weeks.' A few weeks later, he modestly added, he set up an unofficial world record by flying a glider at a speed of eighty miles an hour at a level altitude for a duration of twelve minutes.

The *USS Kittery* arrived at Port au Prince, Puerto Rico, on 4

November. The log book records that L. R. Hubbard left the ship along with his fellow passengers, but by then he had plans other than volunteer relief work. Somewhere between Norfolk, Virginia, and Port au Prince it seems that Ron decided to abandon the Red Cross and strike out into the hills in search of the gold he was convinced must have been left behind on the island by the Conquistadores.

He would later claim that he spent at least six months prospecting in Puerto Rico: 'Harboring the thought that the Conquistadores might have left some gold behind, I determined to find it . . . After a half year or more of intensive search, after wearing my palms thin wielding a sample pack, after assaying a few hundred sacks of ore, I came back, a failure.'[18]

It is possible that his real motive was not so much a genuine expectation of striking gold as a desire to escape the dreary clutches of the Red Cross. As he noted in an article written on his return to the United States: 'Gold prospecting in the wake of the Conquistadores, on the hunting grounds of the pirates in the islands which still reek of Columbus is romantic, and I do not begrudge the sweat which splashed in muddy rivers, and the bits of khaki which have probably blown away from the thorn bushes long ago.'

Quite how long he spent splashing through muddy rivers was not documented. Certainly at one point during his short sojourn on the island, he appears to have been employed as a field representative for a prospecting company called West Indies Minerals and a photograph exists of him standing disconsolately in a pith helmet, hands in his pockets, watching a party of three or four labourers digging on a hillside.

But if he was supervising the first mineralogical survey of Puerto Rico, it was a survey destined never to materialize in any archive. Indeed, it rather seems as if the 'West Indies Minerals Survey' derived from a trip undertaken, at the insistence of Ron's angry and disappointed father, more as a penance than an expedition.

Chapter 4

Blood and Thunder

'His first action on leaving college was to blow off steam by leading an
expedition into Central America. In the next few years he headed
three, all of them undertaken to study savage peoples and cultures to
provide fodder for his articles and stories. Between 1933 and 1941 he
visited many barbaric cultures and yet found time to write seven
million words of published fact and fiction.' (*A Brief Biography of L.
Ron Hubbard*, 1959)

Precious little care went into compiling the many biographies of L.
Ron Hubbard. Had anyone bothered to research Hubbard's published
output, it would immediately have been obvious that he had not
written anything like seven million words during this period. Between
1933 and 1941, he published about 160 articles and stories, almost all
of them in pulp magazines. The nature of the medium proscribed
lengthy literary efforts, thus pulp fiction tended to be short, with few
stories running to more than 10,000 words. If he had written seven
million published words, the *average* length of each of his contributions would have been an impossible 44,000 words.

A little intelligent inquiry would also have established that Hubbard
never left North America during the years in question: the 'fodder' for
his stories derived not from expeditions to faraway places, but from
past experiences embellished by his fecund imagination. Neither did
he visit 'barbaric cultures', except, perhaps, those to be found in New
York and Los Angeles . . .

* * * * *

Ron arrived back in Washington DC in February 1933, not too
disappointed at his failure as a gold prospector and hotly anxious to
renew his acquaintanceship with a young lady he had met on a gliding
field shortly before his father sent him packing to Puerto Rico.

The object of his ardour was a twenty-six-year-old farmer's daughter from Elkton, Maryland. Her name was Margaret Louise Grubb,
but everyone called her Polly. She was a bright, pretty girl with
bobbed blond hair and an independent streak in keeping with the age
of Amelia Earhart who, nine months earlier, had become the first

woman to fly solo across the Atlantic. Earhart inspired thousands of American women to take an interest in aviation and at weekends Polly used to like to walk out to an airfield near her home to watch the gliders wobble uncertainly into the air behind a tow from an aged and rusting Ford.

An only child whose mother had died years earlier, she both looked after her father and supported herself financially (she had got her first job, working in a shoe shop, at the age of sixteen). But despite her responsibilities, she was soon determined to learn to fly and was well on the way to getting her own licence[1] when a young man with startling red hair showed up at the airfield one weekend.

Polly could hardly fail to register Ron's arrival since he was immediately the focus of attention among the little group of leather-helmeted pilots waiting for a tow. They seemed to gather naturally around him, laughing frequently while he talked non-stop, slicing the air with his hands to illustrate his various aerial exploits. For his part, it was not long before Ron noticed the attractive young woman in flying gear and strolled over to talk to her.

Although she was nearly four years older than Ron, the difference in their ages did not bother Polly in the least. Other, less open-minded, women might never have considered the possibility of a romance with a man younger than themselves, but Polly found Ron to be an irresistible companion – kind, considerate, entertaining and always able to make her laugh. He talked a great deal about his travels in the East, but she was never bored; indeed, she was constantly amazed at all the things he had seen and done. He was so much more mature, so much more *worldly*, than the young men she knew around Elkton, a rural community of less than six thousand people close to the north-east corner of Chesapeake Bay. Most of *them* had never been further than Wilmington, Delaware, ten miles up the road.

Polly's father was, understandably, faintly alarmed to learn that his daughter was 'walking out' with Ron Hubbard. It was not that he did not like the young man; he, too, thought Ron was charming. Nor was he concerned that Ron was younger than Polly. What worried him was the fact that Ron had neither money nor career prospects and apparently had no intention of looking for a job, since he planned to support himself by writing. In Mr Grubb's eyes, being a writer was not a *job*, and nothing Ron could do or say would convince him otherwise, particularly since he could only produce two articles from the *Sportsman Pilot* as evidence of his earning potential.

However, both Mr Grubb and Ron's parents recognized the futility of trying to oppose the match. Polly was quite as headstrong as Ron and if she had made up her mind to marry him, there was nothing anyone in the world could do to stop her. And Ron, still the adored only child, always got his own way with his parents. Blessings were reluctantly bestowed and the marriage took place in Elkton on Thursday 13 April. Many of the guests correctly speculated about the whirlwind nature of the courtship and the speed with which the ceremony was arranged. Polly and Ron moved into a little rented house in Laytonsville, Maryland, where she had a spontaneous abortion. In October, she discovered she was pregnant again.

In May Ron received an assignment from the *Sportsman Pilot* to cover an amateur flying competition at College Park Airport, near Washington. His report was competent enough and written in his usual breezy prose: 'Since I was, perforce and per poverty, among the spectators, I can speak only from the ground view and venture the point that those six [pylon] races suffered on only one score. They inherited the disadvantage of all conventional pylon races – we on the ground had nothing to watch save an empty sky as the ships disappeared for their swing around the course. The finishes, though, made up for that temporarily empty sky. The home stretch brought the ships down a brisk wind, through some bumps for which the field's tree-trimmed boundaries must be blamed, and down across the finish line in a power dive to fifty feet. That satisfied the spectators; it looked meteoric and heroic. And you know spectators.'

The article was published in the May/June issue of the magazine, with photographs also provided by Ron. It was his first published piece as a professional writer and he was very proud of it, but it could hardly be described as a promising start to his career. Months would pass before his by-line appeared again.

For a short while it seemed it did not much matter that Ron was finding it difficult to make a living as a writer, for on Friday 18 August, a headline in the *Washington Daily News* proclaimed: 'Youthful DC Adventurer Finds Gold in Nearby Maryland After Trek Fails.' The three-column story reported that L. Ron Hubbard, while on furlough from his job as general manager of West Indies Minerals Inc, had discovered gold on his wife's farm in Maryland.

Much was made of the irony of a prospector striking gold in his own back yard: 'Hubbard, still in his twenties, left here last year for Antilles, West Indies, in search of gold so that he might return and marry the girl he met shortly before his departure. He returned a short time ago empty handed and considerably weakened from fever . . . "Imagine me going 1300 miles in search of gold when it lay right at the back door of my bride-to-be," Hubbard said dejectedly.'

Ron told the newspaper that mining would soon be under way 'on a large scale' and he had also encountered several specimens of a curious white metal he believed was either platinum or iridium. Two photographs accompanied the story, one of Polly, fetchingly attired in boots and jodhpurs, panning for gold, and another of the young couple examining a large chunk of rock with an explanatory caption: 'L. Ron Hubbard, the prospector, says the boulder in the above photo is the largest specimen of gold quartz he has ever seen.'

Paradoxically, despite having struck gold, Ron's financial situation remained precarious. In September, his glider pilot licence expired and he was unable to renew it as he had not completed the necessary ten hours' solo flying in the previous six months. The problem was simply that he had no money, but in a plaintive letter to the Bureau of Aeronautics he side-stepped confessing he was broke by claiming the difficulty was that there was 'no glider within two hundred miles in which I would care to risk my neck'. The Washington Glider Club had offered him the use of their Franklin but it was in such a sorry condition he had to 'beg off' and he did not want to use a primary glider because 'I cracked one up once in Port Huron, Michigan, for the simple reason that most primaries won't fly.'

Ron was, as always, optimistic about the future. He said he was planning to get his own glider, a Franklin, in the spring. He was particularly anxious not to let his licence lapse as he had to wait two months for good flying days in order to take his commercial exam and he did not want to go through the whole rigamarole again. He added that he had flown a great deal more than most glider pilots and slyly suggested that perhaps the Bureau of Aeronautics had seen one of his glider articles in aviation magazines. 'Here's my plea', he concluded. 'Isn't there some way you can extend this thing in view of the circumstances . . . Isn't there something you can do about it?'[2]

It was a naïve hope: no bureaucracy is structured to indulge the roseate ambitions of young men and the Bureau of Aeronautics was no exception. Its dour reply was brief: 'It is regretted that your glider pilot's licence . . . cannot be extended as requested. Also it is the policy of this Department not to extend licences.'[3] Officially it was the end of Ron's gliding career, for he never again held a licence although he would apply, a couple more times, for a student pilot's licence.

In October, Ron contributed another feature to the *Sportsman Pilot*, this time a profile of Chet Warrington, a well-known Washington pilot, and in November he wrote an article about the infant science of radio navigation. His lack of a licence notwithstanding, he always adopted a chatty, aviator-to-aviator style: 'Personally, I abhor navigation. It takes too much algebra and I don't speak good algebra . . . It's my ambition to step into a ship some day and take off in rain and fog with the other coast in mind as a destination. But I don't like circular rules and too many gadgets. I'm lazy, I want someone to tie a piece of string to the hub of the prop and lead me right where I want to go. That's my ambition, and I'll bet my last turnbuckle in a power dive that it's yours too.'

In addition to his three pieces for the *Sportsman Pilot*, Ron also sold an article titled 'Navy Pets' to the *Washington Star* in 1933. But that was the sum of his published output for the year.

The going rate for freelance writers around that time was a cent a word. Polly, whose thickening waistline added greatly to her worries, calculated at the end of 1933 that her husband had managed to earn, during the course of that year, rather less than $100.

There were better times ahead, however, for Ron soon discovered his natural habitat as a writer – the blood and thunder world of 'the pulps'.

Pulp magazines had an honorable literary genesis in the United States and an eclectic following: John Buchan wrote *The Thirty-Nine Steps* in 1915 for *Adventure* magazine, which at one time counted among its subscribers such unlikely fellow travellers as Harry Truman and Al Capone. Writers like C.S. Forester, Erle Stanley Gardner and Joseph Conrad were introduced to huge new audiences through the pulps, as were unforgettable characters like Buffalo Bill, boy detective Nick Carter and the ever-inscrutable Dr Fu Manchu. The most successful of all pulp heroes, Edgar Rice Burrough's 'Tarzan of the Apes', made his first appearance in the pages of *All-Story* magazine and went on to spawn the longest-running adventure comic strip and Hollywood's biggest money-making film series.

By the early '30s, pulp fiction was a major source of inexpensive entertainment for millions of Americans and a convenient means of escape from the anxieties and realities of the Depression. For as little as a dime, readers could enter into an action-packed adventure in which the heroes slugged their way out of tight spots in various exotic corners of an improbable world. Good invariably triumphed over evil and sex was never allowed to complicate the plot, for no hero ever proceeded beyond a chaste kiss and no heroine would dream of expecting anything more.

In 1934, more than 150 pulp magazines were published in New York alone. *Black Mask* was considered the best of the bunch by writers, largely because it paid its top contributors as much as a nickel a word, but *Argosy*, *Adventure*, *Dime Detective* and *Dime Western* were all said to offer more than the basic rate of a cent a word to the best writers. As the average 128-page pulp magazine contained around 65,000 words and as many of them were published weekly, the market for freelance writers was both enormous and potentially lucrative.

Of all this L. Ron Hubbard knew virtually nothing until he began to cast around for new outlets as a matter of urgency after his first disastrous year as a writer. 'He told me', said his Aunt Marnie, 'that he went into a bookstall and picked up all the pulp books from the rack. He took a big pile home to see what it was that people wanted to read. He thought a lot of it was junk and he knew he could do better. That's how he started writing mystery stories.'[4]

More importantly, perhaps, it dawned on Ron that he had been writing in the pulp genre for most of his life. The swashbuckling short stories he had scribbled across page after page of old accounts books when he was in his teens were, he belatedly realized, precisely the sort of material that was to be found between the lurid covers of the most popular 'pulps'.

Polly was fast expanding and every week they were deeper in debt. Ron knew he *had* to earn money somehow and the 'pulps' seemed to offer the best hope. He began writing one story after another, winding page after page into his typewriter without a break, often hammering away all night. Typing at phenomenal speed, never needing to pause for thought, never bothering to read through what he had written, he roamed the entire range of adventure fiction with red-blooded heroes who were gunslingers, detectives, pirates, foreign legionnaires, spies, flying aces, soldiers of fortune and grizzled old sea captains. For a period of six weeks he wrote a complete story of between 4,500 and 20,000 words every day, gathered up the pages when he had finished and mailed it to one or another of the pulps in New York without a second look.

It did not take long to pay off. One morning Ron went out to collect the mail and found there were two cheques waiting for him, totalling $300 – more money than he had ever earned in his life. The first was from *Thrilling Adventures* for a story called 'The Green God', the second from *The Phantom Detective* for 'Calling Squad Cars'. More acceptances soon followed – 'Sea Fangs' was bought by *Five Novels Monthly*, 'Dead Men Kill' by *Thrilling Detective*, 'The Carnival of Death' by *Popular Detective* . . .

By the end of April Ron had earned enough money to take Polly on a short holiday to California. They took a cheap hotel room at Encinitas, a resort a few miles north of San Diego, but Polly, now seven months into her pregnancy, found the unaccustomed heat somewhat debilitating. On 7 May 1934, she decided to take a dip in the ocean to cool off and got caught in a rip tide. She was a strong swimmer but only just managed to get back to the beach and the exertion brought on labour. Later that day she gave birth to a son.

The baby weighed only 2lb 2oz and clung to life by the most gossamer of threads. Praying he would survive, they named him Lafayette Ronald Hubbard Junior. Ron constructed a crude incubator, first out of a shoe box, then by lining a cupboard drawer with blankets and keeping it warm with an electric light bulb; Polly wrapped the mewling mite in cotton wool and fed him with an eye-dropper. For two months they maintained a day and night vigil, taking it in turns to watch over the infant and marvelling at its will to live. While Polly was pregnant, Ron's father always used to ask her how 'his Nibs' was doing and by the time the danger period had passed L. Ron Hubbard Junior was known to the entire family as 'Nibs', a name that would stick for the rest of his life.

Fatherhood in no way moderated Ron's desire to be seen as a devil-may-care adventurer and fearless aviator and he assiduously promoted this image at every opportunity. In July, for example, he was the subject of a glowing tribute in the 'Who's Who' column of the *Pilot*, 'The Magazine for Aviation's Personnel', which described him as 'one of the outstanding glider pilots in the country'. The author, H. Latane Lewis II, made no secret of his admiration.

'Whenever two or three pilots are gathered together around the Nation's Capital,' he wrote, 'whether it be a Congressional hearing or just in the back of some hangar, you'll probably hear the name of Ron Hubbard mentioned, accompanied by such adjectives as "crazy", "wild" and "dizzy". For the flaming-haired pilot hit the city like a tornado a few years ago and made women scream and strong men weep by his aerial antics. He just dared the ground to come up and hit him . . . Ron could do more stunts in a sailplane than most pilots can in a pursuit job. He would come out of spins at an altitude of thirty inches and thumb his nose at the undertakers who used to come out to the field and titter.'

It was not too surprising that Ron was considered to be eminently suitable for inclusion in the 'Who's Who' column, for it was patently obvious that he had been at pains to project himself as the most colourful of characters: 'Before he fell from grace and became an aviator, he was, at various times, top Sergeant in the Marines, radio crooner, newspaper reporter, gold miner in the West Indies and movie director-explorer . . .' Among his other achievements, it seems he taught himself to fly powered aircraft ('He climbed into a fast ship and, without any dual time at all, gave the engine the soup and hopped off . . .'), then became a barnstormer and 'flew under every telephone wire in the Middle West', before settling down to become director of the flying club at George Washington University. H. Latane Lewis II concluded that Ron was 'one of aviation's most distinguished hell-raisers'. It was a sobriquet with which the subject heartily concurred.

When Nibs was bawling and burping like other contented babies, the twenty-three-year-old 'distinguished hell-raiser' decided it was time to make the acquaintance of his fellow pulp writers. Leaving Polly and the baby at home, he caught a train for New York and checked into a $1.50-a-night room at the Forty-fourth Street Hotel, which he had been assured was where many visiting writers stayed.

In 1934, with the country still in the stranglehold of the Depression, there were few tourists in New York, but even before the Wall Street Crash the Forty-fourth Street Hotel had rarely attracted much tourist trade. It was a seedy establishment on Times Square largely patronized by out-of-work actors, third-rate vaudeville performers, wrestlers, touts and bookies. Frank Gruber, the only pulp writer resident when Ron arrived, accurately characterized his fellow quests as 'all-round no-goods and deadbeats'.

Gruber was an aspiring writer from Mount Morris, Illinois, who had come to New York to make his fortune on the strength of selling one story to *Secret Agent X* magazine and a couple more to *Underworld*. That he was not succeeding soon became evident when he explained to Ron how to get a free bowl of tomato soup at an Automat. All you had to do, he said, was pick up a bowl, fill it with hot water, skip the nickel slot which dispensed soup powder and grab a couple of bags of crackers. You took your bowl of hot water to a table, crumbled the crackers into it, then tipped in half a bottle of tomato ketchup. 'Presto!' said Gruber triumphantly. 'Tomato soup.'

Not entirely motivated by charity, Ron offered to buy Gruber a meal. Sitting in Thompson's Restaurant on Sixth Avenue, just around the corner from the hotel, Ron pumped the other man for information about which editors were easiest to see, who was buying what kind of material and which magazines paid most. He made a list of the commissioning editors at the most important publishers – Street and Smith, the Frank A. Munsey Company, Popular Publications and Dell Magazines.

A few days later, Gruber took Ron along to Rosoff's restaurant on 43rd Street, where members of the American Fiction Guild met for lunch every Friday. Most of the successful pulp writers in New York were members of the Guild and most of them gathered at Rosoff's at lunchtime on Fridays. They were names familiar to millions of pulp readers: Lester Dent, creator of Doc Savage; George Bruce, acknowledged ace of battle-in-the-air yarns; Norvell Page, who was said to earn $500 a month for his stories in the *Spider*; and Theodore Tinsley, a regular contributor to *Black Mask*. President of the Guild was Arthur J. Burks, who had been dubbed 'King of the Pulps' in a *New Yorker* profile and quoted as saying that any pulp writer who did not make at least $400 a month was not worth his salt. It was a remark that was to cause him considerable embarrassment, for it was common knowledge in the Guild that Burks never earned that much, despite turning out around two hundred thousand words every month.

Ron was not the kind of young man to be overawed by such

illustrious company and he walked into the Guild lunch at Rosoff's as if he was quite as famous and successful as any man present. He was also a good deal younger than most of the members, but acted as if he had seen and done more than any of them. By the end of the lunch, he was confidently presiding over one end of the table, holding the attention of everyone within earshot with an enthralling blow-by-blow account of his expedition to explore pirate strongholds of the Spanish Main.

It was accepted, at the American Fiction Guild lunches, that members might be inclined to blur the distinction between fact and fiction. What mattered more than strict adherence to literal truth was that the stories should be entertaining, and on that score young Hubbard could not be faulted. He was a natural story-teller, able to set the scene quickly and evocatively, describe the action in rich detail, recount credible dialogue and interject humour with an acute sense of timing. Arthur Burks was happy to welcome him as a new member of the Guild, after he had paid his $10 membership fee, of course.

Ron did well in New York. He made the rounds of the pulp publishers, talked his way into the offices of the important editors, sold a few stories and generally made himself known. In the evenings he used to sit in Frank Gruber's room at the Forty-fourth Street Hotel, kicking ideas around with other young writers and holding forth, although his host eventually tired of Ron's apparently endless adventures. One evening Gruber sat through a long account of Ron's experiences in the Marine Corps, his exploration of the upper Amazon and his years as a white hunter in Africa. At the end of it he asked with obvious sarcasm: 'Ron, you're eighty-four years old aren't you?'

'What the hell are you talking about?' Ron snapped.

Gruber waved a notebook in which he had been jotting figures. 'Well,' he said, 'you were in the Marines seven years, you were a civil engineer for six years, you spent four years in Brazil, three in Africa, you barnstormed with your own flying circus for six years . . . I've just added up all the years you did this and that and it comes to eighty-four.'

Ron was furious that his escapades should be openly doubted. 'He blew his tack,' said Gruber.[5] He would react in the same way at the Guild lunches if someone raised an eyebrow when he was in full flow. Most of the other members *expected* their yarns to be taken with a pinch of salt, but not Ron. It was almost as if he believed his own stories.

Back home with Polly and the baby, Ron continued writing for 'the pulps' at a ferocious rate, turning out endless variations on a hairy-chested theme. His protagonists thrashed through jungle thickets pursued by slavering head-hunters, soared across smoke-smudged skies in aerial dog-fights, wrestled giant octopi twenty fathoms beneath storm-tossed seas, duelled with cutlasses on blood-soaked decks strewn with splintered timbers and held dervish hordes at bay by dispensing steel-jacketed death from the barrel of a machine-gun. Women rarely made an appearance except to be rescued from the occasional man-eating lion or grizzly bear. The titles he gave to his stories vividly attested to their genus – 'The Phantom Patrol', 'Destiny's Drum', 'Man-Killers of the Air', 'Hostage to Death' and 'Hell's Legionnaire'.

Interspersed between these gripping sagas, Ron still wrote occasional features for the *Sportsman Pilot* in his capacity as aerial hell-raiser. 'There are few men in the United States – nay, the world – as well qualified as I to write upon the subject of cross-country flying,' he began a piece in the September 1934 issue. 'It so happens I hold the world's record in dead reckoning. I just have to marvel about it. Probably no other pilot in the world could do it. Probably no other pilot in the world actually has done it so well.'

The braggadocio was a tease, as he soon made clear. On a fifty-mile flight from New London to Mansfield, Ohio, navigating by the sun, he claimed to have missed his destination by a record margin. 'The ship bumped to a beautiful landing. But, and but again, Mansfield was nowhere in sight. We grabbed a farmer's suspender and snapped it for attention. We asked, disdainfully, where we might be. Well, there's no use dragging this out. We were 37 miles off . . . That, I maintain, is a world record.'

In December he was offering readers tips about flying to the West Indies: 'With the long, long shores of Cuba behind you, you hit Port au Prince. Right now we start assuming definitely that your plane has floats on it, though we've been assuming it vaguely all along. Otherwise, you'll get your wheels wet. Port au Prince isn't favoured unless you can wangle the Gendarmerie du Haiti into letting you use their fields. You'd have to be a better wangler than we are . . .'

Two months after this feature was published, on 25 February 1935 Ron again applied for a student pilot's licence. He never got round to taking the test to become a qualified pilot and never actually applied for another licence[6], but he blithely continued writing for the *Sportsman Pilot*, offering advice to fellow aviators and filling many pages of the magazine with dashing accounts of his aerial exploits.

Ron's published work in 1935 included ten pulp novels, three 'novelettes', twelve short stories and three non-fiction articles. In October, *Adventure* magazine invited him to introduce himself to readers in their 'Camp Fire' feature, 'where readers, writers and adventurers meet'. Ron began in jocular fashion – 'When I was a year old, they say I showed some signs of settling down, but I think this is merely rumour . . .' – and touched on all the familiar highspots of his dazzling career, his 'Asiatic wanderings', his expeditions, his 'barn-storming trip through the Mid-West', and so on.

Perhaps because the same issue of *Adventure* also published one of his 'leatherneck yarns', Ron chose to elaborate on his experiences as a 'top-kicker' in the Marines. 'I've known the Corps from Quantico to Peiping, from the South Pacific to the West Indies,' he wrote. 'To me the Marine Corps is a more go-to-hell outfit than the much lauded French Foreign Legion ever could be . . .' Expressing the hope that his thumbnail sketch would be a passport to the readers' interest, he ended with the promise: 'When I get back from Central America, where I'm going soon, I'll have another yarn to tell.'[7]

Ron did not go to Central America but to Hollywood, where one of his stories, 'The Secret of Treasure Island', had been bought by Columbia to be filmed as a fifteen-part serial for showing at Saturday morning matinées. An advertisement in the *Motion Picture Herald* boasted that L. Ron Hubbard, 'famous action writer, stunt pilot and world adventurer' had written an 'excitement-jammed yarn with one of the best box office titles in years'.

Ron, of course, was pleased to add the title of 'Hollywood scriptwriter' to his ever-increasing roll-call of notable accomplish-ments and he would soon be claiming screenwriting credit for a number of successful movies, among them John Ford's classic, *Stagecoach*,[8] and *The Plainsman*, starring Gary Cooper. Most biographies of L. Ron Hubbard describe his Hollywood career, inevitably, as a triumph: 'In 1935, L. Ron Hubbard went to Hollywood and worked under motion picture contracts as a script-writer of numerous films making an outstanding reputation there with many highly successful films. His work in Hollywood is still remem-bered.'[9] He was also said to have salvaged the careers of both Bela Lugosi and Boris Karloff by writing them into scripts when they were out of work. In short, Ron became another 'Hollywood legend'.[10]

Sadly, it appears he was an unsung legend for his name cannot be found on any 'highly successful films', with the exception of *The Secret of Treasure Island*. But this lack of recognition never prevented Ron from reminiscing about his golden days in Hollywood: 'I used to sit in my penthouse on Sunset Boulevard and write stories for New York and then go to my office in the studio and have my secretary tell everybody I was in conference while I caught up on my sleep because they couldn't believe anybody could write 136 scenes a day. The Screen Writers' Guild would have killed me. Their quota was eight.'[11]

Ron did not stay long in Hollywood knocking out 136 scenes a day and by the end of the year he was back in New York. Polly was pregnant again and mindful of what had happened with Nibs, they decided she should have the baby in a New York hospital. On Wednesday 15 January 1936, she produced a daughter, Catherine May. Unlike Nibs, Catherine was a lusty, full-term baby, perfect in every way except for a birthmark on one side of her face. Not long after she was born, the Hubbards travelled by train to visit Ron's parents in Bremerton, Washington.

Harry Ross Hubbard had been promoted to Lieutenant-Commander, at the age of forty-eight, in December 1934 and the following July he was posted, for the third time, to Puget Sound Navy Yard, Bremerton, as an Assistant Supply Officer. For Ron's mother it was a particularly welcome move: her much-loved sister, Toilie, was by then also living in Bremerton and their younger sister, Midgie, lived across the bay in Seattle. May and Harry had already decided they would retire to Bremerton after he left the Navy and so they bought a small house at 1212 Gregory Way, just two blocks from the Navy Yard.

Ron's seventy-two-year-old grandmother, Ida Waterbury, was still at 'the old brick' in Helena, but in October 1935 Helena was hit by an earthquake. The first tremor was felt during one of President Roosevelt's Friday night 'fireside chats' on the radio. Throughout the following week, fifty-six further shocks were recorded, none of them serious, but at ten o'clock on the evening of 18 October a series of violent tremors shook the town, reducing many of the public buildings to rubble and generating widespread panic. 'The old brick' survived the earthquake, but in a dangerous condition. Next day, old Mrs Waterbury caught a train for Bremerton to stay with May and Hub at Gregory Way.

It was in these circumstances that Polly, Ron and their two small children were welcomed into the bosom of the Waterbury family when they arrived in Bremerton in the spring of 1936. All the Waterburys liked Polly. 'She was a lot of fun,' said Marnie, 'a good sport.' Polly reciprocated their warmth, was comfortable with the family and happy to have grandparents and great-aunts around to help take care of the boisterous Nibs while she looked after the baby.

Such was the conviviality of the milieu that Polly and Ron soon began looking for a home of their own in the Bremerton area. Property was cheap in rural Kitsap County and they found a little wooden house at South Colby, a small community with a post office and general store facing Yukon harbour to the south of Bremerton. The house was set among cedar trees on a steep hillside overlooking orchards and meadows sloping down to Puget Sound; from the front porch at nights you could see the lights of Seattle on the other side of the water. Polly fell in love with the place and named it 'The Hilltop'.

Although the house had three rooms upstairs, Ron decided he needed more privacy for writing and employed a local carpenter to build a rough pine cabin in the trees at the back of the property which he could use as a 'studio'. He put in a desk and typewriter and went back to work, churning out such stirring epics as 'The Baron of Coyote River' for *All Western*, 'Loot of the Shantung' for *Smashing Novels* and 'the Blow Torch Murder' for *Detective Fiction*.

The responsibilities of fatherhood weighed lightly on Ron's shoulders and he ignored any suggestion that he should adapt his working habits to accommodate family life. He liked to work all night and sleep all morning, sometimes not making an appearance until two or three o'clock in the afternoon, at which time Polly would be expected to produce 'breakfast'.

Although he was selling stories almost every week, they never seemed to have enough money and the owner of the general store in South Colby was frequently threatening to cut off their credit. Ron was completely unconcerned by the mounting bills. One day he took the ferry into Seattle and came back with an expensive phonograph that he had bought on credit at the Bon Marche department store. When Polly despairingly asked him how he was going to meet the payments he replied, with a grin, that he had no intention of making any. He figured it would be at least six months before Bon Marche got round to repossessing their property, meanwhile they could enjoy it.

Financial worries apart, Polly was perfectly content at The Hilltop. She enjoyed being a mother and was a keen gardener, spending much of her spare time clearing the ground around the house and planting shrubs and flowers. Ron was less easily satisfied by the quiet charm of South Colby and made frequent trips to New York 'on business'. As his absences became longer and longer, Polly suspected, correctly, that he might be seeing other women – she was also acutely aware that there was absolutely nothing she could do about it.

It was not philandering that took Ron away from home so much as the reality that being stuck out in the backwater of South Colby was uncomfortably at odds with his perception of himself. He had spent much of his adult life vigorously and successfully promoting himself as a 'dare-devil adventurer'. It was a description that would be used about him time and time again and he never tired of it. But it was also an image that needed to be sustained, bolstered here and there, and he could hardly do that sitting in a cabin in Kitsap Country. No, he needed to be in New York holding his fellow writers in thrall with epic tales and making sure everyone knew that Ron 'Flash' Hubbard (he sometimes admitted to 'Flash' as a nickname) was 'quite a character'.

Who dared doubt it? Absolutely not the editor of *Thrilling*

Adventure, who was pleased to share his conviction with his readers: 'I guess L. Ron Hubbard needs no introduction. From the letters you send in, his yarns are among the most popular we have published. Several of you have wondered too how he gets the splendid color which always characterizes his stories of far-away places.

'The answer is, he's been there, brothers. He's been and seen and done. And plenty of all three of them!'

In July 1936, New York literary agent and columnist Ed Bodin added a further feather to Ron's crowded cap by reporting in one of his columns that Ron had hit a staggering one million words in print. It was a claim as pointless as it was absurd, yet it would be remorselessly escalated over the years until by 1941 Ron was being variously credited with an output of between seven and fifteen million words.[12]

Whatever the real figure, Ron was certainly proud of his productivity, the sheer number of words he was able to hammer out of his typewriter, and there is no question that he was a truly prolific writer. By 1937 he was using a roster of marvellously improbable pen names – Winchester Remington Colt, Kurt von Rachen, René Lafayette, Joe Blitz and Legionnaire 148 among them. His legendary writing speed led to rumours that he typed on to a continuous roll of paper that fed automatically into an electric typewriter with a keyboard of his own design featuring single keys for commonly used words like 'and' and 'the'. It was also said that editors in New York sent messengers to Ron's hotel room with a cover illustration and note asking him if he would be kind enough to write a story to fit the picture. The punchline was that the messengers *would be told to wait* while Ron dashed off the story, such was the prodigious fertility of his imagination.

Towards the end of 1937, Ron sold his first hardback novel. *Buckskin Brigades*, published by Macaulay, was said to have been inspired by his experiences as a small boy in the wilds of Montana when he became a blood brother of the Blackfoot Indians. The theme of the book revolved around the mistreatment of the Indians by the Hudson Bay Company, although the message did not perhaps get across too forcibly because the Hudson Bay Company sent Ron a case of whisky after publication.

Polly was very pleased that Ron had been able to cross the divide between pulp fiction and 'respectable' publishing, although she was even more pleased that Macaulay had offered an advance of $2500 for *Buckskin Brigades*. It was money they badly needed to clear their debts. They both waited – Ron was back from New York – with considerable impatience for the cheque to arrive.

On the morning the local post office telephoned to say there was a money order for collection, Ron rushed out of the house and was gone for hours. He returned in the late afternoon in a state of high excitement and announced to Polly that he had bought a boat, a wonderful boat, a thirty-foot ketch called the *Magician*. It was a double-ended Libby hull, the kind they used to catch salmon up in Alaska. It had a small cabin and he was going to put a new engine in it and change the rigging and . . . Polly could hardly believe her ears. She had a drawer full of unpaid bills and her husband had just blown all their money on a boat!

Ron's best friend in Bremerton was a thrusting young insurance salesman by the name of Robert MacDonald Ford. 'Almost the first thing Ron did when he got the boat', Ford recalled, 'was to get some letter-heads printed. Ron was always having letter-heads printed, always on the best bond paper. The heading was "Yukon Harbor Marine Ways". There was no such company, but that didn't bother Ron – he only wanted the letter-head so he could buy things for the boat at wholesale prices.'

Ford met Ron because he was always on the look-out for new business. When one of his policy holders ran into a car owned by a Lieutenant-Commander H.R. Hubbard and caused $15 worth of damage, he delivered the settlement draft personally at 1212 Gregory Way in the hope of selling some more insurance. Ron's mother was home when Ford called. 'She was a funny little woman,' he said, 'sort of wrinkled and dried up. When I asked her if she knew anyone who needed insurance she said her son, who lived out at South Colby, didn't have any. She telephoned him right then, offered to pay half the cost and we wrote the business over the 'phone. I figured if she was going to pay I'd have a good chance of collecting the premiums.'

A couple of weeks later, Ford decided to pay his new policy holder a visit, accompanied by his wife, Nancy. It took them a little while to find The Hilltop at South Colby and when they finally arrived at the house Polly answered the door and said her husband was still asleep as he had been working all night. She apologized and invited them to return for dinner that evening.

The Fords and the Hubbards liked each other on sight and quickly discovered they had much in common. They had children of similar ages, both wives were avid gardeners and excellent cooks, and Ron and Mac were the same age, keen on sailing and loved to talk. That first evening spent together at The Hilltop ended with much hilarity when the two men skulked off to the County gravel pile in the dead of night to fill ballast bags Polly had been sewing for the boat.

Thereafter, Ford was a frequent visitor. He used to sit in the cabin with Ron drinking China tea and playing chess by candlelight, using the exquisitely carved chess set he said he had brought back from the

East – even the pawns were fearsome little warriors carrying swords. Sometimes they would shoot at a target pinned to the cabin wall with Ron's air pistol; sometimes they would just talk for hours on end, well into the night. They often discussed what was happening in Europe, what Hitler was up to and whether or not there would be a war.

'He was a sharp guy,' said Ford, 'very stimulating and fascinating to be around. He was interested in a lot of things and was pretty well informed. When he talked about the things he'd done, sometimes I would think he was feeding me a line, but then you'd find out that it had actually happened. He told me once that when he was gliding a guy wire had snapped and smoothed off the ends of his fingers, leaving them very sensitive. I'm pretty sure that happened. When we went to see *Stagecoach* – the original one with John Wayne – he told me he'd worked on the script. I looked for his name on the credits, but didn't see it, although I didn't necessarily disbelieve him. It's possible he exaggerated his exploits a little, but he was a writer and did have a very fertile imagination. Certainly he got into a lot of things.

'He and Polly were on pretty good terms. She was an independent sort of gal, wouldn't take a lot of crap from anybody. They had their arguments, yes, but by and large it wasn't that bad. She'd take a drink, but never much. We didn't drink too much in those days. They were in fairly dire straits for money; the grocer was always pressing them to pay his bill. It would take Ron two or three nights to finish a novelette. Whenever he got some money in, he'd see the grocer was satisfied and then he'd play for a while on his boat, the *Maggie*.'[13]

The Fords and the Hubbards joined Bremerton Yacht Club at the same time and whenever there was a dance they could be found at the same table, usually laughing and always enjoying themselves. In some combination the two families were involved in any number of madcap projects and outings – Polly and Nancy once took a ferry across to Victoria in Canada to visit a horticultural show and returned with dozens of stolen cuttings stuffed into their bras.

On another memorable occasion, Ron and Mac decided they would build an experimental sail-boat with inflatable rubber wheels on the theory that it would be subject to less friction than a conventional hull. They constructed a crude timber frame with three axles and six wheels made out of inner tubes on wooden drums and borrowed a mast and sail from a small boat in the harbour. It was agreed that Ron, the more experienced sailor of the two, would conduct the first trials. He kitted himself out for the occasion in sea boots, cap and yachting rig, and they towed the strange craft out into the Sound with a row-boat. Ron confidently stepped on board and as he did so there was an ominous crack. One of the crucial joints of the frame snapped under his weight and the entire contraption rapidly disintegrated.

The sight of Ron in his natty sailor suit clinging grimly to the wreckage and bellowing to be taken off was too much for Ford. He collapsed in the bottom of the row-boat and the more he laughed the angrier Ron became. In the end, Ford rowed ashore and let someone else pick up his friend. 'He had a real temper and I sure as hell wasn't going to let him catch me when he had his temper up like that,' he explained. 'He would have killed me if he'd got his hands on me at the time. I stayed out of sight for a couple of hours but he soon cooled down. We had dinner together that night.'

Undaunted by the failure of the rubber-wheeled boat, the two friends could soon be found testing a model boat with an unusual V-shaped keel of their own design in Polly's washing machine, trying to figure out an accurate method of measuring the drag. Then they spent several days on the *Maggie* with a complicated arrangement of zips and canvas sleeves with which they hoped to improve the efficiency of the sails.

While the men were playing, it was inevitable that Polly and Nancy would spend a great deal of time together with their children. Thus Nancy knew that Polly suspected Ron of having affairs with other women during his frequent absences back East. Nancy told Mac, who said he was sure Polly was wrong.

A few weeks later, the Hubbards arrived separately at the regular Saturday night dance at Bremerton Yacht Club. Polly drove alone from The Hilltop and Ron sailed across in The *Maggie*, making no attempt to conceal his surly demeanour. 'They were not speaking to each other,' said Ford, 'and it took us a while to find out what had happened. It seems Ron had written letters to a couple of girls in New York and left them in the mail box to be picked up. Polly found them and got so mad that she opened the envelopes, switched the letters and put them back in the box. She didn't tell him what she had done until they had been picked up. Polly was a great girl, a lot of fun.'

Next morning, Ron packed his bag and caught a train for New York, still in a vile temper.

Chapter 5

Science Fictions

'By 1938, Hubbard was already established and recognized as one of the top-selling authors . . . [and] was urged to try his hand at science fiction. He protested that he did not write about "machines and machinery" but that he wrote about people. "That's just what we want," he was told. The result was a barrage of stories from Hubbard that expanded the scope and changed the face of the literary genre . . .' (*About L. Ron Hubbard*, Writers of the Future, Volume II, Bridge Publications Inc, 1986)

* * * * *

To science-fiction fans, 1938 marked the dawn of a new era they were pleased to call the 'Golden Age'. Before then, science-fiction pulps with gosh-wow titles like *Amazing*, *Wonder*, *Planet Stories* and *Startling* had usually been ridiculed if not ignored. Crowded into the darkest corner, or on to the lowest shelf of the news-stand, they were only sustained by the devotion of a small group of passionately loyal enthusiasts who, dreaming of time machines and space travel in the grimly haunted days of the Depression, were widely considered to be dotty.

The sad truth was that the nineteenth century heritage of Mary Shelley, Jules Verne, Edgar Allen Poe and H.G. Wells had largely degenerated, by the early 'thirties, into trash – uninspiring tales of slavering robots and talking animals written in penny-dreadful prose, mediocre fiction without the science. Bug-eyed monsters figured prominently, either invading earth with the intention of enslaving the human race or carrying away our 'fairest maidens' for use as love-toys on some alien planet. Readers needed considerable faith to relish repeated workings of the same tedious themes, but then science-fiction fans were acknowledged to be particularly fanatical, if not particular.

It was possible to date, precisely, the metamorphosis that ushered in the Golden Age because it began with the appointment of John W. Campbell Junior as editor of *Astounding* magazine, at the age of twenty-seven, in early 1938. Campbell was the man who dragged science fiction out of the pulp mire and elevated it to an art form.

Opinionated, overbearing and garrulous, he was a chain-smoking intellectual dynamo bursting with ideas which he would expound at length, driving home every point by stabbing the air with his long black cigarette holder. His first science-fiction story, 'When The Atoms Failed', was published in *Amazing* in 1930 and he quickly made a name for himself as an original, imaginative and sophisticated writer. One of his best stories was transformed, through no fault of his, into one of Hollywood's worst movies, *The Thing From Outer Space*.

As an editor, Campbell used his magazine to speculate on the implications – emotional, philosophical and sociological – of future scientific discoveries. He expected style, skill, ingenuity and technical proficiency from his contributors. Few of the existing pulp writers could meet his exacting standards and so he set out to nurture new talent. Almost all the biggest names of the Golden Age – Isaac Asimov, Robert Heinlein, A.E. van Vogt and many others – were first published in *Astounding*. Campbell never compromised. Faulty plots were ruthlessly rejected with pages of closely typed criticism – Theodore Sturgeon once got a story back with a seven-page explanation as to why a particular fission of light metals was not feasible. Yet Campbell's critiques to writers were always accompanied by a flood of new ideas and suggestions for other stories. 'No editor was ever more helpful,' said Jack Williamson, one of his contributors. 'He read every story submitted. Those he rejected came back with useful comments, and many a letter accepting one story also included ideas for another.'[1] The mechanical ants in Williamson's novel, *The Moon Children*, were Campbell's idea.

Isaac Asimov always remembered his first meeting with Campbell in the Seventh Avenue offices of Street and Smith, the publishers of *Astounding*. 'I was eighteen and had arrived with my first story submission, my very first. He had never met me before, but he took me in, talked to me for two hours, read the story that night and mailed the rejection the following day along with a kind, two-page letter telling me where I had gone wrong.'[2]

Campbell was both a visionary and a realist. He believed in supernatural power and space travel and rockets and a multiplicity of worlds, but he also fervently believed that science fiction should live up to its name. His writing was studded with extraordinary technical detail explaining how complex machines worked, yet his scientists were always real people with human emotions and foibles.

One of what he called his 'pet ideas' was that less than a quarter of the functioning capacity of the brain was used. 'Could the full equipment be hooked into a functioning unit,' he wrote in *Thrilling Wonder Stories* in 1937, 'the resulting intelligence should be able to conquer the world without much difficulty.' Working on this doubtful premise, Campbell made unremitting attempts to encompass telepathy, ESP and other odd psychic phenomena into a science he called 'psionics'.

As the reputation of Campbell's *Astounding* grew, new magazines appeared on the streets thick and fast – *Marvel Science Stories* was out first, closely followed by *Startling Stories*, *Dynamic Science Stories* and *Fantastic Adventures*. To distance his own magazine from the more garish pulps, Campbell changed the title to *Astounding Science Fiction*, which he thought sounded more dignified and more accurately reflected the content.

Campbell first met L. Ron Hubbard at about the time he took over as editor. Ron provided a typically bombastic account of the circumstances: 'I got into science fiction and fantasy because F. Orlin Tremaine, at the orders of the managing director of Street and Smith, brought me over and ordered John W. Campbell Jr . . . to buy whatever I wrote, to freshen up the mag, up its circulation, and to put in real people and real plots instead of ant men. John, although we became dear friends later, didn't like this a bit.'[3]

Tremaine was an editorial director of Street and Smith and might well have effected the introduction – he would certainly have known Ron, since Ron had contributed many stories to Street and Smith's stable of adventure pulps. But it was inconceivable that Campbell would have been *ordered* to buy everything Ron wrote. Campbell was an editor of total dedication and a notorious perfectionist – he would never have relinquished his right to edit or to ask contributors for a rewrite if he thought it was necessary. 'Those who could not meet his requirements,' said Isaac Asimov, 'could not sell to him.'

Whatever the circumstances of their meeting, it was clear that the young editor and the young writer hit it off, for in April 1938 Campbell wrote Ron a long, funny letter, full of friendly gobbledegook, to chide Ron for not making contact when he was recently in New York. 'HUBBARD SNUBBARD: HUBBARD SNUBBARD: HUBBARD SNUBBARD,' Campbell began. 'When I was a little boy, on me fodder's knee, he says to me, says he to me (yes, I was a little boy, and I did have a fodder, and he did have a knee, and he did say to me): "Never take offense, where offense isn't meant." So thata is data . . .'

He continued in similar vein for several pages, invited Ron to contribute some anecdotes about himself for a feature he was writing on the pulp magazine industry and ended: 'My best to your wife and kiddies. I am now about to sign off. By the way, forgive the bad copy; I only learned to type a couple of weeks ago, and can't control the engine sometimes. Addio, John.'[4]

Ron's first story for *Astounding*, and his first venture into science fiction, was 'The Dangerous Dimension', published in the July 1938 issue. It was a diverting little tale about a mild-mannered university professor, Henry Mudge, who works out a philosophic equation enabling him to transport himself to any part of the universe by thought alone. Teleportation causes him endless difficulties since every time he thinks about a place he finds himself whisked there with no more than a 'whup!' By and large, he is remarkably unperturbed, as when he thinks himself to Mars ("Oh dear," thought Mudge. "Now I've done it!").

'The Dangerous Dimension' was followed later in the year by a three-part novelette, 'The Tramp', which also dealt with fantastic powers of the mind. The tramp, one 'Doughface Jack', falls from a train and suffers severe head injuries. After an operation to save his life during which a silver plate is inserted into his head, he discovers he has the power to heal, or to kill, with a single glance. The surgeon is so envious of his patient's remarkable new powers that he decides to have the operation, too, with less happy results.

When, by and by, it became important to promote an image of Ron as one of the world's great thinkers and philosophers, these two stories would be presented as clear evidence that L. Ron Hubbard had begun his research into the workings of the mind. Science fiction, it was explained, was 'merely the method Ron used to develop his philosophy'.[5]

It was a philosophy which was supposedly fully expounded in *Excalibur*, an unpublished book Ron was first said to have written in 1938. Modestly described as 'a sensational volume which was a summation of life based on his analysis of the state of Mankind',[6] much would be heard of this great work in later years; indeed, it would become a cornerstone of the mythology built around his life. It was claimed that the book derived from Ron's 'discovery' that the primary law of life was to survive, although, naturally, the part played by 'his explorations, journeys and experiences in the four corners of the earth, amongst all kinds of men, was crucial'.[7]

The first six people to read the manuscript were said to have been so overwhelmed by the contents that they went out of their minds. Curiously, however, few of Ron's fellow writers were aware of the existence of the book, with the exception of Art Burks: 'Ron called me one day and said, "I want to see you right away, I have written *the* book." I never saw anybody so worked up. Apparently he had written it without sleeping, eating, or anything else and had literally worked himself into a frazzle.

'He was so sure he had something "away out and beyond" anything else that he said he had sent telegrams to several book publishers telling them that he had written *the* book and that they were to meet him at Penn Station and he would discuss it with them and go with whoever gave him the best offer. Whether he did this or not, I don't know, but it is right in line with something he would do.

'He told me it was going to revolutionize everything: the world, people's attitudes to one another. He thought it would have a greater impact upon people than the Bible.'[8]

Burks's recollection of the manuscript was that it was about seventy thousand words long and began with a fable about a king who gathered all his wise men together and commanded them to bring him all the wisdom of the world in five hundred books. He then told them to go away and condense the information into one hundred books. When they had done that, he wanted the wisdom reduced into one book and finally into one word. That word was 'survive'.

Ron developed an argument that the survival instinct could explain all human behaviour and that to understand survival was to understand life. Burks particularly remembered a passage in which Ron explained how emotions could be whipped up to the point where a lynch mob was formed. 'It made the shivers move up your back from your heels to the top of your head,' he said.

Burks was sufficiently impressed by *Excalibur* to agree to write a brief biographical sketch of Ron for use as a preface. It was the usual 'red-headed fire-eater' material, with only one surprising new claim – that 1934 was the year Ron 'rounded off his application of analytical geometry to aerial navigation'.

The preface also mentioned a facet of Ron's character which few members of the American Fiction Guild had noticed – his unwillingness to talk about himself. 'Long ago he discovered that his most concrete adventures raised sceptic eyebrows and so, without diminishing his activities, he has fallen back on silence. We hear of him building a road in the Ladrone Islands or surveying the Canadian border and bellowing squads east and west with the perfection of a trained military man and delve though we may, that is as far as we can get.'

Burks concluded with a tactful reference to the difficulty of reconciling the adventurer with the author of a philosophic treatise: 'One envisions the philosopher as a quiet gray-beard, timid in all things but thought. It is, withal, rather upsetting to the general concept to think of L. Ron Hubbard as the author of *Excalibur*.'

Although *Excalibur* was never published – Burks was convinced that Ron was deeply disappointed he could not find a publisher – Ron assiduously stoked rumours about its existence and its content. 'He told me once that he had a manuscript in his trunk that was going to revolutionize the world,' said his friend Mac Ford. 'He said it was called *Excalibur*, but that's all I know about it. I never saw it.'[9]

Unquestionably, Ron himself believed in *Excalibur*, for in October 1938 he wrote a long and emotional letter to Polly in which he expressed his hope that the manuscript would merit him a place in history.

Polly had recently had a riding accident which resulted in her losing the tip of one finger. Ron tried to cheer her up with a funny catalogue of his own imagined ailments and promised her a jewelled Chinese fingernail holder which she could be 'snooty' about. He wrote of his frustration about his work, the constant shortage of money ('I still wonder how much money we owe in incidental bills. It's grave, I know . . .) and the need to spend so much time in New York, away from her and the children.

Then he turned to the subject that was clearly in the forefront of his mind—his unpublished manuscript, *Excalibur*. He said that in writing the book and assembling his ideas he had given himself an education far better than that available from any university. If he was to enter politics, he averred, he would engender enthusiastic support from all classes of people, from the unemployed as well as industrials, from white-collar workers to blue-collar labourers. 'I have high hopes', he wrote 'of smashing my name into history so violently that it will take a legendary form . . .'

This supreme self-confidence was interspersed, in the letter, with passages exhibiting crushing self-doubt. He fretted about writing pulp fiction for a penny a word, the time it was occupying and the possible damage it was causing to his reputation as a serious writer. He was clearly nervous about his precarious finances and was subject to fits of depression. He wrote of life being a 'grim joke' and the difficulties he was experiencing in surviving and maintaining his equilibrium. But it was also evident that he was expecting great things from the publication of *Excalibur*, in terms of personal and professional recognition.

Ron's nickname for Polly was 'Skipper' and hers for him was 'Red'. The letter finished with a single encouraging line: 'I love you, Skipper, and all will be well. The Redhead.'

While Ron's philosophical work languished for want of a publisher, his literary endeavours in other fields continued to find wide favour. Apart from marking his début in science fiction, 1938 was the year Ron rode the range of Western adventure. His name appeared in *Western Story* magazine almost every month with a series of two-gun titles designed to set the pulse racing – 'Six Gun Caballero', 'Hot Lead Payoff', 'Ride 'Em Cowboy', 'The Boss of the Lazy B', 'The Ghost Town Gun-Ghost', 'Death Waits at Sundown', etcetera.

Campbell thought Ron was wasting his time with Westerns and told him so in a letter dated 23 January 1939: 'I don't, personally, like Westerns particularly, and, in consequence, haven't read your Western stuff. But I'm convinced that you do like fantasy, enjoy it, and have a greater gift for fantasy than for almost any other type. The fact that editor after editor has urged you to do that type seems to me indication that you always have had that ability, and that, in avoiding it heretofore, you've suppressed a natural, and not common, talent. There are a lot of boys that run out readable Westerns, but only about three or four men in a generation that do top-notch fantasy.'[10]

Campbell wanted Ron to contribute to *Unknown*, a new magazine he was in the process of launching which was to specialize in bizarre fantasy, and promised to reserve space for him with a proviso that only 'genuinely first-rate fantasy' would be considered. In response Ron produced a story called 'The Ultimate Adventure', which was used as the lead novel in the April 1939 issue and marked the beginning of a tenure during which his name was virtually a permanent fixture in the magazine.

The protagonist in 'The Ultimate Adventure' was a favourite Hubbard stereotype – a wimp transported by magic to another, vaguely Oriental, world and miraculously mutated into a roistering adventurer. The wimp in this case was a destitute orphan. Beguiled by a mad professor, he finds himself in a scene from *The Arabian Nights*, is condemned to death as a suspected ghoul, shoots his way out, falls in with a band of genuine ghouls who eat human heads, rescues a fair princess from the cliché castle and finally turns the tables on the mad professor. It was rip-roaring stuff.

A second L. Ron Hubbard story, 'Slaves of Sleep', appeared in the July issue of *Unknown*. This time the hero was not a penniless orphan but an heir to a shipping fortune, although quite as ineffectual. Another wicked professor (Ron did not have much time for academics) causes the young man to be cursed with eternal sleeplessness, banishing him to a world where he is a seventeenth-century sailor on the Barbary coast embroiled in hair-raising adventures. Fortunately, he has a magic ring for use in really tricky situations – as when he single-handedly defeats an enemy fleet by obdurately ordering the ships to fall apart.

Compared to previous years, Ron's output in 1939 was positively dilatory – just seven novels and two short stories. But then he had other things on his mind. A year earlier, his friend H. Latane Lewis II, who was by then working for the National Aeronautic Association, had recommended him to the War Department in Washington as the right man for an advisory post in the Air Corps.

In a letter to Brigadier General Walter G. Kilner, Assistant Chief of the Air Corps, H. Latane Lewis II unexpectedly promoted Ron to the rank of 'Captain', perhaps to enhance his case: 'When you asked me last week to procure advice on the problem of bringing a more agreeable and adventurous type of young man into the Air Corps, I did not know I would be fortunate enough to receive a call today from Captain L. Ron Hubbard, the bearer.

'Captain Hubbard, whom you know as a writer and lecturer, is probably the best man to consult on this subject due to his many connections. He has offered to deliver his views in person.

'As a member of the Explorers Club he has occasion to address thousands of young men in various institutions concerning his sea adventures and his various expeditions. Though he only pursued soaring and power flight long enough to emass [*sic*] story information, he is still much respected in soaring societies for the skill and daring which brought him two records. He often speaks at Harvard . . .'[11]

Nothing came of Ron's offer to deliver his views in person, possibly because the Brigadier General discovered L. Ron Hubbard was not a Captain, not a member of the Explorers Club, not a lecturer, held no flying records and had never addressed Harvard.

Ron, as ever, was unabashed but as the situation in Europe deteriorated – the newspapers were full of alarming reports that a German invasion of Poland was imminent – he became increasingly enamoured with the idea that his panoply of talents should be available to Washington.

On 1 September, the day England and France declared war on Germany, he wrote to the Secretary of the War Department: 'Because of the possibility that our nation may, in the near future, find itself at war and because I well know the difficulty of finding trained men at the height of such a crisis, I wish to offer my services to my government in whatever capacity they might be of the greatest use . . .' He continued with a resumé of his career which was, for Ron, a model of restraint and veracity. It was just possible that he inadvertently implied he had only left university in order to lead an expedition to the Caribbean, and his military experience was perhaps just a little over-emphasized, but by and large he stuck to the facts. He even had the grace to point out that though he had spent five years studying psychology and human behaviour it was purely for his own benefit. His 'pioneering' notes on emotional reactions, he added, would be published in the coming year.

Unfortunately for Ron, two days later, President Roosevelt declared the neutrality of the United States, temporarily thwarting his ambition to play a role in the defeat of Hitler.

Following the move to South Colby, Ron became accustomed to spending summers at The Hilltop, burning the midnight oil in his little cabin in the woods and sailing the ruffled reaches of Puget Sound in the *Maggie* at weekends, and winters in New York, where he could enjoy the amiable and cosmopolitan company of his fellow writers.

He usually stayed in the cheapest hotel room he could find, but in the fall of 1939 he scraped together enough money to rent a small apartment in Manhattan, on the Upper West Side at 95th and Riverside. To make a place where he could work without distraction, he rigged up a curtained enclosure about the size of a telephone booth, lit with a blue electric bulb to cut down the reflected glare from his typing paper.

Most of the top science fiction writers of the day tended to gather in John W. Campbell's cluttered office in the Street and Smith building on Seventh Avenue and it was there that other contributors to *Astounding* and *Unknown* made the acquaintance of L. Ron Hubbard. L. Sprague de Camp thought that he looked like a 'reincarnated Pan who had been doing himself a bit too well on the ambrosia'[12] and Isaac Asimov, who greatly admired Ron's work, became quite flustered at meeting him for the first time.

'He was a large-jawed, red-haired, big and expansive fellow who surprised me,' Asimov recalled. 'His heroes tended to be frightened little men who rose to meet emergencies, and somehow I had expected Hubbard to be the same. "You don't look at all like your stories," I said. "Why? How are my stories?" he asked. "Oh they're *great*," I said enthusiastically and all present laughed while I blushed and tried to explain that if the stories were great and he was not like his stories, I didn't mean he was *not* great.'[13]

While he was in New York, Ron lobbied assiduously and moved inexorably towards the fulfilment of a long-standing ambition – to be accepted as a member of the Explorers Club. He had often hinted, over the years, that he was a member, but in reality it was an accolade that had proved singularly elusive. The club occupied a handsome red brick and stone building of suitable neo-Gothic dignity on East 70th Street, but its worth as a prime piece of Manhattan real estate was as nothing compared to the privilege of being allowed to walk through the wrought iron gates as a member. Membership of the snooty Explorers Club of New York, founded in 1904, conferred prestige, social standing and influence. Ron longed to join this exalted fraternity, not least because it would, at a stroke, forever legitimize his doubtful career as an explorer and adventurer.

He could be the most charming and sociable of men when he so desired and he worked hard to make the right connections. On 12

December 1939, he was formally proposed for membership of the Explorers Club on the basis of what appeared to be an impressive application, citing the valuable data he had obtained for the Hydrographic Office and the University of Michigan during his expedition to the Caribbean, his pioneering mineralogical survey of Puerto Rico and his survey flights in the United States, undertaken to 'aid adjustment of field and facility data'.

The club's membership committee did not, it seems, require any of these claims to be checked and on 19 February 1940, L. Ron Hubbard was duly elected, to his enormous and undisguised pleasure. Thereafter, he would rarely forgo the satisfaction of giving his address as 'Explorers Club, New York.'

It not being in his nature to blush quietly on the sidelines, Ron was soon making his presence felt. Within a matter of months the club magazine was reporting rumours that 'our red-headed Captain Ron Hubbard' liked to wrestle fully-grown brown bears. Ron wrote a good-natured denial, slyly contriving to portray himself as both sport and saint: 'I do not make a practice of going around picking on poor, innocent Kodiak bears. The day I arrived in New York City, this thing began: I picked up my phone to hear a cooing voice say, "Cap'n, do you *like* to wrassle with bears?" And since that day I have had no peace. How the story arrived ahead of me I do not know, I mean the whole thing is a damned lie!

'A man can spend endless months of hardship and heroic privation in checking coast pilots; he can squeeze his head to half its width between earphones calculating radio errors; he can brave storm and sudden death in all its most horrible forms in an attempt to increase man's knowledge, and what happens? Is he a hero? Do people look upon his salt-encrusted and exhausted self with awe? Do universities give him degrees and governments commissions? *No*! They all look at him with a giggle and ask him if he likes to wrassle bears. It's an outrage! It's enough to make a man take up paper-doll cutting! Gratitude, bah! Attention and notoriety have centred upon one singular accident – an exaggerated untruth – and the gigantic benefits to the human race are all forgotten!'

In the early months of 1940, Ron was forced to abandon the pursuit of further gigantic benefits for the human race in favour of earning a living. Working under the blue light in the curtained cubicle in his apartment on the Upper West Side, he produced three stories that would come to be regarded as classics – 'Fear', 'Typewriter in the Sky' and 'Final Blackout'.

'No one who read "Fear" in *Unknown* during their impressionable years would ever forget it,' claimed Brian Aldiss, science fiction writer and historian.[14] The stream-of-consciousness narrative, akin to literary psychoanalysis, charts the disintegration of an academic who writes an article debunking the existence of spirits and demons and is punished by being dragged into a nightmare of black magic and hallucinations. In contrast, 'Typewriter In The Sky' was a typical Hubbard swashbuckler about a character called Mike de Wolfe who finds himself trapped in the past as the unwilling victim of a science fiction writer named Horace Hackett. Transported to the Spanish Main, de Wolfe is saddled with the implausible name of Miguel Saint Raoul Maria Gonzales Sebastian de Mendoza y Toledo Francisco Juan Tomaso Guerrero de Brazo y Leon de Lobo and is required to duel with English sea dog Tom Bristol for the hand of the fair Lady Marion, 'flame-headed, imperious and as lovely as any statue from Greece'. It was an ingenious little tale, but hardly great literature, particularly since the protagonists were given to uttering lines like 'God's breath, milord, you jest!' and 'By gad, he's got spunk!' or even 'Peel your peepers!'

Final Blackout was a novel which many science-fiction fans considered Hubbard's finest work and led to hopeful comparisons with Jules Verne and H.G. Wells. (When it was published in hardback later, Ron contrived, unsuccessfully, to appear self-effacing in a jacket note: 'I cannot bring myself to believe that *Final Blackout*, as so many polls and such insist, is one of the ten greatest stories ever published.')

Serialized in the April, May and June issues of *Astounding*, *Final Blackout* precipitated furious controversy in fan magazines and bitter accusations that it was Communist or Fascist propaganda. The story was set in a Europe laid waste by generations of war and populated only by marauding bands of renegade soldiers. Leading a brigade of 'unkillables', the hero, identified only as the 'Lieutenant', fights his way to England, where he establishes a benign military dictatorship until he is overthrown by his former commanding officers, with the backing of the United States.

It was a peculiarly grim and apposite story to be published in the spring of 1940. Viewed from the United States, the war in Europe seemed like a prelude to Armageddon, the potential destruction of civilized life under the heel of the jackboot. While American liberals were campaigning for positive action from the government to aid the Allies in the fight against Fascism, the anti-war neutralist lobby was equally vociferous. Partisans of both left and right read political significance into *The Final Blackout*: it was pro-war, anti-war, Communist or anti-Communist, depending on the reader's political inclinations.

Even Ron's friends could not agree about his intentions. Ron was a member of a war-game circle which had been started by Fletcher Pratt, a naval historian who also enjoyed writing science fiction. Using scale models of real warships made from balsa wood, they re-enacted naval battles on the floor of the living-room in Pratt's New York apartment until the group became too large and it was necessary to transfer the battleground to a hired hall on East 59th Street. While the balsa battles were being fought, they often discussed the war and its attendant politics.

'Hubbard gave a varied impression of himself,' recalled L. Sprague de Camp, who was also a member of the war-game circle. 'Some thought him a Fascist because of the authoritarian tone of certain stories. But one science-fiction writer, then an idealistic left-liberal, was convinced that Hubbard had profound liberal convictions. To others, Hubbard expressed withering disdain for politics and politicians, saying about the imminence of war: "Me, fight for a *political* system?"'[15]

There was certainly no doubt that Ron was anti-German, for on 16 May he wrote a letter to the FBI in Washington on his exotic personalized stationery featuring his initials and a charging cavalryman: 'Gentlemen; May I bring to your attention an individual whose Nazi activities, in time of national emergency if not at present, might constitute him a menace to the state?'

This luckless individual was a German steward at the Knickerbocker Hotel in New York whose sister, according to Ron, was a member of the Gestapo. Ron accused him of being anti-American, an illegal immigrant and 'definitely fifth column'. 'My interest in this is impersonal,' he added, 'though possibly shaded by the feeling of dislike which he always inspires in me.'

J. Edgar Hoover replied promptly, thanked Ron for the information and promised an investigation. But when an FBI agent called at Ron's apartment on Riverside Drive, he discovered that Ron had moved out on 1 June. The agent reported that Ron had told neighbours he was moving to Washington DC, but as he left no forwarding address, the case was closed.[16]

Ron had not gone to Washington DC but to Washington State, back to The Hilltop and to Polly and the children. There was perhaps little time for a lengthy family reunion, however, for he was deeply involved in the planning of his next great adventure – the Alaskan Radio-Experimental Expedition. He was, of course, the leader and would be carrying with him, for the first time, the flag of the Explorers Club.

The signal honour of carrying the club flag was jealously guarded and only granted to members taking part in expeditions with proven serious scientific objectives. Every application was obviously subjected to rigorous scrutiny by the Flag and Honors Committee, lest the significance of its award be devalued. Thus Captain Hubbard proposed eminently laudable aims for his Alaskan Radio-Experimental Expedition, notably to rewrite an important navigation guide – the US Coast Pilot, Alaska, Part 1 – and to investigate methods of radio position-finding with experimental equipment and a new system of mathematical computation. In a committee room at the Explorers Club, these creditable aspirations clearly met with unhesitant approval.

In and around Bremerton, members of the Waterbury family had a rather more prosaic perspective on the Alaskan Radio-Experimental Expedition, referring to it simply as 'Ron and Polly's trip'. As far as the family was concerned, Ron was going to take Polly on a cruise up to Alaska. Aunt Marnie viewed the venture as a wangle entirely typical of her nephew. 'Ron dreamed up the trip as a way of outfitting the *Maggie*,' she said. 'His brain was always working and when he was trying to figure out how he could afford to outfit the boat he wrote letters to all these different manufacturers of instruments and equipment offering to test them out.'

The letters were written on crisply designed notepaper headed 'ALASKAN RADIO-EXPERIMENTAL EXPEDITION', with a sub-heading 'Checking data for the US Coast and Geodetic Survey and the US Navy Hydrographic Office'. The expedition's base was given as Yukon Harbor, Colby, and its address, inevitably, was the Explorers Club of New York. With such impressive credentials, it was no surprise that manufacturers responded positively to letters from 'Captain L. Ron Hubbard, Director AREE '40' asking for equipment to be submitted for scientific testing.

Aunt Marnie knew all about 'Ron and Polly's trip' because they had asked her to look after Nibs and Katie at The Hilltop while they were away. She and her husband, Kemp, were living in Spokane, but Kemp had been unemployed throughout the Depression and they were happy to move into The Hilltop as Kemp thought he might find work at the Navy Yard in Bremerton. 'It was a beautiful spot,' said Marnie. 'Polly had fixed up the house and the garden real nice. She was very clever with flowers, very good at gardening. From the garden you could see the ferry boats coming over from Seattle.'

A few days before they were due to leave, Ron offered to take Marnie and Toilie for a trip round the bay in the *Maggie*. It was not an outing that augured well for the Alaskan Radio-Experimental Expedition. 'We were quite a ways out', Marnie recalled, 'when the engine suddenly went phut-phut – out of gas. Polly was furious and shouted at Ron, "I thought you were going to re-fuel it." He had forgotten to do it. We prayed for a wind to blow so we could get in under sail. In the end we had to drain the little oil lamps. That gave us enough fuel to give the engine a shot to get us moving, then we would drift for a bit and give it another shot and finally we got back. That was my last trip on the *Maggie*.'[17]

The 'expedition' departed its Yukon Harbor 'base' in July, with May, Marnie, Toilie and Midge and their various children waving farewell from the quayside. Marnie and Kemp settled into The Hilltop with Nibs and Katie, their own two children and Marylou, the daughter of Marnie's sister, Hope. For the next several months their only contact with Ron and Polly was through letters posted from various ports in British Columbia as the *Maggie* sailed erratically northwards along the Pacific coast of Canada.

From the start, the *Maggie*'s new engine, fitted only a few weeks before they left Puget Sound, gave trouble. On their second day out, nosing through thick fog in the Juan de Futa Strait, between Vancouver Island and the US coast and barely eighty miles from Bremerton, the engine spluttered and died. They very nearly ran aground before Ron could get it going again. The same thing happened in Chatham Sound, off Prince Rupert, also, coincidentally, in a pea-souper.

On Friday 30 August, the *Maggie* limped into the harbour at Ketchikan, Alaska, with the engine crankshaft banging ominously. Ketchikan was a small fishing and logging community surrounded by spruce forests on the southern tip of the Alaskan panhandle, some seven hundred miles from Bremerton. The *Maggie*'s arrival merited a story in the *Ketchikan Alaska Chronicle*, although no mention was made of the expedition:

'Captain L. Ron Hubbard, author and world traveler, arrived in Ketchikan yesterday in company with his wife aboard the vest pocket yacht, *Magician*. His purpose in coming to Alaska was two-fold, one to win a bet and another to gather material for a novel of Alaskan salmon fishing.'

It seems Ron told the newspaper that friends had wagered it was impossible to sail a vessel as small as the *Maggie* to Alaska and he was determined to prove them wrong. 'Captain Hubbard covered their bets and, now that he has arrived, will have the satisfaction of collecting.'

Ron no doubt wished the story was true, for he had hopelessly underestimated the cost of the trip and they were already so short of money that they could not afford to get the engine repaired. More in hope than anticipation, he sent an angry cable to the engine supplier in Bremerton demanding a replacement crankshaft, free of charge.

Meanwhile, they were effectively marooned in Ketchikan.

While Ron and Polly were carefully saving wherever they could, a letter arrived from Marnie saying that Nibs had been up crying all night with a toothache and she had taken him to the dentist. Ron was angry that Marnie should involve them in further expense and dashed off an irritable reply telling her it was none of her business and she should have waited until they got back. Marnie responded furiously: 'What kind of heel are you?'

Despite these trials, Ron did his best to invest the trip with scientific purpose. In mid-September, he despatched a package of sailing directions and eleven rolls of film to the Hydrographic Office in Washington DC with a note expressing the hope that they would prove of value. He was also able to report favourably to the Cape Cod Instrument Company in Hyannis on the accuracy of its 'Cape Cod Navigator', which he had tested with 721 bearings on radio beacons. 'It has at all times performed its duties like a true shipmate,' Ron wrote.

A solution to their predicament presented itself later that month in the shape of Jimmy Britton, the owner and president of the local radio station. KGBU Radio was a home-spun operation which proclaimed itself to be 'The Voice of Alaska' since it was virtually the only radio station in the area. Jimmy Britton made all the announcements, read the news, conducted interviews, played records and filled in time as best he could.

KGBU was usually so short of material that anyone in Ketchikan was welcome on the air to talk about almost anything. It was hardly surprising, then, that the arrival in town of Captain Hubbard, leader of a scientific expedition carrying the flag of The Explorers Club of New York, was nothing short of a godsend to Britton, particularly as Hubbard was not only willing to broadcast, he seemed positively *eager* to do so. He was soon regaling listeners with a gripping account of his expedition and his adventures navigating through fog-bound, tide-bedevilled and uncharted waters.

Britton recognized that Ron was a natural broadcaster and story-teller, with a seemingly limitless reservoir of material, and his talks on KGBU became a regular and popular feature for several weeks. In one of them he revealed how, after only a week in Alaskan waters he had discovered, with the help of his advanced radio navigational instru-ments, a source of interference which had baffled the local coastguard and signal station. In another he described his role in tracking down a German saboteur who had been sent to Alaska with orders to cut off communications with the United States in the event of war. And his dramatic and sometimes hilarious account of how, on a fishing expedition with a friend, he lassooed a swimming brown bear which then climbed on to their boat, had listeners everywhere glued to their sets. Off the air, at Jimmy Britton's request, Ron re-organized the station and wrote new programming schedules with all the confidence of a man who had spent a lifetime in broadcasting.

With little interference from other radio stations, KGBU's signal, on 900 watts and 1000 kilocycles, carried for hundreds of miles and could often be heard as far south as Seattle and Bremerton. It was for this reason that Ron always contrived to mention that he and his wife were stranded in Ketchikan because the Regal Company of Bremerton had refused to meet its obligations and replace their defective crankshaft. When a new crankshaft arrived in early December, Ron was convinced it was his constant needling on the air that was responsible.

As soon as the new crankshaft was fitted, Ron and Polly set sail for home. No one was more sorry to see them go than Jimmy Britton: he felt that KGBU had hardly begun to tap Ron's fund of stories. The *Maggie* sailed back into Puget Sound on 27 December 1940. Ron bought Marnie a yellow canary to thank her for looking after the children and not a word was said about the dentist.

Beset once more by debts, Ron went straight back to work to earn some money. For many weeks a light could be seen burning all night in the window of the little cabin at the back of The Hilltop as the stories rolled relentlessly out of his typewriter. In one of them, 'The Case of the Friendly Corpse', published in *Unknown*, Ron cheekily disposed of Harold Shea, the hero of a story by L. Sprague de Camp that had appeared in the magazine two months previously. Ron had his own hero meet Harold Shea and demonstrate a magic wand which turned into a serpent and proceeded to swallow up poor Harold. L. Sprague de Camp fans were outraged that Hubbard should so brusquely dispatch someone else's hero.

When he was not working, Ron spent a lot of time, as before, with his friend Mac Ford, who had recently been elected to the state legislature. During the hours they spent playing chess they talked at length about the war in Europe and the likelihood of the United States becoming involved. Ron seemed somewhat subdued after his return from Alaska; he was convinced that the Japanese were planning to attack the West coast mainland and gloomily prophesied that US forces would be driven back to the Rockies before they could stem the tide of the invasion.

Unbeknown to Ford, Ron had made up his mind to join the Navy and was making painstaking preparations to ensure he was offered a commission, tenaciously cultivating useful contacts and soliciting letters of recommendation wherever he could. Jimmy Britton of KGBU Radio was naturally happy to oblige and despatched a two-page eulogy to the Secretary of the Navy on 15 March 1941, listing Ron's abundance of accomplishments. Among them he mentioned that Ron was a 'good professional photographer' whose work he had seen in *National Geographic Magazine*. No one else had, for *National Geographic* had never published any of Ron's pictures.[18] 'I do not hesitate', Britton enthused, 'to recommend him without reserve as a man of intelligence, courage and good breeding as well as one of the most versatile personalities I have ever known.'

Ten days later, Commander W. E. McCain of US Naval Powder Factory at Indian Head, Maryland, added his support: 'This is to certify that I have personally known Mr L. Ron Hubbard for the past twenty years. I have been associated with him as a boy growing up and observed him closely. I have found him to be of excellent character, honest, ambitious and always very anxious to improve himself to better enable him to become a more useful citizen . . . I do not hesitate to recommend him to anyone needing the services of a man of his qualifications.' (McCain was the Lieutenant who had shown Ron and his mother around Manila in 1927 and whom Ron mentioned in his journal.)

Meanwhile, Ron was in touch with his Congressman, Warren G. Magnuson, who was a member of the Committee on Naval Affairs. Ron had suggested to Magnuson that the US Navy should set up its own Bureau of Information, both to improve the Navy's public relations and to counter the 'defeatist propaganda' about naval affairs which Ron claimed was 'flooding the press'. At Magnuson's request, he produced a nine-page report which the Congressman submitted with an introduction which cannot have displeased the author: 'This plan of organization has been prepared by Captain L. Ron Hubbard, a writer who is well-known under each of five different pen names. His leadership in the Authors' League and the American Fiction Guild, his political and professional connections and the respect in which he is held by writers and newsmen make his aid in this organization valuable. His participation in this organization will give to it an instantaneous standing in the writing profession, and bring to it a standard of high ideals . . .'

As if this was not enough, the Congressman also took it upon himself to write to no less a person than President Roosevelt to extol the virtues of 'Captain' Hubbard. The letter, dated 8 April, added yet another laurel to Ron's crown with the improbable claim that he held more marine licences than anyone else in the country. It also introduced an aspect of his personality that was certainly not obvious to other people who knew Ron Hubbard – his 'distaste for personal publicity'.

'Dear Mr President,' Magnuson wrote. 'May I recommend to you a gentleman of reputation? L. Ron Hubbard is a well-known writer under five different names. He is a respected explorer as Captain Bryan, Navy Hydrographer, will confirm. [Bryan acknowledged the sailing directions and films that Ron sent to the Hydrographic Office from his Alaskan trip.]

'Mr Hubbard was born into the Navy. He has marine masters papers for more types of vessels than any other man in the United States.

'He has written for Hollywood, radio and newspapers and has published many millions of words of fact and fiction in novels and national magazines. In writing organizations he is a key figure, making him politically potent nationally.

'An interesting trait is his distaste for personal publicity. He is both discreet and resourceful as his record should indicate.

'Anything you can do for Mr Hubbard will be appreciated . . .'

On 18 April, Ron reported to the Naval Reserve Headquarters in Washington DC for a physical examination. Next day, he persuaded the Dean of the School of Civil Engineering at George Washington University to write a letter to the Navy Yard recommending him for a commission. Professor Arthur Johnson complimented Ron's leadership, ingenuity, resourcefulness and personality and strove to explain why such a paragon had failed to graduate: 'His average grades in engineering were due to the obvious fact that he had started in the wrong career. They do not reflect his great ability.'

Unquestionably the most lyrical of all the letters of recommendation was that signed by Senator Robert M. Ford on the notepaper of the House of Representatives for the State of Washington. Ford was not the kind of man to be too bothered by protocol or paperwork. 'I don't know why Ron wanted a letter,' he said. 'I just gave him a letter-head and said, "Hell, you're the writer, you write it!"'[19]

Ron was unstinting in praise of himself. 'To whom it may concern,' he began. 'This will introduce one of the most brilliant men I have ever known: Captain L. Ron Hubbard.

'He writes under six names in a diversity of fields from political economy to action fiction and if he would make at least one of his pen names public he would have little difficult entering anywhere. He has published many millions of words and some fourteen movies.

'In exploration he has honourably carried the flag of the Explorers Club and has extended geographical and mineralogical knowledge. He is well known in many parts of the world and has considerable influence in the Caribbean and Alaska.

'As a key figure in writing organizations he has considerable political worth and in the Northwest he is a powerful influence.

'I have known him for many years and have found him discreet, loyal, honest and without peer in the art of getting things done swiftly.

'If Captain Hubbard requests help, be assured that it will benefit others more than himself.

'For courage and ability I cannot too strongly recommend him.'

On 19 July 1941, L. Ron Hubbard was commissioned as a Lieutenant (Junior Grade) in the US Naval Reserve.

Chapter 6

The Hero Who Never Was

'Commissioned before the war in 1941, by the US Navy, he [Hubbard] was ordered to the Philippines at the outbreak of war in the US and was flown home in the late spring of 1942 in the Secretary of the Navy's private plane as the first US returned casualty from the Far East.' (*A Brief Biography of L. Ron Hubbard*)

'He served in the South Pacific, and in 1942 was relieved by fifteen officers of rank and was rushed home to take part in the 1942 battle against German submarines as Commanding Officer of a corvette serving in the North Atlantic. In 1943 he was made Commodore of Corvette Squadrons, and in 1944 he worked with amphibious forces. After serving in all five theaters of World War II and receiving 21 medals and palms, in 1944 he was severely wounded and was taken crippled and blinded to Oak Knoll Naval Hospital.' (*Facts About L. Ron Hubbard*)

* * * * *

By July 1941, the United States was effectively, although unofficially, at war. US marines had taken over the British garrison in Iceland and US warships were already escorting convoys of lend-lease supplies across the North Atlantic. The isolationist lobby bitterly accused President Roosevelt of needlessly leading the nation into the conflict, but the momentum was irreversible. When Germany invaded Russia, Roosevelt immediately promised US aid, declaring the defence of Russia to be 'vital to the defence of the United States'.

In August, as the apparently invincible Nazi Panzer divisions pushed the Red Army back towards the outskirts of Leningrad, Roosevelt met the British Prime Minister, Winston Churchill, off the coast of Newfoundland and signed the Atlantic Charter, confirming US-Anglo co-operation and calling for 'the right of all peoples to choose the form of Government under which they will live'. A few days later, a German U-Boat unsuccessfully attacked an American destroyer, the *USS Greer*, south of Iceland and Roosevelt issued orders to 'shoot on sight'. In October, the US Navy suffered its first casualty when another destroyer, the *USS Kearney*, was sunk by a submarine in the North Atlantic. After the loss of the *Kearney*, the United States embarked on an undeclared naval war against Germany.

Lieutenant L.R. Hubbard, US Naval Reserve, did not exactly play a central role in these events. In moments of fantasy he could no doubt picture himself on the bridge of the *Kearney*, heroically choosing to go down with his ship, a wry smile playing on his lips as the last of his crew was rescued; in reality, he was being shunted from one desk job to another in public relations.

In the light of his success as a writer, it was not surprising that the US Navy assigned Lieutenant Hubbard to a job in publicity, even though the fledgling officer's literary talent was largely confined to the abstruse field of science fiction, far divorced from the sober requirements of military public relations.

But Ron naturally considered himself supremely well qualified and he had barely been in uniform five minutes before he was offering the benefit of his advice to his senior officers. On 21 July, with two full days' service completed, he wrote to Congressman Magnuson thanking him for his help in obtaining a commission and mentioning that he had already submitted three ideas to accelerate recruiting, all of which were 'going into effect'.[1] Magnuson replied; 'Glad to hear your commission went through. Know you will be right at home in your work with Navy Press Relations.'

A week later, Ron had other plans. In a second letter to Magnuson, dated 29 July and written from The Explorers Club in New York, he said that 'as Press Relations was getting along well enough' he had offered to write two articles every week for national magazines, with the aim of selling the 'American bluejacket' to the public. He had, he said, been given a 'free helm' and 'because this program will net about three times as much as Navy pay I think it no more than right that I return anything above pay and expenses to Navy Relief. So all goes along swimmingly.'

Well, not quite swimmingly: it transpired that Ron was a little over-confident about his ability to sell US Navy stories to national magazines. He might have written two articles every week, but none was published.

When it became clear to the Navy that Lieutenant Hubbard was wasting his time, it was decided to send him to the Hydrographic Office in Washington to annotate the photographs he had taken during his trip to Alaska with Polly. He arrived on 22 September and stayed two weeks. In a memo to the Assistant Hydrographer, it was noted that several dozen of his photographs were 'fairly clear' and of 'some navigational interest'. Ron had also suggested changes and amplifications to the Sailing Directions for British Columbia. Some were unimportant, the memo continued, 'but in the aggregate they repre-sent a very definite contribution'.[2]

It was a contribution that marked the end of Ron's career in public relations. On 24 November, after six weeks' leave, he was posted to Headquarters, Third Naval District, in New York, for training as an Intelligence Officer.

Throughout this period, his father was stationed at the Navy Yard on Mare Island in San Pablo Bay, California, as officer in charge of the commissary. Now fifty-five and still a Lieutenant-Commander, Harry Hubbard's relationship with his son had deteriorated over the years and they saw little of each other. Any pleasure Hub might have experienced when he learned Ron was following him into the Navy could not outweigh his overall disapproval of, and disappointment with, his son. Harry Hubbard was a deeply conservative, utterly conventional plodder, a man ruled by routine and conformity. He could never come to terms with what he viewed as his son's eccentricities – his refusal to get a job, his habit of staying up all night and sleeping all day, his prolonged absences from home, his lack of regard for his family. Hub was extremely fond of Polly and adored his two grandchildren – Nibs, then seven years old, and Katie, who was five. Sometimes he felt he was closer to them than their own father and he was saddened that this should be the case.

As far as Ron was concerned, he had nothing in common with his father who had spent virtually his entire life pushing paper in the Navy with nothing in prospect but a pension. To Ron it was a grey and unappealing existence compared to his own world, at least as it existed in his thoughts. Ron still saw himself as an adventurer cast in the mould of his fictional heroes and never missed an opportunity to promote himself as a fearless, devil-may-care, globetrotter. It was no wonder father and son inexorably drifted apart – their characters were simply too different to be compatible.

Ron was still at HQ Third Naval District in New York when, a few minutes after three o'clock on the afternoon of Sunday 7 December, an announcer broke into a New York Philharmonic concert being broadcast on CBS: 'We interrupt this program to bring you a special news bulletin. The Japanese have attacked Pearl Harbor.' At that very moment, bombs were still falling on the ships in Pearl Harbor and before the Japanese pilots headed for home, five US battleships had been sunk or beached, three others damaged, ten smaller warships disabled and some 2400 men killed. Next day, the President signed a declaration of war.

If Ron was chafing to get into action he was to be disappointed. On 18 December, he was posted to the Philippines, but got no farther than Brisbane, Australia, where while waiting for a ship to Manila, he so antagonised his senior officers that in February 1942 he was on his way home again on board the *USS Chaumont*. 'This officer is not satisfactory for independent duty assignment,' the US Naval Attaché in Melbourne reported on 14 February. 'He is garrulous and tries to give impressions of his importance. He also seems to think he has unusual ability in most lines. These characteristics indicate that he will require close supervision for satisfactory performance of any intelligence duty.' It was claimed that Ron assumed authority without bothering to obtain official sanction and attempted to perform duties for which he had no qualifications, thus becoming 'the source of much trouble'.[3]

At Headquarters Twelfth Naval District in San Francisco, it was decided that Ron's talents might be more profitably employed in censoring cables. In a despatch dated 22 April, the Chief Cable Censor in Washington recommended that no disciplinary action be taken following the report from Melbourne 'as it is thought that the Subject's qualifications may find a useful outlet in the Office of the Cable Censor, New York'.

Ron did not enjoy his desk job at the Office of the Cable Censor and in June he put in a request for sea duty on a patrol boat, preferably in the Caribbean area, 'the peoples, language and customs of which I know and of which I possess piloting knowledge.' His request was approved – he was taken off cable censorship work and ordered to report to a shipbuilding yard in Neponset, Massachusetts, to supervise the conversion of a heavy beam trawler, the *Mist*, into a US Navy gunboat to be classified as *USS YP-422*. When she was ready to put to sea he was to take over as Commanding Officer.

Here at last was his opportunity to prove he was the hero he devoutly believed himself to be. (Had he not fought and won countless battles in the pages of his fiction?) Fighting men of calibre were certainly desperately needed, for the months following Pearl Harbor saw some of the darkest days of the war for the United States. Although jukeboxes around the country were tinnily cranking out patriotic jingles like 'Goodbye, Mama, I'm Off To Yokohama' and 'You're a Sap, Mister Jap', the initial euphoria that had greeted the war soon began to fade as the Allies were routed in the Pacific: Guam fell, then Manila, then Singapore, Bataan and Corregidor.

It was, then, with a certain sense of fulfilling his destiny that Lieutenant Hubbard travelled to Neponset, his orders contained in a signal in his pocket: 'LTJG LAFAYETTE R HUBBARD DVS USNR HEREBY DETACHED PROCEED IMMEDIATELY NEPONSET MASS . . . DUTY CONNECTION CONVERSION YP422 AT GEORGE LAWLEY AND SONS AND AS CO OF THAT VESSEL WHEN PLACED IN FULL COMMISSION.'

The conversion work was carried out swiftly and on 9 September

1942, Ron despatched a message to the Commandant of Boston Navy Yard reporting that *USS YP-422* was in excellent condition, crew training was 'approaching efficiency' and morale was high. 'As soon as a few deficiencies are remedied,' he added 'this vessel will be in all respects ready for sea and is very eager to be on her way to her assigned station or task force.'

Like his father, Ron tended to be somewhat absent-minded about personal debts. While he was supervising the conversion of the *YP-422* he was being pursued by tailors in Brisbane and Washington DC for unpaid uniform bills and he still owed $265 to the Bank of Ketchikan. When the Alaskan bank reported Lieutenant Hubbard's debt to the Bureau of Navigation in Washington, Ron wrote an indignant letter to the cashier: 'You are again informed that the reason for non-payment of this note is the sharp decrease in pay which I was willing to take to help my country. Until this war is ended I can only make small and irregular payments.'

The implication was that Lieutenant Hubbard was far too busy fighting a war to be bothered by trifling debts, but sadly, when the *USS YP-422* set out on her shakedown cruise, Lieutenant Hubbard was nowhere to be seen on board. On 1 October, Ron was summarily relieved of his command and ordered to report to the Commandant, Twelfth Naval District 'for such duty as he may assign you'. No explanation was contained in his orders, although earlier he had been involved in an unwise altercation with a senior officer at the shipyard. Considerable tension had developed between the officers in charge of the conversion work and those officers assigned to crew the ten YPs being converted at the Neponset shipyard, culminating in an extraordinary order prohibiting YP officers from approaching the conversion office or even speaking to any of the shipyard workers. Ron had taken it upon himself to fire off a memorandum to the Vice-Chief of Naval Operations in Washington, naming the officer responsible and pointing out that the YP commanding officers were all 'startled' by the order.[4] He might have been better advised to keep quiet: on 25 September the Commandant of Boston Navy Yard sent a signal to Washington stating his view that Hubbard was 'not temperamentally fitted for independent command.'

With his dreams of glory temporarily crushed, Ron waited for his next assignment without much optimism, anticipating he would probably be put back in command of a desk. However, he perked up considerably when his orders came through – he was to be sent to the Submarine Chaser Training Center in Miami, Florida. This immediately opened up a vista of wonderful new images – 'Ron the Fox', ace sub hunter, fearless scourge of the Japanese submarine fleet, etcetera.

Wearing dark glasses, Lieutenant Hubbard arrived at the Training

Center on 2 November and quickly made friends with another officer
on the course – a young Lieutenant from Georgetown, Maine, by the
name of Thomas Moulton. Ron light-heartedly explained that he was
obliged to wear dark glasses as he had received a severe flash burn
when he was serving as Gunnery Officer on the destroyer *Edsel*. He
had been standing close to the muzzle of a five-inch gun which fired
prematurely and while his injuries did not impair his vision, he found
any kind of bright light painful without dark glasses. Moulton,
understandably, was impressed.

By judiciously lacing his conversation with jargon and anecdotes,
Ron possessed an uncanny ability to be totally convincing. It was soon
'common knowledge' at the Center that he had served on destroyers;
indeed, said Moulton, he was 'used as something of an authority in the
classroom'.[5] While they were training together in Miami, mastering
the intricacies of tracking and attacking enemy submarines, Moulton
was treated to further details of his new friend's astonishing exploits in
the early months of the war. His strong recollection was that Ron was
a reticent sort of hero, reluctant to talk about himself, but over the
weeks his story came out bit by bit.

On the day the Japanese attacked Pearl Harbor, it seemed that Ron
was landed from the *Edsel* on the north coast of Java in the Dutch East
Indies, not far from the port of Surabaya, to carry out a secret
mission. The *Edsel* was sunk a couple of days later [not quite accurate
– she was sunk in March 1942] and went down with all hands. When
the Japanese occupied the island, Ron took off for the hills and lived
rough in the jungle. Once he was almost caught by a Japanese patrol
and was hit in the back by machine-gun fire before he was able to make
his escape. Those wounds still troubled him, he confessed. He often
suffered severe pain in his right side and the bullets had damaged his
urinary system, making it difficult for him to urinate.

He was in bad shape for quite a while after being shot, but
eventually he teamed up with another officer and they constructed a
raft on which they sailed across the shark-infested Timor Sea to within
one hundred miles of the Australian coast, where they were picked up
by a British or Australian destroyer. It was, Moulton thought, a
remarkable piece of navigation.

In January 1943, Ron was sent on a ten-day anti-submarine warfare
course at the Fleet Sound School in Key West, Florida, prior to being
posted to Portland, Oregon, as prospective Commanding Officer of
USS PC-815, a 280-ton submarine-chaser under construction at the
Albina Engine and Machine Works. Ron asked Moulton if he would
be his Executive Officer. Moulton was really hoping for a ship of his
own, but he so admired Ron that he agreed.

While the *PC-815* was being built, the two officers found time to enjoy life a little in the pleasant city of Portland. Moulton's wife came over from the East Coast and Polly was able to visit from Bremerton, which was only 150 miles to the north. As a foursome they enjoyed each other's company and frequently had dinner together, despite rationing, in one of the restaurants overlooking the green valley of the Willamette river and the distant snow-capped peak of Mount Hood. On one well-remembered occasion, the prospective Commanding Officer of *PC-815* and his Executive Officer drove up to Seattle for a dance at the tennis club. Ron was wearing his mysterious dark glasses, as usual, and was being gently teased by one of the women in their group. When he explained why they were necessary, the woman raised her eyebrows as if she did not believe him. Moulton was quite shocked. However, to prove what he was saying, Ron took off his glasses and within five or ten minutes his eyes began watering and were clearly sore. His friend was deeply gratified.

At ten o'clock on Tuesday 20 April 1943, the *USS PC-815* was commissioned. Ron noted the event in a pencilled entry on the first page of the ship's log book, signing his name with a proud flourish. Two days later, the *Oregon Journal* published a photograph of Ron and Moulton in uniform with an article about the commissioning of the new ship. Ron wore his dark glasses and an intrepid expression, his coat collar was turned up and he gripped a pipe in his right hand: he looked just like a man ready to go to war.

In the story, Ron was described as a 'veteran sub-hunter of the battles of the Pacific and Atlantic . . . an old hand at knocking tails off enemy subs'. To add a little local interest, it seems he told the reporter that he had grown up in Portland and came from a long line of naval men. He said his grandfather, 'Captain' Lafayette Waterbury, and his great-grandfather, 'Captain' I.C. DeWolf, had both helped make American naval history, although naturally he did not elaborate on their contribution. [His great-grandfather's name was Abram; 'I.C.' were his grandmother's initials.]

His membership in the Explorers Club received a prominent mention, of course, along with the fact that he had commanded three 'internationally important' expeditions. He was also persuaded to reveal that during the Caribbean Motion Picture Expedition he had become the first man ever to use a bathysphere for underwater filming.

When the reporter asked Ron for a comment about his new ship, he obliged with a picturesque quote that began by sounding like Humphrey Bogart and ended like the President: 'Those little sweethearts are tough. They could lick the pants off anything Nelson or Farragut ever sailed. They put up a sizzling fight and are the only answer to the submarine menace. I state emphatically that the future of America rests with just such escort vessels.'

On the evening of 18 May, the *USS PC-815* sailed from Astoria, Oregon, on her shakedown cruise. Her destination was San Diego, but she had only been at sea for five hours when, at 0230 hours off Cape Lookout on the coast of Oregon, she encountered at least one, perhaps two, enemy submarines in the middle of a busy shipping lane!

Ron provided a graphic account of the engagement that followed in a secret Battle Report to the Commander-in-Chief, Pacific Fleet:[6]

'Proceeding southward just inside the steamer track an echo-ranging contact was made by the soundman then on duty . . .The Commanding Officer had the conn and immediately slowed all engines to ahead one third to better echo-ranging conditions, and placed the contact dead ahead, 500 yards away.

'The first contact was very good. The target was moving left and away. The bearing was clear. The night was moonlit and the sea was flat calm . . .The *USS PC-815* closed in to 360 yards, meanwhile sounding general quarters . . . Contact was regained at 800 yards and was held on the starboard beam while further investigation was made. Screws were present and distinct as before. The bearing was still clear. Smoke signal identification was watched for closely and when none appeared it was concluded the target must not be a friendly submarine. All engines were brought up to speed 15 knots and the target was brought dead ahead . . .'

On its first attack run, the *USS PC-815* dropped a barrage of three depth charges. When it had re-established contact, a second attack was made at 0350 hours, this time laying down a pattern of four depth charges.

Ron lapsed into rather unmilitary lyricism to describe the ensuing events: 'The ship, sleepy and sceptical, had come to their guns swiftly and without error. No one, including the Commanding Officer, could readily credit the existence of an enemy submarine here on the steamer track and all soundmen, now on the bridge, were attempting to argue the echo-ranging equipment and chemical recorder out of such a fantastic idea . . .

'At 0450, with dawn breaking over a glassy sea, a lookout sighted a dark object about 700 yards from the ship on the starboard beam. When inspected the object seemed to be moving . . . Although very probably this object was a floating log no chances were taken and the target was used to test the guns which had not been heretofore fired structurally. The gunners, most of whom were men of experience, displayed an astonishing accuracy, bursts and shells converging on the target.

'The target disappeared for several minutes and then, to test the guns not brought to bear on the first burst, the ship was turned in case the object reappeared. The object appeared again closer to the ship. Once more fire was opened and the target vanished . . .'

Ron stressed that he considered it likely this target was no more than driftwood, but he thought it was good for the morale of the gunners to ensure the newly-installed guns worked. The *USS PC-815* mounted four further attacks on the elusive submarine in the hope of forcing it to the surface, without success. At the end of the sixth attack the ship's supply of depth charges was exhausted. Urgent signals requesting more ammunition at first met with no response.

At nine o'clock in the morning, two US Navy blimps, *K-39* and *K-33*, appeared on the scene to help with the search. By noon, Ron believed that the submarine was disabled in some way, or at least unable to launch its torpedoes, since the *PC-815*, lying to in a smooth sea, presented an easy target and had not been attacked. In the early afternoon a second, smaller, sub-chaser, the *USS SC-536* arrived, but was unable to make contact with the target.

On the bridge of *PC-815*, Ron offered to lead the other ship on an attack run, blowing a whistle to signal when to drop its depth charges. 'With the bullnose of the SC nearly against our flagstaff,' Ron wrote, 'we came to attack course . . .' Five depth charges were dropped on the first run and two on the second.

'The observation blimps began to sight oil and air bubbles in the vicinity of the last attack and finally a periscope. This ship also sighted air bubbles . . . At 1606 oil was reported again and this ship saw oil. Great air boils were seen and the sound of blowing tanks was reported by the soundman . . . All guns were now manned with great attention as it was supposed that the sub was trying to surface. Everyone was very calm, gunners joking about who would get in the first shot.'

But the submarine did not surface. Far from being discouraged, it seemed that Ron was by then convinced that there was not just one but two submarines lurking somewhere beneath them. His sonar operator had reported making a second, separate, contact a few hours earlier.

Shortly before five o'clock, a Coast Guard patrol boat brought in further supplies of ammuntion. Manoeuvring alongside, twenty-seven depth charges were transferred on to the *USS PC-815* and made ready for firing. Not long afterwards, a second Coast Guard patrol boat, the *Bonham* arrived, followed by another sub-chaser, the *USS SC-537*. There was now a total of five ships and two observations blimps involved in the search for the enemy submarines off the coast of Oregon.

All through the next day, sweep and search operations continued, although not all the Commanding Officers were as keen or convinced as Ron. 'Neither the *SC-537* nor the *Bonham*', he noted 'showed any

understanding whatever and refused by their actions to cooperate.'
The *SC-537*, he added with barely concealed disgust, failed to drop a
single depth charge. As if in compensation, the *USS PC-815* made one
attack run after another, forging back and forth at high speed,
dropping barrage after barrage.

Still no wreckage, no bodies, floated to the surface. Ron was not in
the least deterred. 'Because we had three times found two sub targets
on the previous day, we considered from her failure to surface that one
sub was gone down in 90 fathoms. The other still had batteries well up
for it made good speed in subsequent attacks . . .

'All during the following night, the *USS PC-815* kept the area swept
as well as it could. The moonlight showed up an oil slick which we
investigated, though the slick was too thin for samples . . . A report
that the sub had surfaced off Sand Lake caused all vessels except the
Bonham to go flying north to that position. But before flank speed was
attained the reported "sub" was reported as a fishing vessel . . .

'At 0700, May 21, 1943, being near the area of the attacks the night
before this ship stopped to search . . . Suddenly a boil of orange
colored oil, very thick, came to the surface immediately on our port
bow . . . The Commanding Officer came forward on the double and
saw a second boil of orange oil rising on the other side of the first. The
soundman was loudly reporting that he heard tanks being blown on
the port bow.

'Every man on the bridge and flying bridge then saw the periscope,
moving from right to left, rising up through the first oil boil to a height
of about two feet. The barrel and lens of the instrument were
unmistakeable . . . On the appearance of the periscope, both gunners
fired straight into the periscope, range about 50 yards. The periscope
vanished in an explosion of 20mm bullets.'

The *USS PC-815* made one further attack run and dropped its last
two depth charges. At midnight, after being in action for some
sixty-eight hours, Ron received orders to return to Astoria.

He noted in his report, rather sourly, that they were greeted with
'considerable scepticism' on their return. Nevertheless, his conclusion
was unequivocal: 'It is specifically claimed that one submarine,
presumably Japanese, possibly a mine-layer, was damaged beyond
ability to leave the scene and that one submarine, presumably
Japanese, possibly a mine-layer, was damaged beyond ability to return
to its base.

'This vessel wishes no credit for itself. It was built to hunt
submarines. Its people were trained to hunt submarines. Although
exceeding its orders originally by attacking the first contact, this vessel
feels only that it has done the job for which it was intended and stands
ready to do that job again.'

Despite the scepticism, the US Navy mounted an immediate investigation of the incident. Ever since Pearl Harbor, Americans had been jittery about the possibility of an attack on the mainland by Japanese submarines. In February 1942, a lone enemy submarine had surfaced about a mile offshore north of Santa Barbara, California, and lobbed twenty-five shells at an oil refinery. If it happened once, it could presumably happen again and the Navy certainly needed to know if the *USS PC-815* had indeed stumbled across enemy submarines close to the coast of Oregon.

The Commanding Officer and Executive Officer of *PC-815* were ordered to report immediately to Admiral Frank Jack Fletcher, Commander Northwest Sea Frontier, in Seattle. Fletcher studied Ron's eighteen-page Battle Report and interviewed the Commanding Officers of the four other ships and two blimps involved. The tape from the *PC-815*'s attack recorder, which recorded the strength and characteristics of the sonar signals, was evaluated by experts. When all the reports were in, Fletcher swiftly came to the conclusion that the hundred depth charges dropped during the 'battle' had probably killed a few fish but no Japanese.

In a secret memorandum to the Commander-in-Chief, Pacific Fleet, dated 8 June 1943, Fletcher stated: 'An analysis of all reports convinces me that there was no submarine in the area. Lieutenant Commander Sullivan [Commander of the blimps] states that he was unable to obtain any evidence of a submarine except one bubble of air which is unexplained except by turbulence of water due to a depth charge explosion. The Commanding Officers of all ships except the *PC-815* state they had no evidence of a submarine and do not think a submarine was in the area.'[7]

Fletcher added that there was a 'known magnetic deposit' in the area in which the depth charges were dropped. The implication was clear: Lieutenant Hubbard, Commanding Officer of *USS PC-815*, had fought a two-day battle with a magnetic deposit.

Neither Ron nor Moulton would accept this verdict. They believed that denying the existence of the submarines was a political decision taken to avoid spreading alarm among the civilian population. Moulton pointed out that the *Reader's Digest* had recently published a story about the attack on the oil refinery near Santa Barbara and it had caused something approaching panic among people living along the coast of California. It was hardly surprising, they concluded, that the top brass wanted to hush up the fact that US Navy ships had been fighting enemy submarines only about ten miles off the coast of Oregon.

The disconsolate crew of the *USS PC-815*, who had no doubt expected to return home as conquering heroes, had to be satisfied with this explanation and forego public recognition of their battle. It was a bitter pill for them to swallow. The only reward their Commanding Officer could arrange was a rare treat recorded in the ship's log on the day they returned to Astoria: 'Ice cream brought on board.'

As Commanding Officer, Lieutenant Hubbard's record was unquestionably blighted by the Admiral's damning report, although there was no suggestion that he should be relieved of his command. There was plenty of good-natured joshing in the service about the man who had attacked a magnetic field, but it would probably have been forgotten eventually and need not have affected Ron's career, except that the luckless *USS PC-815* was soon in even worse trouble.

Towards the end of May, the *PC-815* was detailed to escort a new aircraft carrier from Portland to San Diego. Thankfully this voyage was completed without incident. On arrival in San Diego Ron said goodbye to his friend Tom Moulton, who had been transferred to HQ Thirteenth Naval District in Seattle for further assignment.

San Diego is the most southerly coastal town in California, only ten miles from the Mexican border at Tijuana. Just offshore from Tijuana there is a small group of islands known as Los Coronados, used by local fishermen to dry their nets.

On the afternoon of 28 June, the *PC-815* steamed unknowingly into Mexican territorial waters and fired four shots with its 3-inch gun in the direction of the Coronados islands. She then anchored off the island and fired small arms – pistols and rifles – into the water.

The Mexican government may not have considered that the United States was launching a surprise attack, but the incident was deemed sufficiently serious for an official complaint to be lodged. Lieutenant Hubbard, fresh from his notorious battle with a magnetic deposit, was not exactly well placed to be forgiven for this new blunder.

On 30 June, a Board of Investigation was convened on board the *PC-815* in San Diego Harbor. Lieutenant Hubbard was first to give evidence and stoutly denied that he had done wrong. He had ordered the gunnery practice because he was anxious to train his crew and he believed he had authority to be in the area. When asked why he had anchored for the night he admitted that he had not wanted to spend the entire night on the bridge. 'On three separate occasions,' he added, 'when leaving my officers in charge of the bridge they have become lost.'[8]

The next witness was the Gunnery Officer, who cheerfully confessed that he thought the Coronados Islands belonged to the United States. After listening to more than thirteen hours of evidence, the three-man Board of Investigation concluded that Lieutenant Hubbard had disregarded orders, both by conducting gunnery practice and by anchoring in Mexican territorial waters without proper authority.

It was recommended, in the light of the short time he had been in command, that he should be admonished in lieu of the more drastic disciplinary action that the offences would normally have deserved.[9] But it was also decided that he should be transferred to other duties.

On 7 July, after just eighty days as Commanding Officer of his own ship, Ron signed his last page of the *PC-815*'s deck log: '1345, Signed on Detachment, L. R. Hubbard.'

In a fitness report covering his brief career as a Commanding Officer, Rear-Admiral F.A. Braisted, Commander, Fleet Operational Training Command, Pacific, rated Lieutenant L.R. Hubbard as 'below average' and noted: 'Consider this officer lacking in the essential qualities of judgement, leadership and cooperation. He acts without forethought as to probable results. He is believed to have been sincere in his efforts to make his ship efficient and ready. Not considered qualified for command or promotion at this time. Recommend duty on a large vessel where he can be properly supervised.'[10]

Ron was posted to temporary duty in the Issuing Office at Headquarters, Eleventh Naval District in San Diego, where he almost immediately reported sick with a variety of ailments ranging from malaria to a duodenal ulcer to pains in his back. He was admitted to the local naval hospital for observation and remained there as an in-patient for nearly three months. He wrote home to inform the family that he was in hospital because he had been injured when he picked up an unexploded shell from the deck of his ship; it had exploded in mid-air as he threw it over the side.[11]

In later years Ron would tell a story of how he had helped the staff at San Diego Naval Hospital during this period.[12] It seemed a regiment of marines had been shipped home with a disease called filoriasis about which the doctors knew nothing. Ron, because of his experience in 'the South Pacific', advised them that although there was a serum available to treat the condition, his understanding was that a spell in a cold climate would work equally well. Accordingly, the regiment was despatched to Alaska where, Ron said, 'I am sure they all recovered.'

This good deed done, in October 1943 Ron was sent on a six-week course at the Naval Small Craft Training Center on Terminal Island, San Pedro, California. In December he learned he was to be given another opportunity to go to sea – as the Navigating Officer of the *USS Algol*, an amphibious attack cargo ship under construction at Portland, Oregon.

To judge from an entry in his private journal, he was not particularly thrilled about going back to sea, nor indeed, about being in the Navy at all. 'My salvation is to let this roll over me,' he noted gloomily on 6 January 1944, 'to write, write and write some more. To hammer keys until I am finger worn to the second joint and then to hammer keys some more. To pile up copy, stack up stories, roll the wordage and generally conduct my life along the one line of success I have ever had.'[13]

'The only thing that ever affected me as a writer,' he recalled years later in a newspaper interview,[14] 'was the US Navy when their security regulations prohibited writing. I was quiet for about two years before I couldn't take it any more and went and took it out on a typewriter and, wearing a stetson hat in the middle of a battle theater, wrote a costume historical novel of 60,000 words which has never seen the light of day.'

For the first six months of 1944, Ron remained in Portland during the fitting out of the *Algol*. News of the war in the Pacific was of bitter fighting and heavy casualties. US Marines were working their way from island to island towards Japan, but at shocking cost. In the attack on Tarawa Atoll, more than a thousand Americans were killed and two thousand wounded: news pictures of the beaches littered with dead Marines shocked the nation and brought home the terrible reality of war. On 15 June, two divisions of US Marines began an assault on Saipan in the southern Marianas, and in the battle that followed 16,500 Americans were killed or wounded.

The *USS Algol* was commissioned in July and immediately put to sea for trials. Through August and most of September she was exercizing at sea; as Navigating Officer, Ron signed the ship's deck log every day, but there was little to report except 'under way, as before'. He seemed to have had second thoughts about wanting to see action, for on 9 September he applied for an appointment to the School of Military Government, citing among his qualifications his education as a civil engineer, membership in the Explorers Club, wide travel in the Far East and experience of handling natives. The *Algol*'s Commanding Officer approved Ron's application, noting on his fitness report that while Lieutenant Hubbard was a capable and energetic officer, he was 'very temperamental and often has his feelings hurt'. On 22 September, the *Algol* was at last ordered to Oakland, California, to start taking on supplies in preparation for sailing to war. The excited rumour among the crew was that the ship was to take part in a major new offensive in the Pacific aimed at the final defeat of the Japanese.

At 1630 on the afternoon of 27 September – the day before Ron was due to leave for Princeton – the ship's deck log recorded an unusual incident: 'The Navigating Officer reported to the OOD that an attempt at sabatage [*sic*] had been made sometime between 1530–1600. A coke bottle filled with gasoline with a cloth wick inserted had been concealed among cargo which was to be hoisted aboard and stored in No 1 hold. It was discovered before being taken on board. ONI, FBI and NSD authorities reported on the scene and investigations were started.'[15]

No further mention was made of the incident. There was no explanation of why Lieutenant Hubbard, the Navigating Officer, was poking around in cargo being loaded on to the ship or of how he had managed to find the 'petrol bomb'. Neither was the result of the investigations recorded. Shortly after ten o'clock that evening a brief signal was received 'Lt Lafayette Ron Hubbard, D-v (S), USNR 113392, is this date detached from duty.'

On 4 October, the *USS Algol* sailed for Eniwetok Atoll in the Marshall Islands, from where she would take part in the invasion of Luzon in the Philippines and the landings on Okinawa, earning two battle stars. Her erstwhile Navigating Officer, meanwhile, was on a four-month course in 'Military Government' at the Naval Training School, Princeton, prompting him to claim ever after that he finished his education at the venerable Ivy League university of the same name.

While he was at Princeton, Ron was invited to join a group of science-fiction writers who met every weekend at Robert Heinlein's apartment in Philadelphia to discuss possible ways of countering the Kamikaze menace in the Pacific. They were semi-official, brainstorming sessions that Heinlein had been asked to organize by the Navy, in the faint hope of coming up with a defence against young Japanese pilots on suicide missions. 'I had been ordered to round up science fiction writers for this crash project,' Heinlein recalled, 'the wildest brains I could find.'[16]

Heinlein's apartment was only three hundred yards from Broad Street Station in downtown Philadelphia and the group gathered on Saturday afternoons, arriving on Pennsylvania Railroad trains which ran every half hour into Broad Street. 'On Saturday nights there would be two or three in my bed,' said Heinlein, 'a couple on the couch and the rest on the living-room floor. If there was still overflow, I sent them a block down the street to a friend with more floor space if not beds.'

Heinlein tried to avoid asking Ron to walk down the street as Ron had said that both his feet had been broken when his last ship was bombed. 'Ron had had a busy war – sunk four times and wounded again and again,' Heinlein explained sympathetically.

Sunday morning was set aside for the working session, after which everyone sat around swapping stories and jokes. Ron often got out his guitar and entertained them in a rich baritone voice with songs like 'Fifteen Men on a Dead Man's Chest' and 'I Learned about Women from Her'. He could also reduce the assembled company to helpless laughter with his repertoire of fast-moving burlesque skits in which he played all the roles.

On Saturday 2 December, Jack Williamson, then a Sergeant in the US Army, hosted a dinner in Philadelphia for fellow science-fiction writers and their wives. He was to be sent overseas in a couple of days and this was his farewell party. Among those present were the Heinleins, the de Camps, the Asimovs and L. Ron Hubbard. 'The star of the evening', Isaac Asimov recalled, 'was Ron Hubbard. Heinlein, de Camp and I were each prima donna-ish and each liked to hog the conversation – ordinarily. On this occasion, however, we all sat as quietly as pussycats and listened to Hubbard. He told tales with perfect aplomb and in complete paragraphs.'[17]

The host was less impressed. 'Hubbard was just back from the Aleutians then,' said Williamson, 'hinting of desperate action aboard a Navy destroyer, adventures he couldn't say much about because of military security.

'I recall his eyes, the wary, light-blue eyes that I somehow associate with the gunmen of the old West, watching me sharply as he talked as if to see how much I believed. Not much.'[18]

Heinlein's group never came up with any ideas about how to prevent US Navy losses from Kamikaze pilots, but it did not matter much because the war was drawing to a close and Japan was running out of aircraft and pilots to fly them. The last big Kamikaze strike was launched in January 1945 against the US fleet (including Ron's old ship, the *USS Algol*) taking part in the invasion of Luzon. That same month Ron was transferred to the Naval Civil Affairs Staging Area in Monterey, California, for further training, having finished about mid-way among the 300 students on his course at the school of Military Government. In April he again reported sick and a possible ulcer was diagnosed.

On 2 September 1945, after the horror of Hiroshima and Nagasaki, the Japanese signed the surrender instrument on the quarterdeck of the *USS Missouri*, anchored in Tokyo Bay. Three days later, Ron was re-admitted to Oak Knoll Naval Hospital, Oakland, not as a result of heroic war wounds, but to be treated for 'epigastric distress'. It was in this rather inglorious situation, suffering from a suspected duodenal ulcer, that the war ended for Lieutenant L. Ron Hubbard, US Navy Reserve.

He, of course, saw it somewhat differently: 'Blinded with injured optic nerves, and lame with injuries to hip and back, at the end of World War Two I faced an almost non-existent future . . . I was abandoned by family and friends as a supposedly hopeless cripple and a probable burden upon them for the rest of my days . . . I became used to being told it was all impossible, that there was no way, no hope. Yet I came to see and walk again . . .'[19]

If his own account of his war experiences is to be believed, he certainly deserved the twenty-one medals and palms he was said to have received. Unfortunately, his US Navy record indicates he was awarded just four routine medals – the American Defense Service Medal, awarded to everyone serving at the time of Pearl Harbor, the American Campaign Medal, the Asiatic-Pacific Campaign Medal and the World War Two Victory Medal, this last received by everyone serving on V-J Day.

Chapter 7

Black Magic and Betty

'Hubbard broke up black magic in America . . . because he was well known as a writer and philosopher and had friends among the physicists, he was sent in to handle the situation [of black magic being practised in a house in Pasadena occupied by nuclear physicists]. He went to live at the house and investigated the black magic rites and the general situation and found them very bad . . . Hubbard's mission was successful far beyond anyone's expectations. The house was torn down. Hubbard rescued a girl they were using. The black magic group was dispersed and never recovered.' (Statement by the Church of Scientology, December 1969)

* * * * *

Hubbard was a patient at Oak Knoll Naval Hospital for three months after the war, although the doctors were undecided as to precisely what was wrong with him. He was certainly neither blind nor crippled, but seemed to be suffering from endless minor aches and pains. His medical record shows that he was examined exhaustively, almost every week, complaining of headaches, rheumatism, conjunctivitis, pains in his side, stomach aches, pains in his shoulder, arthritis, haemorrhoids . . . there seemed to be no end to his suffering. Sometimes the doctors could find symptoms, sometimes they could not. In September, for example, he was declared 'unfit for service' because of an ulcer, but in November his ailments were described as 'minimal'.

It may be, of course, that Ron was simply preparing the ground to claim a veteran's disability pension, for he certainly wasted no time putting in his application. Lieutenant Hubbard was 'mustered out' of the US Navy on 5 December 1945, and on the following day he applied for a pension on the basis of a sprained left knee, conjunctivitis, a chronic duodenal ulcer, arthritis in his right hip and shoulder, recurrent malaria and sporadic undiagnosed pain in his left side and back.[1]

On the claim form, Ron said his wife and children were living with his parents at 1212 Gregory Way, Bremerton, until he was able to get a house of his own. He described himself as a freelance writer with a monthly income of $0.00; before he joined the Navy he claimed his average earnings had been $650 a month.

Satisfied he had presented a convincing case for a pension, Ron drove out of the Officer Separation Center in San Francisco at the wheel of an old Packard with a small trailer in tow, both of which he had recently acquired. Home and the family were to the north, up in Washington State. But Ron headed south, towards Los Angeles, to a rendezvous with a magician in a bizarre Victorian mansion in Pasadena.

John Whiteside Parsons, known to his friend as Jack, was an urbane, darkly handsome man, not unlike Errol Flynn in looks, and the scion of a well-connected Los Angeles family. Then thirty-one years old, he was a brilliant scientist and chemist and one of America's foremost explosives experts. He had spent much of the war at the California Institute of Technology working with a team developing jet engines and experimental rocket fuels and was, perhaps, the last man anyone would have suspected of worshipping the Devil.

For Jack Parsons led an extraordinary double life: respected scientist by day, dedicated occultist by night. He believed, passionately, in the power of black magic, the existence of Satan, demons and evil spirits, and the efficacy of spells to deal with his enemies.[2]

While still a student at the University of Southern California, he had become interested in the writings of Aleister Crowley, the English sorcerer and Satanist known as 'The Beast 666', whose dabblings in black magic had also earned him the title 'The Wickedest Man In The World'. Crowley's *The Book of the Law* expounded a doctrine enshrined in a single sentence – 'Do what thou wilt shall be the whole of the Law' – and Parsons was intrigued by the heady concept of a creed that encouraged indulgence in forbidden pleasures.

In 1939, Parsons and his young wife, Helen, joined the OTO, Ordo Templi Orientis, an international organization founded by Crowley to practise sexual magic.[3] A lodge had been set up in Los Angeles and met in a suitably sequestered attic. Meetings were conducted by a priestess swathed in diaphanous gauze, who climbed out of a coffin to perform mystic, and painstakingly blasphemous, rites.[4] Parsons quickly rose to prominence in the OTO and by the early '40s he had begun a regular correspondence with Crowley, always addressing him as 'Most Beloved Father' and signing his letters 'Thy son, John'.

When Parsons's father died, his son inherited a rambling mansion and adjoining coach-house on South Orange Grove Avenue in Pasadena. South Orange Grove was where the best people lived in Pasadena in the '20s and '30s, and although its discreet gentility was fading by the end of the war, most of the large houses in the area were still in single occupancy, the paintwork had yet to peel and the lawns were regularly watered and manicured.

The residents of South Orange Grove Avenue did not welcome the arrival of young Jack Parsons, for the elegant three-storey family mansion, shaded by huge palms and flowering magnolias and set in its own grounds, was rapidly transformed, under his ownership, into a rooming-house of dubious repute – the only way he could afford to keep the house was by renting rooms. This might not have caused too much upset in the neighbourhood, except that when he advertized for tenants in the local newspaper, he specified that only atheists and those of a Bohemian disposition need apply. Thus were the myriad rooms at 1003 South Orange Grove Avenue occupied by an exotic, argumentative and peripatetic assortment of itinerants and ne'er-do-wells – out-of-work actors and writers, anarchists and artists, musicians and dancers, all kinds of questionable characters and their equally questionable friends of both sexes. Noisy parties continued for days on end, guests slept on the floor when they could not find a bed and sometimes they simply forgot to leave.

Understandably the neighbours were outraged, although they would undoubtedly have been even more alarmed had they known that the house was also destined to become the headquarters of a black magic group which practised deviant sexual rites. Parsons converted two large rooms into a private apartment for himself and a temple for the OTO lodge. In his bedroom, the biggest room in the house, there was an altar flanked by pyramidal pillars and hung with occult symbols. The other room was a wood-panelled library lined with books devoted to the occult and dominated by a huge signed portrait of Crowley hanging over the fireplace.

No one was allowed into these two rooms unless specifically invited by Parsons; when members of the OTO turned up for a meeting, the doors remained firmly closed. Other residents sometimes glimpsed Parson or one of his followers moving about the house in black robes, but no one really knew what went on in the 'temple'.[5] On one occasion, two smirking policemen arrived at the front door to investigate a complaint that the house was being used for black magic orgies. They had been told, they said, something about a ceremony requiring a naked pregnant woman to leap nine times through a sacred fire, but they made it so obvious that they considered the whole thing to be a joke that Parsons had no difficulty convincing them he was a bona fide and respectable scientist, and persuaded them to leave without conducting a search.

Among his other interests, Parsons was also a science-fiction fan and occasionally turned up at meetings of the Los Angeles Fantasy and

Science Fiction Society, where devoted fans gathered every week to meet the top science fiction writers. Jack Williamson, a regular contributor to *Science Wonder Stories*, encountered Parsons at a meeting in 1941 and was surprised to learn he was a scientist. 'He had read my novel *Darker Than You Think*, which deals with the supernatural,' Williamson recalled. 'I was astonished to discover he had a far less sceptical interest in such things than I did.'[6]

To Parsons there was an attractive affinity between magic and science fiction and on Sunday afternoons in the summer his science-fiction friends tended to congregate in his kitchen for endless discussions about the relative merits of sci-fi writers, their ideas and stories. One of the fans who regularly took the streetcar to South Orange Grove Avenue on Sunday afternoons was a young man called Alva Rogers, who would eventually become a 'semi-permanent resident' – an arrangement that was not in the least unusual. On an early visit he met and fell in love with a young art student who was renting a room in the mansion and thereafter he would spend the night with her whenever he could.

Rogers was fascinated by the house, its owner and the occupants. 'Mundane souls were unceremoniously rejected as tenants,' he said. 'There was a professional fortune teller and seer who always wore appropriate dresses and decorated her apartment with symbols and artefacts of arcane lore. There was a lady, well past middle age but still strikingly beautiful, who claimed to have been at various times the mistress of half the famous men of France. There was a man who had been a renowned organist in the great movie palaces of the silent era. They were characters all.'

According to Rogers, Parsons never made any secret of his interest in black magic or his involvement with Aleister Crowley. 'He had a voluminous correspondence with Crowley in the library, some of which he showed me. I remember in particular one letter from Crowley which praised and encouraged him for the fine work he was doing in America, and also casually thanked him for his latest donation and intimated that more would shortly be needed. Jack admitted that he was one of Crowley's main sources of money in America.

'I always found Jack's insistence that he believed in, and practised, magic hard to reconcile with his educational and cultural background. At first I thought it was all fun and games, a kick he was on for its shock value to his respectable friends. But after seeing his correspondence with Crowley, and the evidence of his frequent remittances to Crowley, I had to give him the benefit of the doubt.'[7]

In the summer of 1944, Helen Parsons left her husband and ran off with another member of the lodge, by whom she was pregnant.

Parsons consoled himself by transferring his affections to Helen's younger sister, Sara Northrup, who was then eighteen, a beautiful and vivacious student at the University of Southern California. Within a few months, Sara dropped out of her course and moved in with Parsons, to the great distress of her parents. At South Orange Grove Avenue she became known as Betty (her middle name was Elizabeth). Completely under the spell of her lover, she was soon inculcated onto the OTO and assisting in its ceremonies. In accordance with the teachings of 'the Beast', Parsons encouraged Betty to enjoy sex with other members of the lodge, or indeed any man who took her fancy. It would not affect their relationship, he loftily explained to anyone who cared to listen, since jealousy was a base emotion unworthy of the enlightened and fit only for peasants.

'Betty was a very attractive blonde, full of joie de vivre,' said Rogers. 'The rapport between Jack and Betty, the strong affection, if not love, they had for each other, despite their frequent separate sextracurricular activities, seemed pretty permanent and shatterproof.'[8]

It was soon to prove an illusion. One afternoon in August 1945, Lou Goldstone, a well-known science-fiction illustrator and a frequent visitor to South Orange Grove Avenue, turned up with L. Ron Hubbard, who was then on leave from the Navy. Jack Parsons liked Ron immediately, perhaps recognized in him a kindred spirit, and invited him to move in for the duration of his leave.

Ron, ebullient as always, was not in any way intimidated by the egregious company and surroundings; on the contrary, he felt instantly at home. Most evenings he could be found dominating the conversation at the big table in the kitchen, where the roomers tended to gather, telling outrageous stories about his adventures. One night he unbuttoned his shirt to display the scars left by arrows hurled at him when he encountered a band of hostile aborigines in the South American jungle.

Like almost everyone in the house, Alva Rogers thought Hubbard was an enormously engaging and entertaining personality. Rogers also had red hair and Ron confided to him his belief, confirmed by extensive research he had undertaken at the 'Royal Museum' in London, that all redheads were related, being descended from the same line of Neanderthal man. 'Needless to say,' Rogers recalled, 'I was fascinated.'

For a while, Ron shared a room with Nieson Himmel, a young reporter who had also met Parsons through a shared interest in science fiction. Perhaps because of the inbred scepticism of newspapermen, Himmel was less impressed than most by his new room-mate: 'I can't stand phoneys and to me he was so obviously a phoney, a real con man. But he was certainly not a dummy. He was very sharp and quick, a fascinating story-teller, and he could charm the shit out of anybody. He talked interminably about his war experiences and seemed to have been everywhere. Once he said he was on Admiral Halsey's staff. I called a friend who worked with Halsey and my friend said "Shit, I've never heard of him."

'I was not one of his favourite people because I liked to try and trip him up. One time he told a story about how he was walking down a corridor in the British Museum when he was suddenly grabbed by three scientists who dragged him into an office and began measuring his skull because it was such a perfect shape. I said, "Gee, Ron, that's a great story – didn't I read it in George Bernard Shaw?" Another time he said he was in the Aleutians in command of a destroyer and a polar bear jumped from an ice floe onto his ship and chased everyone around. I recognized it as an old, old folklore story that goes way back.

'He was always broke and trying to borrow money. That was another reason he didn't like me – I would never lend him a cent. Whenever he was talking about being hard up he often used to say that he thought the easiest way to make money would be to start a religion.'[9]

Parsons shared none of Himmel's mistrust. He considered that Ron had great magical potential and took the risk of breaking his solemn oath of secrecy to acquaint Ron with some of the OTO rituals.[10] Betty, too, was much enamoured with the voluble naval officer, so much so that she soon began sleeping with him. True to his creed, Parsons tried to pretend he was not concerned by this development, but others in the house thought they detected tension between the two men. Himmel, who was himself in love with Betty, was furious that she had been seduced by Hubbard. 'Betty was beautiful, the most gorgeous, intelligent, sweet, wonderful girl. I was so much in love with her and I knew she was a woman I could never have. Then Hubbard comes along and starts having affairs with one girl after another in the house and finally fastens on to Betty. I couldn't believe it was happening. There he was, living off Parsons' largesse and making out with his girlfriend right in front of him. Sometimes when the two of them were sitting at the table together, the hostility was almost tangible.'[11]

Alva Rogers, too, sensed that Parsons was suffering. 'Jack had never boggled at any of Betty's previous amorous adventurings, but this time it seemed somehow different . . . although the three of them continued to maintain a surface show of unchanged amicability, it was obvious that Jack was feeling the pangs of a hitherto unfelt passion, jealousy. As events progressed, Jack found it increasingly difficult to keep his mind on anything but the torrid affair going on between Ron and Betty and the atmosphere around the house became supercharged with tension.'

Nevertheless, Parsons clearly remained convinced that Ron possessed exceptional powers. After Ron had left to report back to Oak Knoll Naval Hospital, Parsons wrote to his 'Most Beloved Father' to acquaint him with events: 'About three months ago I met Captain L. Ron Hubbard, a writer and explorer of whom I had known for some time . . . He is a gentleman; he has red hair, green eyes, is honest and intelligent, and we have become great friends. He moved in with me about two months ago, and although Betty and I are still friendly, she has transferred her sexual affection to Ron.

'Although he has no formal training in Magick, he has an extraordinary amount of experience and understanding in the field. From some of his experiences I deduced that he is in direct touch with some higher intelligence, possibly his Guardian Angel. He describes his Angel as a beautiful winged woman with red hair whom he calls the Empress and who has guided him through his life and saved him many times. He is the most Thelemic person I have ever met and is in complete accord with our own principles . . . I think I have made a great gain and as Betty and I are the best of friends, there is little loss. I cared for her rather deeply but I have no desire to control her emotions, and I can, I hope, control my own. I need a magical partner. I have many experiments in mind . . .'[12]

In early December 1945, Ron showed up again at South Orange Grove Avenue, still in uniform, having driven directly from the Officer Separation Centre in San Francisco. He parked his Packard and his trailer at the rear of the house and walked back into the complicated, enigmatic lives of Jack Parsons and Betty Northrup. To Parsons's secret distress, Betty and Ron immediately resumed their affair.

Alva Rogers and his girlfriend were perhaps the only two people in the house who really knew how much their friend was suffering. 'Our room was just across the hall from Jack's apartment,' Rogers recalled, 'and in the still, early hours of a bleak morning in December we were brought out of a sound sleep by some weird and disturbing noises as though someone was dying or at the very least was deathly ill.

'We went out into the hall to investigate the source of the noises and found that they came from Jack's partially open door. Perhaps we should have turned around and gone back to bed at this point, but we didn't. The noise, which by this time we could tell was a sort of chant, drew us inexorably to the door, which we pushed open a little further in order to better see what was going on.

'What we saw I'll never forget, although I find it hard to describe in any detail. The room, in which I had been before, was decorated in a manner typical of an occultist's lair, with all the symbols and appurtenances essential to the proper practice of black magic. It was dimly lit and smoky from a pungent incense; Jack was draped in a black robe and stood with his back to us, his arms outstretched, in the centre of a pentagram before some sort of altar affair on which several indistinguishable items stood.

'His voice, which was actually not very loud, rose and fell in a rhythmic chant of gibberish which was delivered with such passionate intensity that its meaning was frighteningly obvious. After this brief and uninvited glimpse into the blackest and most secret center of a tortured man's soul, we quietly withdrew and returned to our room, where we spent the balance of the night discussing in whispers what we had just witnessed.'[13]

Rogers was convinced that Parsons was trying to invoke a demon in order to despatch his rival, or harm him in some way. It clearly did not work, however, for Ron remained in the best of spirits. Despite what Alva Rogers and his girlfriend had seen on that unforgettable December night, the fragile three-cornered relationship continued. Parsons seemed determined to try and overcome what he considered to be an unworthy emotion. 'I have been suffered to pass through an ordeal of human love and jealousy,' he noted in his 'Magical Record', adding, 'I have found a staunch companion and comrade in Ron . . . Ron and I are to continue with our plans for the Order.'[14]

Their plans were unprecedented. Parsons wanted to attempt an experiment in black magic that would push back the frontiers of the occult world. With the assistance of his new friend, he intended to try and create a 'moonchild' – the magical child 'mightier than all the kings of the earth', whose birth had been prophesied in *The Book of the Law* more than forty years earlier.

Aleister Crowley professed 'the great idea of magicians of all times' was to bring into being an Anti-Christ, a 'living being in form resembling man, and possessing those qualities of man which distinguish him from beasts, namely intellect and power of speech, but neither begotten in the manner of human generation, nor inhabited by a human soul'.[15] To find a mother for this new Messiah, Parsons envisaged invoking an elemental spirit of the 'whore of Babylon', the scarlet woman of St John's Revelation: 'I saw a woman sit upon a scarlet coloured beast, full of names of blasphemy, having seven heads and ten horns. And the woman was arrayed in purple and scarlet colour, and decked with gold and precious stones and pearls, having a golden cup in her hand full of abominations and filthiness of her fornication. And upon her forehead was a name written, Mystery, Babylon the Great, the Mother of Harlots . . .'

On 4 January 1946, Jack Parsons began a series of elaborate mystic rituals, known as the 'Babalon Working', which he hoped would lead to the invocation of a scarlet woman whose destiny was to be mother to the moonchild. For the benefit of future magicians, he kept a detailed, day-by-day account in a manuscript he called the 'Book of Babalon'.

Magical rites began in the temple at South Orange Grove at nine o'clock that evening, with Prokofiev's *Violin Concerto* playing in the background. First Parsons prepared and consecrated various magical weapons, tablets and talismans, then he carried out eleven separate rituals, beginning with 'Invoking Pentagram of Air' and 'Invocation of Bornless One' and ending with 'License to Depart, Purification and Banishing'.

The nightly ritual of incantation and talisman-waving continued for eleven days, at first without much effect. Parsons noted that a strong windstorm blew up on the second and third days, but he had obviously been hoping for rather more startling results. 'Nothing seems to have happened,' he wrote in a letter to Crowley. 'The wind storm is very interesting, but that is not what I asked for.'[16]

On the seventh day, Parsons was woken at midnight by seven loud knocks and he discovered that a table lamp in the corner of his bedroom had been thrown violently to the floor and smashed. 'I have had little experience with phenomena of this sort,' he recorded. 'Magically speaking, it usually represents "breaks" in the operation, indicating imperfect technique. Actually, in any magical operation there should be no phenomena but the willed result.'

Not until 14 January was the frustrated magician able to report an encouragingly mysterious occurrence. 'The light system of the house failed at about 9 pm. Another magician [Hubbard] who had been staying at the house and studying with me, was carrying a candle across the kitchen when he was struck strongly on the right shoulder, and the candle knocked out of his hand. He called me, and we observed a brownish yellow light about seven feet high in the kitchen. I brandished a magical sword and it disappeared. His right arm was paralyzed for the rest of the night.'

Next morning, the magicians had more prosaic business to attend to. For some time, Ron, Betty and Jack had been discussing the prospect of going into business together, buying yachts on the East Coast and sailing them to California to sell at a profit. On 15 January the three of them signed their names to an agreement setting up a business partnership with the hopeful title of 'Allied Enterprises'. It was not exactly an equitable financial arrangement, since Parsons put up more than $20,000, Ron only managed to vouchsafe $1200 and Betty contributed nothing. Under the articles of co-partnership, it was vaguely stated that Allied Enterprises would indulge in activities of a 'varied and elastic nature', presumably with an eye to subsequent expansion into other fields.[17]

That evening, the new business partners resumed their magical activities and there was a further strange incident involving Ron who was by then occupying the role of 'scribe'. Parsons noted that the scribe had 'some sort of astral vision' and saw one of his old enemies standing behind him clad in a black robe with an 'evil, pasty face'; Ron promptly launched an attack and pinned the phantom figure to the door with four throwing knives. 'Later, in my room,' Parsons wrote, 'I heard the raps again and a buzzing, metallic voice crying, "Let me go free." I felt a great pressure and tension in the house that night.'

The tension continued for four days, until the evening of 18 January. The magician and his scribe had ventured out into the Mojave Desert on some unexplained mystical mission and, at sunset, the stress that Parsons had recently been experiencing drained away. He was suffused instead with a sense of well-being and turned to Ron and said simply: 'It is done.'

When the two men returned to South Orange Grove Avenue, they found the 'scarlet woman' waiting for them. Her name was Marjorie Cameron and in truth she was not very much different from many of the unconventional and free-spirited young women who had gravitated to the Bohemian lodging-house in Pasadena. But Parsons was convinced that she was his libidinous elemental spirit, not least because it transpired she was not only willing, but impatient, to participate in the magical and sexual escapades he had in mind. 'She is describable', he wrote in the 'Book of Babalon', 'as an air of fire type, with bronze red hair, fiery and subtle, determined and obstinate, sincere and perverse, with extraordinary personality, talent and intelligence.'

A few days later he wrote exultantly to Crowley: 'I have my elemental! She turned up one night after the conclusion of the Operation and has been with me since . . . She has red hair and slant green eyes as specified . . . She is an artist, strong minded and determined, with strong masculine characteristics and a fanatical independence.'

Crowley replied: 'I am particularly interested in what you have written to me about the elemental, because for some little time past I have been endeavouring to intervene *personally* in this matter on your behalf . . .'

Towards the end of February, Ron went on a trip to the East Coast, perhaps to investigate the yacht market on behalf of Allied Enterprises. On 28 February Parsons drove alone into the lonely reaches of the Mojave Desert to perform an invocation of the goddess Babalon. During this invocation, he said, the presence of the goddess came upon him and commanded him to write a mystical communication, couched in picturesque biblical terminology and beginning: 'Yea, it is I, Babalon. And this is my book . . .'

The seventy-seven clauses Parsons excitedly scribbled in his notebook became the centrepiece of the 'Book of Babalon'. He believed he was taking instructions for the impregnation of his scarlet woman, although it would not have been immediately obvious to non-believers: 'Now is the hour of birth at hand. Now shall my adept be crucified in the Basilisk abode. Thy tears, thy sweat, thy blood, thy semen, thy love, thy faith shall provide . . .'

Some of the message was also suspiciously contemporary: 'Thou fool, be thou also free of sentimentality. Am I thy village queen and thou a sophomore, that thou should have thy nose in my buttocks?'

Parsons returned to Pasadena in a state of considerable agitation which was greatly increased when his magical partner arrived back the next day and announced he had had a vision of a 'savage and beautiful woman riding naked on a great cat-like beast' and had an urgent message to deliver.

That night, in the temple at South Orange Grove, the two magicians made preparations to receive the message. Candles were lit, incense burned and a magical altar was laid with flowers and wine. Hubbard, the scribe, wore a white-hooded robe and carried a lamp; Parsons, the high priest, wore a black robe and carried a cup and dagger. An automatic tape recorder was set up and at Hubbard's suggestion Rachmaninoff's 'Isle of the Dead' was played as background music.

At eight o'clock, Hubbard began to intone his message from the astral world: 'These are the preparations. Green gold cloth, food for the Beast, upon a hidden platter, back of the altar. Disclose only when the doors are bolted. Transgression is death. Back of the main altar. Prepare instantly. Light the first flame at 10 pm, March 2, 1946. The year of Babalon is 4063 . . .'

After a few minutes, Parsons noticed that his scribe was pale and sweating profusely. Hubbard rested for a few moments, then continued: 'Make a box of blackness at ten o'clock. Smear the vessel which contains flame with thine own blood. Destroy at the altar a thing of value. Remain in perfect silence and heed the voice of our Lady. Speak not of this ritual or of her coming to any person . . .

'Display thyself to Our Lady; dedicate thy organs to Her, dedicate thy heart to Her, dedicate thy mind to Her, dedicate thy soul to Her, for She shall absorb thee, and thou shalt become living flame before She incarnates . . .'

When Hubbard finished dictating, the scarlet woman, naked under a crimson robe, was brought into the temple. 'Oh circle of stars,' the high priest intoned, 'whereof our Father is but the younger brother, marvel beyond imagination, soul of infinite space . . .'

Marjorie Cameron had been well rehearsed in the necessary response. 'But to love me is better than all things . . .' she chanted. 'Put on the wings and arouse the coiled splendour within you. Come unto me, to me! Sing the rapturous love songs unto me! Burn to me the perfume! Drink to me for I love you! I am the blue-lidded daughter of sunset, I am the naked brilliance of the voluptuous night sky . . .'

With passions mounting, the three black magicians intoned a chorus: 'Glory unto the Scarlet Woman, Babalon, the Mother of Abominations, that rideth upon the Beast, for She hath spilt their blood in every corner of the earth and lo! she hath mingled it in the cup of her whoredom . . .'

The scribe remained at the altar declaiming and describing what was supposed to be happening on an astral plane while the high priest excitedly inserted his 'wand' into the scarlet woman and they began copulating furiously.

At midnight the unholy troika retired to bed, exhausted. Next morning one of the lodgers in the house disturbed Parsons while he was meditating in the temple – he flew out in a rage and put a curse on the man, who, he said, was very soon taken ill. After this incident, Parsons confessed that he succumbed to a black mood. His temper cannot have improved when he discovered that the roof of the guest-house had caught fire and been partially destroyed the previous night while he was otherwise occupied. He darkly deduced that the fire had started at the very moment, during the night's black festivities, when he had smashed an image of Pan.

'That evening,' Parsons wrote, 'the scribe and I resumed our work.' This time a white sheet smeared with menstrual blood was laid out on the floor of the temple and a red star, cut from the high priest's robe, was symbolically burned on the altar. As Parsons performed the 'Invocation of the Wand' on the naked body of the scarlet woman, the scribe droned: 'Embrace her, cover her with kisses. Think upon the lewd lascivious things thou couldst do. All is good to Babalon. *All* . . . The lust is hers, the passion yours. Consider thou the Beast raping.'

On the third and final day, the rituals began four hours before dawn and ended with a long poem titled 'The Birth of Babalon' extolling 'holy whoredom':

Her mouth is red and her breasts are fair and her loins are full of fire,
And her lust is strong as a man is strong in the heat of her desire,

And her whoredom is holy as virtue is foul beneath the holy sky,
And her kisses will wanton the world away in passion that shall not die.
Ye shall laugh and love and follow her dance when the wrath of God is gone,
And dream no more of hell and hate in the birth of Babalon.[18]

In the 'Book of Babalon', Parsons was completely convinced that the magic had worked and that his scarlet woman would be delivered of a moonchild in nine months. 'Babalon', he wrote confidently, 'is incarnate upon the earth today awaiting the proper hour of her manifestations.'[19]

But in his 'Magical Record' he was less assured: 'For the last three days I have performed an operation of birth, using the air tablet, the cup and a female figure, properly invoked by the wand, then sealed up in the altar. Last night I performed an operation of symbolic birth and delivery. Now I can do no more than pray and wait.'[20]

On 6 March, Parsons sat down to compose a letter to his Satanic Master in England, apprising him of the momentous events that had recently taken place. 'I can hardly tell you or decide how much to write,' he began. 'I am under command of extreme secrecy. I have had the most important, devastating experience of my life . . . I believe it was the result of the IXth degree working [the class of sexual magic designed to produce a higher being] with the girl who answered my elemental summons. I have been in direct touch with One who is most Holy and Beautiful as mentioned in *The Book of the Law*. I cannot write the name at present. First instructions were received direct through Ron, the seer. I have followed them to the letter. There was a desire for incarnation. I do not yet know the vehicle, but it will come to me bringing a secret sign. I am to act as instructor guardian for nine months; then it will be loosed on the world. That is all I can say now . . .'[21]

Crowley, who was by then in his seventies, chronically addicted to heroin and facing death, was irritated by his disciple's secrecy. On 19 April he despatched a terse reply: 'You have got me completely puzzled by your remarks about the elemental . . . I thought I had a most morbid imagination, as good as any man's, but it seems I have not. I cannot form the slightest idea of what you can possibly mean.' On the same day he wrote to Karl Germer, head of the OTO in the United States: 'Apparently Parsons or Hubbard or somebody is producing a Moonchild. I get fairly frantic when I contemplate the idiocy of these louts.'

While Parsons fretted over Crowley's letter, his faithful scribe was facing more earthly, and much more familiar, problems. Having contributed his meagre savings to Allied Enterprises, Hubbard was badly in need of money. He had written virtually nothing since leaving the Navy and his wife was rapidly losing patience with his repeated excuses as to why he was unable to send any money home to support her and the children.

Polly recognized by this time that there was little chance of saving her marriage. Towards the end of the war, she and Ron had briefly discussed moving to California when he was discharged from the Navy, but Polly refused to uproot the children. She had a nightmare vision of trying to raise a family while trailing forlornly after her husband, backwards and forwards from one coast to the other.[22] Nibs and Katie were happily settled in Bremerton, enjoyed school, and had friends and family all around. Polly had left The Hilltop and moved in with Ron's parents to be closer to the facilities of Bremerton; it was an arrangement she found perfectly satisfactory. Both Harry Hubbard, who had retired from the Navy and found a job as manager of Kitsap County Fair, and his wife enjoyed having their grandchildren around.

But while Polly was content to live with her in-laws, she still needed money to feed and clothe herself and the children and, not unreasonably, she expected her husband to provide it. Ron's problem in this regard was not just that he was broke (nothing unusual), but that he had reached the limit of his credit with the residents of 1003 South Orange Grove Avenue, having borrowed from everyone who was prepared to lend.

In February, the Veterans Administration had awarded him a pension of $11.50 a month for a ten per cent disability caused by his ulcer. Ron did not consider this miserable amount to be nearly sufficient and on 18 March, two weeks after completing his duties as a black magic scribe, he lodged an appeal, producing a dramatic new disability which he had somehow neglected to mention on his original claim form. 'I have lost between sixty and eighty per cent of my vision,' he claimed in a letter typed on his distinctive initialled notepaper, 'and as my profession is that of writer, my present inability to read or use my eyes seriously affects my income. I cannot work either long hours or under the slightest adverse conditions. My income at the present time, due entirely to service connected injuries, is zero. Would you please advise me as to the steps I should take to gain further pension?'[23]

After his years in the Navy, Ron was well aware of the speed with which the wheels of bureaucracy moved and his need for money was urgent. His solution was to persuade Parsons that the time had come to activate Allied Enterprises. Towards the end of April, Ron and Sara [she was only called Betty at South Orange Grove] left for Florida with $10,000 drawn from the Allied Enterprises account at the Pasadena First Trust and Savings Bank. Parsons approved the withdrawal so that the partnership could purchase its first yacht in the east; it was agreed that Ron and Sara would then either sail it back to California for re-sale, or transport it overland, whichever proved to be cheaper.

It seemed a perfectly simple and sensible business arrangement, although Parsons presumably did not know that on 1 April Ron had written to the Chief of Naval Personnel requesting permission to leave the United States to visit South America and China.[24] However, not many weeks passed before Parsons began to worry, for he heard not a word from either Ron or Sara. He realized, with mounting frustration, that they had gone off with $10,000 of his money and he had little idea of where they might be. He confessed his concern to Louis Culling, another member of the OTO lodge, and swore he was going to get his money back and dissolve the partnership.

The next day Ron telephoned from Florida, reversing the charges. Culling was at South Orange Grove when the call came through and he was amazed to find that Parsons was completely dominated by Hubbard. After what had been said the previous day, Culling expected Parsons to be cool towards his wayward partner at the very least. But Parsons made no mention of his disquiet, did not complain about being kept in the dark and said nothing about dissolving the partnership. He was soon laughing happily into the telephone as if he had not a care in the world and the conversation ended with Parsons saying, 'I hope we shall *always* be partners, Ron.'

Greatly disturbed, Culling took it upon himself to make some inquiries and on 12 May he wrote to Karl Germer: 'As you may know by this time, Brother John signed a partnership agreement with this Ron and Betty whereby all money earned by the three for life is equally divided between the three. As far as I can ascertain, Brother John has put in all of his money . . . Meanwhile, Ron and Betty have bought a boat for themselves in Miami for about $10,000 and are living the life of Riley, while Brother John is living at rock bottom, and I mean *rock bottom*. It appears that originally they never secretly intended to bring this boat around to the California coast to sell at a profit, as they told Jack, but rather to have a good time on it on the east coast . . .'[25]

Germer naturally informed Crowley, who replied by cable on 22 May: 'Suspect Ron playing confidence trick. Jack evidently weak fool. Obvious victim prowling swindlers.' In a letter seven days later, Crowley wrote, 'It seems to me on the information of our brethren in California that Parsons has got an illumination in which he has lost all his personal independence. From our brother's account he has given away both his girl and his money. Apparently it is the ordinary confidence trick.'[26]

While Crowley and fellow members of the OTO were already in

agreement that Brother Parsons had been conned, Brother Parsons was painfully arriving at a similar conclusion and at the beginning of June he packed a case and caught a train East, determined to track down the errant lovers and get his money back.

In Miami, Parsons discovered to his astonishment that Allied Enterprises had already purchased three boats – two auxiliary schooners, the *Harpoon* and the *Blue Water II*, and a yacht, the *Diane*. It seemed that Ron had raised mortgages totalling more than $12,000 to buy the schooners.

Parsons traced the *Harpoon* to Howard Bond's Yacht Harbor on the County Causeway, but there was no sign of either Ron or Sara. The *Blue Water* was found at the American Ship Building Company docks on the Miami river; again, there was no one on board.

One evening a few days later, Parsons received a telephone call from the harbour. The *Harpoon*, he was told, had set sail at five o'clock that afternoon, with Ron and Sara on board apparently intent on making an escape. In his Miami hotel room, Parsons donned his magic robes and traced a circle on the floor with his magic wand. At eight o'clock, he stepped into the ring and performed the 'Banishing Ritual of the Pentagram', the preliminary to all magic, followed by a full invocation of Bartzabel, the spirit of Mars, whose help he sought to restrain his fleeing partners. In a letter to Crowley describing his actions, he was able to report a highly satisfactory result: 'At the same time, so far as I can check, his ship was struck by a sudden squall off the coast, which ripped off his sails and forced him back to port, where I took the boat in custody.'[27]

On 1 July, the magician sought redress through more conventional means: he filed suit in the Circuit Court for Dade County, accusing Ron and Sara of breaking the terms of their partnership, dissipating the assets and attempting to abscond.[28] A receiver was appointed to wind up the affairs of Allied Enterprises and a restraining order was placed on the defendants, preventing them from leaving Miami or disposing of any of the partnership's assets.

'Here I am in Miami pursuing the children of my folly,' Parsons wrote gloomily to Crowley on 5 July. 'I have them well tied up. They cannot move without going to jail. However, most of the money has already been dissipated. I will be lucky to salvage $3000 to $5000.'

On 11 July, the three partners signed an agreement, drawn up by Parsons' lawyer, dissolving the partnership. Ron and Sara handed over the *Blue Water* and the *Diane* and agreed to pay half Parsons' legal costs. For his part, Parsons allowed Ron and Sara to keep the *Harpoon* in return for a $2900 promissory note which covered his financial interest in the schooner. Jack Parsons returned to Pasadena satisfied that he had made the best deal he could under the circumstances and not too distressed at the loss of his former lover and his former best friend. He never saw either of them again.

In Miami, Ron and Sara were returned to their accustomed state of penury after their brief fling at the expense of Allied Enterprises. Their most immediate and pressing problem was how to maintain payments on the $4600 mortgage still outstanding on the *Harpoon*. Ron, who had never allowed money matters to worry him over-much, clung to the belief that he would eventually be able to wheedle a larger pension from the Veterans Administration. On 4 July, Independence Day, he had spent part of the holiday composing yet another stirring appeal against his pension award and introducing a further hitherto unmentioned disability, this time a 'chronic and incapacitating bone infection'.

On the claim form, he painted a harrowing picture of a veteran gamely struggling against disabilities which he rated at one hundred per cent. His original duodenal ulcer had mysteriously multiplied; his 'ulcers', he pointed out, had caused him to abandon his old profession of 'ship-master and explorer' and severely hampered his work as a writer. 'I can do nothing involving nervous strain without becoming dangerously ill.' As for his failing eyesight, he now found it difficult to read for more than three or four minutes without suffering from headaches, making it virtually impossible for him to do any research. His problems had begun, he noted, after 'prolonged exposure to tropical sunlight in the Pacific'. Furthermore, he was lame as the result of a bone infection in his right hip, contracted at Princeton University because of 'the sudden transition from the tropics to the slush and icy cold of Princeton'. He was unable to walk without suffering severely.

'My earning power, due to injuries, all service connected,' he concluded, 'has dropped to nothing. I earned one thousand dollars a month prior to the war as a writer. I cannot now earn money as a writer and attempts to find other employment have failed because of my physical condition.'

To support his case, Hubbard persuaded Sara to write to the Veterans Administration as an old friend to provide independent corroboration of his rapidly deteriorating health. She put her parents address in Pasadena on the top of the letter.

'I have know Lafayette Ronald Hubbard for many years,' she began, inauspiciously and untruthfully, 'and wish to testify as to the condition of his health as I have observed it since his separation from the Navy.

'Before the war, he was an extremely energetic person in excellent health and spirits . . . Since his return in December last year he is entirely changed. He cannot read because of his eyes, which give him much pain. He is rather lame and cannot take his accustomed hikes . . . He has tried to work at three different jobs and each he has had to leave because of an increase in his stomach condition. He seems to need an enormous amount of rest . . .

'I do not know what he is going to do for income when his own meagre savings are exhausted, because I see no chance of his condition improving to a point where he can regain his old standards. He is becoming steadily worse, his health impaired again by economic worries . . .'[29]

In fact, a short-term solution to his economic worries was immediately and obviously at hand: the *Harpoon*. Faced with the impossibility of repaying the mortgage, Ron decided to sell the boat in the hope of clearing his most pressing debts. Solvent again, temporarily at least, he asked Sara to marry him. She accepted unhesitatingly. At the beginning of August the lovers left Florida and caught a train for Washington DC. On 10 August 1946, twenty-one-year-old Sara Northrup and L. Ron Hubbard were married in a simple ceremony at Chestertown, Maryland.

By a curious coincidence, Chestertown was only thirty miles from Elkton, where L. Ron Hubbard had married Polly Grubb in 1933. Sara knew nothing of Polly and had no idea that her new husband had been previously married. Still less did she know he had never been divorced.

Similarly, Polly, in Bremerton, had yet to learn her husband was a bigamist.

Back at South Orange Grove in Pasadena, Parsons sold the old mansion for development and moved into the coach-house with his scarlet woman, Marjorie Cameron, whom he subsequently married.

It was to be a tragically brief alliance. On the afternoon of Friday 20 June 1952, Parsons was working alone in the garage of the coach-house, which he had converted into a laboratory. At eight minutes past five there was an enormous explosion. The heavy stable doors were blasted from their hinges, the walls blew out and a huge hole was torn in the floor timbers. When the dust had cleared, a partially dismembered body could be seen still bleeding in the rubble.

Further horror was to follow. Police traced Parsons's mother, Mrs Ruth Virginia Parsons, to the home of a crippled woman friend in West Glenarm Street. Informed of the accident and her son's death, Mrs Parsons returned to the room where her friend was sitting in an armchair. She sat down in another chair out of reach, unscrewed a bottle of sleeping tablets and, watched by her helpless and appalled friend, rapidly swallowed the entire contents. Unable to move from her chair, the terrified cripple watched her friend slowly die.[30]

The inquest found that the explosion had been caused by Parsons accidentally dropping a phial of nitro-glycerine. But because of his known interest in the occult, there were inevitably rumours of suicide or even murder; none of his friends could believe that a man so experienced in handling explosives would have dropped nitro-glycerine accidentally.

Whatever the truth, no black magician could have wished for a blacker departure from the world.

Chapter 8

The Mystery of the Missing Research

'In 1948, Mr Hubbard's first writings on the nature of life and the human mind began to circulate privately. Passed from hand to hand, word quickly spread that he had made a revolutionary breakthrough . . .' (*L. Ron Hubbard, The Man and His Work*, 1986)

* * * * *

After their wedding in Maryland, Hubbard and his young bride returned to California and found an apartment at Laguna Beach, a resort much favoured by artists and writers, half-way between Los Angeles and San Diego. John Steinbeck lived there when he was writing his first major novel, *Tortilla Flat*, a factor Ron no doubt took into consideration when he was looking for a place to settle down and resume his career as a writer.

The problem was that he could neither settle down nor write. Indeed, to judge from his bulging file at the Veterans Administration, in 1946 Ron largely directed his literary talents to the diligent pursuit of a bigger pension. On 19 September, he limped into the VA medical centre in Los Angeles with a miserable litany of by now familiar complaints: 'Eyes are sensitive to bright sunlight and I can't read very much and I have severe headaches . . . My stomach trouble keeps me on a very rigid diet – can only eat milk, eggs, ground meat and strained vegetables . . . I tire quickly and become nauseated when I work hard . . . My left shoulder, hip – in fact the entire left side is bothered with arthritic pains – can't sit any length of time at typewriter or desk . . .'

Once again, the doctors did not seem to be able to find anything markedly wrong with the veteran, other than calcified bursitis, a touch of arthritis in his ankles apparently causing him to walk with a 'hobble-like gait' and 'minimal duodenal deformity'. On the examination report it was noted that there were no scars or indications of gunshot wounds or other injuries.[1]

It was perhaps just as well for Ron that the Veterans Administration did not have access to his private journals, for a very different picture was presented therein. Several scrawled pages were filled with

'Affirmations', many of which concerned his health. Had he been a little more circumspect, the 'Affirmations' could have been viewed as a brave attempt to make light of his ailments, or to cure himself through sheer strength of will, for in some of them he seemed to be trying to convince himself that he was fit:

'Your ulcers are all well and never bother you. You can eat anything.

'You have a sound hip. It never hurts.

'Your shoulder never hurts.

'Your sinus trouble is nothing.'

Unfortunately for his place in posterity, he frequently chose to elaborate. Thus he confessed that his stomach trouble was a device he had used to get out of punishment in the Navy, his bad hip was a pose and his foot injury was an alibi: 'The injury is no longer needed. It is well. You have perfect and lovely feet.' A few of the Affirmations were also stamped with the faintly sinister mark of Aleister Crowley, as in 'Men are your slaves' and 'You can be merciless whenever your will is crossed and you have the right to be merciless.'

VA doctors would undoubtedly have found them fascinating reading, not least for the insight they provided into Hubbard's psyche and his attitude towards the VA:

'When you tell people you are ill, it has no effect upon your health. And in Veterans Administration examinations you'll tell them how sick you are; you'll look sick when you take it; you'll return to health one hour after the examination and laugh at them.

'No matter what lies you may tell others, they have no physical effect on you of any kind. You never injured your health by saying it is bad. You cannot lie to yourself.'[2]

By October, Hubbard was once again down to his last few dollars and when a friend offered him a temporary job taking care of a boat at the yacht club on Santa Catalina Island he jumped at the opportunity. After less than six weeks at Laguna Beach, Sara uncomplainingly packed their bags and prepared to move on. It was a situation with which she would become all too familiar in the months ahead.

While staying at the Catalina Island Yacht Club, Ron managed to stir himself to write an article about fishing for the local newspaper, the *Catalina Islander*, but this was his only published work in 1946. On 14 November, he wrote to the Veterans Administration from the Yacht Club to complain that his last two pension cheques had not been forwarded. 'I need this money, little as it is, very badly,' he wrote 'and would appreciate any expedition which the matter can be given.'

A week later, he wrote again to explain why he had failed to show up for another medical examination which the VA had requested in October. 'I was unable to report for further examination because I was both ill and broke . . . I certainly hope you can scare me up something by way of a pension for I am not eating very well these days and this job I have will vanish shortly.'[3]

Vanish it did and by the beginning of December Ron and Sara were in New York, staying at the Hotel Belvedere, West 48th Street. On 8 December he wrote on hotel notepaper to acknowledge receiving orders to report for another examination, explaining his expensive address by saying that a friend had financed his trip back East in return for his advice on an expedition then being planned.

While he was in New York, Ron naturally looked up his old science fiction friends and one of them introduced him to Sam Merwin, who was then editing the 'Thrilling' group of magazines. 'I found him a very amusing guy,' Merwin recalled, 'and bought several stories from him. He was really quite a character. I always knew he was exceedingly anxious to hit big money – he used to say he thought the best way to do it would be to start a cult.'[4]

Ron also called on his old friend and mentor, John W. Campbell, in his familiar office in the Street and Smith building. Campbell was delighted to welcome Ron back from the war; he had written to him a year earlier[5] pleading for contributions ('*Astounding* is in a mell of a hess. I need – and but bad – stories. Any length.') and now he urged Ron to get back to work. He was constantly getting letters from readers, he said, asking when the magazine was going to publish more stories by L. Ron Hubbard. Before he left the building, Ron accepted an assignment to write a five thousand-word feature about the consequences of man landing on the moon for *Air Trails and Science Frontiers*, a new non-fiction magazine which Campbell had recently launched.

Despite his terrible eye-strain and rheumatism and ulcers and everything else, Hubbard managed to put together an imaginative and informative piece. He prophesied that the first moon landing would take place within five or ten years and argued that a lunar military base would have enormous strategic value. 'It is entirely within reason', he wrote, 'that the nation which demonstrates the courage, intelligence and industrial proficiency necessary to establish a base on the moon will rule the world.'

'Fortress in the Sky', under the by-line of Captain B.A. Northorp, was the cover story in the May 1947 issue of *Air Trails*. The reason Hubbard did not use his own name could be found buried deep in the text. Although he packed the feature with authoritative and impressive detail about the composition and environment of the moon, he simply could not resist the opportunity for further self-aggrandisment. In a section discussing the technical problems of reaching the moon by rocket, he wrote: 'Here and there throughout the world many men have been thinking about rockets for some time. I recall that in 1930, L. Ron Hubbard, a writer and engineer, developed and tested – but without fanfare – a rocket motor considerably superior to the V-2 instrument of propulsion and rather less complicated.'

Campbell was still a meticulous editor and a stickler for accuracy. If he believed that his friend was developing rocket motors in 1930 at the age of nineteen, he was also extraordinarily naïve. It is more likely that he turned a blind eye to keep Ron happy in the hope that he would soon return to the pages of *Astounding*.

Ron and Sara only stayed a matter of weeks in New York. In the New Year they were on the move again, this time to the unprepossessing environs of Stroudsburg, Pennsylvania, just south of the Pocono Mountains. There Ron fulfilled Campbell's hopes by writing a novel, *The End Is Not Yet*, about a young nuclear physicist's attempts to prevent the world being taken over by constructing a new philosophical system. It was serialized in three parts in *Astounding* later in the year, although it was not as well received as some of Ron's earlier work.

On 14 April 1947, the long-suffering Polly filed for a divorce in Port Orchard, Washington, on the grounds of desertion and non-support. She was still unaware that her husband had 're-married'; she did not even know he was living with another woman. That situation was soon to change.

Three weeks after Polly set divorce proceedings in motion, Ron scandalized his family by moving into The Hilltop with Sara. 'It was an awful slap in the face for his mother,' said his Aunt Marnie. 'Hub and May deeply disapproved. It was very difficult for them as they had Polly and the children living with them. The family clammed up about it and never mentioned it. When Ron took Sara up to The Hilltop I said to my sister, "Well, we loved him as a child, Midgie, but he's a perfect stranger to us now."'[6]

The family would have been even more shocked had they known that Ron had married Sara; only Ron's friend, Mac Ford, knew the truth and he kept quiet. 'I ran into Ron one evening when he was taking the children to the theatre in Bremerton,' Ford said. 'We hadn't seen each other since before the war and when we were talking in the lobby he mentioned something about marrying again. I thought it was strange because I knew that he was not divorced from Polly, but I did not say anything because I didn't want to get involved.'[7]

Hubbard filed an agreement to the divorce on 1 June and an interlocutory decree was awarded on 23 June. Polly was given custody of the children, costs and $25 a month maintenance for each child. Knowing Ron, she did not cherish much hope of the maintenance payments arriving regularly, if at all.

Ron and Sara left The Hilltop in July and returned to California, to a rented trailer on a lot in the seediest section of North Hollywood, where he began writing the first of the popular 'Ole Doc Methuselah' stories – rousing yarns about a Soldier of Light and his devoted four-armed slave, Hippocrates, who travel around the universe in a golden spaceship saving entire civilizations from death and disease and overthrowing despotic inter-planetary dictators as a sideline.

In August, the month *The End Is Not Yet* began serialization in *Astounding*, Ron acquired a literary agent. Forrest Ackerman was not a big-time Hollywood agent with a fat cigar, but a young man with thick horn-rimmed spectacles who had been addicted to science fiction ever since he first picked up a copy of *Amazing Stories* at the age of nine.

'Forrie' Ackerman would one day be the proud owner of the world's biggest collection of science-fiction magazines and would drive around Los Angeles in a red Cadillac with SCI-FI on the licence plate, but in 1947 he was still struggling to capitalize on his devotion to the genre by persuading science-fiction writers that he could represent them. Then thirty years old, he had actually met Hubbard ten years earlier in Shep's Shop, a second-hand bookshop on Hollywood Boulevard which specialized in science fiction.

'I was browsing in Shep's Shop one night in 1937 when I got into conversation with this young red-haired man who told me he held a world record in gliding. He said his name was L. Ron Hubbard and that he had had a lot of adventure stories published in pulp magazines. I asked him if he had ever tried his hand at science fiction and he said, no, oddly enough, he hadn't. But right there, on the spot, he began to outline the plot for a science fiction story set in California 25,000 years in the future, during a second Ice Age. I never saw that story in print, but it seemed to plant a seed in his mind . . .'

Ackerman liked to believe that their brief encounter in Shep's Shop was the spur that started Ron Hubbard writing science fiction. His first act on his new client's behalf was to take him to meet G. Gordon Dewey and Peter Grainger, two Los Angeles businessmen who wanted to diversify into publishing. The meeting was not a marked success: there was some desultory discussion about buying rights to some of Hubbard's novels, but nothing was concluded. Afterwards, Ron offered to drive Forrie back to his apartment in New Hampshire. It was a journey Ackerman would never forget, for on the way Ron began to tell him the incredible story of how he had died on an operating table during the war.

'I remember he had an old rattletrap of a car and he was chewing tobacco. As he drove he would open the door with one hand and squirt tobacco juice out onto the road. When we got to my apartment we sat outside in the car while he continued with the story. It was after five o'clock in the morning, and the sun was coming up, before he had finished.

'Basically what he told me was that after he died he rose in spirit form and looked back on the body he had formerly inhabited. Over yonder he saw a fantastic great gate, elaborately carved like something you'd see in Bagdad or ancient China. As he wafted towards it, the gate opened and just beyond he could see a kind of intellectual *smorgasbord* on which was outlined everything that had ever puzzled the mind of man. All the questions that had concerned philosophers through the ages – When did the world begin? Was there a God? Whither goest we? – were there answered. All this information came flooding into him and while he was absorbing it, there was a sort of flustering in the air and he felt something like a long umbilical cord pulling him back. He was saying "No, no, not yet!", but he was pulled back anyway. After the gates had closed he realized he had re-entered his body.

'He opened his eyes and found a nurse standing over him looking very concerned. Just as a surgeon walked into the room, Ron said, "I was dead, wasn't I?" The surgeon shot a venomous look at the nurse as if to say, "What have you been telling this guy?" But Ron said "No, no, I know I was dead."

'The next part of the story I would find very difficult to direct realistically if I was a movie director. According to Ron, he jumped off the operating table, ran to his Quonset hut, got two reams of paper and a gallon of scalding black coffee and for the next 48 hours, at a blinding rate, he wrote a work called *Excalibur*, or *The Dark Sword*.

'Well, he kept the manuscript with him and when he left the Navy he shopped it around publishers in New York, but was constantly turned down. He was told it was too radical, too much of a quantum leap. If it had been a variation of Freud or Jung or Adler, a bit of an improvement here and there, it would have been acceptable, but it was just too far ahead of everything else. He also said that as he shopped the manuscript around, the people who read it either went insane or committed suicide. The last time he showed it to a publisher, he was sitting in an office waiting for a reader to give his opinion. The reader walked into the office, tossed the manuscript on the desk and then threw himself out of the window.

'Ron would not tell me much about *Excalibur* except that if you read it you would find all fear would be totally drained from you. I could never see what was wrong with that or why that would cause anyone to commit suicide.'[8]

Ackerman was frankly incredulous, but was impressed by the sincerity and conviction with which Ron told the story. He also recognized, as an aspiring literary agent, that *Excalibur* could be just the kind of thing to get a new publishing venture off the ground.

Later that morning he telephoned Gordon Dewey and Peter Grainger, repeated the story Ron had told him and asked them if they would take a look at the manuscript. His sly hint of the potential risk only served to whet their appetites. 'They were mad keen to see it,' Ackerman said. 'I remember Dewey saying, "No combination of words, ideas or philosophy will have that effect on *me*!"'

Ackerman reported the good news to his client, but Hubbard, suddenly and uncharacteristically bashful, refused to produce the manuscript. 'He said it was in a bank vault and it was going to stay there. I think he was quite sincere. He seemed like a man who had seen too many people go crazy or commit suicide, who had enough on his conscience already. I never did get to see the manuscript or show it to any publisher. In fact, I never encountered anyone who said they had seen it.'

Despite Forrie's best efforts, Ron did not make anything like a living wage as a writer in 1947. After *The End Is Not Yet*, he sold two Ole Doc Methuselah stories to *Astounding*, a short story, 'Killer's Law', to *New Detective* and a novel, *The Chee-Chalker*, to *Five Novels Monthly*. The income generated from these five stories was barely sufficient to support himself, let alone his present wife, his former wife and his two teenage children.

In October, Ron discovered he could qualify for $90 a month subsistence from the VA if he enrolled at college. He promptly signed on as a student at the Geller Theater Workshop on the corner of Fairfax and Wilshire, but he was still determined to pursue a better disability pension. Two weeks later he composed a letter to the VA in Los Angeles unquestionably designed to tug at bureaucratic heartstrings by painting a pathetic picture of a confused and helpless veteran on the brink of a total breakdown:

Gentlemen;

This is a request for treatment . . .
After trying and failing for two years to regain my equilibrium in civil life, I am utterly unable to approach anything like my own competence. My last physician informed me that it might be very helpful if I were to be examined and perhaps treated psychiatrically or even by a psychoanalyst. Toward the end of my service I avoided out of pride any mental examinations, hoping that time would balance a mind which I had every reason to suppose was seriously affected. I cannot account for nor rise above long periods of moroseness and suicidal inclinations, and have newly come to realize that I must first triumph above this before I can hope to rehabilitate myself at all.

I cannot leave school or what little work I am doing for hospitalization due to many obligations, but I feel I might be treated outside, possibly with success. I cannot, myself, afford such treatment. Would you please help me?

Sincerely, L. Ron Hubbard[9]

To its credit, the VA responded to this dramatic cry for help with commendable speed and arrangements were made for Hubbard to attend Birmingham VA Hospital in Van Nuys for another examination. By this time, his medical records were hopelessly confused as he had given so many different versions of his service career, his injuries and ailments. He took the opportunity of this consultation to add another injury to the record, claiming that he had fallen from a ladder on a ship called the *USS Pennant* in 1942, injuring his back, hip, left knee and right heel.

While he was waiting for the results to come through, Ron was greatly discomforted to receive a demand from the VA for $51 which he had been overpaid in subsistence – he had dropped out of college on 14 November, claiming he was too ill to continue studying, but had collected subsistence until the end of the month.

'I cannot imagine how to repay this $51', he whined in a letter to the VA dated 27 January 1948, 'as I am nearly penniless'. Since leaving school in November, he said, he had only made $40 from the sale of two articles to magazines. This money, plus the repayment of a $75 debt, comprised his entire income for the previous two and a half months. Such was his plight that he had been obliged to sell a typewriter for $28.50, which was all he had to support himself and his wife for the next month. Since he was paying $27 a month rent on his trailer, and food, cigarettes and incidentals were setting them back another $80 a month, it was hardly surprising, as he said, that he was very much in debt.

With his usual impudence, Ron suggested that the VA might like to help with a grant or a loan to enable him to finish the novel that he had been asked to write and help him get back on his feet financially.

Nothing came of this hopeful inquiry. A few days later the results of Ron's medical examination arrived, but offered little encouragement that he would be awarded a higher pension. As before, nothing too serious was diagnosed, other than arthritis and myositis, an inflammation of the muscle tissue. There was not even, any longer, any evidence of a duodenal ulcer and no evidence at all of the injuries he said he had sustained when he fell from a ladder.

However, bureaucracy works in strange and unfathomable ways.

Despite the findings of his most recent medical, Ron's bewildering portfolio of infirmities and his dogged determination to be disabled finally paid off. On 27 February he received a letter from the VA regional office with the good news that his combined disability rating had been re-assessed at forty per cent and his pension increased to $55.20 a month.[10] With that, Lieutenant Hubbard USNR had to be satisfied.

Forrest Ackerman, who had noticeably not been getting rich from his ten per cent of Ron's earnings, nevertherless remained on good terms with his client. When Ron came bounding up the stairs to his apartment one afternoon, sweat trickling from under the band of his white straw hat, and said he needed money to get out of town because his ex-wife was after him for alimony, Forrie good-naturedly handed over everything he had in his wallet – $30. 'It was a small fortune to me then,' he recalled.

For some time, Forrie had been trying to persuade Ron to make an appearance at one of the meetings of the Los Angeles Fantasy and Science Fiction Society, of which he was naturally a founding member. The meetings were held every Thursday evening in the basement room of a small hotel on South Bixel Street in downtown Los Angeles and were often attended by writers with an eye to future sales.

Ron first turned up at a 'Lasfas' meeting on 15 April and, as a distinguished guest, was invited to address the members. He gave an impromptu, entertaining little talk about himself and his work, mentioning his 'shame' that he was only able to write about five thousand words a day and touching briefly on his philosophical opus, *Excalibur*, which he had locked in a bank vault when he 'finally realized how dangerous it was'.

'The real surprise of the evening', the club magazine reported, 'came when Hubbard was talking about his friend, Arthur J. Burks. Someone mentioned Burks's story, "Survival", which had been judged one of the best of 1938 when it appeared that year in *Marvel Tales*. "Survival?" questioned Hubbard. "I don't remember reading that one. What was it about?" It concerned an invasion of America by the "yellow men of the East", he was told. "What?" said Hubbard. "And how did they escape the peril?" By burrowing under the ground, he was told. Mr Hubbard was surprised at this. In fact, he said, "Good God! That dog! Wait till I get hold of Burks . . ." He explained the outburst: "Back in '38 I wrote a movie treatment of a story called 'Survival'. It concerned an invasion of America by the yellow men of the East. They escaped by burrowing under the ground! I gave that story and four others to an agent to sell. He lost them. And now I find that Burks has written and sold a story just like it!'"[11]

Among the fans present that evening was a young teletype operator by the name of Arthur Jean Cox. He admitted to mixed feelings about meeting the famous Ron Hubbard for the first time: 'He was an amusing, lively, animated, dynamic man who dominated the conversation, although I had the feeling that he told more lies in the club room in the first half hour than had been told there in the previous month. He talked a lot about his past – I heard the story about the polar bear jumping on his boat dozens of times – but I thought it was all fantasy.

'At that time he was one of the most famous science fiction writers in America, certainly in the top ten. Most of the members of the club were very young and in awe of him, but I didn't like him. His face was pock-marked, as if he'd had smallpox as a child, and I thought he looked like a wolf; he was a very predatory sort of man.'[12]

Hubbard returned to the Los Angeles science fiction society two weeks later to give a talk about immortality and the future of medical science. He had become interested in medical matters, he explained to a mainly spellbound audience, after he had 'died' for eight minutes as a result of wounds received in the war. He was brought back to life 'by the use of several emergency measures'. While convalescing he had plenty of time to satisfy his natural curiosity and he had become convinced that bio-chemists were capable of lengthening life to the point of 'limited immortality'. Joseph Stalin was only being kept alive, he claimed somewhat obscurely, because of a particular serum that had been developed by the Russians.

Afterwards, Ron demonstrated a surprising talent as a hypnotist with a repertoire of parlour tricks. He hypnotized almost everyone in the clubroom: one young man looked at his hand with utter astonishment, convinced he was holding a pair of miniature kangaroos in his palm; another rapidly removed his shoes when he felt the floor getting hot and a third spent a hysterically funny ten minutes on an imaginary telephone trying to fend off a persistent and non-existent car salesman.

It was probable that Hubbard had learned hypnosis from Jack Parsons and he appeared to have no difficulty inducing hypnotic trances – all he needed to do, with some people, was count to three and snap his fingers. But he sometimes forgot to bring a subject out of hypnosis. He told Cox's younger brother, Bill, that he would fall asleep every time he (Hubbard) scratched his nose. Under hypnosis, Bill dutifully obeyed. But later in the evening Hubbard absent-mindedly scratched his nose while he was standing in the centre of a group of fans and Bill Cox instantly collapsed, fortunately falling into the arms of Forrest Ackerman, who was standing behind him.

Hubbard also played a cruel, post-hypnotic trick on Bill Cox. He took him to one side at the meeting and told him that the following afternoon, at two o'clock, he would drop whatever he was doing and meet Hubbard at a building site on the corner of Wilshire and Lucas. Hubbard was waiting there next day when, at precisely two o'clock, Cox showed up. Under Hubbard's instructions, Cox first found he could not take his hands out of his pockets. Then he was ordered to take hold of a nearby railing and discovered he could not let go. As he struggled to release his grip, Hubbard told him the rail would get hotter and hotter until it was red hot. Considerably distressed, Cox writhed in agony until at last Hubbard laughed, patted him on the shoulder, told him he could go home and that he would not remember anything that had happened.

This incident only later came to light because a fellow science fiction writer, A.E. van Vogt, shared Hubbard's interest in hypnotism. One night at a Lasfas meeting, someone described a particularly vivid dream and Hubbard immediately claimed responsibility for it, saying it was a hallucination he had caused while he was 'out strolling in Astral form'.

Van Vogt did not necessarily disbelieve Hubbard but thought it was more likely that he had induced the dream by post-hypnotic suggestion. With the help of a professional hypnotist friend, he decided to check if any members of the club had been hypnotized by Hubbard without being able to remember it. They started with Bill Cox, put him in a deep trance and quickly learned of the ordeal that Hubbard had put him through. Although van Vogt gravely disapproved, he continued, curiously, to hold Hubbard in the highest esteem.

In the world of science fiction, A.E. van Vogt was considered to be in the very top rank of writers and it was Hubbard who requested that they should meet at the end of the war. Van was invited to dinner with Hubbard at Jack Parsons's house in Pasadena and was instantly dazzled by the force of his personality; like everyone else around Hubbard, he rapidly found himself in a vaguely supplicant position. Very soon he would be running around at Hubbard's beck and call.

'When we were first introduced, a hand of steel grabbed mine and squeezed it so hard that I braced myself. He was physically very strong and in fine physical condition. He had been in command of a gunboat in the Pacific. Once he sailed right into the harbour of a Japanese occupied island in the Dutch East Indies. His attitude was that if you took your flag down the Japanese would not know one boat from another, so he tied up at the dock, went ashore and wandered around by himself for three days. Everyone else was scared except Hubbard; he was a brave man, no question about it.

'I knew his work as a writer, of course, and enjoyed it. He wrote about a million words a year, straight on to the typewriter at incredible speed. My guess was that he typed at about seventy words a minute. It just poured out – I have seen typists working at that speed, but never a writer. I was in his apartment a couple of times when he said he had to finish a story and he would sit typing steadily for twenty minutes without a break and without looking up. That would have been totally impossible for me.

'When he was out in the evenings, he would begin to think of a plot for a story and throw ideas around, asking people around the table what they thought of this or that. By the end of the evening he would have it worked out in his mind and when he got home he would spend the night writing, tearing the pages out of the typewriter and throwing them all over the floor. Sara told me it was her job when she got up in the morning to collect the pages and put them in order. He left a note to tell her where to send it and he never looked at it again.

'He never told me where he learned hypnotism, but he was certianly a great hypnotist. There were certain people he could hypnotize instantly. He would talk to them for a few moments, take their mind in a certain direction, then just say "Sleep!"'[13]

Hubbard's efforts to use his facility in a more constructive fashion at the science fiction society were somewhat less successful. He once hypnotized a member who was taking a college examination the following day and ordered him to get straight A's, without that happy result. Another attempt to help someone who felt he had a 'block' about spelling similarly failed. By the time a fan approached Ron to ask if hypnosis could help with his emotional problems, Ron could only lamely suggest he tried reading Dale Carnegie's *How to Win Friends and Influence People*.

That summer, 1948, Hubbard ran into a spot of bother with the law. A trifling misunderstanding over a cheque led to the embarrassment of his being arrested by the San Luis Obispo County Sheriff, fingerprinted and charged with petty theft. He was released on bail of $500 while the Sheriff's Forgery Detail investigated the circumstances of the offence. On 19 August 1948 he was arraigned at San Gabriel Township Justice Court where he entered a plea of not guilty and waived trial by jury. However, by the time the trial date came around on 31 August, Hubbard changed his plea to guilty and was fined $25. Remarkably, he did not need time to pay.[14]

Ron never mentioned the incident to his friends and the court files were destroyed in 1955, so it will never be known precisely what he had done wrong. He was also fortunate that none of the local newspaper reporters was a science-fiction fan and so no one realized that the L.R. Hubbard charged with petty theft at San Luis Obispo was a famous sci-fi writer.

Shortly afterwards, Ron and Sara left California for Savannah, Georgia, where, Ron would claim later, he embarked upon another important stage of his pioneering research into the unexplored recesses of the human mind.

Within a couple of years it would become imperative for L. Ron Hubbard to play down his career as a pulp writer and establish for himself a rather more sober reputation as a scientist, philosopher and guru. Lesser men might have hesitated to undertake such a radical metamorphosis, but not Ron Hubbard, who effortlessly contrived to make it appear as if his whole life had been dedicated to unravelling the mysteries of the psyche.

The story of his childhood in the 'wilds of Montana' and his adoption as a blood brother of an Indian tribe presented a picture of a boy unusually in tune with nature and primitive cultures. His tutelage by a 'personal student' of Freud, his 'wanderings' in the mystic East and his expeditions as an explorer all suggested an upbringing and career of extraordinary dimensions, constantly directed towards a quest for deeper understanding of life's mysteries. Writing science fiction was downgraded to no more than a convenient device designed to finance his 'research'.

During the 'year' he had spent in Oak Knoll Naval Hospital, Ron would claim he had had the run of the medical library and access to the medical records of former prisoners of war. He began experimental psycho-analysis on ex POWs, 'using a park bench as a consulting room', and his research continued ever more intensively through the post-war years. In Savannah, he said, he worked as a volunteer lay practitioner in a psychiatric clinic, helping charity patients no one else would treat.

There was, perhaps, no reason why anyone should question the veracity of Hubbard's research, but his friends must have been puzzled that they knew nothing of it. Mac Ford, for example, who had spent so much time with Ron in the late '30s, sailing on Puget Sound and often talking through the night over a bottle of whisky, had never realized that his friend was engaged in research of any kind. In the heated and wide-ranging discussions that took place in the kitchen of Jack Parsons's house in Pasadena, an ideal forum for Hubbard to talk about his theories, he had said not a word about them. Alva Rogers had frequently heard him tapping away at a typewriter in his room, but there was nothing to indicate he was writing anything but fiction. Not even the amiable Forrest Ackerman had any idea that Ron was about to abandon science fiction in favour of philosophy, although in January 1949 he received an amusing letter from his client hinting at the possibility.

Addressing Ackerman, as always, as '4E', Ron wrote from Savannah to say that he had set up an office in the apartment building where he was living on Drayton Street. It was a very nice place, he said, and could easily become a den of vice, 'so I only allow women over 16 in there'. He had acquired a dictaphone machine which Sara was 'beating out her wits on' transcribing not only fiction but his book on the 'cause and cure of nervous tension', which he was going to call either *The Dark Sword* or *Excalibur* or *Science of the Mind*. He was writing so much fiction, Sara was having to work on the manuscript in fits. 'So far, however,' he wisecracked, 'she has recovered easily from each fit.'

If Ackerman did not take the letter too seriously he could hardly be blamed, for its tone was largely facetious throughout. Ron promised that among the 'handy household hints' contained in the book was information on how to 'rape women without their knowing it, communicate suicide messages to your enemies as they sleep, sell the Arroyo Seco parkway to the mayor for cash, and evolve the best way of protecting or destroying communism'. He had not decided, he added casually, whether to destroy the Catholic Church or 'merely start a new one'.

He continued in similar vein, suggesting promotional gimmicks such as requiring readers to sign a release absolving the author of any responsibility if they went crazy and posting a ten thousand dollar bond to be paid to anyone who could attain equal results with any other known field of knowledge. 'This has more selling and publicity angles', he added, 'than any book of which I have ever heard . . .'

(Publicity angles notwithstanding, he could not have been too confident of the book's success, because shortly after writing to Forrie he wrote to the Bureau of Naval Personnel asking for a transcript of his sea service in order to apply for a licence in the merchant marine. He asked for the request to be dealt with quickly as he had a 'waiting berth'.[15])

The first sci-fi fans knew of L. Ron Hubbard's intention to write a philosophic treatise was an interview with him that appeared in the January 1949 issue of a magazine called *Writers' Markets and Methods*, during which he mentioned that he was working on a 'book of psychology'. But he added that he was also working on a rewrite of a Broadway play, no less than ten novels and a serial for Street and Smith.

This was the conundrum. In 1949, the year in which Hubbard's 'research' was presumably approaching fruition, he once again began writing fiction at a prolific rate: 'Gun Boss of Tumbleweed' and 'Blood on his Spurs' for *Thrilling Western*, 'Gunman' and 'Johnny the Town Tamer' for *Famous Western*, 'Plague' and 'The Automagic Horse' for *Astounding*, 'Beyond the Black Nebula' and 'the Emperor of the Universe' for *Startling Stories*, and many more.

Not a month passed in 1949 without the name of L. Ron Hubbard appearing on the cover of one of the pulp magazines. Nevertheless, rumours began to circulate among science-fiction fans in the summer of 1949 that Ron Hubbard was also writing a book about philosophy and was intending to unveil an entire new 'science of the mind'. What was most surprising to the fans was that Hubbard had found the *time* to produce such a science, for it had long been expected by science-fiction devotees that one of their number would eventually come up with some world-shaking discovery. Many of the technological developments of the previous twenty years, including the atom bomb, had been predicted with uncanny accuracy by science-fiction writers and to the fans it was entirely logical that science fiction should give birth to an important new science.

The rumours were fuelled by the fact that no one had seen Hubbard for months – he had not attended any of the recent gatherings of the Los Angeles science fiction society, neither had he made an appearance in any of the magazine offices in New York. It was said he was holed up somewhere in New Jersey and that John W. Campbell was somehow involved in his plans. But no one knew exactly where Hubbard was or precisely what he was doing or what the new 'science' might entail, although everyone was agreed that Hubbard was on to 'something big', whatever it was.

The first tantalizing details were revealed in an editorial in the December issue of *Astounding Science Fiction*. With an implicit sense of history in the making, Campbell announced that an article was in preparation about a new science called Dianetics. 'Its power is almost unbelievable; it proves the mind not only can but does rule the body completely; following the sharply defined basic laws set forth, physical ills such as ulcers, asthma and arthritis can be cured, as can all other psychosomatic ills . . .' On the facing page, by a curious coincidence, there was a story titled 'A Can of Vacuum' by L. Ron Hubbard, about a practical joke which results in remarkable scientific discoveries.

By January 1950, the rumours had reached the ears of Walter Winchell, the syndicated columnist on the New York *Daily Mirror*. 'There is something new coming up in April called Dianetics,' he wrote in his column on 31 January. 'A new science which works with the invariability of physical science in the field of the human mind. From all indications it will prove to be as revolutionary for humanity as the first caveman's discovery and utilization of fire.'

In the April issue of *Astounding*, Campbell announced that the long-awaited article was at last ready for publication: 'Next month's issue will, I believe, cause one full-scale explosion across the country. We are carrying a 16,000 word article entitled "Dianetics – An Introduction to a New Science', by L. Ron Hubbard. It will, I believe, be the first publication of the material. It is, I assure you in full and absolute sincerity, one of the most important articles ever published. In this article, reporting on Hubbard's own research into the engineering question of how the human mind operates, immensely important basic discoveries are related. Among them:

'A technique of psychotherapy has been developed which will cure any insanity not due to organic destruction of the brain.

'A technique that gives any man a perfect, indelible, total memory, and perfect, errorless ability to compute his problems.

'A basic answer, and a technique for curing – not alleviating – ulcers, arthritis, asthma, and many other nongerm diseases.

'A totally new conception of the truly incredible ability and power of the human mind.

'Evidence that insanity is contagious, and *is not hereditary*.

'This is no wild theory. It is not mysticism. It is a coldly precise engineering description of how the human mind operates, and how to go about restoring correct operation tested and used on some 250 cases. And it makes only one overall claim: the methods logically developed from that description *work*. The memory stimulation technique is so powerful that, within 30 minutes of entering therapy, most people will recall in full detail their own birth. I have observed it in action, and used the techniques myself . . .

'It is not only a fact article of the highest importance; it is the story of the ultimate adventure – an exploration in the strangest of all *terra incognita*; the human mind. No stranger adventure appeared in *The Arabian Nights* than Hubbard's experience, using his new techniques, in plowing through the strange jungle of distorted thoughts within a human mind. To find, beyond that zone of madness, a computing mechanism of ultimate and incredible efficiency and perfection!'

Rarely can any editor have penned such a fulsome and glowing testimonial. The world, or at least the world of science fiction, waited with bated breath.

Chapter 9

The Strange Début of Dianetics

'My vanity hopes that you will secure credit to me for eleven years of unpaid research, but my humanity hopes above that that this science will be used as intelligently and extensively as possible, for it is a science and it does produce exact results uniformly and can, I think, be of benefit.' (Letter from L.R. Hubbard to Dr Joseph Winter, August 1949)

* * * * *

In the spring of 1949, Ron and Sara had moved to the New Jersey shore, to a beach cottage at Bay Head, a discreetly genteel yachting resort on the northern tip of Barnegat Bay. Rich New Yorkers who could not quite afford the Hamptons kept large summer houses at Bay Head where they sailed the ruffled blue waters of the bay, played tennis and attended each other's cocktail parties. The Hubbards' rented cottage was one of the smallest properties, but Sara, who suspected she was pregnant, was delighted with it. She was weary of their peripatetic lifestyle; she calculated that in only three years of marriage they had set up home in seven different States and had never stayed in one place for more than a few months. Bay Head, with its country club aura, did much to lift her spirits.

John Campbell had persuaded them to move from Georgia and had found them the cottage which was less than a hour's drive on the Garden State Parkway from Plainfield, where he and his wife lived. He wanted Ron close by because he wanted, passionately wanted, to be involved in what he considered to be the historic genesis of Dianetics.

It was predictable, in the course of their working relationship as science-fiction editor and science-fiction writer, that Campbell and Hubbard would spend time together discussing ideas and that Ron would test his theories on a man as responsive as the editor of *Astounding*. Campbell was an intellectual maverick: he had studied physics and chemistry at college, had a mechanistic approach to psychology and was fascinated by gimmicks and technology, but he also flirted with psychic phenomena like dowsing, telekinesis, telepathy and clairvoyance. Ron could not have had a more attentive audience when he first began to propound his theory that the brain worked like a computer which could be made markedly more efficient by clearing its clogged memory bank.

Always a persuasive talker, Hubbard possessed a natural ability to marshal a smattering of knowledge into a cogent and authoritative thesis, interwoven with scientific and medical jargon. His 'scientific' approach to unravelling the mysteries of the human psyche precisely accorded with Campbell's own view that humanity could be investigated with the techniques and impersonal methodology of the exact sciences,[1] and although Ron's ideas stemmed more from his exuberant imagination than from any research, to Campbell what Hubbard had to say was tantamount to a revelation on the road to Damascus.

He compared individual memory to a 'time-track' on which every experience was recorded. Using a form of hypnosis, he believed painful experiences could be recalled and 'erased' with consequent beneficial effects to both physical and mental health. Ron offered to demonstrate on a convenient couch at Campbell's home in Plainfield. He drew the blinds, told Campbell to relax, close his eyes on a count to seven and try to recall his earliest childhood experience. Gently prompted by Ron to produce more and more details, Campbell was surprised to find he could resurrect long-forgotten incidents with such clarity that it was as if he had physically returned to the time and place. After a couple of sessions, he seemed to be able to go back far enough to actually re-live the astonishing experience of his birth and at the same time he discovered that the chronic sinusitis that had plagued him all his life was much improved.

Thereafter, Campbell was the first committed disciple of Dianetics, utterly convinced that L. Ron Hubbard had made profound discoveries about the workings of the mind and that the fundamental nature of human life was about to be changed for the better. [Hubbard himself was perhaps as concerned to make money as he was to help humanity and he had some interesting ideas about how to do it. Around this time he was invited to address a science-fiction group in Newark hosted by the writer, Sam Moskowitz. 'Writing for a penny a word is ridiculous,' he told the meeting. 'If a man really wanted to make a million dollars, the best way to do it would be to start his own religion.'[2]]

Determined to help Ron propagate his new 'science', in July 1949 Campbell wrote to Dr Joseph Winter, a general practitioner from St Joseph, Michigan, who had contributed occasional articles on medical subjects to *Astounding*: 'L. Ron Hubbard, who happens to be an author, has been doing some psychological research . . . He's gotten important results. His approach is, actually, based on some very early work of Freud's, some work of other men, and a lot of original research. He's not a professional psychoanalyst or psychiatrist, he's basically an engineer. He approached the problem of psychiatry from the heuristic viewpoint – to get results.'

Campbell described the case of an amputee veteran suffering from severe depression who had been helped by Hubbard after conventional psychiatry had failed to alleviate his condition. Psychiatrists had injected sodium Pentothal to enable the veteran to re-live his war experience, taking him through the moment he was hit by a mortar shell to the moment he recovered consciousness in the aid station, but he continued to be depressed and insist he would be better off dead. Using Dianetics, Hubbard had also taken the veteran back through the shell burst but discovered that *while he was unconscious* medics had said, 'This guy's hopeless, he's better off dead anyway' and chosen to move other casualties first. This incident, it transpired, was the cause of his problems.

Winter was intrigued: he had never considered before that an unconscious patient could in any way be aware of what was going on around him. He wrote to Campbell asking for more information and back came another long letter elaborating on the theory and concluding: 'With cooperation from some institutions, some psychiatrists, he [Hubbard] has worked on all types of cases. Institutionalized schizophrenics, apathies, manics, depressives, perverts, stuttering, neuroses – in all, nearly 1000 cases. But just a brief sampling of each type; he doesn't have proper statistics in the usual sense. But he has one statistic. He has *cured every patient* he worked with. He has cured ulcers, arthritis, asthma.'

While Winter was avowedly incredulous at the idea that a man with no medical training of any kind was able to cure one hundred per cent of his patients, he did not share the tendency of his medical colleagues to dismiss all lay practitioners as dangerous cranks. He had always been fascinated by the enigmas of human behaviour and believed in a holistic approach to medicine which was amenable to unconventional hypotheses. He contacted Hubbard, suggested that he present his findings to the medical profession, and offered to help.

Hubbard quickly replied, promising to forward an 'operator's manual' for Winter's use and thanking him for his interest. When his manual arrived, Winter made several copies and gave them to psychiatrist friends in Chicago, but was disappointed by their negative reactions. They were interested in the ingenuity of Hubbard's ideas, but strongly sceptical of their efficacy. However, Winter still felt the subject was worth pursuing and made arrangements to visit Bay Head to observe Dianetics 'in action'. Ron, who was acutely aware of the potential value of recruiting a doctor to the Dianetic cause, invited Winter to stay with him and Sara at the cottage on the beach.

He arrived in Bay Head on 1 October 1949, and Sara, now several months into her pregnancy, did her best to make the young doctor welcome, despite somewhat cramped conditions. Winter discovered that Hubbard was spending much of his time testing his theories by 'running' science-fiction fans brought in by Campbell. The purpose of 'running' a patient, Hubbard explained, was to send them 'down the time-track' to uncover their 'impediments'.

Winter sat in on several sessions, then agreed to Ron's suggestion that he should be 'run' himself. 'The experience was intriguing,' he said. 'I felt, in general, that I was obtaining some benefits from Hubbard's methods of therapy. I was also aware of the possible inaccuracies of a subjective evaluation of my own progress: I therefore endeavoured to make up for this by observing the other patients closely. It was possible during this short period of observation to note only the differences in their behaviour before and after each therapy session. The changes were obvious: before a session I would see agitation, depression and irritability; after a session the patient would be cheerful and relaxed.'[3]

Although he had some reservations, particularly about Hubbard's absolutism and inclination to make sweeping generalizations, he was unquestionably impressed. He noted the emotional discharge that resulted when patients recalled painful experiences; he himself re-lived the terror he had felt as a child on learning of his grandmother's death and found it dissolving in a fit of sobbing and weeping, after which he felt a great sense of relief.

Winter did not return to Michigan until Thanksgiving, when an incident occurred which finally convinced him of the validity of Dianetics. He arrived home to discover that his six-year-old son was having problems: the boy had developed a paralyzing fear of the dark and of ghosts, which he believed were waiting upstairs to strangle him. Winter recalled that his wife had experienced considerable difficulties during the boy's birth and decided to apply Dianetic techniques to see if there was any connection. He was flabbergasted by the result.

The doctor persuaded his son to lie down, close his eyes and try to recall the first time he had ever seen a ghost. To Winter's amazement the boy described in detail the white apron, cap and mask of the obstetrician who had delivered him and how he felt he was being strangled. Winter and his wife discussed what had happened and concluded with certainty that the only time their son had seen that doctor in his surgical gown was at the moment of his birth. It was evident to them that the boy's fear was connected with his struggle to be born and his phobia soon disappeared.

Believing himself to be at the possible dawn of a 'Golden Age of greater sanity', Winter returned to Bay Head after the holiday enormously optimistic about the prospects for Dianetics. 'I immediately became immersed in a life of Dianetics and very little else,' he recorded. Hubbard and Campbell were deeply involved in the projected article for *Astounding* and Winter began work on the preparation of a paper explaining the principles and methodology of Dianetic therapy, intended for presentation to the medical profession. Ron, who made no secret of his contempt for the medical establishment (often to the considerable embarrassment of Dr Winter), was not in the least surprised by the reception it received: the *Journal of the American Medical Association* and the *American Journal of Psychiatry* both rejected the paper for publication on the grounds of insufficient clinical evidence of the technique's effectiveness.

Undeterred, the three men continued developing and refining Dianetic theory, slowly bringing into their orbit other converts, notably a young electrical engineer by the name of Don Rogers and Art Ceppos, head of Hermitage House, a small medical and psychiatric textbook publisher who had contracted, at Campbell's instigation, to publish a book about Dianetics. The 'Bay Head Circle', as it came to be known, devoted many hours to discussion of terminology. Ron was still using the word 'impediment' to describe painful past experiences, although they all agreed that a new word was needed to avoid confusion. For a while, impediment was replaced by 'norn', the name of the Norse goddesses said to control Man's destiny, but in the end they plumped for 'engram', which was defined in Dorland's *Medical Dictionary* as a 'lasting mark or trace'.

Meanwhile, Ron found time to dash off a feature about Dianetics for the Explorers Club journal, in which he explained that he had developed the therapy as a tool for expedition commanders to maintain the health and morale of their men. 'That it apparently conquers and cures all psychosomatic ills', he added with barely feigned modesty, 'and is of interest to institutions where it has a salutary effect upon the insane, is beyond the province of its original intention.' Untroubled, as always, by facts, Ron nonchalantly informed his fellow members that details of the science could be found, 'where it belonged', in textbooks and professional publications on the mind and body.[4]

[Credit for the inspiration for Dianetics would be variously and fancifully attributed over the years; at one point Hubbard claimed his interest in the mind had been stimulated while at university by comparing the rhythmic vibrations of poetry in English and Japanese, in which language he was, of course, fluent.[5]]

Shortly before Christmas 1949, Hubbard finished the article for

Astounding, but Campbell agreed to delay publication so that it would come out shortly before the book was available and help promote sales. Despite his lingering misgivings about the extravagance of Ron's claims, Winter agreed to write a foreword to the article, an endorsement which would greatly add to the credibility of Dianetics. 'I sincerely feel', he wrote, 'that Ron Hubbard has discovered the key which for the first time permits a true evaluation of the human mind and its function in health and in illness – the greatest advance in mental therapy since man began to probe into his mental make-up.'

In the midst of all this accelerating activity, of writing and revising, proof-reading, 'running patients' and answering the inquiries that were beginning to arrive as a result of the advance editorials in *Astounding*, Hubbard became a father for the third time. On 8 March, 1950, Sara gave birth to a daughter, Alexis Valerie, in the local hospital. Winter, conveniently on hand, supervised the delivery. When she cradled the baby in her arms for the first time, Sara registered with considerable pleasure that her daughter had flaming red hair.

By the beginning of April, Campbell's editorials had stimulated so much interest that it was decided to establish a Hubbard Dianetic Research Foundation to disseminate knowledge of the new therapy and stimulate further research. The Foundation was incorporated in the unlovely environs of Elizabeth, New Jersey, a grimy industrial town on the shores of Newark Bay, opposite Staten Island. The board of directors was made up of Ron and Sara Hubbard, Campbell, Winter, Don Rogers, Art Ceppos and a lawyer by the name of Parker C. Morgan. Dr Winter, who had by then sold his practice in Michigan to devote himself full-time to Dianetics, accepted the post of medical director 'without qualms'.

The Foundation rented the top floor of an old office building on Morris Avenue and furnished it with second-hand sheet-metal desks, Navy surplus lecture-hall chairs and Army surplus cots. Ron and Sara rented a small frame house at 42 Aberdeen Road, Elizabeth, and moved in with the baby. Sara very much regretted leaving Bay Head and viewed Elizabeth with unconcealed distaste, but Ron persuaded her that it was vital for him to be on hand to direct the affairs of the Foundation.

Campbell's wife, Dona, was similarly suffering from her husband's obsession with Dianetics, so much so that she walked out of their marriage, declaring Dianetics to be the 'last straw'. Regular contributors to *Astounding* also began to express concern that the editor no longer seemed interested in anything but Ron Hubbard's wonderful new science and many of them failed to share his enthusiasm. Isaac Asimov read an advance copy of the Dianetics article and thought it was 'gibberish'[6] while Jack Williamson said he thought it was like a 'lunatic revision of Freudian psychology'.

But Campbell's ardour could not be cooled. In a letter to Williamson he said he had witnessed Ron restoring sanity to a 'raving psychotic' in thirty minutes and curing a Navy veteran of ulcers and arthritis. 'I *know* dianetics is one of, if not the greatest, discovery of all Man's written and unwritten history,' he added. 'It produces the sort of stability and sanity men have dreamed about for centuries.'[7]

The May 1950 issue of *Astounding Science Fiction* appeared on the streets in the third week of April. A hairy, ape-like alien with yellow cat's eyes glowered menacingly from the cover. Readers would discover that he was the evil Duke of Kraakahaym, special envoy from the Empire of Skontar to the Commonwealth of Sol, but everyone knew there was something much more diverting in the magazine that month – the long-awaited introduction to Dianetics, the first science ever to be launched in a pocketbook pulp magazine.

So startling were the tidings that Campbell felt obliged to emphasize that the author was entirely serious. 'I want to assure every reader, most positively and unequivocally,' he wrote, 'that this article is *not* a hoax, joke, or anything but a direct, clear statement of a totally new scientific thesis.'

Hubbard might have wished for a more venerable medium in which to launch his new science, but he could hardly have found a more receptive forum. Many science-fiction fans at that time had an engineering and science background and as far as they were concerned Hubbard's dissertation, filling more than forty pages and seemingly resulting from years of diligent research and study, was logical, enticing and thoroughly persuasive.

It was certainly very different from his previous writing. The customary narcissistic swaggering was notably absent and his usual racy prose was replaced by a sober, textbook style sometimes too wordy to be immediately comprehensible: 'When exterior determinism was entered into a human being so as to overbalance his self determinism the correctness of his solutions fell off rapidly.'

Hubbard's approach was that of an engineer seeking practical, scientific solutions to the mysteries of the human mind, constantly testing his postulates against a single, simple criterion: does it work? He began by drawing an analogy between the brain and a computer with an infinite memory bank and perfect function. Every human brain, he argued, had the potential to operate as this optimum computer, with untold benefits to the individual and to mankind, not least restoring sanity to the insane, curing all manner of illnesses and ending wars.

Constraints were presently imposed on the brain by 'aberrations', usually caused by physical or emotional pain. Since pain was a threat to survival, the basic principle of existence, the sane, analytical mind sought to avoid it. Evolution had provided the necessary mechanism by means of what he called the 'reactive mind'. In moments of stress, the 'analytical mind' shut down and the 'reactive mind' took over, storing information in cellular recordings, or 'engrams'.

He provided an example of how an engram was stored. If a child was bitten by a dog at the age of two, she might not remember the incident in later life but the engram could be stimulated by any number of sights or sounds, causing her inexplicable distress. It might be a similar noise to that of the car driving past when the dog attacked, the smell of a dog's fur, or the scrape of skin on concrete when she was knocked to the ground.

The purpose of Dianetic therapy, he explained, was to gain access to the engrams in the reactive memory banks and 're-file' them in the analytical mind, where their influence would be eradicated. To 'unlock' the reactive memory bank it was necessary to locate the earliest engrams, which he claimed were often pre-natal, sometimes occurring within twenty-four hours of conception! A foetus might not understand words spoken while it was in the womb, he asserted, but it would be able to recall them in later life.

Having cleared the reactive mind, the analytical mind would then function, like the optimum computer, at full efficiency – the individual's IQ would rise dramatically, he would be freed of all psychological and psychosomatic illnesses and his memory would improve to the point of total recall.

Dianetics was easy to apply, he asserted, once the axioms and mechanisms had been learned, and he envisaged the science being practised by 'people of intelligence and good drive' on their friends and families. 'To date, over two hundred patients have been treated,' he claimed; 'of those two hundred, two hundred cures have been obtained.'

It was certainly an alluring prospect – a simple science available to ordinary people that invariably succeeded and claimed amazing results. But Hubbard knew better than to reveal, in a twenty-five-cent magazine, *how* to practise his wonderful new science; readers were specifically warned that the article would not contain sufficient information for them to become Dianetic operators. All the techniques would be explained, they were told, in a forthcoming book soon to be published by Hermitage House, price $4.00.

On 9 May 1950, *Dianetics, The Modern Science of Mental Health* by L. Ron Hubbard appeared without fanfare in bookstores across the nation. Hermitage House was not optimistic that it would be a big seller and set the initial print run at a modest six thousand copies.

The book, dedicated to Will Durant, esteemed author of *The Story of Philosophy*, displayed none of the restraint evident in the *Astounding* article. Indeed, Hubbard introduced his new science with breathtaking magniloquence. 'The creation of Dianetics', he declared in the opening sentences of the book, 'is a milestone for Man comparable to his discovery of fire and superior to his inventions of the wheel and the arch . . . The hidden source of all psychosomatic ills and human aberration has been discovered and skills have been developed for their invariable cure.'

Significant among the maladies Hubbard claimed he could cure were the complaints that had figured so prominently in his Veterans Administration file: arthritis, eye trouble, bursitis and ulcers. He also added to the list the most intractable ailment known to medical science – the common cold.

Optimism and confidence in the ability of Dianetics to deal with almost all human problems were the abiding themes of the book. Hubbard's seductive message was simple – a dramatic breakthrough had occurred in psychotherapy. The techniques were easy to learn, were available to everyone and, most important of all, *always worked*!

The first challenge of Dianetics was to get through the book, for the text was abstruse, rambling, repetitive, studded with confusing neologisms and littered with interminable footnotes, which Hubbard seemed to think added academic verisimilitude. Fellow science-fiction writer L. Sprague de Camp frankly admitted he found the book incomprehensible and quoted W.S. Gilbert to explain why a fiction writer who was fluent, literate and readable should produce such impenetrable non-fiction:

'If this young man expresses himself in terms too deep for *me*,
Why, what a very singularly deep young man this deep young man must be!'[8]

Hubbard's anxiety to invest his work with intellectual authority should have deterred him from laying bare his own fierce prejudices, but he could not be restrained. The book exposed a deep-rooted hatred of women, exemplified by a prurient pre-occupation with 'attempted abortions', which he claimed were the most common cause of pre-natal engrams. 'A large proportion of allegedly feeble-minded children', he wrote, 'are actually attempted abortion cases . . . However many billions America spends yearly on institutions for the insane and jails for the criminals are spent primarily because of attempted abortions done by some sex-blocked mother to whom children are a curse, not a blessing of God . . . All these things are scientific facts, tested and rechecked and tested again.'

When the women in Hubbard's 'case histories' were not thrusting knitting needles into themselves, they were usually being unfaithful to their husbands, or they were being beaten up, raped or otherwise abused. Almost without exception, they allowed the wretched embryos in their wombs to be grievously mistreated. 'Fathers, for instance, suspicious of paternity, sometimes claim while trouncing or upsetting mothers that they will kill the child if it isn't like Father. This is a very bad engram . . . it may compel an aberee into a profession he does not admire and all out of the engramic command that he must be like the parent. The same engram, he added mysteriously, could also cause premature baldness or lengthen the child's nose.

Hubbard gave many illustrations of the problems caused by pre-natal engrams, some of which might have strained the credulity of even his most gullible readers. If a husband beat his pregnant wife, for example, yelling, 'Take that! Take it, I tell you. You've got to take it!', it was possible the child would interpret these words literally in later life and become a thief. Or a pregnant woman suffering from constipation might sit straining for a bowel movement muttering to herself, 'Oh, this is hell. I am all jammed up inside. I feel so stuffy I can't think. This is too terrible to be borne.' In this case, he explained, the child might easily develop an inferiority complex from a engram which suggested to him he was too terrible to be 'born'.

Some of the worst pre-natal engrams were caused by naming the child after the father. If the expectant mother was committing adultery, as so many of Hubbard's pregnant women were wont to do, she was likely to make derogatory remarks about her husband while engaged in sexual intercourse with her lover. The foetus, obviously, would be 'listening' and if he was given the husband's name he would assume in later life that all the horrible things his mother had said about his father were actually about *him*.

After women, Hubbard's secondary target was the medical profession, towards which he directed almost rabid hostility, accusing neurosurgeons of reducing their 'victims' to 'zombyism' either by burning away the brain with electric shocks or tearing it to pieces with a 'nice ice-pick into each eyeball'. 'In terms of brutality in treatment of the insane,' he wrote, 'the methods of the shaman or Bedlam have been exceeded by the "civilized" techniques of destroying nerve tissue with the violence of shock or surgery . . . destroying most of his personality and ambition and leaving him nothing more than a manageable animal.'

Indisputably the most portentous section of the book was that which explained to the reader how to put Dianetics into practice. Artfully employing the jargon of modern technology, Hubbard called the process 'auditing'. The practitioner was the 'auditor' and his patient was a 'pre-clear'. To become 'clear' of all engrams was the goal devoutly to be pursued for 'clears' were free from all neuroses and psychoses, had full control of their imaginations, greatly raised IQs and well-nigh perfect memories.

Auditing began in a darkened room by inducing in the pre-clear a condition Hubbard described as 'Dianetic reverie', which could apparently be recognized by a fluttering of the closed eyelids. It was not so much a hypnotic trance, he was careful to point out, as a state of relaxation conducive to travelling back along the time-track. Once the reverie had been induced, the auditor placed the pre-clear back in various periods of his life, moving inexorably towards birth or conception. Most pre-clears, Hubbard advised, would eventually experience a 'sperm dream' during which, as an egg, they would swim up a channel to meet the sperm. Once the earliest engram had been erased, later engrams would erase more easily.

An average auditing session should last about two hours and Hubbard estimated that a minimum of twenty hours' auditing would be needed before the pre-clear began to reap the rewards.

To a nation increasingly inclined to unload its problems on an expensive psychiatrist's couch, the promise of Dianetics was wondrous. It all seemed so eminently logical, pragmatic and alluring, as if human life was about to take on a new sparkle. With the book in one hand, what problems could not be solved? Here at last was a do-it-yourself therapy for the people that friends could offer to friends, husbands to wives, fathers to children. Any doubts were swept aside by the book's overweening absolutism: who would dare make such sweeping claims if they were not true?

Even the immoderate tenor of the author's attack on the medical profession struck many chords. Electric shock therapy and pre-frontal lobotomy were frightening and mysterious techniques disturbingly reminiscent of the experiments that had taken place in Nazi concentration camps, horrors only recently uncovered and still fresh in the mind. It was understandable that people wanted to believe in Dianetics, if for no other reason than to relegate such seemingly medieval practices to history.

For the first few days after publication of *Dianetics, The Modern Science of Mental Health*, it appeared as if the publisher's caution about the book's prospects had been entirely justified. Early indications were that it had aroused little interest; certainly it was ignored by most reviewers. But suddenly, towards the end of May, the line on the sales graph at the New York offices of Hermitage House took a steep upturn.

The first purchasers of *Dianetics* were mostly science-fiction fans and readers of *Astounding*. Primarily they wanted to see if Hubbard's new science really did work. Typical among them was Jack Horner, a psychology graduate at a college in Los Angeles: 'I had been a science-fiction fan since 1934 and I was fascinated by Campbell's editorials in *Astounding*. I ordered the book as soon as I heard about it. I got it on Monday, read it by Tuesday and was auditing on Wednesday. I sat down and audited five people and boy, it worked just like Hubbard said it would. I said to myself, "Gee, he may not have it all, but he's sure got a good piece of it."'[9]

A. E. van Vogt knew the book was coming out because Hubbard had been telephoning him every day from Elizabeth to try and get him interested in Dianetics. Van insisted he was a writer, not a therapist, and had no intention of reading Ron's book. But when an advance copy arrived in the mail he could not resist taking a look and he was piqued to discover how well Dianetic theory dovetailed with his own fiction. His most popular novel, *Slan*, had been about supermen evolving fantastic new powers of the mind very much in the way envisaged by Dianetics.

Van Vogt read *Dianetics* twice, then decided to experiment on his wife's sister, who was visiting them at the time. He began auditing her, following the instructions in the book, and to his utter astonishment found she was soon re-living the moment of her birth. She had been a breech baby and Van and his wife, Edna Mayne, watched in awe as she went through the motions of being born, screaming and yelling as she 'felt' the forceps pulling her out. Next day, Van invited Forrie Ackerman and his wife over.

'Van was the first in town to get Ron's book' said Ackerman. 'He told me that his 'phone was ringing off the hook all day. Everyone wanted to know if Dianetics was phoney or if there was really something in it.

'I was his second guinea pig. He asked me to lie on a couch and explained about the time-track. He said I could think of it as if I was in an elevator going down and stopping at floors equating to different years, or I could imagine I was on a train and watching signs with different dates flash by the window. I got the idea and lay there waiting for something to happen. Suddenly, on a sort of velvety background I saw two disembodied eyes, hard-boiled eyes like those of the actor, Peter Lorre. I said, "I see these popping eyes . . ."

'Van said to concentrate on that and keep repeating "popping eyes". I kept saying it and it gradually got abbreviated to "Popeyes", then "poppies". When I was in High School we memorized a poem about

World War One: "In Flanders fields the poppies grow, by the crosses row on row . . ." I suddenly thought of the poppies growing row on row and in my mind I went right to the grave of my dear brother, Lorraine Ackerman, who didn't quite make it to twenty-one. When I learned he had been killed, I remember I just went round with an empty feeling. All those years later, the sorrow that I had been holding at bay came gushing out and I got it all out of my system. It was quite astonishing to me at the time and gave me the feeling there was certainly something to it.'[10]

All over the country the same thing was happening: science-fiction fans were buying the book and auditing their friends, who then rushed out to buy the book so they could audit *their* friends. In this first flush of enthusiasm, Hubbard's insistence that Dianetics worked seemed indisputable: everyone could uncover an engram somewhere down their time-track and only the most churlish pre-clears would not admit to feeling uplifted after an auditing session. If auditing worked, it was perhaps not unreasonable to give credence to the whole science of Dianetics.

At the offices of *Astounding Science Fiction* in New York, more than two thousand letters had arrived in the fortnight following publication of the Dianetics article and mail continued to pour in by the sackload. Campbell, who liked statistics, calculated that only 0.2 per cent of the letters were unfavourable. At Hermitage House, Art Ceppos was frantically trying to arrange for more copies of the book to be printed and distributed; bookstore owners everywhere were complaining that they were running out of supplies. In Los Angeles, the demand was so great that *Dianetics* was only available on an under-the-counter basis.

In Elizabeth, New Jersey, the Hubbard Dianetic Research Foundation was inundated with inquiries when it was announced in June that L. Ron Hubbard would be teaching the first full-time training course for Dianetic auditors. Hopeful trainees travelled thousands of miles to New Jersey in the hope of getting a place on the course. Jack Horner was one of them. 'I got hold of Hubbard's telephone number and called him and said I wanted to take the course. He said, "It's awful crowded out here, but you're as welcome as the flowers in May." I had a friend with a Cadillac who was also interested and we drove non-stop across the country to get there in time.

'The course cost $500, which was an immense amount of money in those days, but it was worth every cent. There were about thirty-five to forty people in the course, all sorts, men and women. They were a well-educated, literate bunch and if there was a common factor among them it was probably an interest in science fiction.

'Ron lectured every day. He was very impressive, dedicated and

amusing. The man had tremendous charisma; you just wanted to hear
every word he had to say and listen for any pearl of wisdom. We never
discussed where he had got all his knowledge. To me, the source of his
data was irrelevant. I'd been in college studying recent discoveries in
psychology and they were not worth a damn compared to what he had
come up with and what it would do.

'I guess it would be true to say that the early 'fifties was the right
moment to launch Dianetics. The atomic bomb had been dropped,
there was a sense of hopelessness around and there was a great deal of
fear about a nuclear war – people were building cabins out in the
wilderness. McCarthyism was rife and our troops were fighting a war
in Korea which seemed completely unreal to most of us. Then along
comes Hubbard with the idea that if we could increase the overall
sanity of man just a little bit, it would be a partial solution to the threat
of nuclear war. It was no wonder that people wanted to listen to him.'

While Hubbard was lecturing in Elizabeth, Dianetics became,
virtually overnight, a national 'craze' somewhat akin to the canasta
marathons and pyramid clubs that had briefly flourished in the
hysteria of post-war America. Dianetic groups sprang up everywhere,
in every small town and every college; on the West Coast 'Dianetic
parties' became the rage; in Hollywood, where neuroses and dollars
lay thick on the ground, the movie colony joyfully embraced the idea
of a therapy that did not involve all the tedious hours demanded by
psychoanalysts. Everyone wanted to audit everyone else and right
across the nation Americans were excitedly re-living their births,
courtesy of the new guru, L. Ron Hubbard.

The media had so far largely chosen to ignore L. Ron Hubbard and
his new science, but it was clear from the rising level of public interest
that he could not be ignored forever. On 2 July, *Dianetics, The
Modern Science of Mental Health* – now known to converts simply as
'The Book' – reached the top of the bestseller list in the *Los Angeles
Times*, where it would remain for many months. On the same day the
book received its first major review, in *The New York Times*. It was a
predictable savaging by Rollo May, a noted psychologist and writer.

May could find no merit in Dianetics. It was, he said, an over-
simplified form of regular psychotherapy mixed with hypnosis. He
wondered if the author was not writing with his tongue in his cheek
and searched in vain for scientific evidence to support the book's
bizarre theories. 'Books like this do harm', May concluded, 'by their
grandiose promises to troubled persons and by their oversimplification
of human psychological problems.'

In *Scientific American*, a professor of physics at Columbia University declared the book contained less evidence per page than any
publication since the invention of printing. 'The huge sale of the book

to date is distressing evidence', wrote the professor, 'of the frustrated ambitions, hopes, ideals, anxieties and worries of the many persons who through it have sought succor.'[11] *New Republic* weighed in by describing the book as a 'bold and immodest mixture of complete nonsense and perfectly reasonable common sense, taken from long acknowledged findings and disguised and distorted by a crazy, newly invented terminology'.[12]

Following close on the heels of the media pundits came the outraged ranks of the medical profession. The American Psychological Association, pointing out that Hubbard's 'sweeping generalizations' were not supported by empirical evidence, called for Dianetics to be limited to scientific investigation 'in the public interest'.

'If it were not for sympathy for the mental suffering of disturbed people,' Dr Frederick Hacker, a Los Angeles psychiatrist declared, 'the so-called science of Dianetics could be dismissed for what it is – a clever scheme to dip into the pockets of the gullible with impunity. The Dianetic auditor is but another name for the witch doctor, exploiting a real need with phoney methods.'[13] Many medical experts sourly pointed out that there was nothing new in Dianetics and that Hubbard was simply applying new words to common phenomena long known and accepted in psychoanalysis. The 'engram' theory, they explained, was no more than a form of 'abreaction', the psychiatric term for releasing emotions associated with the suppressed memory of some past event.

In the face of such criticism, Dianeticists rose en masse to defend their founder and his ideas, bombarding the offending publications with indignant letters. Leading the protest was Frederick L. Schuman, a distinguished professor of political science from Williamstown, Massachusetts, who had visited Hubbard in New Jersey and been instantly converted. 'History has become a race between Dianetics and catastrophe,' he wrote to *The New York Times*. 'Dianetics will win if enough people are challenged, in time, to understand it.'[14]

The constant publicity spread the word as effectively as a nation-wide advertizing campaign and the more the medical profession railed against Dianetics, the more people became convinced there must be something to it. Only two months after the publication of the book, *Newsweek* reported that more than fifty-five thousand copies had been sold and five hundred Dianetics groups had been set up across the United States.[15]

If the cause of all the fuss was in any way bewildered by his sudden change of circumstances, he was certainly not going to show it. In truth, Hubbard had certainly not anticipated that the book would ever be a bestseller, but he acted as if it was pre-ordained and slipped effortlessly into the role of luminary. He was, naturally, much in demand for interviews and he proved to be a natural interviewee providing reporters with a multitude of picturesque quotes about his colourful life and exhausting years of research 'in the laboratories of the world'.

He was unfailingly polite, amusing, ready to answer any question and always willing to pose for a photograph. He also contrived to provide every reporter with a tit-bit of new information. *Parade* magazine was able to reveal exclusively, for example, that 'the man behind the new mental health craze' was also 'the father of the world's first Dianetics baby'. Alexis Valerie Hubbard, Ron explained, had been carefully shielded in her pre-natal life from noise, bumps and parental conversations in order to protect her from engrams. The result, Ron happily announced, was that the baby was talking at three months, crawling at four months and was free from all phobias.[16]

'Since the overnight success of his book *Dianetics*,' the Los Angeles *Daily News* reported, 'Hubbard has become, in a few swift months, a personality, a national celebrity and the proprietor of the fastest growing "movement" in the United States.'[17]

Chapter 10

Commies, Kidnaps and Chaos

'The United States Government at this time [1950] attempted to monopolize all his researches and force him to work on a project "to make man more suggestible" and when he was unwilling, tried to blackmail him by ordering him back to active duty to perform this function. Having made many friends he was able to instantly resign from the Navy and escape this trap. The Government never forgave him for this and soon began vicious, covert international attacks upon his work, all of which were proven false and baseless.' (*What is Scientology?* 1978)

* * * * *

California, ever enchanted by fads and facile philosophies, was the natural habitat of Dianetics and it was to California that Hubbard returned in triumph at the beginning of August 1950, to be feted by joyful Dianeticists waiting to meet him at Los Angeles airport. Two years earlier, he had left as a penniless pulp fiction author; now he was back as a celebrity with a book firmly lodged at the top of every bestseller list and a growing legion of followers who truly believed him to be a genius.

He had a busy schedule ahead: apart from personal appearances and interviews, he was to lecture at the newly-formed Hubbard Dianetic Research Foundation of California, all the big bookstores wanted him for signing sessions and, most important of all, he was to attend a rally on Thursday 10 August at the Shrine Auditorium. It promised to be Dianetics' finest hour, for on that evening the identity of the world's first 'clear' was to be announced.

The Shrine was a vast, mosque-like building with white stucco castellated walls and a dome in each corner, unforgettably characterized by the music critic of the *LA Times* as being of the 'neo-penal Bagdad' school of architecture. Built in 1925 by the Al Malaikah Temple, it was the largest auditorium in Los Angeles and could seat nearly 6500 people under a swooping ceiling designed to resemble the roof of a tent. When the Hubbard Dianetic Research Foundation booked it for the meeting on 10 August, few people expected more than half the seats to be filled.

Arthur Jean Cox, the young teletype operator who had met Hubbard at the Los Angeles Science Fantasy Society, left early for the meeting by streetcar and was surprised how crowded it was. 'More and more people got on at every stop,' he said. 'I couldn't believe that *everyone* was going to the meeting but when we arrived at the Shrine on Royal Street, everyone got off. I was absolutely amazed. By the time I got inside there were only a few seats left.'[1]

The audience was predominantly young, noisy and good-humoured. Many people carried well-thumbed copies of 'The Book', in the hope of getting them signed by Hubbard, and there was much speculation about 'the world's first clear' and what he or she would be able to do. Dozens of newspapers and magazines, including *Life*, had sent reporters and photographers to cover the event and those cynics who had predicted a sea of empty seats looked on in astonishment as even the aisles began to fill.

When L. Ron Hubbard walked on to the stage, followed by A. E. van Vogt, whom he had recently recruited, and other directors of the Foundation, there was a spontaneous roar from the audience, followed by applause and cheering that continued for several minutes. Hubbard, totally assured and relaxed, smiled broadly as he looked around the packed auditorium and finally held up his hands for silence.

The meeting opened with Hubbard demonstrating Dianetic techniques. With the help of a pretty blonde, he showed how to induce Dianetic reverie and then he 'ran a grief incident' on a girl called Marcia. While the audience obligingly responded when Hubbard spread his arms for applause at the end of each demonstration, it all seemed a little too well rehearsed and there was murmur of approval when someone stood up in the audience and called out: 'Ladies and gentlemen, somehow I can't help but feel that all this has been pre-arranged.'

Immediately people began shouting for Hubbard to demonstrate on someone from the audience and when a young man jumped on to the piano in the orchestra pit, a chant went up: 'Take *him*! Take *him*!' Hubbard, not in the least flustered by this turn of events, invited him up on to the stage. The young man introduced himself as an actor whose father had studied with Freud, which fortuitously gave Hubbard the opportunity of mentioning his own connection with the great analyst, through his old friend 'Snake' Thompson.

Sitting on facing chairs at the front of the stage, Hubbard made a determined attempt to audit the man, but he proved an unresponsive subject, answering almost every question in the negative. The audience soon became bored and restless and began calling, 'Throw him out, throw him out!' Hubbard, perhaps somewhat relieved, shook the man's hand and he stepped down.

The atmosphere throughout had remained perfectly cordial, even if the shouted comments from the audience were increasingly irreverent. When Hubbard was explaining the multitude of mental and physical benefits arising from successful auditing, someone yelled, 'Are your cavities filling up?' and caused a good deal of laughter.

As the highlight of the evening approached, there was a palpable sense of excitement and anticipation in the packed hall. A hush descended on the audience when at last Hubbard stepped up to the microphone to introduce the 'world's first clear'. She was, he said, a young woman by the name of Sonya Bianca, a physics major and pianist from Boston. Among her many newly acquired attributes, he claimed she had 'full and perfect recall of every moment of her life', which she would be happy to demonstrate. He turned slowly to the wings on one side of the stage and said: 'Will you come out now please, Sonya?'

The audience erupted once more in applause as a thin, obviously nervous, girl stepped out of the wings and into a spotlight which followed her to centre stage, where she was embraced by Hubbard. In a tremulous voice she told the meeting that Dianetics had cleared up her sinus trouble and cured her 'strange and embarrassing' allergy to paint. 'For days after I came in contact with paint I had a painful itching in my eyebrows,' she stammered. 'Now both conditions have cleared up and I feel like a million dollars.' She answered a few routine questions from Hubbard, who then made the mistake of inviting questions from the audience: they had clearly been expecting rather more spectacular revelations.

'What did you have for breakfast on October 3 1942?' somebody yelled. Miss Bianca understandably looked somewhat startled, blinked in the lights and shook her head. 'What's on page 122 of *Dianetics, The Modern Science of Mental Health*?' someone else asked. Miss Bianca opened her mouth but no words came out. Similar questions came thick and fast, amid much derisive laughter. Many in the audience took pity on the wretched girl and tried to put easier questions, but she was so terrified that she could not even remember simple formulae in physics, her own subject.

As people began getting up and walking out of the auditorium, one man noticed that Hubbard had momentarily turned his back on the girl and shouted, 'OK, what colour necktie is Mr Hubbard wearing?' The world's first 'clear' screwed up her face in a frantic effort to remember, stared into the hostile blackness of the auditorium, then hung her head in misery. It was an awful moment.

Hubbard, sweat glistening in beads on his forehead, stepped forward and brought the demonstration swiftly to an end. Quick-witted as always, he proffered an explanation for Miss Bianca's impressive lapses of memory. The problem, Dianetically speaking, was that when he called her forward, asking her to come out 'now', the 'now' had frozen her in 'present time' and blocked her total recall. It was not particularly convincing, but it was the best he could do in the circumstances.

Forrie Ackerman, who was at the Shrine that night to see his client perform, summed up the feelings of many people who were there: 'I was somewhat disappointed not to see a vibrant woman in command of herself and situation. She certainly was not my idea of a "clear".'[2]

It would be some time before Hubbard produced another 'Clear', although his followers, in their enthusiasm, would frequently declare that their own protégés had reached that blissful state. One of these was a fifteen-year-old girl of such remarkable powers that she was said to have made her bad teeth fall out and grown new teeth in their place.[3] But no one suggested presenting her at a public meeting.

The débâcle at the Shrine was no more than a hiccup in the rising fortunes of L. Ron Hubbard. When, after the meeting, Ackerman called on his client in his suite at the Frostona Hotel in Los Angeles, Hubbard clapped him on the shoulder and boomed happily: 'Well, Forrie, I'm dragging down Clark Gable's salary.'

It was true: money was literally pouring in. For the first few weeks after van Vogt agreed to take over as head of the Los Angeles Foundation, he recalled doing little but tear open envelopes and pull out $500 cheques from people who wanted to take an auditor's course.[4] Only a few days after the Shrine meeting, the Foundation moved its headquarters into the former official mansion of the governor of California, a sprawling building shaded by palm trees on the corner of South Hoover and Adams, known as the 'Casa' because of its Spanish appearance. Although it cost $4.5 million, enough money had already come in for a down payment. Other branches of the Foundation had opened in New York, Washington DC, Chicago and Honolulu.

But while money was pouring in, it was also pouring out and there was no accounting, no organization, no financial strategy or control. 'One day the bank manager called me,' said van Vogt. 'He told me Mr Hubbard was in the front office and wanted to draw a cashier's cheque for $56,000 and was it all right to give it to him. I said, "He's the boss."'

Trying to hold all the reins, refusing to delegate, Hubbard became ever more authoritarian and suspicious of the people around him. 'He was having a lot of political and organizational problems with people grabbing for power,' said Barbara Kaye [not her real name], a public relations assistant at the Los Angeles Foundation. 'He didn't trust anyone and was highly paranoid. He thought the CIA had hit men after him. We'd be walking along the street and I would ask, "Why are you walking so fast?" He would look over his shoulder and say, "You don't know what it's like to be a target." No one was after him: it was all delusion.'

Barbara Kaye knew a lot about Ron's problems because she was having an affair with him. She was just twenty years old, an exceptionally pretty blonde and a psychology major. 'I wanted to get into public relations and an employment agency sent me along to the Foundation. They were looking for someone to answer the scurrilous attacks that the Press was making on Dianetics. Ron interviewed me for the job and hired me straight away.

'My first impression was of a husky, red-haired man with a full, flabby face – not by any means what one would call handsome. If I'd seen him on the street I wouldn't have given him a second look, but I soon learned he was a very creative, intelligent and articulate individual. He had a marvellous personality and was very dynamic. There was a lot going on in the office at that time and sometimes when I worked late he took me home. One night he kissed me and, well, one thing led to another. That's how it all started. I knew he was married, but I was very young at the time and not as concerned with other men's wives as perhaps I should have been.'

It was an affair squeezed into a hectic timetable. Hubbard was lecturing at the Foundation every day, seven days a week. A. E. van Vogt, who had temporarily abandoned science-fiction writing, got up at 5.30 each morning to drive down to the Casa to open the office. Hubbard arrived an hour later and chaired a daily meeting of the staff instructors, most of whom had received their initial training in Elizabeth, New Jersey. At eight o'clock the first students arrived. Hubbard lectured from eight to nine and demonstrated from nine to ten.

'We had an auditorium that could seat 500 people,' said van Vogt, 'but the lectures were always crowded. You see there was nothing available for ordinary people at that time in the way of therapy. Analysts were a lost cause because they were already charging too much and we offered a complete course for $500. What sticks in my mind was how fluently Ron talked off the top of his head. Every morning it was something different. It amazed me. Where had it all come from? That was the question in my mind. The only thoughts I ever got from Ron were that he had observed things they were doing in China and thought they were pretty good. I think he modified Chinese ideas.'

When he was not lecturing in the evenings, Hubbard spent his time with Barbara, who soon found herself hopelessly in love. She was thrilled when he rented a 'love nest' apartment for them at the Chateau

Marmont Hotel, a fake castle on a hill overlooking Sunset Strip which was a favourite haunt of movie stars. The first night they spent there together, Ron seemed to want to reassure her of the permanence of their relationship. He put his arm round her shoulders and took her through the apartment. 'This is your closet,' he said, 'this is your dressing-table, this is your toothbrush . . .' Barbara was deeply touched.

Two days later, Sara and the baby arrived in town from the East Coast and moved into the love nest. When Barbara turned up for work at the Foundation next morning, she found her toothbrush on her desk, along with the few personal possessions she had left at the apartment. While she stood staring at the pathetic little bundle with tears welling in her eyes, Hubbard came over and hissed his apologies, whispered that his wife was a 'bitch' and that there was nothing he could do. 'I miss you,' he croaked. Then, to Barbara's amazement, he asked her if she would like to have dinner with him and Sara that evening. Speechless, she could do no more than shake her head.

Despite the hurt, Barbara could not bring herself to break off the affair. 'I was completely infatuated. I remember I said to my room-mate – we had a small apartment in Beverly Hills – "If I ever tell you I am marrying this guy I want you to tie me up and not let me out of the door because he's a lunatic." But I didn't trust myself not to do it because I was so enchanted by him. Being with him was like watching a fascinating character playing a role on a stage. I was never bored with him. He was a magical, delightful man, a great raconteur, very bright and amusing and a very gentle, patient and sweet lover.

'At the same time I recognized early on that he was also deeply disturbed. Some of the things he told me were really bizarre, but I never knew what to believe. He said his mother was a lesbian and that he had found her in bed with another woman and that he had been born as the result of an attempted abortion. He talked a lot about his grandfather who could really hold his liquor and played a fiddle with the head of a negro carved on the end, but he never talked about his father and never once mentioned he had children. I did not know he had a son until I read it in the newspapers years later.'

Towards the end of September, Barbara accompanied Hubbard on a lecture tour in the San Francisco area in her capacity as public relations officer of the Hubbard Dianetic Research Foundation. To her acute embarrassment, Sara came to see them off at Union Station and ostentatiously kissed her husband goodbye, at the same time sweeping her eyes up and down Barbara's figure. Hubbard, too, was discomforted and drank a great deal in the club car of the train as it rattled north.

His spirits improved greatly when they arrived in San Francisco and he discovered that a welcoming barbecue party had been arranged at the home of a local Dianeticist. Barbara, however, had an unhappy time – during the course of the evening she wandered into the kitchen and found Hubbard kissing his host's wife. Later that evening when she refused to sleep with him he lost his temper and bellowed, 'They're all against me!' That night, Barbara wrote in her diary: 'I see him now as vain, arrogant, self-centred and unable to tolerate any frustration.'

They soon made it up, as a subsequent passage in her diary recorded: 'Things were better in Oakland. He took a penthouse apartment, I was with him constantly and he fell in love with me a little again and I felt closer to him than ever. He drank excessively and talked in proportion to his intake. Grotesque tales about his family mostly and his hatred of his mother, who he said was a lesbian and a whore . . . He is a deeply unhappy man. He said the only thing to show him affection for the last few years, before he met me, was Calico, his cat.'[5]

In October, Hubbard returned to the East Coast for a few days and was greeted at Elizabeth with the news that the Foundation was approaching a financial crisis – its monthly income could no longer even cover the payroll – and Joseph Winter, the man who had done so much to validate Dianetics, was about to resign.

Winter was deeply disillusioned with the Hubbard Dianetic Research Foundation. He no longer believed that Dianetics was free from risk – two pre-clears had developed acute psychoses during auditing – and he was extremely worried by the Foundation's continuing willingness to accept anyone for training as an auditor.

'People had breakdowns quite often,' said Perry Chapdelaine, a Sears Roebuck clerk from Mason City, Iowa, who was a student at Elizabeth. 'It was always hushed up before anyone found out about it. It happened to a guy on my course, a chemical engineer. They wanted to get him out of the school and I volunteered to stay with him in an adjoining building. He never slept or ate and was in a terrible state, no one could do anything with him and in the end they took him off to an asylum.'[6]

Apart from what he considered to be inherent dangers in allowing anyone to audit anyone, Winter had also begun to doubt whether the state of 'clear' was realistically obtainable. Finally, he was frustrated by the fact that the Research Foundation was making absolutely no attempt to conduct any serious scientific research, which was one of its avowed aims. He had voiced his growing concern on several occasions, only to be airily dismissed by Hubbard. It became clear to Winter that he had no alternative but to resign.[7]

Art Ceppos was largely in sympathy with Winter and also submitted
his resignation. Hubbard's reaction was typically immoderate. Angry
and bitter at what he considered to be a betrayal by two of his earliest
supporters, he spread the word that Winter and Ceppos had been
plotting to seize control of the Foundation and had consequently been
'forced' to resign.[8]

It was not Hubbard's style to be satisfied with simply blackening the
reputation of his enemies – he wanted *revenge*. An opportunity
presented itself in the unlovely form of Senator Joe McCarthy, the
self-seeking demagogue who, in February 1950, had accused the State
Department of being riddled with Communists and Communist
sympathizers. The atmosphere of fear and suspicion generated during
the witch-hunts that followed cast a shadow across America; almost
nothing was worse, during the era of McCarthyism, than to be a
'Commie', or be *thought* to be a 'Commie'. On 3 November 1950, the
general counsel of the Hubbard Dianetic Research Foundation in
Elizabeth contacted the FBI and said that Art Ceppos, president of
Hermitage House, was a Communist sympathizer who had recently
tried to get hold of the Foundation's mailing list of sixteen thousand
names which would be 'valuable to anyone interested in circulating
Communist party literature'.[9]

Hubbard stayed less than a week in Elizabeth and made little
attempt to resolve the financial crisis facing the Foundation. He had
absolutely no interest in balance sheets and operated on the optimistic,
if unrealistic, belief that somehow everything would come out all right
in the end. Further problems, of a more personal nature, arose when
he returned to Los Angeles: he began to suspect his wife was having
an affair. One evening he had insisted on an outlandish double date
with his wife and his lover. Barbara, who hated the idea, reluctantly
showed up to meet Ron and Sara at a Los Angeles restaurant in the
company of Miles Hollister, one of the instructors from the LA
Foundation. 'I think Sara must have known what was going on,' said
Barbara. 'She was very hostile. At one point in the evening we were
talking about guns and she said I looked like the type to carry a
Saturday night special.'

The dinner party back-fired on Hubbard – his lover's date became
his wife's lover. Miles Hollister was twenty-two years old, tall,
dark-haired and strikingly handsome, a graduate of Bard College in
New York State, where he had been president of the student body,
and a sportsman of some repute – he was the first man to land a
swordfish off the coast of Florida using light tackle. In short, he was
everything that Hubbard was not: young, attractive, sporting and
well-connected. It was hardly surprising that Hubbard conceived a
passionate loathing for the young man and predictable that he would

retaliate. His first move was curiously elliptical – he summarily fired two of Hollister's closest friends at the Foundation, claiming they were Communists.

Jack Horner, who was by then working at the Los Angeles Foundation, attempted to intervene on their behalf. 'They were both nice guys and highly trained instructors and I tried to get them off the hook. I went and confronted Hubbard in his office and said, "You can't fire those guys, you don't have any evidence." He ranted and raved, pacing up and down, and said, "You don't understand. I'm fighting a battle here. I might lose some people on the way, but I'm going to win."

'Hubbard was willing to do anything, for him it was any means to an end. A couple of weeks later he got mad at a fellow named Charlie Crail, who had helped set up the LA organization. They had some disagreement about how the place should be run. He called me and another guy into his office and told us to go and steal Charlie's Dianetics certificates. We told him we wouldn't do it and that he shouldn't count on us for that kind of operation. He couldn't understand it. As far as he was concerned, because he had signed the certificates they belonged to him. There were lots of incidents like that, but I was usually prepared to go along with them because I felt his genius far outshone his craziness.'[10]

With his suspicions festering, Hubbard's relationship with Sara deteriorated rapidly. One night they had a violent row and Sara shouted at him, 'Why don't you just go off and spend the weekend with some pretty girl!' Hubbard stormed out of the house, picked up Barbara Kaye and drove to a motel in Malibu, where he spent much of the weekend moodily swigging whisky.

'He was very down in the dumps about his wife,' said Barbara. 'He told me how he had met Sara. He said he went to a party and got drunk and when he woke up in the morning he found Sara was in bed with him. He was having a lot of problems with her. I remember he said to me I was the only person he knew who would set up a white silk tent for him. I was rather surprised when we were driving back to LA on Sunday evening, he stopped at a florist to buy some flowers for his wife.'

Barbara kept a meticulous diary in which she constantly analyzed and re-analyzed her affair with Hubbard, speculated on his mental condition and recorded day-to-day drama. On Monday 27 November, she noted that Hubbard burst into her office that morning 'tremendously emotionally disturbed'. Sara had tried to commit suicide over the weekend by taking sleeping pills, he said, after Barbara had spoken to her on the telephone. He assumed Barbara had told her about their affair.

It was not true. Barbara had telephoned to speak to Hubbard about Foundation business and had only exchanged a few words with Sara after learning Ron was not at home. Hubbard would not believe it: he had audited Sara and 'recovered an engram' indicating that her suicide attempt was triggered by Barbara's telephone call.

An argument inevitably followed and Barbara recontructed the extraordinary 'highlights' in her journal, very much as if she was writing a pulp romance:

'ME: You make a habit of *instilling* engrams, too, don't you? That's fine. That's good behaviour for the founder of Dianetics.

HE: Isn't it exciting for you being a pawn on such a grand chess board? You are playing for the world. Can you think of anything more exciting?

ME: I don't give a good God damn about the world. I want a single, gratifying, human relationship.

HE: You couldn't have one. You're an ambitious woman. You crave power. You're a Marie Antoinette, a Cleopatra, a Lucretia Borgia . . . you must have a Caesar or an Alexander.

ME: No, I don't need a Caesar, though Caesar may need me. I know you now, Ron, and at this moment am closer to you than anyone has ever been.

HE: (Head hung low) And knowing me you don't care for me any more.

ME: I care for you in a different, new and exciting way. (He put his hands on my shoulders and drew me to him.)

HE: I shouldn't do this. (He kissed me.)

ME: You still care for me.

HE: How do you know?

ME: You can't find your hat. You're distracted.

HE: That makes you feel powerful, doesn't it?

ME: It makes me aware of something interesting. You still want me.

HE: Why?

ME: Because you need me. You need me more than I need you.

HE: In 1939 I was very much in love with a girl. She felt that way too. When I knew she had a boyfriend coming up, I waited on the stairway with a gun, just for a moment. Then I said they are flies. I realized who and what I was and left. I told her I would leave her free to marry a sharpie with a cigar in his mouth from Muncie, Indiana. Would you like to be left free?

ME: The alternative is a sharpie with a Kool cigarette from Elizabeth, New Jersey.

HE: That was unwise, very unwise, of you to say that.'

Barbara discovered just how unwise it was when, two days later, she received a terse message via Western Union: 'Would advise you to forget all about me and the Foundation – Ron.' 'I was in shock,' she recalled. 'Here was the man I was supposed to be having a great love affair with telling me I was fired.'

A. E. van Vogt, meanwhile, was striving to keep the Los Angeles Foundation in business. He calculated that the six Hubbard Dianetic Research Foundations had spent around one million dollars and were more than $200,000 in debt. At the beginning of November, while Hubbard was away on the East Coast, van Vogt cut the staff of sixty by half in an attempt to stay solvent. Hubbard was furious and began hiring indiscriminately the moment he returned: within a week, the payroll was back up to sixty-seven people. Van Vogt remonstrated, but Hubbard insisted that the extra staff was needed for research. 'Financial disaster was inevitable,' said van Vogt.[11]

One of the research projects about which Hubbard was very excited was the aptly named 'GUK' programme. 'GUK' was a haphazard cocktail of benzedrine, vitamins and glutamic acid which Hubbard believed facilitated auditing. 'I recall Ron telling a meeting about this great breakthrough in Dianetics,' said Forrest Ackerman. 'He said he had discovered a chemical way to audit yourself called GUK. It comprised huge quantities of vitamins which you took every two hours for at least twenty-four hours. If you took enough, he said, it would release the engrams within you without the need for a partner.

'The Foundation rented a huge complex on Rossmore near Beverly and loads of Dianeticists were holed up there going through the GUK programme but it didn't last too long – I think it was a dead end.'

In December, *Look* magazine published a scathing article under the headline 'Dianetics – Science or Hoax?' The text left the reader in little doubt as to which the magazine thought it was. 'Half a million laymen have swallowed this poor man's psychiatry . . .' it began. 'Hubbard has demonstrated once again that Barnum underestimated the sucker birth rate.' The tens of thousands of people who had swallowed Hubbard's doctrine were characterized as 'the usual lunatic fringe types, frustrated maiden ladies who have worked their way through all the available cults, young men whose homosexual engrams are all too obvious . . .' The article referred to the 'awe, fear and deep disgust' with which the medical profession viewed Dianetics and quoted a doctor at the famous Menninger Clinic in Topeka, Kansas, who conceded that sufferers from mental malaise might find temporary relief from 'Dianetic hocus pocus' just as they sometimes do from hypnotism or voodoo. 'But,' he added, 'the greatest harm to a person would come not because of the vicious nature of Dianetic therapy but because it will lead them away from treatment which they may badly need.'

Hubbard's primary attraction, *Look* concluded, was that his ersatz psychiatry was available to all. 'It's cheap. It's accessible. It's a public festival to be played at clubs and parties. In a country with only 6000 professional psychiatrists, whose usual consultation fees start at $15 an hour, Hubbard has introduced mass-production methods. Whether such methods can actually help you if you're sick is a moot point.'

As always in the face of an attack, particularly from the direction of the despised media, committed Dianeticists closed ranks and there was no lack of cheer at the LA Foundation's Christmas party, attended by staff and students alike. Barbara Kaye turned up and was asked to dance by Hubbard. 'I need some counselling, doctor,' she whispered in his ear. 'What do you do with a pre-clear who keeps dreaming she is in bed with you?' He grinned broadly and replied, 'I have been thinking of beginning a series of empirical tests on the result of substituting the reality for the dream.' Within a few days, their affair resumed: on New Year's Eve, Hubbard missed the party he was supposed to attend with Sara and spent the night with Barbara at her apartment on Dale Drive in Beverly Hills.

In January 1951, the New Jersey Board of Medical Examiners instituted proceedings against the Hubbard Dianetic Research Foundation in Elizabeth, accusing it of teaching medicine without a licence. The Foundation hired an attorney who was confident he could defend the suit, but there was a strong feeling among the directors that they should 'skip'; inquiries were instituted to find a state where they would be more welcome.[12] Hubbard, who clearly thought the prospects in New Jersey looked bleak, asked two reliable students at Elizabeth – John Sanborn and Greg Hemingway, the youngest son of the writer – to load all his personal possessions into his black Lincoln limousine and drive it to Los Angeles.

In the interim, perhaps still hoping to save his marriage, he persuaded Sara and the baby to accompany him to Palm Springs, where he had rented a single-storey adobe house with a small garden of flowering shrubs on Mel Avenue. He wanted to get away from the distractions of Los Angeles, he explained, to start writing a sequel to *Dianetics*. It was to be called *Science of Survival* and would introduce faster, simplified auditing techniques.

Hubbard, Sara and Alexis were joined in Palm Springs by Richard de Mille, son of the film director Cecil B. de Mille, who had recently been appointed Hubbard's personal assistant. 'Although it never occurred to me at the time, I think my name had something to do with it,' de Mille acknowledged. 'He liked to collect celebrities. I had got into Dianetics as early as possible after reading the article in *Astounding* and I was working at the LA Foundation making publications out of Hubbard's lectures when he asked me to go with him to Palm Springs.

'There was a lot of turmoil and dissension in the Foundation at the time; he kept accusing Communists of trying to take control and he was having difficulties with Sara. It was clear their marriage was breaking up – she was very critical of him and he told me she was fooling around with Hollister and he didn't trust her.'[13]

Predictably, Sara did not stay long in Palm Springs – the tension was more than she could stand. Hubbard did not try to detain her and as soon as she and Alexis had departed for Los Angeles, he sent a telegram to Barbara Kaye telling her he loved her and needed her. She caught a bus for Palm Springs on 3 February and was met by Hubbard at the bus station. 'As he walked towards me,' she said, 'I could see that he was ill.'

Kaye, who would later become a psychologist, said she made a clinical diagnosis of Hubbard during the weeks they spent together in Palm Springs. 'There was no doubt in my mind he was a manic depressive with paranoid tendencies. Many manics are delightful, productive people with tremendous energy and self-confidence. He was like that in his manic stage – enormously creative, carried away by feelings of omnipotence and talking all the time of grandiose schemes.

'But when I arrived he was in a deep depression. He had been totally unable to work on his book, which had been originally scheduled for publication that month. That's why he had called me— he was hoping I could help him get through his writers' block. He was very sad and lethargic, lying around feeling sorry for himself and drinking a great deal. Sometimes he would go to the piano and fiddle around, improvising weird melodies of his own composition. He thought that Sara had hypnotised him in his sleep and commanded him not to write. He told me that the people in Elizabeth had tried to "slip him a Mickey" in his glass of milk and another time they attempted to insert a fatal hypo into his eye and heart to try and stop him from ever writing again. Those were the engrams he was running.

'I tried to help him by using a technique I had learned at college, breaking down the problem into small parts and presenting it a step at a time. I got a block of butcher's paper and said to him, "Look, you don't have to write. Just sit down at this table and look at the paper and when you don't want to look at it any more, get up and leave." He sat there for ten minutes on the first day and this went on for several days until one day he picked up a pencil and began to write. Next day he was back at work, very excited and enthused about what he was doing. He was singing and horsing around, talking, laughing and discussing ideas in the kitchen until three o'clock in the morning.'

One of Hubbard's favourite topics of conversation was psychiatrists. One night over dinner at Mel Avenue, he told Barbara about an occasion when he had demonstrated auditing techniques to a group of psychiatrists and one of them had said to him, 'If you claim to cure people by doing that, if you're not careful we'll lock you up.' He laughed excessively, took a bite out of a chicken leg and spluttered, 'They called me a paranoid, can you imagine it?' That night Barbara wrote in her diary: 'My blood ran cold as he was saying that. It was all I could do to keep from weeping.'

Barbara had been in Palm Springs for nearly three weeks when Ron began fretting that 'something was brewing' in Los Angeles. He decided that they should return immediately, even though the book was not yet finished.

'I didn't see him for a week after we got back,' Barbara said, 'then he turned up at my place at about five o'clock one afternoon, very distraught and pale, with his hair all over the place. He paced up and down in my room and told me he had discovered Miles and Sara in bed together. He was afraid that they were plotting with a psychiatrist in San Francisco to get him committed to a mental institution. Sara had telephoned Jack Maloney, the general manager in Elizabeth, and said a doctor had recommended he should be treated for paranoid schizophrenia. He said he had found letters proving that Miles was conspiring with Ceppos and Winter to get control of the Foundation. "Please don't ask me anything," he said. "I'm in a very bad way. I'm going to the desert for a few days alone. Things are very bad."'

Hubbard did not go off into the desert alone. He had other plans: he was going to get Sara committed before she committed him. But first he had to kidnap Alexis.

On the evening of Saturday, 24 February 1951, John Sanborn was babysitting for eleven-month-old Alexis Hubbard at the Casa on Hoover and Adams in Los Angeles. Several of the staff, Sanborn included, lived in one wing of the building. Sanborn and Greg Hemingway used to hang around with Hank and Marge Hunter, who worked in the research department; they'd usually eat together in a little joint down the road called 'The Bread Line'. Marge, who was a friend of Sara's, had a baby daughter the same age as Alexis and Sara occasionally left Alexis with Marge when she wanted to go out.

This particularly Saturday evening, Sanborn was tired and when there was a suggestion that they should all go to the movies, he offered to stay behind and look after the kids. He had done it lots of times before, knew all about changing nappies and giving them bottles. Marge was grateful and went off with the others, happy to have a night out, leaving Sanborn in charge of her daughter, Tam, and 'Lexie'.

At about eleven o'clock there was an urgent rapping at the door. Sanborn opened it and found Frank Dessler, one of Hubbard's aides, standing on the doorstep wearing a long topcoat and wide-brimmed felt hat. His hands were thrust into his coat pockets in such a way that Sanborn was positive he was carrying a gun. 'Mr Hubbard's coming,' Dessler rasped. 'He's here to get Alexis.' Sanborn thought it was a hell of a time of night to do it, but said nothing.

A few minutes later, Hubbard came in, also wearing a topcoat and felt hat. 'We're just taking Alexis,' he said. Sanborn led the way to the room where both children were sleeping. Hubbard leaned over and picked up a toy from Alexis's crib. 'This hers?' he asked. Sanborn shook his head and Hubbard threw it on the floor. While they were getting the baby's things together, Sanborn started to say, 'Listen, if she wakes up in the night there's a certain routine . . .' but Hubbard cut him short. 'I don't care about that,' he snapped. 'We've got a nurse for her and we're taking her to Palm Springs.' He picked Alexis out of her crib, still asleep, and hurried away into the night.

Sanborn wondered idly what was going on, but he went to bed soon afterwards. At one o'clock in the morning he was woken by someone shaking him violently and he sat up with a start to find Miles Hollister standing over his bed. If he had not been so sleepy, he would have laughed: Hollister, too, was wearing a long topcoat and felt hat and also appeared to be carrying a gun. 'Where did Ron take Lexie?' he demanded. Sanborn rubbed his eyes and mumbled, 'Palm Springs'. 'When did they leave?' Hollister asked. It seemed that Sanborn did not respond quickly enough, for Hollister shouted '*When did they leave?*' Sanborn told him and he hurried out of the room. A few minutes later, Sanborn heard Hollister revving his car outside.

Hollister headed out of town at high speed in the direction of Palm Springs, which was exactly what Hubbard had intended him to do. By then, Alexis had been handed over to the twenty-four-hour Westwood Nurses Registry in Los Angeles. Hubbard, posing as a businessman by the name of James Olsen, had asked the agency to arrange for his child, Anne-Marie, to be put in the care of a competent nurse for about a month because his wife had suddenly been taken seriously ill and business commitments required him to leave immediately for the East Coast. Melba McGonigel, the owner of the agency, was deeply suspicious but agreed to take the baby after 'Mr Olsen' had signed a 'To whom it may concern' statement releasing the agency of any responsibility.

Shortly after one o'clock on the morning of 25 February, a black Lincoln drew up outside the Hubbards' apartment at 1251 Westmoreland Avenue in West Los Angeles. Richard de Mille was at the wheel, Hubbard and Frank Dessler were in the back. Inside the house, Sara sat in her nightgown by the telephone, weeping into a handkerchief as she waited for news of Alexis. She jumped up in alarm when she heard a key scraping at the door, but her fear turned to anger when her husband and Dessler appeared in the doorway. 'Where's Lexie?' she screamed. Neither man said a word. They grabbed her by each arm, one of them clamped a hand over her mouth and they bustled her out of the house, across the sidewalk and into the back of the car, which drove off at speed.

Sara fought like a cat in the back of the car, screaming and shouting at Hubbard, who in turn was shouting at her. At one point, when the car stopped at traffic lights, she tried to leap out and thereafter Hubbard gripped her round the neck in a stranglehold while the argument continued. 'She was enraged at being hauled off and was fulminating insults in all directions,' said de Mille. 'She was very bitter about their marriage and his conduct and Ron was fulminating against Miles Hollister and *her* conduct.'

At Los Angeles city limit, Dessler was dropped off and the Lincoln sped on towards San Bernardino, where Ron hoped to get Sara medically examined and declared insane. 'She was eager to get the same opinion about him,' de Mille declared, 'but Ron held all the cards at that point.' There followed a ludicrous farce as they toured the dark streets of San Bernardino trying to find a doctor while Sara alternately screamed at, and pleaded with, her husband to tell her where he had taken Alexis. Eventually, Hubbard went into the county hospital while de Mille guarded Sara in the car. He returned after some few minutes, apparently surprised and disgusted that there was no doctor available in the early hours of the morning willing to declare his wife insane.

At dawn, the Lincoln could be seen trailing a cloud of dust as it headed east across the desert towards the Arizona border; Hubbard had ordered de Mille to drive to the airport at Yuma. The angry squabbling in the back of the car had not let up for a moment. Sara swore again and again that she would have Ron arrested for kidnapping the moment she was free and he swore that if she did she would never see Alexis again. The mutual threats and recriminations continued while Hubbard was thinking hard how he could extricate himself from the situation.

Parked in the watery early morning sunshine in a quiet corner of Yuma airport, the warring couple at last agreed on a temporary truce. Hubbard promised to release Sara and tell her where Alexis was if she signed a piece of paper saying that she had gone with him voluntarily. Sara tearfully signed and Hubbard scribbled a note to Dessler: 'Feb. 25. To Frank – This will authorize Sara to take Alexis to live with her when she has a house. L. Ron Hubbard.' He jotted down the name of the agency he said was caring for Alexis – 'Baby Sitters Inc, Hollywood phone book' – and added, 'Give Sara the baby's address now so Sara can see her.'

Hubbard and de Mille got out of the car and Sara, still in her nightgown, drove back to Los Angeles clutching the piece of paper she believed would enable her to be re-united with her baby. But Hubbard had no intention of permitting such a reunion. 'He believed that as long as he had the child he could control the situation,' de Mille explained.

While Sara was on her way back to Los Angeles, Hubbard was standing in a telephone booth at Yuma airport giving urgent instructions to Frank Dessler. He was to arrange for Alexis to be collected from her nurse before Sara got there. No matter what it cost, he was then to hire a reliable couple to drive the baby to Elizabeth, New Jersey, where Hubbard would meet her.

It did not take long for Sara to discover that Ron had misled her but by the time she had persuaded Dessler to reveal the baby's whereabouts it was too late. She arrived at the Westwood nursery just two hours after Alexis had been taken away. Sara filed a kidnapping complaint with Los Angeles police department, but Hubbard was lucky – the police dismissed the incident as a domestic dispute which was nothing to do with them.

Hubbard did not go directly to Elizabeth because he wanted to block any further attempts Sara might make to have him committed. Accompanied by the loyal de Mille, he caught a commuter plane to Phoenix and from there they flew to Chicago, where Hubbard presented himself for examination by a psychiatrist and a psychologist, both equally bemused.

'He wanted a testimonial from a professional who would say he was OK and that he was not a paranoid schizophrene,' said de Mille. 'He and I went first to a psychiatrist who didn't like the smell of it. He obviously thought he was being manipulated, so we just paid him $10 and left. Then we went to a prominent diagnostic psychologist of that era who did some projective testing on Hubbard and produced an upbeat, harmless report, saying that he was a creative individual upset by family problems and dissension and it was depressing his work and so forth. It was very bland but Hubbard was delighted with it. The main value of it to him was that it didn't say he was crazy, so he could claim he had been given a clean bill of health by the psychiatric profession.'

Before leaving Chicago, Hubbard called at the offices of the FBI to alert them of his suspicions that one of his employees was a Communist. The man's name, he was far from reluctant to reveal, was Miles Hollister.[14] Hubbard and de Mille then flew to New York and caught a taxi to Elizabeth, where the Hubbard Dianetic Research Foundation was still in operation, although besieged by creditors. They checked into a hotel and waited for Alexis to arrive.

While they were there, a further complication entered Hubbard's already entangled private life: Polly Hubbard filed suit in Port Orchard, Washington, for maintenance, alleging that her former husband had 'promoted a cult called Dianetics', had authored a bestseller, owned valuable property and was well able to afford payment of maintenance for his two children, Nibs, then sixteen, and Katie, fifteen. Hubbard responded by claiming that his first wife was not a fit and proper person to have control of the children because she 'drinks to excess and is a dipsomaniac'.

On 3 March 1951, Hubbard, in his role as patriotic citizen, wrote to the FBI in Washington to provide the names and descriptions of fifteen 'known or suspected Communists' within his organization. Heading the list were his wife and her lover:

'SARA NORTHRUP (HUBBARD): formerly of 1003 S. Orange Grove Avenue, Pasadena, Calif. 25 yrs. of age, 5'10", 140lbs. Currently missing somewhere in California. Suspected only. Had been friendly with many Communists. Currently intimate with them but evidently under coercion. Drug addiction set in fall 1950. Nothing of this known to me until a few weeks ago. Separation papers being filed and divorce applied for.

'MILES HOLLISTER: Somewhere in the vicinity of Los Angeles. Evidently a prime mover but very young. About 22 yrs, 6', 180lbs. Black hair. Sharp chin, broad forehead, rather Slavic. Confessedly a member of the Young Communists. Center of most turbulence in our organization. Dissmissed [*sic*] in February when affiliations discovered. Active and dangerous. Commonly armed. Outspokenly disloyal to the U.S.'

FBI director John Edgar Hoover replied promptly: 'I wish to thank you for the information you have made available to this Bureau.'[15]

Four days later, Hubbard kept an appointment, arranged at his request, with an FBI agent from the Internal Security Section. His intention was to press home his accusations against Hollister, as was evident from the agent's report: 'Hubbard advised that he felt that Communists within his organization were undermining its structure. He advised that he had turned over the names of several suspected Communists to the FBI office in Los Angeles. Hubbard could only recall the name of one of these individuals. He stated Miles Hollister was one of the individuals he suspected of being Communistically inclined. Concerning Hollister, Hubbard stated that he was instrumental in driving Hubbard's wife, Sara Elizabeth Northrup, to the point of insanity. Hubbard expressed considerable concern in connection with Hollister's influence on his wife. He stated that his wife, as well as his Army .45 automatic, had been missing for several days . . .'

Later in the interview, Hubbard disclosed that Russia was interested in his work. 'Hubbard stated that he strongly feels that Dianetics can be used to combat Communism. However, he declined to elaborate on how this might be done. He stated that the Soviets apparently realized the value of Dianetics because as early as 1938 an official of Amtorg, while at The Explorers Club in New York, contacted him to suggest that he go to Russia and develop Dianetics there.

'In an apparent attempt to give credence to his statements, Hubbard advised that he was recently psychoanalyzed in Chicago and was found to be quite normal . . .'[16] The FBI agent conducting the interview could not agree: he concluded that Hubbard was a 'mental case'.[17]

During his short stay in Elizabeth, Hubbard managed to alienate his old friend and mentor, John W. Campbell, who resigned from the Foundation and thus joined Hubbard's lengthening list of enemies. In Campbell's view, Hubbard had become impossible to work with and was responsible for the ruinous finances and complete disorganization throughout the Dianetics movement. (Dessler wrote to Hubbard on 9 March to say that none of the staff at the LA Foundation had been paid for more than two weeks, but Hubbard seemed unconcerned.)

Soon after Alexis arrived, Hubbard announced to de Mille that they were going to go south, where it was warmer, so that he could continue with his book. It had been snowing for weeks in Elizabeth and de Mille was not in least the sorry to leave, even though Hubbard had made it clear that it would be his responsibility to care for the baby.

They were unlikely fellow travellers: a large, forty-year-old man with a florid complexion, flaming red hair and a Kool cigarette constantly between his lips; his diminutive companion, twenty-nine years old, rather shy and very much in awe of the older man; and a gurgling twelve-month-old baby in nappies just learning to walk. The three of them arrived in Tampa, Florida, in the middle of March. They took two rooms in a small hotel: Hubbard had a room to himself, de Mille and the baby shared. 'It never crossed my mind that the baby should go in with him,' said de Mille. 'He was the leader and I was the follower. He gave the orders; I was privileged to serve.'

Hubbard pretended to look for property in Tampa, but de Mille noticed that he seemed nervous and ill at ease much of the time. 'One evening I knocked on his door and he opened it carrying a loaded .45 service automatic. I must have looked a bit surprised because he said, "You shouldn't creep up on me like that, Dick." I didn't even know he had a gun until that moment.'

A couple of days later Hubbard said to de Mille: 'I don't like the way things feel around here. I want to go to a place where I can breathe free. We're going to Havana.'

Havana in the early 'fifties, before Castro, was the fun capital of the Western hemisphere – a corrupt, colourful, hedonistic, wide-open city where tourists with money were guaranteed a good time. Americans did not even need a passport to enter Cuba and no one raised an eyebrow at the two men who arrived from Florida in the company of an apparently motherless baby. They took a taxi downtown and checked into a hotel on the Paseo Marti, Havana's bustling main street.

'Hubbard managed to rent a very old Spanish typewriter', de Mille recalled, 'and was madly banging away on it all night, while I was taking care of the baby and trying to sleep with the water pipes rattling in the wall. After we had stayed there a couple of nights, we went to a real estate agent and rented a ground-floor apartment in the Vedado district, the Beverly Hills of Havana. Once we had moved in, we hired two Jamaican women to look after Alexis, which was a great relief to me.'

Comfortably installed in the apartment, Hubbard began working intensively on his book, dictating into a recording machine. As was his usual habit, he worked all night with little to sustain him but a bottle of rum, which was usually empty by dawn.

In the afternoons, he would often sit and talk with de Mille. 'He talked about himself a lot, but as is often true with that kind of person he didn't really give me any confidences: he was telling me his story as he thought I ought to know it. He told me about Jack Parsons and Aleister Crowley and all that. He didn't take any responsibility for the black magic rituals and blamed them on Parsons, but he admitted he was there.

'What I didn't understand about him at the time was his lack of personal attachment. He thought people were there to be used, to serve the user and didn't have any importance in their own right. I don't think he abducted Alexis, for example, with any intention of keeping her; he was just using her to keep control of the situation.

'When I first saw him at the meeting at The Shrine auditorium I was very impressed. I thought he was a great man who had made a great discovery and whatever his shortcomings they must be discounted because he had the answer. He promised heaven. He said I have the key which can open the door, do you want to go there? It did not matter that his qualifications were suspect; he held the key. Actually, he was very widely read, a sort of self-made intellectual. I don't think he did any research in the academic sense, but he knew a lot about Freud, hypnosis, the occult, magic, etcetera, and Dianetics grew out of that knowledge.

bram Waterbury, L. Ron
ubbard's great-grandfather,
aying the fiddle carved
ith a negro's head
at became part of
mily legend.

(BELOW) Ron's grandfather was
supposed to have owned a
quarter of the state of
Montana. Here he is
seen as he really
was, a struggling
veterinarian,
pictured with his
wife and their first
child (Ron's mother)
at Tilden, Nebraska,
around the late
1880s.

Ledora May Waterbury, Ron's mother (left), with an unknown relative, her sisters Toilie and Midgie and brother Ray photographed in their home town of Helena, Montana.

Ron's long-suffering mother. He remembered her sometimes with affection, sometimes with deep dislike.

Harry Ross Hubbard in the dress uniform of an officer of the US Navy. Promotion eluded him and debtors pursued him.

(ABOVE LEFT) The hospital in
[T]ilden, Nebraska, where L. Ron
[H]ubbard was born in 1911. His
[Au]nt Toilie, who worked in the
[ho]spital, is second from the right.

(ABOVE RIGHT) Little Ron in a
[sa]ilor hat. One day he would be
[th]e self-appointed commodore of
[hi]s own private navy.

(RIGHT) The budding science-
[fic]tion writer poses at his
[ty]pewriter during a visit to his
[pa]rents on the island of Guam in
[19]28.

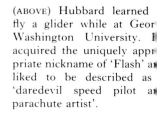

(ABOVE) Hubbard learned to fly a glider while at George Washington University. He acquired the uniquely appropriate nickname of 'Flash' and liked to be described as a 'daredevil speed pilot and parachute artist'.

(LEFT) Dianetics makes its inauspicious début, in the pages of a pulp science fiction magazine.

Between his second and third marriages, Ron dallied with his public relations assistant, luscious Barbara Kaye. She would soon conclude that he was paranoid.

(BELOW) Richard de Mille and Barbara Kaye at the house in Palm Springs where Hubbard plotted to kidnap his daughter Alexis.

(RIGHT) The portly Nibs (second from right) posing with his father and friends in a London garden in the 1950s – the smiles would soon turn to tears when father and son fell out.

Hubbard as 'revolutionary horticultural scientist', proving that plants can feel pain. (*Rex Features Ltd*)

(RIGHT) Dr Hubbard, the 'nuclear scientist', on the steps of Saint Hill, the Georgian manor house he bought out of the proceeds of Dianetics. (*Photo Source Ltd*)

Hubbard as genial family man. From the left Suzette (4), his wife Mary Sue, Quentin (5), Arthur (1) and Diana (7). All were to suffer in various ways. (*Photo Source Ltd*)

Hubbard believed he was a reincarnation of Cecil Rhodes and liked to sport the kind of hat worn by the founder of Rhodesia. Fortunately, he did not know Rhodes was homosexual.

(LEFT) Hubbard with his friend Ray Kemp on a two-day trip to Ireland during which he hoped to solve the 'Irish problem'.

Rare picture of the 'mystery ship', the *Royal Scotman*, in which the commodore sailed the Mediterranean. (*Granada Television Ltd*)

Arthur Hubbard and Doreen Smith, one of the messengers, playing with fire in the Californian desert. Like his father, Arthur collected guns.

The family business: Hubbard and his daughter Diana. At 17, she was a senior officer on the flagship.
(Copyright © Times Newspapers Ltd.)

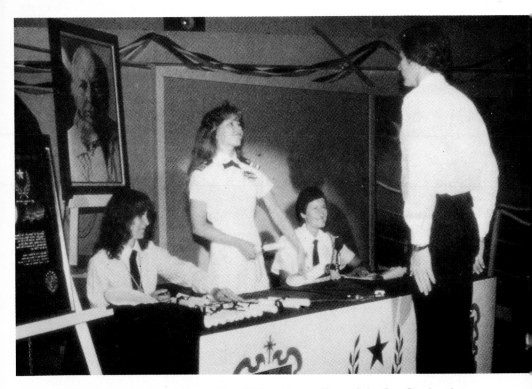

Under a portrait of a benign L. Ron Hubbard, an officer of the Sea Org hands out certificates at Gilman Hot Springs in 1981. The founder of Scientology had already gone to ground.

'I don't think Dianetics were necessarily successful because the time was right. The time is never wrong for a cultist movement. People present new ideas which they say are going to change the world and there are always a certain number of people who believe them. Lenin was the Hubbard of 1917. Hubbard was the Madame Blavatsky of 1950.'

Hubbard's ability to concentrate on his work was subjected to a severe setback when the American newspapers of Thursday 12 April arrived in Cuba. Sara had at last blown the whistle and filed a writ at Los Angeles Superior Court demanding the return of her child. The headlines told the story: 'Cult Founder Accused of Tot Kidnap', '"Dianetic" Hubbard Accused of Plot to Kidnap Wife', 'Hiding of Baby Charged to Dianetics Author'. Most newspapers carried a picture of the distraught mother, smiling broadly.

After digesting this less than welcome news, Hubbard sat down and wrote a letter to Sara. It was dated 15 April and contained all the pulp writer's flair for fantasy:

'Dear Sara,
I have been in the Cuban military hospital and I am being transferred to the United States next week as a classified scientist immune from interference of all kinds.

Though I will be hospitalized probably a long time, Alexis is getting excellent care. I see her every day. She is all I have to live for.

My wits never gave way under all you did and let them do but my body didn't stand up. My right side is paralyzed and getting more so. I hope my heart lasts. I may live a long time and again I may not. But Dianetics will last 10,000 years – for the Army and Navy have it now.

My Will is all changed. Alexis will get a fortune unless she goes to you as she would then get nothing. Hope to see you once more. Goodbye – I love you.
Ron.'

The next day, Hubbard marched into the US Embassy in Havana, insisted on seeing the military attaché and asked for protection from Communists who, he said, were trying to steal his research material. He appealed, as one officer to another, for help. The attaché, clearly sceptical, murmured something about 'seeing what he could do' and cabled the FBI in Washington for 'any pertinent information' about his wild-eyed visitor. Back came the reply that Hubbard had been interviewed on 7 March last and that 'agent conducting interview considered Hubbard to be mental case'.

De Mille had not noticed the paralysis Hubbard mentioned in his moving letter to Sara, nor indeed was he aware that Hubbard was interned in a military hospital, but he certainly registered a drooping in his spirits. 'He began to get very nervous again and complained that he wasn't feeling well. He said he had to move downtown, so we broke our lease and moved into the Packard Hotel, which faced the park and overlooked the entrance to the harbour and the prison. There he proceeded to get sick. It was probably an ulcer, but he said it was the result of pain-drug hypnosis which Sara and Winter had done way back.'

The news from Los Angeles was not calculated to make him feel any better. On 23 April, Sara filed for divorce, citing 'extreme cruelty, great mental anguish and physical suffering'. Her allegations were sensational. Apart from charging Hubbard with bigamy and kidnapping, Sara claimed he had subjected her to 'systematic torture, including loss of sleep, beatings, and strangulations and scientific experiments'. Because of his 'crazy misconduct' she was in 'hourly fear of both the life of herself and of her infant daughter, who she has not seen for two months'.

All the salacious details were included in the divorce complaint. While they were living at the Chateau Marmont, Sara said Ron had told her he no longer wanted to be married to her but did not want a divorce as it might damage his reputation. His suggestion was that she 'should kill herself if she really loved him'. Subsequently he prevented her from sleeping for a period of four days and then gave her sleeping pills 'resulting in a nearness to the shadow of death'.

Sara accused her husband of frequently trying to strangle her; on one occasion, shortly before Christmas 1950, he had been so violent he ruptured the Eustachian tube in her left ear. The following month, at Palm Springs, he had started his car in gear while she was getting out and knocked her to the ground.

As a result of Hubbard's behaviour, the divorce complaint continued, the 'plaintiff and her medical advisers . . . concluded that said Hubbard was hopelessly insane, and, crazy, and that there was no hope for said Hubbard, or any reason for her to endure further; that competent medical advisers recommended that said Hubbard be committed to a private sanitarian for pshychiatric observation and treatment of a mental ailment known as paranoid schizophrenia . . .'[18]

Caryl Warner, Sara's flamboyant Hollywood attorney, did his best to ensure the case received maximum publicity. The reporters covering the Divorce Court for the *LA Times* and the *Examiner* were both women and early feminists. 'Before the case I made sure they knew what a bastard this guy Hubbard was,' said Warner. 'I told them he was a sadist, that he'd kept his wife awake for days and burned her with cigarettes and that he was crazy, crazy like a fox. They could hardly wait for me to file the complaint.

'I liked Sara and Miles a lot. They eventually married and got a house in Malibu and we became friends; I remember they introduced me to pot. I believed Sara absolutely; there was no question about the truth in my opinion. When she first came to me with this wild story about how her husband had taken her baby I was determined to help her all I could. I telephoned Hubbard's lawyer in Elizabeth and warned him: "Listen, asshole, if you don't get that baby back I'm going to burn you."'[19]

The first singe was inflicted by the damaging headlines in newspapers across the country the day after the kidnapping complaint was filed on 11 April. (The only unforeseen setback to Warner's carefully laid plans was that President Harry S. Truman inconveniently chose the same day to sack General Douglas MacArthur for insubordination in Korea and thus rather hogged the front page.) The divorce itself received more extensive coverage and was better handled: the pictures of Sara smiling broadly were replaced by pictures of her weeping pitifully and being comforted by her attorney.

In Cuba, Hubbard's condition regressed. 'I think what really caught up with him,' said de Mille, 'was that he felt he was losing control of the organization. That's what it amounted to.'

There was no question that Hubbard's fortunes had undergone a radical revision in the twelve months since his emergence as the adored founder of Dianetics. His personal life was in disarray, the Hubbard Dianetic Research Foundations in Elizabeth and Los Angeles were disintegrating, most of the money had somehow been frittered away, he was months behind with his second book and he was stuck in Cuba with Alexis and he had no idea what to do with her.

What he needed was a saviour, preferably a saviour with plenty of ready cash. And there was one obvious candidate – Don Purcell, a businessman in Wichita, Kansas. Mr Purcell was not only an enthusiastic Dianeticist, he also happened to be a millionaire.

Towards the end of April, Hubbard sent a telegram to Purcell from Havana saying he needed help. De Mille followed up with a long-distance telephone call urging Purcell to 'do something' because Ron was dying. Purcell acted without delay. He sent a private plane to Cuba with a registered nurse on board to collect Ron and Alexis and bring them back to Kansas. (De Mille had been instructed to stay behind and finish transcribing Ron's plastic recording discs.)

As a follower of Dianetics, Purcell was delighted and honoured to be able to play host to L. Ron Hubbard in Wichita. It was a pleasure that would be short-lived.

Chapter 11

Bankrolling and Bankruptcy

'Fur coats, Lincoln cars and a young man without any concept of honor so far turned the head of the woman who had been associated with me that on discovery of her affairs, she and these others, hungry for money and power, sought to take over and control all of Dianetics.' (L. Ron Hubbard, *Dianetics: Axioms*, October 1951)

* * * * *

Don Purcell was a shy, unassuming man who was once a short-order chef in a little fourteen-stool cafe opposite the Orpheum Theater in downtown Wichita before he made his fortune in oil and real estate during the post-war boom. Very tall and thin – he was usually described as all 'skin and bones' – he turned to Dianetics in the hope of finding a cure for his chronic constipation.[1]

He attended an auditor's course at Elizabeth with his wife in the autumn of 1950 and returned to Wichita brimming with enthusiasm for the new science. Although he never mentioned if it had eased his constipation, he did frequently claim that Dianetics had given him the ability to work a twenty-two-hour day, which was useful to a real estate developer in Wichita in 1951. The farming town in the heart of the winter wheat belt had been transformed by the arrival of the oil and aircraft industries and it was expanding at a phenomenal rate. Roads, houses, schools, churches, office blocks and factories were being built everywhere. Between 1950 and 1951, the population of Wichita rose by more than 30,000, pushing the figure above 200,000 for the first time.

Purcell's real estate company, Golden Bond Homes, was building

150 houses in the south-west of the city, an ambitious development which put him in the burgeoning ranks of Wichita's post-war millionaires. Yet despite his success and wealth, he never aspired to social prominence in the town; imbued with the quintessential hardworking, godfearing values of the mid-West, he preferred to remain quietly in the background, perfectly content with his reputation as a businessman of integrity and a good Christian.

Like most early Dianeticists, Purcell was a true believer, both in the efficacy of the science and the genius of its founder. When he heard the Elizabeth Foundation was in difficulties, he immediately offered to 'lend a hand', with both short-term finance and practical business advice. He also provided the funds to set up a branch of the Foundation in Wichita, in a two-storey building sandwiched between Hope's Hamburger Hut and an auto repair firm at 211 West Douglas Avenue, Wichita's main street.[2]

It was, then, entirely to be expected that Purcell would respond unhesitatingly to Hubbard's dramatic plea for help. Ron told him over the telephone from Havana of his plans to set up the headquarters of the Dianetics movement in Wichita and, as far as Purcell was concerned, if the great L. Ron Hubbard chose to make his home in Wichita, it could do the town nothing but good.

Hubbard stepped from Purcell's chartered aeroplane at Wichita airport wearing a lightweight tropical suit and a cream silk Ascot, an item of apparel not often seen in Sedgwick County. Purcell was waiting to greet him, along with a reporter from the *Wichita Eagle*, to whom Ron delivered a carefully prepared statement designed to appeal to the good folk of Wichita. After Los Angeles and Havana, Wichita might have appeared somewhat lacking in glamour, but Hubbard had the good sense not to make invidious comparisons. 'Dianetics is a pioneer mental science,' he announced, 'therefore it is only natural that we should prefer to centralize where the American pioneering spirit and cultural interests are still high. It is impossible to take Dianetics to every interested person, so we have established our headquarters here where those interested can come to Dianetics.'[3] He also took the opportunity to point out that seventy per cent of insane people throughout the world could be returned to normality with Dianetics. 'Hope for Insane is Claimed for Dianetics by Founder' was the headline in the evening edition.

Hubbard checked into the Broadview Hotel, where Purcell had reserved and paid for a suite for him. Alexis, who was becoming accustomed to a succession of surrogate mothers, remained in the care of the nurse who had looked after her on the plane from Havana. The two men were soon discussing plans for the consolidation of Dianetics in Wichita, plans that would be speedily brought to the attention of the FBI.

On 4 May, 1951, the FBI agent in Wichita received an anonymous letter: 'Investigate No 211 West Douglas, under the "Hubbard Dianetics Research Foundation", they are conducting a vicious sexual racket. There are four women and a larger number of men. If they have moved go after them. They are bad, I know because I am one of the victims . . .' This execrable piece of rumour-mongering was added to Hubbard's FBI file, along with a memo from the special agent in charge in Wichita noting: 'General gossip at Wichita has it that the Los Angeles branch of the Hubbard Dianetic Research Foundation went broke and the cost of operation in New Jersey necessitated establishing headquarters of the organization in the central United States . . .'[4]

Hubbard did not know he had been accused of running a 'vicious sexual racket', which was probably just as well because he already had so much to worry about that he was finding it exceedingly difficult to give his full attention to the affairs of the Foundation. The main problem, entirely of his own making, was that his private life remained in complete turmoil.

While his first wife was pursuing him for maintenance and he was still involved in a messy divorce from Sara, Hubbard invited his lover in Los Angeles to be his third wife. Almost as soon as he arrived in Witchita he had telephoned Barbara and asked her to join him, following up with a cable: 'DO NOT THINK I SHOULD OFFER YOU ANYTHING LESS HONORABLE THAN MARRIAGE. SHOULD YOU CONSIDER IT I MUST DOUBLY CLARIFY EXISTING STATUS TO BE SURE. WITH ALL MY HEART AND MUCH LOVE. RON.' Barbara realized that Ron remained as paranoid as ever, as a second cable arrived at her Beverly Hills apartment two hours later: 'BETTER KEEP OUR PLANS A CLOSE SECRET AS I DO NOT KNOW WHAT THEY WOULD TRY TO DO TO YOU IF THEY KNEW. BE VERY CAREFUL. ALL MY LOVE. RON.'

Barbara had no idea who 'they' were and was understandably concerned about marrying a man accused of bigamy, kidnapping and torture. 'Darling, yo sho is in a mess o' trouble,' she replied by letter. 'Do you dare give me any idea of the sort of future awaiting us? God knows I don't want what could be a wonderful and productive partnership between us to wind up with you in jail or continually on the lam from the law . . .'[5]

While Barbara was pondering Ron's proposal, Sara filed a further complaint in Los Angeles, claiming she had been unable to serve divorce papers on her husband because he had fled to Cuba. To support her petition, she included the letter Hubbard had written to her from Havana and a letter, dated 2 May, she had received from his first wife in Bremerton. Polly had read about the divorce in the newspapers and felt moved to offer her sympathy. 'Sara, if I can help in any way, I'd like to,' she wrote. 'You must get Alexis in your custody. Ron is not normal. I had hoped you could straighten him out. Your charges probably sound fantastic to the average person, but I've been through it – the beatings, threats on my life, all the sadistic traits which you charge – 12 years of it.'

The newspapers were happy to report this further development in the domestic troubles of the 'mental-movement mogul', as Hubbard was described with laboured alliteration in the *LA Times*. In Wichita, State Marshal Arthur W. Wermuth was surprised to read that Hubbard had 'fled to Cuba' because he had just read of his arrival in Wichita in the *Evening Eagle*. Wermuth, who happened to be a well-known local war hero, sent a message to Los Angeles acquainting the authorities with Hubbard's whereabouts. Next day the newspapers reported that the 'missing mental-movement mogul' had been 'discovered' in Wichita by the 'legendary one-man army of Bataan'.

Prompted by the news from Wichita, on 14 May Sara's attorney filed another petition asking for Hubbard's assets in Los Angeles to be placed in receivership. The petition noted that Hubbard had been found 'hiding' in Wichita 'but that he would probably leave town upon being detected'.

Coincidentally, on the same day Hubbard despatched a seven-page letter to the Department of Justice in Washington, clearly seeking revenge against Sara. Even for Hubbard, the rambling, venomous missive was a breathtaking concoction of lies, vituperation and wild allegations rendered all the more dangerous by the rise of McCarthyism.

Describing himself as 'basically a scientist in the field of atomic and molecular phenomena', he accused Communists of destroying his half-million dollar business, ruining his health and withholding material of interest to the US Government. The architect of his misfortune was none other than 'a woman known as Sara Elizabeth Northrup . . . whom I believed to be my wife, having married her and then, after some mix-up about a divorce, believed to be my wife in common law'.

Sara, he stressed, was responsible for breaking up the 'American Institute of Advanced Therapy', an organization he had established in 1949, and the following year she was the primary cause of all the trouble at the Hubbard Dianetic Research Foundation, along with Art Ceppos, who was '"formerly" a member of the Communist Party' and Joseph Winter, who 'seemed to have Communist connections' and was a 'psycho-neurotic' who had been discharged from the US Army Medical Corps.

Playing the role of fearfully browbeaten husband, he said his 'alleged wife' had caused him to make out a will leaving her shares in the copyrights and Foundations. Later, when he was asleep at his home in New Jersey he was 'slugged'. He had unwisely done nothing about it at the time as he had no witnesses, but his health had been poor thereafter. Arriving in Los Angeles, his wife left their baby unattended in a car and he was arrested for it – 'I could never understand why.'

Much worse was to come. 'On December 5, while asleep in my apartment on North Rossmore in Los Angeles, I was again attacked and knocked out. When I woke I debated considerably about going to the police but was again afraid of publicity for again I did not know who might have done this. It never occurred to me to suspect that my wife had any part in this.

'I had become so ill by January 1st and was so long overdue in writing my second book that I went to Palm Springs. I returned from Palm Springs in late February to find my wife apparently ill, in bad mental condition, and my baby more or less forgotten in a back room of the Los Angeles Foundation. I instantly took steps, what steps I could, to give my wife help. She seemed to recover.

'I was in my apartment on February 23rd, about two or three o'clock in the morning when the apartment was entered, I was knocked out, had a needle thrust into my heart to give it a jet of air to produce "coronary thrombosis" and was given an electric shock with a 110 volt current. This is all very blurred to me. I had no witnesses. But only one person had another key to that apartment and that was Sara.'

Hubbard went on to describe how he had found love letters to his wife from Miles Hollister, a 'member of the Young Communists', and an ominous telegram containing the phrase 'Lombardo should live so long'. Lombardo, he explained, was a name Sara sometimes called him. Then he described how they had plotted to have him committed and how he had tried to get his wife away by taking her to Palm Springs. She consented to go with him, he said, and he had her signed statement to prove it. Sara's real motive in filing for divorce, he claimed, was to get control of the Foundation.

All the attacks she had mounted against him had held up research he was intending to offer to the Government. 'In August 1950 I found out a method the Russians use on such people as Vogeler, Mindszenty and others to obtain confessions. I could undo that method. My second book was to have shown how the Communists used narco-synthesis and physical torture and why it worked as it did. Further, I was working on a technology of psychological warfare to present it to the Defense Department. All that work was interrupted. Each time I tried to write, a new attack was launched.'

Hubbard declared his concern to prevent Dianetics falling into the hands of Communists and appealed for a 'round-up' of the 'vermin Communists or ex-Communists' who were trying to take over the potent forces of the Foundation. He suggested the 'round-up' should start with Sara:

'I believe this woman to be under heavy duress. She was born into a criminal atmosphere, her father having a criminal record. Her half-sister was an inmate of an insane asylum. She was part of a free love colony in Pasadena. She had attached herself to a Jack Parsons, the rocket expert, during the war and when she left him he was a wreck. Further, through Parsons, she was strangely intimate with many scientists of Los Alamo Gordos [Alamogordo in New Mexico was where the first atomic bomb was tested]. I did not know or realize these things until I myself investigated the matter. She may have a record . . . Perhaps in your criminal files or on the police blotter of Pasadena you will find Sara Elizabeth Northrup, age about 26, born April 8, 1925, about 5'9", blond-brown hair, slender . . . I have no revenge motive nor am I trying to angle this broader than it is. I believe she is under duress, that they have something on her and I believe that under a grilling she would talk and turn state's evidence.'

Hubbard made it clear he felt his life was in danger and concluded: 'Frankly, from what has happened, I am not certain I will live through this. If I do not, know that I have only these enemies in the entire world.'[6]

If Hubbard's letter had been a little more moderate and his FBI file not already voluminous, his letter might easily have resulted in Sara's arrest. The 'Red Scare' was at its height and the American people had succumbed to an irrational fear of subversion and disloyalty encouraged by McCarthy, the cold war, Korea, a series of sensational spy trials and the Truman administration's loyalty programme. Many reputations and careers were destroyed by accusations a great deal milder than those levelled by Hubbard against his wife.

But by 1951, Hubbard was well known to the FBI. The opinion of the agent who had interviewed him in Newark that he was a 'mental case' figured prominently in his file, as did Sara's divorce allegations that he was 'hopelessly insane'. It was a diagnosis with which the FBI was inclined to concur and Hubbard's letter was tucked into his file and ignored, no doubt after the filing clerks had had a good laugh.

At the end of May, Barbara Kaye arrived in Wichita, having decided that she would marry Ron. 'If love can break men's hearts it can restore them too,' she had written to him. 'Yours shall be regenerated with my love and it will grow stronger.'

She found a hand-written note from Ron waiting for her at the Broadview Hotel: 'Hello! I am happy you are here! I love you! Ron.'

Its cheery tone encouraged her greatly and she was thus doubly shocked by Hubbard's appearance when he showed up at the hotel soon after she had checked in.

'He had visibly deteriorated both physically and mentally. He was extremely unkempt, like a street person. His fingernails were uncut and his hair was long and stringy; he looked like Howard Hughes in his last days. He talked in a monotone all the time and seemed on the verge of tears; he was obviously clinically depressed. He told me he had borrowed $50 from Purcell to pay for my room but no one was to know I was in Wichita because Purcell had opposed me coming.'

Hubbard took her out to a jewellery store to buy her an engagement ring, but she was already having second thoughts. 'I felt extremely distanced from him because he was so strange, he was like a different person. I began to think I could never marry this man; I was frightened of him.' Next morning, Barbara hurriedly returned to Los Angeles, leaving Hubbard a note saying she didn't want to come between him and his patron.

As the prospective third Mrs Hubbard swept out of town, Sara arrived to parley for the return of Alexis. 'She got the baby back', said Richard de Mille, who had by then joined Hubbard in Wichita, 'by agreeing to let him divorce *her* and by not saying anything bad about him.'[7]

On 9 June 1951, Sara signed a handwritten statement scrawled on the notepaper of The Hubbard Dianetic Foundation Inc of Wichita agreeing to cancel her receivership action and divorce suit in California in return for a divorce 'guaranteed by L. Ron Hubbard' in mid-June.

Two days later she signed a typed statement categorically retracting the allegations she had made against her husband:

> I, Sara Northrup Hubbard, do hereby state that the things I have said about L. Ron Hubbard in courts and the public prints have been grossly exaggerated or entirely false.
>
> I have not at any time believed otherwise than that L. Ron Hubbard is a fine and brilliant man.
>
> I make this statement of my own free will for I have begun to realize that what I have done may have injured the science of Dianetics, which in my studied opinion may be the only hope of sanity in future generations.
>
> I was under enormous stress and my advisers insisted it was necessary for me to carry through an action as I have done.
>
> There is no other reason for this statement than my own wish to make atonement for the damage I may have done. In the future I wish to lead a quiet and orderly existence with my little girl far away from the enturbulating influences which have ruined my marriage.
> Sara Northrup Hubbard.

The statement bore all the hallmarks of having been written by Hubbard, even down to the use of one of his own invented words, 'enturbulating'. The English language was insufficiently rich and diverse for Hubbard and he often made up new words to compensate for its inadequacies – to 'enturbulate' was a neologism meaning to 'bring into a confused state'.

On 12 June, Hubbard was awarded a divorce in Sedgwick County Court on the basis of Sara's 'gross neglect of duty and extreme cruelty'. The court agreed to an emergency hearing after Hubbard testified that the breakdown of the marriage had brought about severe damage to his health and peace of mind and he feared that any delay would cause him to 'suffer further nervous breakdown and impairment to health'.[8]

Sara did not give evidence in court. All she cared about was that she was awarded custody of Alexis. Clutching her baby, she caught the first Greyhound bus out of Wichita and out of the life of L. Ron Hubbard.

A few months later, Hubbard took a final swipe at his former wife. Writing in *Dianetics: Axioms* he claimed that the 'money and glory' inherent in Dianetics was too much for those with whom he had the misfortune to associate himself, most notably 'a woman who had represented herself as my wife and who had been cured of severe psychosis by Dianetics, but who, because of structural brain damage would evidently never be entirely sane . . .'

Every Dianeticist knew he was referring to the hapless Sara.

It did not take Don Purcell long to discover the role Hubbard expected him to play as president of the Hubbard Dianetic Foundation of Wichita — to provide money, uncomplainingly.

Hubbard, the vice-president and chairman, was spending Purcell's money at a prodigious rate. He had moved into a large, comfortably furnished frame house on North Yale opposite the snooty Wichita Country Club and in the heart of a select residential area called Sleepy Hollow. Following Barbara's abrupt departure he hired a comely housekeeper, a lady in her early forties, who very soon succumbed to his advances and as a consequence was summoned to his bed most nights. 'Ron enjoyed women,' explained Richard de Mille. 'He didn't see any point in having an attractive woman around without making use of her.'

At the Foundation on West Douglas, staff were hired and fired arbitrarily as Hubbard's attention and enthusiasm flitted from project to project, from one grandiose scheme to another. He had a fiction writer's gift for dreaming up impressive titles for every venture, even if it only existed as an idea. Thus, courtesy of Hubbard, Wichita was briefly the home of an organization called 'The International Library of Arts and Sciences', which no doubt caused some head-scratching among the local farmers and factory workers.

Five-hundred dollar training courses for Dianetic auditors were run on a continuous basis and although there was still a reasonable number of applicants making their way to Wichita, the excitement of the previous summer had faded away. To thousands of people across America, Dianetics was no more than a passing whim.

A major conference of Dianeticists organized in Wichita at the end of June 1951 only attracted 112 delegates, but Hubbard continued to behave as if the movement was going from strength to strength. Heedless of demand, the Foundation published a never-ending stream of booklets, bulletins and pamphlets on arcane elements of the science – 'Child Dianetics', 'Handbook for Pre-clears', 'Lectures on Effort Processing', etcetera – which piled up at 211 West Douglas despite the best efforts of the staff to press them on to every visitor.

Hubbard's second book, *Science of Survival*, was published by the Wichita Foundation in August. Dedicated to 'Alexis Valerie Hubbard, For Whose Tomorrow May Be Hoped a World That Is Fit To Be Free,' it delved into metaphysics and reincarnation and elaborated on what Hubbard called the 'tone scale', a device for measuring an individual's emotional state and a key to the interpretation of personality. Hubbard provided a veneer of authority for the book by acknowledging the influence of a long list of philosophers from Aristotle and Socrates, through Voltaire and Descartes, to Freud and Korzybski. But despite their contribution, *Science of Survival* significantly failed to follow *Dianetics* on the *New York Times*'s bestseller list.

For students taking courses at the Foundation, the highlight of the week was the lecture Hubbard delivered every Friday evening. Helen O'Brien, a young woman from Philadelphia who had negotiated a bank loan in order to train as a professional auditor, described the scene: 'He would appear at the back of the crowded hall and walk down the centre aisle to the platform, amid applause. It was well staged. He spoke against a background of rich drapes, bathed in spotlights that set off his red hair and weird, enthusiastic face . . .

'Hubbard was a marvellous lecturer, and he spoke quite frankly then, introducing the soberest and wildest ideas without apology, seeming to share the uproarious delight of some of the members of his audience at his flights of intellectual audacity. His rhetoric had a tempo that usually carried everyone along in at least pseudo acceptance of everything he said, although some of it was far afield of the "science of mental health" which had brought us all together.'[9]

Helen O'Brien soon became a member of Hubbard's 'honour

guard', a small group of awed, intensely loyal admirers who considered it the highest privilege to be in Ron's presence. 'It was not like
being with a human being,' she said. 'He was shaking with energy and
there was a sort of light around him, a cloak of power.

'Sometimes at his house he would play the organ and sing songs he
had composed in college. Ron told me quite a bit about his life. He
said his father was some sort of conman, a very shadowy kind of
character, who he suspected was trying to take over Dianetics. Ron
said he'd destroy the whole thing if that happened. He talked a lot
about Sara. When she ran off with another man Ron followed them
and they locked him in a hotel room and pushed drugs up his nose,
but he managed to escape and went to Cuba.

'He was not promiscuous, but he was available sexually. I had sex
with him one night. Several of us were working late with him, taking
notes and we all went out to a coffee shop. Ron and I left the others
there and went up to bed. It was real matter of fact.'[10]

Among the motley collection of well-meaning people who trekked
to Wichita in the summer of 1951 was a slim, pretty girl from
Houston, Texas, by the name of Mary Sue Whipp. Born in Rock-
dale, Mary Sue was a nineteen-year-old coed at the University of
Texas intent on making a career in petroleum research. She arrived
in Wichita with a friend, Norman James, who had read about
Dianetics in *Astounding* and had persuaded her to join him on the
course. Blue-eyed and auburn-haired, Mary Sue aroused predictably mixed feelings at the Hubbard Dianetic Foundation. Most of
the men liked her; most of the women did not. 'She was a nothing,'
said Helen O'Brien sourly. 'Her favourite reading was *True
Confession.*'

It did not take long for Hubbard to register the arrival of this
attractive pre-clear from Texas and he took a particular interest in
her progress. Mary Sue was flattered by the great man's attention and
within a matter of a few weeks she had moved in with him at 910
North Yale, to the fury of the housekeeper, who found herself
relegated to more conventional duties. Mary Sue rapidly qualified for
her Hubbard Dianetic Auditor's Certificate and joined the staff of the
Foundation as an auditor, all thoughts of a career in the petroleum
industry abandoned.

Auditing was the major activity at the Foundation, for staff and
students alike. Everyone was auditing everyone else and someone,
naturally, had to audit Hubbard. This dubious honour was variously
bestowed and on one occasion it passed to Perry Chapdelaine, who
was working as a research assistant at the Wichita Foundation. 'I
assumed I would have to stick rigidly to the techniques we had been
taught at the Foundation,' said Chapdelaine, 'but it was very differ-

ent from what I expected. He just lay down on the bed in his bedroom, closed his eyes and started to talk. I sat on a chair by the bed and snapped my fingers a time or two, like we had been taught, directing him to go back to the earliest moment he could recall but he opened his eyes, glared at me, closed his eyes again and continued talking. He was relating, very vividly, what was happening to him as a clam or a jellyfish, in terms of effort and counter-effort. It was fascinating, but I didn't know what to make of it. I learned then, pretty well, what he meant by research – it was him talking and the auditor listening.

'The problem for many people involved in Dianetics was that they accepted every word Hubbard said as literal truth, rather than a framework around which you could do things. I remember at a lecture one night he told people if they did this or that they would no longer need to wear glasses and that they would be able to throw them away forever. He pointed to a big bowl at the bottom of the steps leading up to the rostrum and at the end of the lecture people were throwing their glasses into this bowl. Don Purcell was one of them.

'Hubbard thought it was a great joke. He told me about it afterwards, making a snide remark about Purcell and describing how he took off his glasses, threw them into the bowl and groped his way out of the lecture hall. Hubbard was laughing that people would do something like that just because of what he said. Of course, it didn't work. Like every one else, Purcell had a new pair of glasses in a couple of days.

'There was no question Hubbard had an extraordinary ability to transmit to other people. He audited me once in his front room in Wichita and it was the one and only time in my life I had a perfect perception of being in embryo. I'll never forget it, it was the most amazing experience of my whole life.'[11]

In August, Hubbard had to submit to the indignity of another medical examination to avoid losing his pension from the Veterans Administration. 'This veteran gives a long history of three years of sea duty,' the examining physician noted in his report. 'It was gathered from what he says that the duty was rather strenuous, his first assignment in 1942 being with a merchant ship which was assigned to transporting troops. Later, he states, he served with escorts in the North Atlantic. One one occasion, in 1942, he fell down a ladder and struck his right hip, but there were no facilities aboard ship and it was necessary for him to go on without any aid . . . He is a writer by profession and states he has some income from previous writing that helps take care of him.'

Hubbard presented his usual laundry list of injuries and ailments, but the doctors could find symptoms for none of them. 'This is a well nourished and muscled white adult', the examination report concluded, 'who does not appear chronically ill.'[12]

Understandably, the VA saw no cause to increase the veteran's pension, but on this occasion the veteran was perhaps not too concerned since Don Purcell was still providing ample funds for his activities, even though their relationship was fraying. It had been agreed between them that Purcell would be responsible for the management and business affairs of the Foundation while Hubbard looked after training, processing and research, but a simple division of responsibility proved to be unworkable.

'Things went along fine for a while, then Ron began to encroach on my territory,' Purcell recorded. 'The more he did this the ornerier I got. Ron established an overhead structure that far exceeded the gross income. I began to hold out for an organizational structure that could exist within its income with the idea of expanding the structure as our income increased. This idea did not satisfy Ron. He kept telling me that I had agreed to pay off all the old debts and underwrite a new start for the Foundation and why didn't I go ahead and do it?'[13]

Purcell's Wichita lawyer, Jean Oliver Moore, was present on many occasions when money was discussed. 'The bills were reaching astronomical proportions,' he said. 'Ron believed one thing should be done and Don another and there was a divergence of opinion. But in the end it had to be a matter of prudent business judgement – the Foundation was losing money hand over fist at a rate faster than Purcell could replace it.'[14]

Money was not the only problem. Purcell and Hubbard were in fundamental disagreement over the issue of 'past lives'. From the earliest days of auditing, pre-clears invited to travel back along the time-track had occasionally progressed beyond birth or conception to previous, often romantic, existences, recalling their adventures as medieval knights or centurions in ancient Rome. It happened to Helen O'Brien, who re-lived the experience of being a young peasant woman in Ireland in the early nineteenth century who was killed by a British soldier when she tried to prevent him raping her.

Hubbard was at first ambivalent about the validity of 'past lives', but by the time he got to Wichita he had embraced the concept so enthusiastically that he showed up for one of his regular Friday night lectures with a dreadful limp; he explained to the audience that he had returned on his genetic time-track to a moment when he was shot in the leg during the Civil War and had not had time to complete 'running' the incident.

Purcell, who was still hoping that Dianetics would achieve academic and professional recognition, considered the notion of 'past lives' to be unscientific and wanted it dropped. Hubbard resented his interference in his 'research' and was anyway disinclined to heed the views of a pragmatic real estate developer. 'Ron's motive was always to limit Dianetics to the authority of his teachings,' Purcell noted. 'Anyone who had the effrontery to suggest that others beside Ron could contribute creatively to the work must be inhibited.' Friction between the two men increased markedly.

Meanwhile, the FBI, ever vigilant, continued to fret about what Hubbard was up to, at the same time displaying a remarkable talent for obfuscation. On 1 October 1951, for example, the FBI office in Kansas City, which apparently did not read newspapers, asked Washington for any information about a school or clinic of 'Dyanetics' operated by an L. Ron Hubbard in Wichita. The reply indicated that the FBI was quite as paranoid about Hubbard as Hubbard was about the FBI. Prominent mention was made of allegations that the activities of the Foundation were of 'particular interest to sexual perverts and hypochondriacs' and that Sara had accused her husband of being 'mentally incompetent'. The file failed to note that she had retracted her accusations.[15]

In November and December, Hubbard played a starring role in FBI communications when he became enthused, temporarily, by an extraordinary enterprise straight from the pages of his own science fiction and smacking faintly of world domination. His idea was to establish an alliance of leading international scientists and to store all the latest scientific research on microfilm in an atom-bomb-proof archive somewhere in Arizona. In this way, he argued somewhat obscurely, individual nations would be denied the technical capacity to wage a nuclear war. Hubbard called the project 'Allied Scientists of the World' [the name of an organisation that had featured in his novel 'The End Is Not Yet'] and chose Perry Chapdelaine to supervise its inauguration.

'Ron telephoned me at three o'clock in the morning and said he needed me real bad,' Chapdelaine recalled. 'I got dressed and went over to his house and we sat in the front room where he told me all about his plan for Allied Scientists of the World. His stated goal was to stop war in the world. He thought with Allied Scientists he could control war and in that way control the world. That was what he wanted, no question.'

Chapdelaine was despatched in great secrecy – 'Hubbard told me to make sure no one knew he was behind it, I've no idea why' – to Denver, Colorado, where the headquarters of Allied Scientists of the World was to be established. His orders were to organize a mass mailing of scientists and technicians who would be informed that they had been awarded fellowships in Allied Scientists of the World in recognition of their scientific achievements and invited to send in annual dues of $25.

The timing could not have been worse. 'Thousands of leaflets went out,' said Chapdelaine, 'but only one or two came back.' Instead, the FBI was deluged with requests from recipients of the mail-shot to investigate the organization as a possible Communist front organization – such was the power of McCarthyism. The FBI soon established that L. Ron Hubbard was behind Allied Scientists: inter-Bureau memoranda now contained the information that 'several individuals' alleged he was 'mentally incompetent' and a report from the Kansas City office noted that he had 'delusions of grandeur'.[16]

When Post Office inspectors began an investigation of Allied Scientists for possible violation of mail fraud statutes, Hubbard beat a rapid retreat and abandoned the venture. But he was, as always, untroubled by trouble. At the Foundation's New Year party, which was held in a Wichita hotel and featured a live orchestra and a floor show, he was the life and soul of the festivities. 'He danced a great deal,' said Helen O'Brien, 'with a light and exact rhythm that was completely without grace. There was something attention-arresting in the way he handled himself. Many almost worshipped him in those days, but there were other individuals who looked at him askance, with something close to fear.'

For Don Purcell, the Allied Scientists fiasco was almost, but not quite, the last straw. According to Chapdelaine, Purcell was 'frantic, almost hysterical' over the ill-starred enterprise. 'He was scared to death that it would reflect on him,' said Chapdelaine. 'He was afraid of what Hubbard might do next.'

With the relationship between the two men at its lowest ebb, it fell to lawyers to deliver the final blow. Ever since Hubbard's arrival in Wichita, Purcell had been fending off creditors who had been left in the lurch as, one after another, the original Hubbard Dianetic Research Foundations closed their doors. At one point he had had to lodge an $11,000 bond with the district court to prevent the Wichita Foundation being placed in State receivership.

'During this time,' he noted, 'I was negotiating with attorneys trying to effect a settlement of the State receivership. I purchased all of the accounts involved in the deal and heaved a sigh of relief. The mess was cleaned up.'[17]

His relief was premature. Early in 1952, a court ruled that the Hubbard Dianetic Foundation in Wichita was liable for the very considerable debts of the defunct Hubbard Dianetic Research Foundation in Elizabeth, New Jersey. It was a disaster. Purcell, now deeply suspicious that his partner had all along deliberately suppressed the truth about the financial situation in Elizabeth, believed the only option was to file for voluntary bankruptcy.

Hubbard would not countenance such a move, but was outvoted at an emergency meeting of the board of directors held on 12 February. He resigned immediately and announced his intention to establish a 'Hubbard College' on the other side of town. After some discussion, he shook hands on a 'gentlemen's agreement' to continue co-operating with Don Purcell and the Wichita Foundation.

The 'gentlemen's agreement' was worthless, for Purcell had crossed Hubbard and had thus become an enemy to be attacked and harrassed at every opportunity. The millionaire got a taste of what lay in store ten days later when, on the day the Foundation filed for bankruptcy, he received a telegram from Hubbard: 'YOU ARE ADVISED THAT A $50,000 BREACH OF FAITH AND CONTRACT SUIT IS BEING FILED AGAINST YOU PURSUANT TO FAILURE TO DISCHARGE CREDITOR OBLI-GATIONS AND THAT ANOTHER SUIT FOR BAD MANAGEMENT FOR A SIMILAR AMOUNT IS BEING FILED. I AM SORRY TO BE PRESSED TO THIS EXTREMITY. SORROWFULLY, L. RON HUBBARD.'

The final accounts for the Hubbard Dianetic Foundation of Wichita revealed an income of $142,000 and expenditure of $205,000. Hubbard had received fees amounting to nearly $22,000 while salaries for all the remaining staff only accounted for $54,000. The assets of the Foundation largely comprised copyright of all the tapes, books, techniques, processes and paraphernalia of Dianetics, including the name.

Both Purcell and Hubbard claimed ownership and during the bitter feud that inevitably followed, Hubbard mounted a campaign of vilification against his former partner and took to referring to him as 'that little flatulence'. He accused Purcell of plotting to steal Dianetics and of accepting a $500,000 bribe from the American Medical Association to destroy the movement. Purcell was out of his depth: one day he arrived at the Foundation offices on West Douglas and found that all the address plates for the mailing list were missing. Later James Elliott, a Hubbard aide, admitted 'inadvertently' remov-ing them. (They were kept in three boxes, each two feet long and three feet high and weighing more than twenty-five pounds.) Subse-quently a number of taped lectures went missing and when a court ordered the tapes to be returned Purcell discovered every third or fourth word had been erased.[18]

In March, Hubbard took a break from hostilities to marry Mary Sue Whipp, who was by then two months pregnant. To avoid the three-day waiting period required by the state of Kansas, they drove across the state line into Oklahoma where it was possible to be married instantly by a Justice of the Peace. Mary Sue would later provide friends with two versions of the circumstances: one had Hubbard knocking on her door in the middle of night shouting, 'Susie, you're the girl I'm going to marry. Get your things, we're leaving.' In the other, they eloped with her parents in hot pursuit and got a JP out of bed to perform the ceremony, still in his pyjamas.[19]

Back in Wichita, the new Mrs Hubbard assumed partial responsibility for running the Hubbard College, which occupied the second floor of a modern office building on North Broadway. It only stayed in business for just six weeks, but it was long enough for the founder to gather together, by telegram, as many loyal followers as he could find to attend a convention at which he promised to present 'important new material'.

About eighty people turned up for the event, which was held in the banqueting hall of a Wichita hotel. Hubbard first introduced an ingenious little gadget called an E-meter, which he claimed was capable of measuring emotions accurately enough to 'give an auditor a deep and marvellous insight into the mind of his pre-clear'. It was a black metal box with a lighted dial, adjustment knobs and wires connected to two tin cans. He demonstrated how it worked by inviting a member of the audience to hold the tin cans and then pinching him – the needle of the dial flickered in response. Then he asked him simply to imagine the pinch and the needle fluctuated again!

The excitement generated by the E-meter was as nothing compared to Hubbard's next revelation. He had, he said, discovered an entirely new science which transcended the limitations of Dianetics. It was a science of *certainty* and he already had a name for it – he was going to call it Scientology.

Chapter 12

Phoenix Rising

'Many awards and honors were offered and conferred on L. Ron Hubbard. He did accept an honorary Doctor of Philosophy given in recognition of his outstanding work on Dianetics and, as an inspiration to the many people . . . who had been inspired by him to take up advanced studies in this field.' (*Mission Into Time*, 1973)

* * * * *

At the beginning of April 1952, Hubbard packed his belongings into the back of his yellow Pontiac convertible and headed out of Wichita on the Kansas Turnpike with his teenage bride of four weeks beside him on the front seat. Their destination, one thousand miles to the west, was Phoenix, Arizona, where loyal aides had already put up a shingle outside a small office at 1405 North Central Street, announcing it as the headquarters of the Hubbard Association of Scientologists.

Phoenix was so named because it was built on the ruins of an ancient Indian settlement on the Salt River, which had risen like the legendary phoenix. Hubbard, who had had more than enough of Wichita, could not think of a more appropriate location for the rise of his astounding new science from the still-smoking ruins of Dianetics.

The word Scientology was derived from the Latin *scio* (knowing in the fullest sense) and the Greek *logos* (study). Hubbard erroneously believed it to be his own invention: but curiously and coincidentally, almost twenty years earlier in 1934, a German scholar by the name of Dr A Nordenholz had written an obscure work of philosophical speculation titled *Scientologie, Wissenschaft von der Beschaffenheit und der Tauglichkeit des Wissens* (Scientology, the Science of the Structure and Validity of Knowledge). It was unlikely, however, that Hubbard was plagiarizing Dr Nordenholz – the book had not been translated into English and Hubbard's knowledge of German was rudimentary.

Hubbard would introduce Scientology as a logical extension of Dianetics, but it was a development of undeniable expedience, since it ensured he would be able to stay in business even if the courts eventually awarded control of Dianetics and its valuable copyrights to 'that little flatulence', the hated Don Purcell. The difference between Dianetics and Scientology was that Dianetics addressed the body, whereas Scientology addressed the soul. With his accustomed bombast, Hubbard claimed that he had 'come across incontrovertible, scientifically-validated evidence of the existence of the human soul'.[1]

To underpin his new science, Hubbard created an entire cosmology, the essence of which was that the true self of an individual was an immortal, omniscient and omnipotent entity called a 'thetan'. In existence before the beginning of time, thetans picked up and discarded millions of bodies over trillions of years. They concocted the universe for their own amusement but in the process became so enmeshed in it that they came to believe they were nothing more than the bodies they inhabited. The aim of Scientology was to restore the thetan's original capacities to the level, once again, of an 'operating thetan' or an 'OT'. It was an exalted state not yet known on earth, Hubbard wrote. 'Neither Lord Buddha nor Jesus Christ were OTs according to the evidence. They were just a shade above Clear.'[2]

Throughout the early summer months of 1952, Hubbard promulgated the theory of Scientology at a series of lectures delivered at the Hubbard Association of Scientologists in Phoenix. He was addressing, for the most part, committed Dianeticists, people who truly believed him to be a genius, and so the audiences tended to be somewhat uncritical. But if validation of the cosmology was needed, it was constantly provided by the 'past lives' which were by now a prominent and fascinating feature of auditing.

Thetans were obviously not restricted to this universe and auditing sessions revealed innumerable accounts of space travel and adventures on other planets very similar to those found in the pages of *Astounding Science Fiction*, to which the founder of Scientology had so recently been contributing. One report described how a pre-clear had arrived on a planet 74,000 years ago and battled 'black magic operators' who were using electronics for evil purposes. 'He now goes to another planet by spaceship. A deception is accomplished by hypnosis and pleasure implants (rather like opium in their effects) whereby he is deceived into a love affair with a robot decked out as a beautiful red-haired girl . . .'[3]

'Past lives' were further confirmed by the flickering needle of the E-meter, which was enthusiastically adopted as propitious technological support. Invented by a Dianeticist called Volney Mathison, the E-meter was basically a device which measured galvanic skin response – the changes in electrical conductivity of the skin that occur at moments of even quite slight excitement or emotional stress. It proved to be such a useful auditing tool that it would eventually become invested with an almost mystical power to reveal an individual's innermost thoughts. It also provided a useful source of income, for every self-respecting Scientologist wanted to have his own E-meter and the only place to buy them was from the Hubbard Association of Scientologists.

In July, the Scientific Press of Phoenix (another Hubbard enterprise) published a book originally titled *What To Audit* and later re-named *The History of Man*. Introduced as a 'cold-blooded and factual account of your last sixty trillion years', Hubbard intended the book to establish the foundations of Scientology and he had no desire to be unduly modest about its potential. With the knowledge gained by Scientology, he wrote in the third paragraph, 'the blind again see, the lame walk, the ill recover, the insane become sane and the sane become saner.'

Even judged by the standards of his science fiction, *The History of Man* was one of Hubbard's most bizarre works and possibly the most absurd book ever written, although it was treated with great reverence by his followers. An amalgam of mysticism, psychotherapy and pure science fiction, the content invited the derision which was inevitably forthcoming. 'To say it is an astonishing document does not adequately convey the peculiar qualities or contents of *The History of Man . . .*' one government report[4] noted. 'For compressed nonsense and fantasy it must surpass anything theretofore written.'

In a narrative style that wobbled uncertainly between schoolboy fiction and a pseudo-scientific medical paper, Hubbard sought to explain that the human body was occupied by both a thetan and a 'genetic entity', or GE, a sort of low-grade soul located more or less in the centre of the body. ('The genetic entity apparently enters the protoplasm line some two days or a week prior to conception. There is some evidence that the GE is actually double, one entering on the sperm side . . .') The GE carried on through the evolutionary line, 'usually on the same planet', whereas the thetan only came to earth about 35,000 years ago to supervise the development of caveman into homo sapiens. Thus the GE was once 'an anthropoid in the deep forests of forgotten continents or a mollusc seeking to survive on the shore of some lost sea'. The discovery of the GE (Hubbard hailed every fanciful new idea as a 'discovery') 'makes it possible at last to vindicate the theory of evolution proposed by Darwin'.

Much of the book was devoted to a re-working of evolution, starting with 'an atom, complete with electronic rings' after which came cosmic impact producing a 'photon converter', the first single-cell creature, then seaweed, jellyfish and the clam. This knowledge was important to Scientologists since it enabled them to identify the kind of engrams a GE might have picked up when occupying a prehistoric life form.

Many engrams, for example, could be traced back to clams. The clam's big problem was that there was a conflict between the hinge that wanted to open and the hinge that wanted to close. It was easy to restimulate the engram caused by the defeat of the weaker hinge, Hubbard pronounced, by asking a pre-clear to imagine a clam on a beach opening and closing its shell very rapidly and at the same time making an opening and closing motion with thumb and forefinger. This gesture, he said, would upset large numbers of people.

'By the way,' he warned, 'your discussion of these incidents with the uninitiated in Scientology can cause havoc. Should you describe the "clam" to some one [sic], you may restimulate it in him to the extent of causing severe jaw pain. One such victim, after hearing about a clam death, could not use his jaws for three days.'

After the clam came the 'Weeper' or the 'Boohoo', a mollusc that rolled in the surf for half a million years, pumping sea water out of its shell as it breathed, hence its name. Weepers had 'trillions of misadventures', prominent among them the anxiety caused by trying to gulp air before being swamped by the next wave. 'The inability of a pre-clear to cry,' Hubbard explained, 'is partly a hang-up in the Weeper. He is about to be hit by a wave, has his eyes full of sand or is frightened about opening his shell because he may be hit.' Fear of falling also had its origins in the luckless Weepers, which were freqently dropped by predatory birds.

Progressing along the genetic time-track, evolution arrived at the sloth, which 'had bad times falling out of trees', the ape and the famous Piltdown Man, which was the cause of a multitude of engrams, ranging from obsessions about biting to family problems. These could be traced back to the fact that 'the Piltdown teeth were enormous and he was quite careless as to whom and what he bit.' Indeed, so careless was the Piltdown Man, Hubbard recorded, that he was sometimes guilty of 'eating one's wife and other somewhat illogical activities'.

(Unfortunately for Hubbard, just twelve months after *The History of Man* was published, the supposed fossil remains of primitive man found in gravel on Piltdown Common in the south of England were exposed as a hoax. The Piltdown Man had never existed. Hubbard was describing engrams caused by GEs occupying a fictitious early life form dreamed up in 1912 by Charles Dawson, the English amateur archaeologist responsible for the Piltdown fraud.)

The History of Man drifted into pure science fiction when Hubbard came to the point of explaining how thetans moved from body to body. Thetans abandoned bodies earlier than GEs, it appeared. While the GE stayed around to see the body through to death, thetans were obliged to report to a between-lives 'implant station' where they were implanted with a variety of control phases while waiting to pick up another body, sometimes in competition with other disembodied thetans. Hubbard revealed that most implant stations were on Mars, although women occasionally had to report elsewhere in the solar system and there was a 'Martian implant station somewhere in the Pyrenees'.

After publication of the epoch-making *The History of Man*, Hubbard was not of a mind to rest on his dubious laurels. The Hubbard Association of Scientologists and the Scientific Press of Phoenix produced a veritable avalanche of publications during 1952, including another book, *Scientology: 8-8008,* which appeared only a few months after *The History of Man*. Continuing his tradition of audacious introductions, the author wrote: 'With this book, the ability to make one's body old or young at will, the ability to heal the ill without physical contact, the ability to cure the insane and the incapacitated, is set forth for the physician, the layman, the mathematician and the physicist.'

Both books were required reading for new Scientologists and were studied as if they were serious scientific textbooks, indicating the extraordinary hold Hubbard was beginning to exert over his followers. Non-Scientologists could never understand how he achieved a position of such omnipotence, but the power he wielded was far from unprecedented. Scientology already exhibited the classic characteristics of a religious sect, offering salvation through secret knowledge and totally dominated by a leader claiming a monopoly on the source of the knowledge. Many such 'manipulationist sects' flourished at different periods of Christian history.[5]

There were also striking parallels between Scientology and the quirkier pseudo-sciences like phrenology, Count Alfred Korzybski's general semantics and 'iridiagnosis', which taught that all physical ailments could be diagnosed through the iris of the eye. Many such pseudo-sciences were built on a structure of the wildest assumptions, yet attracted a devoted following. They were invariably the creation of a single, highly charismatic, individual viewed by his followers as a genius of divine inspiration. Absolute power was vested in the leader, critics were derided, successes loudly trumpeted and failures ignored. Opponents were darkly accused of ulterior motives in wanting to prevent the advancement of the human race – Hubbard's frequent plaint.

While Hubbard was writing and lecturing in Phoenix in the summer of 1952, a somewhat unexpected event occurred – his son, L. Ron Hubbard Junior, turned up in town apparently intent on becoming a

Scientologist. Nibs was then eighteen years old, a plump young man with a shining, cherubic countenance topped by wispy curls of pale orange hair. He had been living with his grandparents in Bremerton for the previous two years, but had been unable to settle down in high school and had decided to join his father in Phoenix. Mary Sue, preoccupied with her thickening waistline, raised no objection when her husband suggested that Nibs should move in with them, in the modern house they had rented near Camel Back Mountain, on the outskirts of town. And since she was only about a year older than Nibs, she felt under no obligation to be a dutiful stepmother.

Nibs enrolled at a correspondence school in an attempt to complete his high school education and his father gave him a job at the Hubbard Association of Scientologists, at the same time arranging for him to be audited intensively. As the son and namesake of the founder, Nibs was treated with some deference by other Scientologists and made rapid progress in the organization – he was soon designated as 'professor' of the 'Advanced Clinical Course', one of a number of courses on offer to ambitious Scientologists in Phoenix. He also acquired a number of initials after his name to support his professorial status.

In September 1952, Hubbard and Mary Sue left Phoenix for their first visit to Europe. The trip was explained to fellow Scientologists somewhat illogically: 'Amid the constant violence of the turncoat Don J. Purcell of Wichita and his suits which attempted to seize Scientology, Mary Sue became ill and to save her life, Ron took her to England.' It was never spelled out why taking Mary Sue to England would save her life; indeed, since she was eight months pregnant it would have been much safer not to travel. But Hubbard wanted to go to London to establish his control over the small Dianetics group which had formed there spontaneously and Mary Sue insisted on accompanying him. The Hubbards' first impressions of London were gloomy. As they drove into the city from the airport, they were shocked by the extent of the bomb damage which they could see from the back of their taxi. The people on the streets seemed drab and dispirited, the shop windows were empty – rationing was still in force – and Hubbard thought there was an air of 'quiet desperation' about the place. He was also quietly desperate himself, having discovered that American cigarettes were unavailable. However, their spirits lifted somewhat when the taxi drew up outside 30 Marlborough Place, Maida Vale, the house that had been rented for them by local Dianeticists. It was a handsome, double-fronted late Edwardian villa with light, airy rooms, not far from Regent's Park and the West End.

Two nights later, Ron and Mary Sue were guests of honour at a welcoming dinner party arranged by a member of the Dianetics group who had an apartment only ten minutes' walk from Marlborough

Place. Among the guests was a woman called Carmen D'Alessio who, like most of those present, admitted to being 'totally fascinated' by Dianetics. She was, of course, greatly looking forward to meeting Hubbard, not least because she was hoping that he might be able to cure her of the unexplained attacks of panic she had suffered since she was a child.

'My first impression was of a big, tall man with a highly coloured face and brilliant red hair combed back from a high forehead. He was a very magnetic, powerful man, not really very attractive, but you couldn't ignore him. He dominated the evening, talking about energy, electronics, tractor beams, etcetera. I heard him say he'd been in the Navy and had some trouble with his leg and got the impression he was talking about a war injury.

'After dinner, when we were all sitting around, I told him about my problem and he immediately began to audit me. I was sitting on a sofa against a wall and he told me to do something that would prompt most people to think he was mad, although I thought I knew what he was talking about. What he said to me was, "Be three feet back of your head" – those were his exact words. I thought I would have to go into the wall, or the room behind, but I attempted to do it in my imagination. He gave me quite a long session, with everyone sitting around completely silent, but it did nothing.'

Not long afterwards, Carmen D'Alessio attended Hubbard's introductory lecture at his house in Marlborough Place. 'About 30 or 40 people were foregathered in the sitting-room and when Hubbard walked in it was obvious to me he had a bloody awful cold,' she recalled. 'He had a very high colour, much more so than normal, he was sweating profusely, his eyes were streaming and he kept blowing his nose. He even *talked* like man with a cold, but he told us that he was suffering from the effect of leaving his body and visiting another planet. While he was advancing across the floor of this other planet, he said, something like a bomb blew up in his face. Everyone was taking it very seriously, but I didn't believe it. I thought, "the man's a thumping liar." I was right. A nurse was living in the house at the time because Hubbard's wife was extremely pregnant. She was a friend of mine and she told me afterwards that he had flu. She'd even given him an injection for it.'

The nurse was soon obliged to direct her ministrations elsewhere: on 24 September, less than three weeks after arriving in London, Mary Sue gave birth to a daughter, Diana Meredith de Wolfe Hubbard. Ron cabled the good news back to Phoenix, adding a terse plea for cigarettes: 'SEND MORE KOOLS.'

Miss D'Alessio, meanwhile, was continuing to be audited by Hubbard, at his instigation, despite an unnerving experience during a second session at Marlborough Place. 'While I was sitting there trying to do what he told me, I suddenly opened my eyes and saw that he was sitting opposite me laughing silently. I didn't like that at all.'

She was disappointed to register no improvement in her condition. 'It seemed quite useless, it wasn't helping at all. Two or three days afterwards I was feeling very disorganized, ragged and out of sorts. Friends kept telling me to ring Ron, but I didn't want to bother him. Eventually someone rang him and he said, "Put her on the line." He gave me a long session over the telephone lasting at least two hours, possibly three.

'At that time he was very interested in energy. He said, "I want you to mock up a small amount of energy, like a little ball and tell me when you have done it." Then he said, "Now blow it up, make it explode." This was going on subjectively in my imagination; I had no difficulty doing it. Then he said, "Now you have exploded it, gather it all together again and reduce it all down to the small ball of energy, make it solid again." I did that and he said, "Now explode it again." That is all the session consisted of.

'After I had been doing this for a while, possibly half an hour, my physical body began to react in an extraordinary way. It began of its own accord to jerk about unintentionally, first quite gently. I told him what was happening and he told me not to worry but continue doing what he told me. The jerking became stronger, almost out of my control. I felt quite frightened, but he remained very calm and gentle. Finally it seemed my body was being flung out of the chair and I had to hold the chair and the telephone with might and main. I could not possibly have made my body do what it was doing, I would have had to have been an acrobat or trained contortionist. I thought my heart was going to burst. My friends sitting in the room watching me were aghast, terrified.

'The explosions, which had become more and more violent, became less violent by degrees and in the end instead of violent explosions of vast energy it was more like a stone thrown into pond sending out ripples. The ripples became very pleasant and as they did so my body calmed down and became quite tranquil, as if I was lying in the sun on a hot day. All around me were beautiful colours like the Aurora Borealis, colours out of this world, very soothing and harmonious and completely restorative. This went on until I felt quite all right and then he said it was the end of the session.'

Hubbard was clearly pleased by the results he had obtained with Carmen D'Alessio and at his next public lecture, in a small hall near Holland Park, he invited her to tell the audience about her experience. Unfortunately, Miss D'Alessio began her account by describing how her heart had nearly stopped and Hubbard hastily interrupted. 'He didn't want me to say any more,' she recalled. 'He never allowed anyone to say anything negative about him.'[6]

In October, a British edition of *Scientology: 8-8008* was published, with a note about the author from an unnamed editor: 'Some think of his work as the only significant enlargement of the mind since Freud's papers in the late 19th century; others think of it as the Western World's first workable organization of Eastern philosophy. It has been called by two of the leading writers in America: "The most significant advance of mankind in the 20th century" . . . Probably no philosopher of modern times has had the popularity and appeal of Hubbard or such startling successes within his own lifetime.'

At the end of November, Hubbard returned to the United States, with Mary Sue and the baby, to deliver a series of lectures in Philadelphia, where the Scientology franchise was being run by Helen O'Brien and her husband, who paid ten per cent of their gross earnings to Hubbard for the privilege. The O'Briens agreed to pay Hubbard a $1000 fee for the lectures; in addition they arranged a car for his use and rented an ultra-modern terraced apartment at 2601 Parkway, high above River Drive. Hubbard was pleased with it, declared it to be a 'science-fiction writer's dream' and at the same time tried to manoeuvre Helen O'Brien into signing the rental agreement. She knew him too well to be caught out like that. 'I told him, "It's your apartment, you sign the lease,"' she said. 'He was tricky like that.'[7]

Hubbard lectured for a total of seventy hours in Philadelphia to an audience of thirty-eight devotees, speaking without preparation or notes on three evenings and six afternoons each week between 1 and 19 December. Every word was recorded on high-fidelity tapes and later lucratively marketed as the 'Philadelphia Doctorate Course', along with a spiral-bound book of the fifty-four crayon drawings with which he illustrated his talks. Many of the seventy hours were devoted to elaborating the cosmology of Scientology, but he also talked about ways of 'exteriorizing' from the body and demonstrated a new auditing technique called 'creative processing', similar to the 'mock-up' routine he had tried out on Carmen D'Alessio.

'What made it interesting,' said Fred Stansfield, one of the students on the course, 'was the feeling that you were involved in the birth of a new, developing science. It looked like something you could do something with, not just some theory that was utterly useless.'[8]

The only small hiccup in the smooth running of the Philadelphia Doctorate Course occurred on the afternoon of 16 December, when US marshals thundered up the stairs of the Hubbard Dianetic Foundation at 237 North 16th Street, Philadelphia, waving a warrant for the arrest of L. Ron Hubbard. Nibs, who was present and who had inherited something of his father's talent for story-telling, would later talk about an 'incredible Western-style' fight ensuing, with two hundred Scientologists battling on the stairs against FBI agents, US marshals and Philadelphia police.[9]

Helen O'Brien can recall no such mêlée. 'I was on the door so I know what happened. There was no fight. Two detectives in plain clothes and a policeman in uniform came in. I asked them what they wanted and they said, "We are here to arrest Ronald Hubbard". We were always apprehensive about plots to arrest Ron and I ran upstairs and told him what was happening. He went up to the third floor, but there was no escape. One of the students who had only one arm waved his hook at the cops and they backed down a bit, but they said, "We've got a warrant for Hubbard and we are going to take him". My husband and I got in the paddy-waggon with Ron. They fingerprinted him and put him in a cell—it was the only time he was ever behind bars. I called my brother, who was a lawyer, and he got Ron out on $1000 bail later that afternoon.'

The cause of this spot of bother was Don Purcell, who was still doggedly pursuing Hubbard through the courts in an attempt to get some of his money back and keep the Wichita Foundation in business. When he heard Hubbard was in Philadelphia, Purcell filed an affidavit in Pennsylvania District Court accusing him of wrongfully withdrawing $9286 from the bankrupt Wichita Foundation. 'Throughout his Dianetic career,' the affidavit noted, 'Hubbard has displayed a fine talent for profiting personally although his firms and institutions generally fail.'[10]

Hubbard was examined before the bankruptcy court on 17 and 19 December, agreed to make restitution and was discharged. Very soon afterwards he flew back to London, where the Hubbard Association of Scientologists International, or HASI, had opened for business in a couple of draughty rooms above a shop in Holland Park Avenue in West London. They were unprepossessing premises for a science offering immortality, but Hubbard was not finding it easy to establish a base for Scientology in Britain. Helen O'Brien received a despairing letter from a friend describing the HASI offices in London: 'There was an atmosphere of extreme poverty and undertones of a grim conspiracy over all. At 163 Holland Park Avenue was an ill-lit lecture room and a bare-boarded and poky office some eight by ten feet, mainly infested by long-haired men and short-haired, tatty women.'

In February 1953, Hubbard decided it was necessary to bolster his status wth the phlegmatic British by acquiring some academic qualifications. He knew precisely where they were available – from Sequoia University in Los Angeles. The 'university' of Sequoia was owned by

Dr Joseph Hough, a chiropracteur and naturopath who ran a successful practice from a large house in downtown Los Angeles and conferred 'degrees' on whoever he thought merited them. Richard de Mille was awarded a Ph.D. from Sequoia, somewhat to his surprise, for a slim volume he had written under the title *An Introduction to Scientology*.

On 27 Feburary, de Mille, who was then living in Los Angeles, received an urgent telegram from Hubbard in London: 'PLEASE INFORM DR HOUGH PHD VERY ACCEPTABLE. PRIVATELY TO YOU. FOR GOSH SAKES EXPEDITE. WORK HERE UTTERLY DEPENDANT ON IT. CABLE REPLY. RON.' De Mille found Hough thoroughly agreeable and replied the following day: 'PHD GRANTED. HOUGH'S AIRMAIL LETTER OF CONFIRMATION FOLLOWS. GOOD LUCK.' It was in this way that Hubbard acquired the distinction of appending letters to his name – a mysterious 'Doctorate of Divinity' would follow shortly, along with a 'D. Scn'.

It was clear from correspondence around this time that Hubbard was beginning to ponder the future of Scientology. Few of the franchises in the United States were generating much income and the organization had grown haphazardly into a cumbersome conglomeration of corporations spread around the country and increasingly difficult to control. He was also facing the relentless, if covert, opposition of J. Edgar Hoover and the FBI. Hoover's agents rarely failed to mention, in answer to inquiries about Hubbard, that his former wife claimed he was 'hopelessly insane'.[11]

At the beginning of March, Hubbard wrote to Helen O'Brien from London and asked her to go to Phoenix, close down the publishing operation and move it to Philadelphia. On the day she arrived, she learned that burglars had broken into Hubbard's house on East Tatem Boulevard, near Camel Back Mountain. She drove out there and found the house had been ransacked. Although she had no way of knowing what had been stolen, she assumed the thieves had been looking for the fabled manuscript of *Excalibur*. Two guns were certainly missing and she reported their serial numbers to the FBI.

With her usual efficiency, O'Brien packed up the 'communications center', shipped everything to Philadelphia and assumed editorship of the bi-monthly magazine, the *Journal of Scientology*, which was the primary channel of communication between Hubbard and his followers. In truth, editing the magazine was not too onerous a task, since almost everything was written by Hubbard. (Whenever he wished to discuss his own wondrous work in glowing terms, he signed the articles 'Tom Esterbrook'.)

On 10 April, Hubbard wrote another long letter to Helen O'Brien discussing the possibility of setting up a chain of HASI clinics, or

'Spiritual Guidance Centers'. They could make 'real money', he noted, if each clinic could count on ten or fifteen pre-clears a week, each paying $500 for twenty-four hours of auditing. He had clearly previously discussed the prospect of converting Scientology into a religion. 'I await your reaction on the religion angle,' he wrote. 'In my opinion, we couldn't get worse public opinion than we have had or have less customers with what we've got to sell. A religious charter would be necessary in Pennsylvania or NJ to make it stick. But I sure could make it stick.'

Perhaps inspired by such considerations, Hubbard's next published work bore a distinctly Old Testament flavour. *The Factors* was a summation of his '30-year examination' of the human spirit and the material universe: 'Factor No. 1: Before the beginning was a Cause and the entire purpose of the Cause was the creation of effect.' At the end of the thirty factors was a valediction reading, 'Humbly tendered as a gift to Man by L. Ron Hubbard.'

Three weeks later, the humble tenderer of gifts to mankind was writing to Helen O'Brien in a rather less pious fashion about a particular member of the species who continued to be a thorn in his side—Don Purcell. It was obvious to Hubbard that Purcell was trying to stir up public odium against him and take control of Dianetics, and Hubbard employed some choice phrases to vent his anger. Purcell, he wrote, was patently insane, probably the most hated man in Wichita, about as safe to have around as a mad dog and would inevitably soon run up against someone who would put a bullet through him. The only surprising part of all this, he concluded, was that by paying attention to Purcell the American public demonstrated its complete incompetence and 'desire to be swindled'.

At the end of May, Hubbard announced his intention to stir up some interest in Scientology on the continent and he left London for Spain by car, with Mary Sue, who had recently discovered she was pregnant again, and baby Diana, then eight months old. They stayed first in Sitges, a small resort on the Mediterranean coast, then drove further south to Seville. It seems they did little other than enjoy an extended holiday, although Helen O'Brien, who was virtually running Scientology in the United States, continued to receive long, rambling letters in Hubbard's untidy scrawl.

On 19 July, he wrote nine pages asking her to get one of her 'electronic eager beaver' friends to construct an extraordinary machine with which he believed he would be able to cure insanity. The device was to be disguised as an ordinary briefcase with the trigger incorporated in the lock and it was to be capable of delivering a concentrated supersonic beam alternating approximately between breathing and heart rates, thus inducing hypnosis. He wanted to be able, he said, to walk into a sanitorium with his secret machine, confront an insane patient and make him sane in a few seconds. 'This would mean', he wrote, 'the immediate end of psychiatric resistance to Scientology.' O'Brien was to get the machine made up as a matter of urgency and air-freight it to him in Spain with a spurious explanation of its function for the benefit of the Customs officals.

On 15 August he wrote again, pleading with her to make sure the machine was finished by the time he arrived back in the United States in mid-September. He added that he had been working with children very successfully: 'I can make kids walk in a few minutes who were crippled . . . I can solve any case and teach people to solve any case without failure. I know the mind like a surveyor knows a map. That sets me free, like the genie of the uncorked bottle.'

The 'genie' returned to Philadelphia at the end of September in time to address the three-day International Congress of Dianeticists and Scientologists at the Broadwood Hotel. With more than three hundred delegates attending, the event was a great success, but by this time the organizers, Helen O'Brien and her husband, were exhausted and disillusioned. They had been at Hubbard's beck and call for most of the year, receiving little in return. 'As soon as we became responsible for Hubbard's interests,' Helen O'Brien recorded, 'a projection of hostility began, and he doubted and double-crossed us, and sniped at us without pause.' They had no desire to take it any more and resigned. Helen O'Brien would forever recall her parting, regretful words to Hubbard: 'You're like a cow who gives a good bucket of milk, then kicks it over.'

In October and November, Hubbard lectured to the Hubbard Assocation in Camden, New Jersey, just across the Delaware River from Philadelphia. Mary Sue would normally have been present at every lecture, but she was forced by her pregnancy and the endless demands of an active toddler, to spend most of the time at home—yet another rented house, this time at Medford Lakes, about twenty miles from Camden. Nibs, who had recently married his long-time girl-friend, Henrietta, in Los Angeles, came to visit and was given a job in the Camden 'org', a Scientology abbreviation for organization.

The Hubbards returned to Phoenix for Christmas, to the house near Camel Back Mountain, and on 6 January 1954, Mary Sue gave birth to her second child, a son, Geoffrey Quentin McCaully Hubbard.

Deprived of the services of Helen O'Brien, Hubbard tried to entice Richard de Mille back into the fold, only to discover that he, too, had become disillusioned. 'I wanted to find the true answer to everything,' de Mille explained, 'but I didn't like all the contradictions and I was becoming more and more sceptical of the whole thing. There was a constant pyramiding of claims, but the performance was always deficient. The answer to the deficiency was that we didn't have a particular step quite right, but now we had *another* step and this time it's going to be right.

'When Hubbard called me and said, "I miss you. Why don't you come back?" I was somewhat critical and expressed my scepticism. His reaction was typical. "Who's gotten to you, Dick?" he asked. To him, there was no such thing as simply being unconvinced.'

Despite the defections, Scientology prospered in Phoenix, so much so that in April 1954, the HASI moved into sumptuous new premises on a corner site at 1017 North Third Street. Formerly an apartment building, the new headquarters had wide Spanish-style colonnaded porches offering shade from the fierce Arizona sun on both first and second floors. Outside there was a large parking lot lined with palm trees and inside an auditorium with the latest recording facilities, more than twenty auditing rooms, comfortable offices for the executives and a swimming pool. In a brochure printed to celebrate the move, a picture of a beaming L. Ron Hubbard, C.E., D. Scn., D.D. could be found on the inside front cover and a similarly beaming L. Ron Hubbard Jr., H.G.A., D.Scn., on the inside back cover. 'Ten thousand years of thinking men have made this science possible,' the introduction proclaimed. 'L. Ron Hubbard has spent more than 30 years perfecting Dianetics and Scientology to the point of practical application.'

The house at Camel Back, where the Hubbards were enjoying an unaccustomed period of residential stability, became a gathering place for whichever courtiers happened to be in favour at the time. One of them was an Englishman by the name of Ray Kemp, who had no doubt that Hubbard possessed supernatural powers. 'He could certainly move clouds around in the sky,' said Kemp. 'I saw him do that. If there were a lot of little puffy clouds in the sky he could move one in one direction and one in another and then get them to join up. It was nothing particularly special for him; it was just a fun thing to do.'

Kemp liked to say he had found Scientology in a wastepaper basket. He was serving as a Royal Navy radar technician in Malta and was looking for something to read at a dull party when he spotted a discarded copy of *Astounding Science Fiction*. It was the Dianetics issue. He read it avidly, then bought the book and enrolled for an auditing course at Holland Park Avenue when he was next in London on leave. By 1954 he had made his way to Phoenix, where he was working for the org as an auditor.

'I spent quite a bit of time with Ron and Mary Sue out at Camel

Back. We used to swap war stories and try to cap each other's yarns. He was a wonderful story-teller and he'd make a story fit whatever point he was trying to make. I don't think he ever expected me to take his war stories seriously, although I knew he had been wounded because one night he kept complaining of a pain in his side and when he stood up a little bit of shrapnel fell out from under his shirt. He said it was something that often happened—fragments of shrapnel still in his body were slowly working their way out.

'One of the things he liked to do was ride his motorcycle – he had an Indian, a real monster – out into the desert. He played a game he called point to point. He'd pick a spot on the horizon and go for it, straight as he could, without deviating, regardless of what was in the way, cactus or whatever. Nibs and Dick Steves, from the org, used to chase him on their motorcycles, but Ron's favourite trick was to put up dust devils behind him. That's another thing he could do – manipulate dust devils. He could whip them up and move them around at will. I often saw him do that.'[12]

Ray Kemp exemplified a propensity in Hubbard's disciples to build myths around him. There was also a marked tendency to treat everything he said as gospel, which led to frequent misunderstandings as Hubbard liked to make jokes. Once, during a lecture in Phoenix, he made a crack about a Colt .45 being an 'enormously effective' method of exteriorization. As this ludicrous piece of wisdom was disseminated, a story grew that Hubbard had drawn a gun during the lecture and fired a round into the floor. Nibs swore later that he had seen the hole in the floorboards.

Jack Horner joined the circle close to Hubbard that summer of '54. Like so many of the early Dianeticists he had fallen out with Hubbard, in his case after Hubbard had accused him of fiddling the accounts, but typically he found he could not stay away. He pretended he was in Phoenix to see some friends who were working for the org and naturally ran into Hubbard.

'He asked me what I was doing and I said "teaching school" and he said, "we'll soon fix that" and he began to run a process on me right there and then. He told me to go and touch certain things in the room and then sit down at a desk. Then he said, "Now *you* go touch them" and I knew exactly what he meant. While I was sitting there I suddenly found myself looking at the underside of the desk. I had a definite, certain reality of myself out of my body. I said "Oh my God, I'm out of my body!" At that point I knew what he meant by exteriorization.

'Later, when I was working for him doing research in Phoenix, I was out at his home late one afternoon with Jim Pinkham, who did all the recording at the org, and someone knocked at the door. Ron went and talked to a guy outside for about five minutes and came back with a big grin on his face. He said the guy at the door wanted to give him a cheque for $5000 for a copy of *Excalibur*. Then he laughed out loud and said, "One of these days I'll have to get round to writing it." We cracked up. It was the only time Ron ever admitted there was no such book.

'It didn't matter too much to us. From our standpoint at that time Scientology was the only game in town and it was Ron's game. It was like exploring the moon, like being in the space programme, except that we were exploring the mind instead of space. Religion didn't cut it, psychology didn't cut it. If Ron wanted to tell tall stories about himself to make himself look good, so what? We didn't worry a whole lot about it. His genius outflowered his craziness.'[13]

Many of Ron's most fervent admirers, Horner included, found it difficult to include Mary Sue in their devotion. 'I hated her,' said Horner. 'She was a real tight-lipped Baptist. One night I got into a fight with her because she called my girlfriend a whore. I really tore into her verbally and Hubbard threw me out of the house.'

Hubbard would never allow anyone to criticize Mary Sue and although he rarely showed much affection for her in public, it seemed, after two failed marriages and innumerable affairs, that he had at last formed a stable relationship, improbable as it had first appeared. They were indeed an unlikely couple – a flamboyant, fast-talking extrovert entrepreneur in his forties and a quiet, intense young woman twenty years his junior from a small town in Texas. But anyone who underestimated Mary Sue made a big mistake. Although she was not yet twenty-four years old, she exercized considerable power within the Scientology movement and people around Hubbard quickly learned to be wary of her. Fiercely loyal to her husband, brusque and autocratic, she could be a dangerous enemy. She also had a remarkable capacity for motherhood; only four months after Quentin was born, she was pregnant again.

In June, the Hubbard Association of Scientologists International produced an imaginative re-working of Hubbard's biography in a letter to the Better Business Bureau in Phoenix, clearly designed to improve HASI's standing in the town. Much new information was included, not all of it entirely comprehensible.

The mysterious Commander Tompson [*sic*], for example, was said in the letter to have 'instituted psychoanalysis in the US Navy for use in flight surgery'. A Dr William Alan White, superintendent of St Elizabeth's, a government asylum in Washington, made his debut as someone under whom Hubbard had trained and mention was made of a hitherto unmentioned book: 'In 1947 Hubbard published a book for the Gerontological Society and the American Medical Association called *Scientology. A New Science*.'

This non-existent publication, it seemed, was 'politely received', but thereafter events had conspired against the scientist-author. Like 'almost any nuclear physicist' he had often written science fiction 'for amusement' and unscrupulous publishers took advantage of this fact. While poor Ron wanted nothing for himself but to be left in peace to continue his study and research, he was pressurized to produce a popular book for Hermitage House, who then 'unwisely' published an article in a pulp magazine. The sorry tale continued with Hubbard constantly being taken advantage of by all and sundry, with everyone but Ron trying to make money out of his discoveries and his wicked estranged wife threatening to stir up a 'great deal of scandal'.

However, the biography had a happy ending in Phoenix in the Hubbard Association of Scientologists – the first organization in the field to be under Hubbard's sole control and therefore untainted by all the previous manoeuvrings. It had established a two-year record of good repute and responsibility, paid its bills promptly 'as any Phoenix business firm with which it deals can attest' and was following a policy of quiet, orderly business. It was soon intending to make Scientology available to the disabled 'as a public service'.

The letter was signed by John Galusha, the secretary of the HASI board of directors. It was, no doubt, written in good faith, for Galusha was a thoroughly decent, deeply committed Scientologist. He had been working on the railroad in Colorado when he first heard about Dianetics and had thrown himself into it wholeheartedly. 'I thought it was a privilege to work for Ron,' he said. 'Maybe he was a charlatan and a liar – I didn't care. The point was that the tech was good. It *worked*.'[14] The 'tech' was the commonly used contraction for what Hubbard, the engineer, liked to describe as 'the technology' of Scientology.

Galusha did not get to know Hubbard particularly well, but then very few people did. Jack Horner recalled a strange remark Hubbard once made: 'We were out the back of his house and he was draining the radiator of his car because it was going to be unexpectedly cold that night. I said to him, "You know Ron, it would be nice if we could be closer friends." There was a silence for a moment, then he replied, "Yeah, it would be nice, but I can't have any friends."'

For Hubbard, the best news of 1954 came towards the end of the year when he heard from Wichita that Don Purcell was giving up the fight for control of Dianetics. Purcell had tired of the seemingly endless litigation and the constant attacks from Scientologists. He had also became interested in an offshoot of Dianetics called Synergetics and when he decided to devote his future resources to Synergetics he handed the Wichita Foundation's copyrights and mailing lists back to Hubbard, thankful to disentangle himself from the man he had once considered a saviour.

Purcell's retreat could not have come at a more apposite moment. With Dianetics and Scientology at last firmly under his control, Hubbard was ready to follow his own often-voiced advice: 'If a man really wanted to make a million dollars, the best way to do it would be to start a religion.'

Chapter 13

Apostle of the Main Chance

'A historic milestone in the personal life of L. Ron Hubbard and in the history of Dianetics and Scientology was passed in February 1954, with the founding of the first Church of Scientology. This was in keeping with the religious nature of the tenets dating from the earliest days of research. It was obvious that he had been exploring religious territory right along.' (*Mission Into Time*, 1973)

* * * * *

Hubbard had been quietly planning the conversion of Scientology into a religion for more than twelve months, ever since his return from Europe in the autumn of 1953. It made sense financially, for there were substantial tax concessions available to churches, and it made sense pragmatically, for he was convinced that as a religion Scientology would be less vulnerable to attack by the enemies he was convinced were constantly trying to encircle him.

Furthermore, religion was booming in post-war America. All the churches were increasing their membership, there was a new interest in revivalism, epitomized by Billy Graham's spectacular crusades, and even theologians were fostering the concept of the church as integral to contemporary culture, reflected in the popularity of songs like 'I Believe' and epic films like *The Ten Commandments*. Politicians, too, spoke of 'piety on the Potomac' and President-elect Dwight D. Eisenhower declared in late 1952: 'Our government makes no sense unless it is founded on a deeply felt religious faith – and I don't care what it is!' In 1954 Congress boosted the new piety by adding the phrase 'under God' to the pledge of allegiance.

Hubbard was quick to recognize there was a religious bandwagon rolling and equally quick to leap nimbly aboard. In December 1953, he incorporated three new churches – the Church of American Science, the Church of Scientology and the Church of Spiritual Engineering – in Camden, New Jersey. On 18 February 1954, the Church of Scientology of California was incorporated. Its objects, inter alia, were to 'accept and adopt the aims, purposes, principles and creed of the Church of American Science, as founded by L. Ron

Hubbard'. Another Church of Scientology was incorporated in Washington DC and throughout 1954 Hubbard urged franchise holders around the United States to convert their operations into independent churches. Executives of the Hubbard Association of Scientologists International henceforth described themselves as 'ministers', and some of the more flamboyant even took to wearing clerical collars and pre-fixing their names with 'Reverend'.

At the beginning of 1955, Hubbard moved his headquarters from Phoenix to Washington DC, declaring his belief that the church's constitutional rights were safer under the jurisdiction of Federal, rather than State, courts. Travelling with him to Washington was a veritable family entourage, including his heavily pregnant wife and their two small children, his son Nibs and his wife, Henrietta, also pregnant. On Sunday, 13 February, Mary Sue gave birth to a daughter, Mary Suzette Rochelle Hubbard, her third child in rather less than three years of marriage.

The Hubbards moved into a two-storey house in the leafy Maryland suburb of Silver Spring, just outside the Washington DC metropolitan area, and it was from there that Ron resumed his correspondence with the Communist Activities Division of the FBI. On 11 July 1955, he wrote a maundering three-page letter about Communists and wicked accountants conspiring with renegade IRS agents to destroy him, so inane that the recipient at the FBI scribbled on it a notation 'appears mental'.[1] Thereafter, the FBI no longer acknowledged communications from Hubbard 'because of their rambling, meaningless nature and lack of any pertinence to Bureau interests'.[2] No doubt somewhat to the Bureau's chagrin, Hubbard was not in the least deterred from writing.

Two weeks later, on smart new printed notepaper headed 'L. Ron Hubbard D.D., Ph.D.', he wrote again to say he had received an invitation to go to Russia. It had come from an 'unimpeachable source' who suggested that as he was about to be ruined by the IRS he might as well accept the offer. It seemed, he wrote, that he could go to Russia as an adviser or consultant and not only be provided with his own laboratories but also receive very high fees. Passport formalities were already more or less complete—all he had to do was go to Paris, where he would be picked up by a Russian plane. He did not wish to reveal the name of his contact, he added, 'because he is a little too highly placed on the [Capitol] Hill'.

It seemed Hubbard was able to resist blandishments from beyond the Iron Curtain, for through the sweltering summer months in Washington DC he could be found lecturing at the 'Academy of Religious Arts and Sciences', in a ten-roomed house at 1845 R Street, in the north-west section of the city. He was still maintaining a

one-way communication with the FBI and on 7 September, he wrote
to complain about the persecution of Scientologists, some of whom he
alleged were being mysteriously driven insane, possibly by the use of
LSD, 'the insanity producing drug so favoured by the APA [Ameri-
can Psychological Association]'. Another poor wretch, a 'half-blind
deaf old man' had been arrested for practising medicine without a
licence in Phoenix by a County attorney promising to 'get to the
bottom of this thing about Hubbard and Scientology'.

On a personal basis, Hubbard pointed out that it was not uncom-
mon 'to have judges and attorneys mad-dogged about what a terrible
person I am and how foul is Scientology . . . All manner of defama-
tory rumours have been scattered around me, questioning even my
sanity . . .'

It certainly was a question in the forefront of the FBI file, although
Hubbard was not to know that. He continued: 'I am trying to turn out
some monographs on matters in my field of nuclear physics and
psychology for the government on the subject of alleviating some of
the distress of radiation burns, a project I came east to complete.' He
also promised to forward information about the latest brain-washing
techniques in Russia.

The horror of 'brain-washing' had been an emotive talking point in
the United States ever since the end of the Korean war and the
revelation that United Nations prisoners had been brain-washed for
propaganda purposes. Timely as always, Hubbard entered the debate
by distributing a pamphlet entitled 'Brain-Washing: A Synthesis of
the Russian Textbook on Psychopolitics', which he claimed was a
transcript of a lecture delivered in the Soviet Union by the dreaded
Lavrenty Pavlovich Beria, architect of Stalin's purges.

It was this pamphlet he forwarded in due course to the FBI with a
note explaining that it was the Church of Scientology's printing of
'what appeared to be a Communist manual'. The Bureau's Central
Research Section examined it and concluded that its authenticity was
doubtful, since it lacked documentation of source material, did not use
normal Communist words and phrases and contained no quotations
from well-known Communist works, as would be expected. Had the
Central Research Section been familiar with the works of L. Ron
Hubbard, they might have noted certain similarities in the narrative
style.

The FBI did not acknowledge receipt of the pamphlet, but this did
not dissuade the Hubbard Dianetic Research Foundation of Silver
Spring, Maryland, from mailing the pamphlet to influential individuals and organizations around the country with a covering letter
claiming that 'authorization' had been received to release the material
after the FBI had been supplied with a copy.

While Hubbard was skirmishing with the FBI, he was also tightening his grip on the Scientology movement and urging his followers to take action against anyone attempting to practise Scientology outside the control of the 'church'. He derided apostates as 'squirrels' and recommended merciless litigation to drive them out of business. 'The law can be used very easily to harass, and enough harassment on somebody who is simply on the thin edge anyway, well knowing that he is not authorized, will generally be sufficient to cause his professional decease,' he wrote in one of his interminable bulletins, casually adding, 'If possible, of course, ruin him utterly.'

In the same bulletin he offered the benefit of his advice to any Scientologists unlucky enough to be arrested. They were instantly to file a $100,000 civil damages suit for molestation of 'a Man of God going about his business', then go on the offensive 'forcefully, artfully and arduously' and cause 'blue flames to dance on the courthouse roof until everybody has apologized profusely'. The only way to defend anything, Hubbard wrote, was to attack. 'If you ever forget that, you will lose every battle you are ever engaged in.'[3] It was a philosophy to which he would adhere ardently all his life.

At the end of September, the Hubbards packed their bags once again, closed the house at Silver Spring and departed the United States with their three young children for another extended visit to London. Hubbard had taken a lease on a large apartment in Brunswick House, a mansion block in Palace Gardens Terrace, a few minutes walk from Kensington Gardens. It became, temporarily, the address of the Hubbard Communications Office, which maintained links with embryonic Scientology groups in other countries (satellite churches had already been established in South Africa, Australia and New Zealand).

Hubbard immediately took over the day-to-day running of the Hubbard Association of Scientologists International, which was still operating from its dreary premises at 163 Holland Park Avenue, although it had grown considerably in size. There was now a full-time staff of twenty auditors, most of them young, like Cyril Vosper, who had been a nineteen-year-old biology student when he first read about Dianetics and was a qualified professional auditor by the time he was twenty.

'I had no doubt that Hubbard's arrival in town was a historic event,' he recalled. 'I believed in him totally, believed he was a genius and was convinced he knew a lot more about the human species and the human condition than anyone else. The only reason I had any slight difficulty in accepting that he was the world's greatest human being was that, to English eyes, he didn't *look* like a Messiah. He used to wear very brash American clothes – loud check jackets and bootlace ties and brothel-creepers. It wasn't quite the image we expected. But he gave a number of public lectures around town and was interviewed by the media and was pretty well received. The newspapers at that time were quite complimentary, they viewed him as an oddball who might just have come up with something good.

'Ron presided over the staff meeting at the HASI at five o'clock every afternoon. It was all Christian names at the HASI, everyone called him Ron, but there was no doubt he was absolutely in charge. He wouldn't brook any other input: all the books were written by him, all the policy letters were written by him. No one would ever question anything he said or wrote. I had read *The History of Man* and I knew, as a biology student, that it was a load of bleeding nonsense but I explained it to myself as an allegorical work. In any case, I could never have said to him, "Now listen, Ron, that's just not true." No one would ever have done that.

'One of the things that began to worry me about Ron was that he was unpredictable. He could be very thoughtful and kind one minute and quite hideous the next. We were auditing about 50 hours a week and I remember one afternoon a girl auditor burst into tears when she was telling Ron about a particularly difficult case she had. He put his arm round her and said, "Jenny, anything we can do for this pre-clear is better than doing nothing. She needs help and a bit of attention and that is what you are giving her. Just keep on doing the same thing you're doing and you will resolve it in due course. You can't expect miracles overnight." That struck me as a very humane and comforting thing to say to her. There was no question he had something to contribute in the psychological area. I mean, just to sit down with someone and listen to them for a couple of hours did them good.

'But then I have also seen him behave in a grotesque fashion. One afternoon during a lecture a woman in the audience was coughing rather badly and he walked to the front of the stage, red-faced and visibly angry, and shouted, "Get that woman out of this lecture hall!" She was one of his most fervent supporters and she was also desperately ill – she died three weeks later of lung cancer.'[4]

Aside from occasional temper tantrums, Hubbard considered things were going very well in London. In a letter to Marilyn Routsong, an aide left behind in Washington to keep an eye on his interests, he wrote to say how busy he was, how everything was rolling along at high speed and how he was hoping to have some promotional films ready for use soon. He ended with a titbit of information that must have made Miss Routsong's nerves tingle: 'Just between ourselves, I actually do have a method of as-ising the atom bomb. Anyway I'm not quite as far away as you think. Love, Ron.'

In the peculiar argot of Scientology, 'as-isness' was a process of making something disappear. What Hubbard was apparently saying was that he was well on the way towards removing nuclear weapons from the face of the earth. However, something must have gone wrong since he would soon be applying his awesome imagination to the problem of dealing with radiation.

The Hubbards' closest friends in London were Ray Kemp, now back home from Phoenix, and his pretty girlfriend, Pam, both of whom worked at the HASI. Hubbard, as a minister of the Church of American Science, performed the ceremony when they married in February 1956, in the lecture room at the HASI, and Mary Sue was Pam's maid of honour. 'Ron and Mary Sue had dinner with us the night before the wedding,' Pam said, 'and Ron told us he had written the ceremony specially for us. He was a very good friend – he even fixed our honeymoon, made arrangements for us to use an apartment in Tangier owned by a friend of his and paid for our air tickets.

'When we got back, we used to see a great deal of them, two or three times a week. Ron would telephone and say, "I'm coming over to dinner and I'm bringing a chicken." Then we would sit up for hours playing Cluedo and the men would start telling stories and there would be lots of laughter. It was a lot of fun – I'd usually end up falling asleep and Mary Sue would go to bed. Their relationship seemed OK, but there never seemed to be a lot of love between them. She was not the affectionate type, she was more efficient than affectionate. They used to have fierce husband and wife domestic arguments.

'We had a big old apartment in Palace Court, Kensington, with a huge living-room with a full-size concert grand in the corner and we used to have parties every night. Ron was always the life and soul, great fun. He loved to dance, play the guitar or ukulele; he was a real actor. He would drag me up to sing with him and then we'd make up rude songs about him and auditing and he would top each verse and roar with laughter and think it was terribly funny. I thought he was always very *aware* as an individual. He would make a comment about something and he'd invariably be right and I'd look at him and think "How did you know that?"'[5]

At the end of March 1956, Ray Kemp accompanied Hubbard on a trip to Dublin. 'He wanted to see if there was something he could do for Ireland,' Kemp explained. 'He felt that Ireland's troubles were based on the fact that it was a bit like a Third World nation and had never been able to apply the skills of its people. We were there for two or three days and he spent the whole time talking to people. We'd be walking down the street and all of a sudden he wasn't there. I'd look back and see him deep in conversation with someone, asking them if they had a job, what their skills were, things like that. Believe it or not, he'd actually run a little process on them there and then and they'd feel better and he'd walk away. His idea was to open a Personal Efficiency Foundation in Dublin to teach people how to apply whatever skills they had got, but I don't think anything ever came of it.'

Back in London, Hubbard applied himself to proselytizing for his fledgling church. Never short of ideas, he told Kemp to try putting an advertisement in the London evening newspapers with a telephone number and the offer, 'I will talk to anyone about anything.' It instantly tapped the deep well of loneliness which exists in every big city and generated an extraordinary response. 'We were inundated with calls,' said Kemp. 'Everyone from potential suicides to a girl who couldn't decide which of three men to marry.'

So successful was this campaign that Hubbard then tried targeting specific, and potentially vulnerable, groups, starting with the victims of one of the most feared diseases of the 'fifties. The classified columns of the evening newspapers soon began carrying the following, apparently innocuous, advertisement: 'Polio victims. A research foundation investigating polio desires volunteers suffering from the effects of that illness to call for examination . . .' The 'research foundation' followed up with similar advertisements aimed at asthmatics and arthritics.

'Casualty Contact' was another thoroughly distasteful recruiting method advocated by Hubbard. He recommended that ambitious auditors looking for new pre-clears should cut out stories in the newspapers about 'people who have been victimized one way or the other by life. It does not much matter whether that victimizing is in the manner of mental or physical injury . . .' Then they should make a call on the bereaved or injured person as speedily as possible, representing themselves as 'a minister whose compassion was compelled by the newspaper story'.

By the summer of 1956 Scientology was prospering mightily and so, at last, was its founder. Hubbard's gross receipts for the fiscal year ending June 1956 amounted to $102,604 – a handsome income by any standards.[6] His salary from the Church of Scientology was only $125 a week, but he earned commission from the sale of training processes and E-meters, in addition to substantial royalties from his innumerable books. More than sixty books on Scientology by L. Ron Hubbard were in print by this time and a new one was appearing approximately every two months, usually containing new processes and procedures superseding those currently in use.

The church could easily afford the expense of allowing its founder to become an early transatlantic commuter and Hubbard made frequent visits back to Washington during the year, collecting lecture fees on each trip. In November, the Academy of Religious Arts and Sciences (also known as the Academy of Scientology) moved to 1810-1812 19th Street, adjoining grey-brick townhouses with two flights of stone steps leading up to the front door in a tree-lined street of eminent respectability. The Hubbards took a lease on a handsome four-storey brownstone on the other side of the street for their use when they were in Washington.

In March 1957, the Church of Scientology adopted a compensation scheme known as a 'proportional pay plan' under which Hubbard would henceforth receive, in lieu of salary, a percentage of the church's gross income. The effect was dramatic: before the end of the 'fifties the founder of the Church of Scientology would be coining around $250,000 a year, a great deal more than the President of the United States.

By April it seemed that Hubbard had given up his heroic, single-handed attempt to rid the world of nuclear weapons by 'as-ising' the atomic bomb, for in that month he hired the Royal Empire Society Hall in London in order to preside over the 'London Congress on Nuclear Radiation and Health'. The various lectures delivered at this extraordinary event were later condensed into an even more extraordinary book titled *All About Radiation* and written by 'a nuclear physicist' and 'a medical doctor'.

The doctor was anonymous, but the 'nuclear physicist' was none other than L. Ron Hubbard offering the benefit of his advice with customary scant recourse to the laws of science. He asserted, for example, that a sixteen-foot wall could not stop a gamma ray whereas a human body could, an assertion later described by an eminent radiologist as 'showing complete and utter ignorance of physics, nuclear science and medicine'.[7] In line with his philosophy that most illnesses were caused by the mind, Hubbard avowed, 'The danger in the world today in my opinion is not the atomic radiation which may or may not be floating through the atmosphere but the hysteria occasioned by that question.' Radiation, he added, was 'more of a mental than a physical problem'.

Fortunately, however, no one needed to worry about radiation, since Hubbard had devised a vitamin compound called 'Dianazene' (after his first child by Mary Sue?) which provided protection: 'Dianazene runs out radiation – or what appears to be radiation. It also proofs a person against radiation to some degree. It also turns on and runs out incipient cancer. I have seen it run out skin cancer. A man who didn't have much liability to skin cancer (only had a few moles)

took Dianazene. His whole jaw turned into a raw mass of cancer. He
kept on taking Dianazene and it disappeared after a while. I was
looking at a case of cancer that might have happened.'

The doctor, writing under the pseudonym Medicus, confirmed in
his section of the book that 'some very recent work by L. Ron Hubbard
and the Hubbard Scientology Organization has indicated that a simple
combination of vitamins in unusual doses can be of value. Alleviation
of the remote effects and increased tolerance of radiation have been the
apparent results . . .'

The Food and Drugs Administration in the United States was
inclined, after studying a copy of *All About Radiation*, to disagree.
FDA agents swooped on the Distribution Center Inc, a Scientology
company in Washington, seized 21,000 Dianazene tablets and
destroyed them, alleging that they were falsely labelled as a preven-
tative treatment for 'radiation sickness'.

In July 1957, Hubbard addressed the 'Freedom Congress' at the
Shoreham Hotel in Washington; during the lecture he carried out a
christening ceremony for the first time. Its function, he explained,
was simply to help get the thetan oriented in its new body and
informality was the keynote, as was made evident in a booklet titled
'Ceremonies of the Founding Church of Scientology'. After introducing the child to its parents and godparents, the ceremony proceeded:
'Here we go. (To the child): How are you? All right. Now your name
is ---. You got that? Good. There you are. Did that upset you? Now,
do you realize that you're a member of the HASI? Pretty good, huh?'
Thereafter the parents and godparents were introduced to the child
and the ceremony concluded: 'Now you're suitably christened. Don't
worry about it, it could be worse. OK. Thank you very much.
They'll treat you all right.'

His image as a family man was a pose, since he evinced little interest
in his own children. Nibs rarely managed to please his father and his
sister, Catherine, then twenty-one, had started working for the
organization in Washington but saw little of Hubbard. She married a
Scientologist in 1956 which would have pleased her father except he
did not like the man; the marriage could not survive his disapproval
and she divorced in 1957. Hubbard made no attempts to see Alexis.

The same month as the Freedom Congress, the Central Intelligence
Agency opened a file, No. 156409, on L. Ron Hubbard and his
organization. CIA agents trawled through police, revenue, credit and
property records to try and unravel Hubbard's tangled corporate
affairs. It was a task of herculean difficulty, for the Church of
Scientology was a cryptic maze of ad hoc corporations. The printed
notepaper of the Academy of Scientology gave only a hint of its
labyrinthine structure – on the left-hand side of the page was a list of no

less than seventeen associated organizations, ranging from the American Society for Disaster Relief to the Society of Consulting Ministers.

Agents traced a considerable amount of property owned either by Hubbard, his wife, son, or one of the daunting number of 'churches' with which they were associated, but the report quickly became bogged down in a tangle of names and addresses: 'The Academy of Religious Arts and Sciences is currently engaged as a school for ministers of religion which at the present time possesses approximately thirty to forty students. The entire course consists of $1500 to $1800 worth of actual classroom studies . . . The public office is located at 1810-12 19th Street N.W. The corporations rent the entire building . . .

'The Hubbard Guidance Center, located at 2315 15th Street, N.W., occupies the entire building which consists of three floors and which was purchased by the SUBJECT Organization. The center also rents farm property located somewhere along Colesville Road in Silver Spring, Maryland, on a short-term lease. The center formerly operated a branch office at 8609 Flower Avenue, Silver Spring, Maryland. In addition to the Silver Spring operation, the center has a working agreement with the Founding Church of Scientology of New York, which holds classes at Studio 847, Carnegie Hall, 154 West 57th Street, New York City. Churches of this denomination number in excess of one hundred in the United States . . .'

One agent was assigned the thankless task of reading through all Hubbard's published work at the Library of Congress in order to gain an 'insight' into Scientology. 'Hubbard's works', he noted glumly, 'contain many words, the meaning of which are not made clear for lay comprehension and perhaps purposely so.'

The District of Columbia Income Tax Division reported that the 'church' had applied for a licence to operate as a religion in Washington DC probably in an attempt to claim tax-free status, and the Personal Property Division reported that it was having difficulty persuading the church to produce its records so that a personal property tax could be levied. Repeated telephone calls had produced nothing but excuses as to why the records could not be produced.

In the end, the CIA file could do no more than chronicle a multitude of vague suspicions; it certainly uncovered no hard evidence of wrong-doing and it revealed curiously little about the remarkable career of the founder of the Founding Church of Scientology. 'Dr Hubbard', it noted simply, 'received a Doctor of Divinity degree in 1954 and throughout his adult career has been a minister.'

The increasingly obvious success of Scientology from 1957 onwards unquestionably prompted federal agencies to keep a closer eye on Hubbard. The Washington Field Office of the FBI, for example, maintained an extensive file which included film and sound recordings as well as photographs and doggedly noted every example of Hubbard's exuberant irreverence to authority.

When the Academy of Scientology delivered twelve thousand feet of film to a Washington laboratory for processing, outraged technicians forwarded it to the FBI for investigation, alleging that the speaker on the film was 'anti-American'. The film covered six one-hour lectures by Hubbard, during which he made a crack about the Government developing the hydrogen bomb in order to 'kill more people faster'.

He also talked about his experience, when 'he was a policeman', in dealing with the criminal mind. 'The FBI thinks there's such a thing as the criminal mind – always a big joke,' he said. 'There's a criminal mind and a non-criminal mind. The FBI have never shown me a non-criminal mind. Of course, these are terrible things to say – simply comments on J. Edgar who is an awfully good guy, stupid, but awfully good.' The Washington Field Office, which perhaps lacked Hubbard's sense of humour, solemnly took note of this analysis of their director and diligently forwarded to him the advice that L. Ron Hubbard thought he was 'stupid'.[8]

Largely unaware of the extent of federal interest in his activities, Hubbard had remained in Washington after the Freedom Congress to lecture on a more permanent basis at the Academy of Scientology. Mary Sue and the children joined him from London and they all moved into the brownstone house on 19th Street. Although she was soon pregnant once more, Mary Sue was appointed 'Academy Supervisor' and remained a powerful figure in the organization. On 6 June 1958, she gave birth to her fourth child—a son, Arthur Ronald Conway Hubbard. Like his older brother and sisters, Arthur emerged into the world with a wispy topping of bright red hair.

Through most of 1958 Hubbard lectured in Washington at the Academy. In one famous lecture, taped for posterity and marketed for profit, he recounted the colourful 'story of Dianetics and Scientology', interlacing the resumé with anecdotes and jokes, all delivered with a fine sense of timing and generating roars of laughter from an appreciative audience. It was essentially the story of his own life as it had come to be compiled in his mind, with extraordinary adventures tagged on to a slender framework of facts.

The story started, he said, when he was twelve years old and met Commander Thompson, an explorer and 'one of the great men of Freudian analysis'. Thompson, who was called 'Crazy Thompson' by his enemies and "Snake" by his friends, apparently had no children of his own and took a shine to little Ron when they found themselves together on a US Navy transport. The first thing the 'great man of Freudian analysis' taught the boy was how to train cats. Thompson's own cat, Psycho, had a crooked tail, Ron recalled, and would perform tricks.

He continued the story in similar vein. Finding himself in Asia while still a teenager, he discovered he was able to 'operate in the field of Asian mysticism'; in college he was 'never in class' but got through by persuading other students to take his mathematics examinations while he did their psychology papers. It was easy, he said. He simply read the textbooks the night before and sat the exam next morning. During the Prohibition years he knocked around with newspaper reporters and drank bathtub gin acquired from the 'very best gangsters'.

In 1938, having 'associated rather thoroughly with twelve different native cultures, not including the people in the Bronx', he identified the urge to survive as the common denominator of all forms of life. In hospital at the end of the war, 'recuperating from an accumulation of too much wartime Scotch and overdoses of lead', he continued his research. 'I found out that by taking off one collar ornament I became an MD. They don't let anybody in a medical library except doctors but by stopping off with one collar ornament and for a couple of bucks having a marine on crutches come by and say, "Good morning, doctor", I was able to get in a year's study at the medical library.'

After leaving hospital he bought a yacht, took a cruise to the West Indies, then used his wartime back pay to finance further research – 'I went down to the middle of Hollywood, rented an office, wrapped a towel round my head and became a swami.'

Perhaps the most revealing thing Hubbard said about himself during the lecture was a comment on one of Commander Thompson's favourite little aphorisms. It appeared that the Commander used to tell Ron, 'If it's not true for you, it's not true.' It aligned with his own personal philosophy, Hubbard explained, 'because if there is anyone in the world calculated to believe what he wants to believe it is I'. Never did L. Ron Hubbard speak a truer word.

In October, Hubbard flew back to London to preside over a six-week 'Advanced Clinical Course' at HASI's smart new West End offices in Fitzroy Street. Cyril Vosper was one of the students on the course hoping for a Bachelor or Doctorate of Scientology and he noticed a marked change in Hubbard's appearance: 'The flashy American clothes were gone. Now he was wearing grey tweed suits and silk shirts. He looked like a well-dressed professional gentleman and there was a feel of money and class about the whole thing.'[9]

Much of the course, Vosper recollected, was devoted to students investigating one another's past lives. As Hubbard made frequent mention in his lectures of past lives on other planets, with zapp guns, flying saucers, mother ships, galactic federations, repeller beams and suchlike, Vosper reported that many of the past lives excitedly revealed during the course sounded like 'Flash Gordon' adventures.

Nibs, who was one of the instructors, proved to be enormously resourceful in the past lives area. 'When a student was having difficulty in making his past life gel,' said Vosper, 'Nibs would helpfully fill in bits. Students knew that unless they could bring forth a past life with full recall, pain, emotion, full perception, the lot, they would be regarded as something less than real Scientologists. There was a good deal of rivalry as to who could dig up the most notable or extraordinary past life. Jesus of Nazareth was very popular. At least three London Scientologists claimed to have uncovered incidents in which they were crucified and rose from the dead to save the world. Queen Elizabeth I, Walter Raleigh and the venerable Bede were also popular. Funnily enough, I never met anyone who claimed to know anything about Attila the Hun, Genghis Khan or Pontius Pilate.'

Hubbard returned to Washington for Christmas, but in the New Year he began making plans to move back to London with his family. Pam and Ray Kemp wrote to say that they were moving and that their house in North London, on the Finchley Road in Golders Green, would be available if Ron was looking for somewhere to live. The Hubbards – Ron, Mary Sue, Diana, aged six, Quentin, five, Suzette, four and Arthur, eight months – arrived in London at the end of February and agreed to rent the Kemps' house in Golders Green.

'My daughter Suzanne was born on Ron's birthday,' said Pam Kemp. 'Ron came over with a beautiful, bright orange, angora shawl for me. He said everyone brings presents for the baby but everyone forgets it is the mother that has been doing all the work so he was bringing a present for the mother. That was typical of him.

'It was also typical of him that he stiffed us for the rent and he stiffed the greengrocer. Before they moved in, the greengrocer on the other side of the road asked us if he could trust the new tenants and we said "Of course." Ron proceeded to run up a huge bill which he never paid. And he never paid us any rent. We asked him dozens of times for the money. He told us to ask Mary Sue and she always said they didn't have any money.

'Then one day Ron came over on his motorcycle, very excited and pleased with himself. He said, "Guess what I've done?" '[10]

The Kemps were dumbfounded by their friend's news. He announced that he had bought the Maharajah of Jaipur's estate in Sussex.

Chapter 14

Lord of the Manor

'My own life is rather dull these days. I sort of won the Maharajah of Jaipur's luxury Sussex estate in a poker game . . .' (Note in the Explorers Log from Dr L. Ron Hubbard, *Explorers Journal*, February 1960)

* * * * *

Saint Hill Manor was a Georgian mansion on a landscaped estate two miles from the little market town of East Grinstead in Sussex. The countryside thereabouts was much favoured by the landed gentry in the eighteenth century for the beauty of its verdant, gently rolling hills and its proximity to the court in London, only a few hours away by horse and carriage, and Saint Hill was one of a number of large country houses in the area.

Built for a wealthy landowner in 1733, the manor could not be described as one of the glories of Georgian architecture (indeed, its sandstone façade had a faintly brooding aspect), but it was sufficiently imposing to merit a ballroom with marble columns and grounds of fifty acres with a lake, surrounded by a dense boundary hedge of rhododendrons. By the time it passed into the ownership of the Maharajah of Jaipur, the house boasted eleven bedrooms, eight bathrooms and an outdoor swimming-pool. While the Maharajah spent a considerable sum on interior improvements, including commissioning the artist John Spencer Churchill to paint a mural in one of the first-floor rooms, he only lived in the house intermittently. When the fortunes of the Indian princes wavered after Independence in 1947, he decided to put his English estate on the market and was happy to find a buyer in the unlikely shape of L. Ron Hubbard.

The arrival of an American family at Saint Hill Manor in the spring of 1959 occasioned almost as much excitement in East Grinstead as that of the exotic Maharajah had done some years earlier. Alan Larcombe, a young reporter on the East Grinstead *Courier* was despatched to interview the new owner and found him to be extremely co-operative, happy to pose for a photograph with his wife and children and more than willing to talk about himself.

'An American and his delightful family find a haven at Saint Hill', the *Courier* reported in its issue of 29 May 1959. Describing 'Dr Hubbard' as a 'tall, heavily built man whose work for humanity is known throughout the world', Larcombe made no attempt to explain the nature of Dr Hubbard's work, but contented himself with a recap of his subject's career, starting, naturally, with breaking broncos and hunting coyotes on his grandfather's cattle ranch. 'When he inherited his grandfather's cattle estates in Montana and all its debts, he wrote it into solvency, turning his hand to anything: essays, fiction and film scripts.'

The inheriting of his grandfather's insolvent cattle estates was a titbit of information Hubbard had not previously disclosed, as was his revelation that he was deeply involved in the study of plant life. 'The production of plant mutations is one of his most important projects at the moment. By battering seeds with X-rays, Dr Hubbard can either reduce a plant through its stages of evolution or advance it.'

It was, perhaps, inevitable that Hubbard would become an expert gardener the instant he moved into the English countryside and the fact that Saint Hill Manor had well-stocked greenhouses undoubtedly helped fire his interest. But his horticultural experiments also helped divert attention from the real reason he had bought the estate: his intention was that it should become the world-wide headquarters of Scientology. Hubbard surmised, no doubt correctly, that the people of East Grinstead were not quite ready for this piece of information.

In August, the *Courier* reported that the experiments being conducted at Saint Hill by the 'nuclear scientist, Dr Hubbard' promised to revolutionize gardening. By treating seeds with 'radioactive rays' he was growing tomato plants 16 feet high, with an average of 15 trusses and 45 tomatoes on each truss. He had also discovered that an 'infra-red ray lamp' provided complete protection against mildew, a discovery that was likely to save market gardeners 'thousands of pounds'.

The reporter, again, was Alan Larcombe: 'He showed us some very big tomatoes and I remember thinking at the time that anyone could have grown them that size with fertilizers, but he was very keen we should take a photograph of them, so we did.'[1] The picture the newspaper used was of little Quentin, five years old, standing on duckboards in his father's greenhouse, staring solemnly at the camera through a forest of tomato and maize plants.

Dr Hubbard's experiments soon came to the attention of *Garden News*, to which publication he revealed, gardener to gardener, his conviction that plants felt pain. He demonstrated by connecting an E-meter to a geranium with crocodile clips, tearing off its leaves and showing how the needle of the E-meter oscillated as he did so. The

Garden News correspondent was enormously excited and wrote a story under the sensational headline 'PLANTS DO WORRY AND FEEL PAIN, describing Hubbard as a 'revolutionary horticultural scientist'.[2]

It was not too long before television and Fleet Street reporters were beating a path to Saint Hill Manor demanding to interview Hubbard about his novel theories. Always pleased to help the gentlemen of the press, he was memorably photographed looking compassionately at a tomato jabbed by probes attached to an E-meter – a picture that eventually found its way into *Newsweek* magazine, causing a good deal of harmless merriment at his expense. Alan Whicker, a well-known British television interviewer, did his best to make Hubbard look like a crank, but Hubbard contrived to come across as a rather likeable and confident personality. When Whicker moved in for the kill, sarcastically inquiring if rose pruning should be stopped lest it caused pain and anxiety, Hubbard neatly side-stepped the question and drew a parallel with an essential life-preserving medical operation on a human being. He might have whacky ideas, Whicker discovered, but he was certainly no fool.

Scientologists around the world could have been forgiven for wondering what their beloved leader was up to, but an explanation was soon forthcoming. The purpose of Ron's experiments, they were told, was to 'reform the world's food supply'. He had already produced 'ever-bearing tomato plants and sweetcorn plants sufficiently impressive to startle British newspapers into front-page stories about this new wizardry'.[3]

Soon after Hubbard moved into Saint Hill, the Church of Scientology commissioned a bust of its founder from the sculptor Edward Harris. Harris liked his sitters to talk while he was working and asked his friend, Joan Vidal, to attend the sittings and chat with Hubbard. 'My first impression of him', she said, 'was that with his very pink skin and light red hair he looked like a fat, pink, scrubbed pig. I remember one of the first things he told me was that you could hear a tomato scream if you cut it and that's why he never ate tomatoes. He talked a lot about whether vegetables could feel pain and about all his past lives. It was very entertaining; it was obvious he had a good mind and was widely read.

'After the bust was finished we were invited to dinner with him and his wife at Saint Hill. When we arrived we were met by Mary Sue. She was a rather drab, mousy, nothing sort of person quite a bit younger than him. She showed us into a book-lined study and he waited a few minutes, rather theatrically, before making an entrance. I don't think they had finished work on the house because we had dinner in the kitchen. It was all white tiled, very antiseptic, and the meal was served by a woman wearing a white overall, white shoes and stockings. There

was nothing to drink but Coca-Cola or water and the food was awful—we
had frozen plaice fillets, a few vegetables and ice cream, but he had an
enormous steak overhanging his plate. It was obvious that everything
revolved around him. He was almost like Oswald Mosley, he had the
same sort of power. Both of them talked a lot about past lives; they told
me that their daughter had previously been a telephone operator who
had died in a fire. We didn't stay late and when we got back to Victoria
Station Eddie and I were both so hungry that we went in the buffet and
had delicious roast lamb sandwiches.'[4]

In October, Dr Hubbard unveiled yet another of his interests.
Learning that East Grinstead had been unable to fill a vacancy for a
Road Safety Organizer, he volunteered for the job. As he explained to a
meeting of the East Grinstead Road Safety Committee, he was anxious
to make a contribution to the community and he felt that the experience
he had gained serving on 'numerous' road safety committees in the
United States could be put to good use in East Grinstead. He gave an
interesting talk on road safety campaigns in the United States, put
forward many ideas on how to reduce accidents locally, confidently
answered questions and was unanimously elected as the town's new
Road Safety Organizer by a grateful committee.

He was not able to give road safety considerations his attention for too
long, however, for he had arranged to visit Australia in November to
lecture to Scientologists in Melbourne. He left London on 31 October,
flying first-class on BOAC via Calcutta and Singapore. At the Hubbard
Communications Office in Spring Street, Melbourne, he was greeted by
an ecstatic crowd of Scientologists who cheered noisily when he
announced his belief that Australia would be the first 'clear continent'.
Between lectures, he spent hours with local HASI executives discussing
ways of persuading the Australian Labour Party and trades union
movement to adopt Scientology techniques. Hubbard was convinced
that Scientology could help Labour win the next election in Australia,
thus creating a favourable climate for the development of the church
and neutralizing the unabated hostility of the Australian media.

While he was still in Melbourne, Hubbard received an urgent
telephone call from Washington with bad news. Nibs, he was told, had
'blown'. To Scientologists, 'blowing the org' (leaving the church) was
one of the worst crimes in the book: it was almost unbelievable that the
highly-placed son and namesake of the founder would take such a step.
Nibs had simultaneously held five posts in Scientology's increasingly
cumbersome bureaucratic structure: he was Organizational Secretary
of the Founding Church of Scientology, Washington DC; Hubbard
Communications Office-in-Charge, Washington DC; Chief Advanced
Clinical Course Instructor; Hubbard Communications Office World
Wide Technical Director; and a Member of the International Council.

Despite his portentous titles, Nibs was frustrated by not being able to make any money out of Scientology and he left a letter to his father explaining that this was the only reason for his resignation: 'Over the past few years, I have found it increasingly difficult to maintain basic financial survival for myself and my family. This I must remedy. I fully realize that I have not handled my financial affairs in the most optimum manner. But for six years I have managed to provide, at least the basic necessities, in some manner. In doing so I have depleted all my reserves and have become deeply in debt . . .'

Hubbard, who was not exactly a pillar of rectitude in fiscal matters, was nevertheless furious with his son. Nibs had been in and out of debt ever since he had first turned up on Hubbard's doorstep in Phoenix. The problem was that he had his father's casual attitude towards money, but none of his talent for making it and none of his luck. In his resignation letter, Nibs said he was going to look for a full-time job, but hoped to be able to continue practising Scientology in his spare time. He failed to take into account the fact that his father would automatically view his defection as an act of treachery. Hubbard would never have allowed Nibs to continue trying to make money out of Scientology. He quickly scribbled an airmail letter to Marilyn Routsong on 25 November: 'Nibs was trying to get more money by loans from us. This may make a field upset but we'll survive. If he goes into practice anywhere or starts up a squirrel activity have HCO cancel all certificates and awards of his. He won't ever be hired back.'

A few days later Hubbard received more, equally unwelcome, family news when his Aunt Toilie telephoned from Bremerton to say that his seventy-four-year-old mother had had a stroke, was very ill and not expected to live. Hubbard had had little contact with his parents, or the Waterbury family, since the end of the war. Toilie was the only one who tried to keep in touch, writing to him once or twice a year, and it fell to her to find Ron when May was taken to hospital. Hubbard told her, over a crackling inter-continental telephone line that he could not get away, he was too busy.

Toilie was quite as forceful a personality as a grey-haired old lady as she had been as a young woman. 'You're coming home,' she told him. 'I want you to catch the next flight out. That is orders, Ron. You owe that much to your mother and I pray to God you get here before she's dead.'

By the time Hubbard arrived in Bremerton, his mother was in a coma. He went in to see her, held her hand and talked to her; he told the family afterwards he was sure she knew he was there. She died the following day. 'Ron didn't stay for the funeral,' said his Aunt Marnie. 'He organized the burial, ordered the stone, paid all the expenses and made arrangements for a man from the Church of Scientology to come up and accompany the body with Hub and Toilie to the funeral in Helena. Then he flew back to England from Bremerton. I thought he should have stayed for the funeral. I don't know what could have been so pressing that he had to get back to England.'[5]

In March 1960, the gentle burghers of East Grinstead learned a little more about their Road Safety Organizer when he published a book titled *Have You Lived Before This Life?* in which were described a number of startling 'past lives' revealed during auditing. One case history concerned a previous existence as a walrus, another as a fish, a third had witnessed the destruction of Pompeii in AD 79 and a fourth had been a 'very happy being who strayed to the planet Nostra 23,064,000,000 years ago'.

The *Courier* reported that the book caused a 'storm of controversy' in the town, as might have been anticipated, and Hubbard was prompted to issue a statement seeking to explain something of Scientology: 'Scientific research work on Dianetics and Scientology has been carried out by Dr L. Ron Hubbard, and skilled persons employed by him, over the past 30 years. Only since 1950 has the knowledge gleaned from this exacting and penetrating work into the functions of the mind been released to the general public in the form of special and skilled treatment . . . In connection with Dr Hubbard's book *Have You Lived Before This Life?* the contents are merely reported from an observer's point of view . . .'

In an internal memo to his press officer, Hubbard stressed the need to emphasize constantly that he was working in the field of 'nuclear physics on life sources and life energy' in order to avoid being tagged as a psychiatrist or spiritualist. 'This will take some doing, perhaps,' he added, in a rare moment of candour.[6]

Hubbard need not have worried overmuch as far as East Grinstead was concerned, since the weather and the Royal Family were topics of much greater perennial interest than whatever was going on at Saint Hill Manor. The cast list of the upcoming, absorbing and long-running British royal soap opera was just being drawn up in spring 1960 – the Queen's third child, Prince Andrew, was born in February and Princess Margaret was due to marry in May. To add a little spice to the conversation in East Grinstead pubs, there was also the forthcoming obscenity trial of D. H. Lawrence's masterpiece, *Lady Chatterley's Lover*.

This last event was being followed closely by Mary Sue as her husband had recently uncovered a previous life coincidentally revealing her to have been none other than D. H. Lawrence! In a letter to her friend Marilyn Routsong, Mary Sue explained the considerable problems she had experienced as D. H. Lawrence. It seemed the great writer had difficulty constructing plots, thought poetry was a joke and believed little of what he wrote.

On the strength of this previous incarnation, Mary Sue confessed that she, too, was going to write a book and outlined the plot with a somewhat unpromising grasp of grammar and spelling. She wrote that it would be completely anti-Christ. The first sentence begins 'In the small town of Balei, a bastard child was born.' She then intended to show how he was really a mongrel and the son of three fathers (a joke on the Trinity of God) because the mother had, the night in question, slept with three of the town's most virile men and not knowing whose sperm had reached her womb, had thereupon decided to call him Ali, Son of ----, Son of ----, and Son of ---- which impressed the local inhabitants and created a stir throughout the country. She concluded that she wouldn't have it in her name, for obvious reasons.

In the same letter, Mary Sue mentioned the rumpus that had been caused when Ron ordered all the staff at Saint Hill to be checked out on an E-meter. She noted that three office staff refused and five domestic staff refused. She was surprised and wrote that they were all scared to death of the E-meter and pretending that it was something that would only happen in America, adding that they evidently have something to hide because of their fear to go on the E-meter.[7]

Hubbard's insistence that everyone who worked for him be interrogated on the E-meter was part of the routine 'security checking' he deemed necessary to identify potential trouble-makers, dissidents and spies. No one in Scientology now doubted the capability of the E-meter to expose visceral emotions and ever more elaborate 'sec-checks' would become a common feature of life in the Scientology movement – evidence of Hubbard's persistent paranoia about his enemies, both those that existed in reality and those that thronged his imagination.

Despite the not unreasonable reluctance of some of the servants at Saint Hill Manor to be interviewed about their private lives while grasping tin cans attached to a mysterious electric machine, the Hubbards had settled in comfortably by the spring of 1960. The painters and decorators had finished their work and the family was enjoying the Elysian delights of gracious living in an English country house. On their 'personal staff' there were a secretary, housekeeper, cook, butler, valet, nanny and tutor for the children.

The former billiards room, leading directly from the grand entrance hall, had been re-modelled into Hubbard's private office, with a bench seat upholstered in red leather down one side of the room and a personal teleprinter installed alongside his desk. Also accessible from the hall was the family dining-room, which included a bar stocked with Coca-Cola (Hubbard's preferred drink), a large lounge and a television room. Upstairs, Hubbard had his own suite comprising a sitting-room, bedroom and bathroom, adjoining Mary Sue's office, bedroom and bathroom. The children had bedrooms at the other end of the house and the 'Monkey Room', named after the murals painted by John Spencer Churchill, was converted into a school-room and equipped with trampoline. Apart from the kitchen, most of the remaining rooms in the manor were used as offices.

It was the first time that the Hubbards as a family had remained in one place for any length of time and the children were particularly enchanted by Saint Hill Manor, with its maze of rooms and sweeping grounds. At weekends the four of them could usually be found, muddy-kneed, exploring the estate or paddling in rubber boots on the fringes of the lake; twice a week Diana and Suzette attended dancing lessons at the local Bush Davies school.

Hubbard, too, liked to stroll the grounds at weekends, taking photographs with one or the other of his new cameras. Photography was a recently acquired hobby and his framed pictures could be found in many of the rooms at Saint Hill. Mainly landscapes and portraits, they were of course universally praised, even those that were slightly out of focus.

All in all, visitors to Saint Hill at this time would have observed little amiss with the nice American family who had taken up residence. Certainly no one would have guessed that Hubbard possessed the dubious distinction of being probably the only owner of an English country house under the continuous surveillance of the FBI. His file, Number 244-210-B, was much thumbed and even included an interview with his first wife, Polly, by then re-married, who was able to say very little except that her first husband was a 'genius with a misdirected mind'.

To some extent, the FBI's interest in Hubbard was a situation of his own making, for the frequently intemperate bulletins and policy letters which flowed from Saint Hill in an endless stream for distribution to Scientologists around the world were bound to generate the attention of J. Edgar Hoover's staff. On 24 April 1960, for example, Hubbard issued a bulletin to US franchise holders asking them to do everything in their power to deny the presidency to 'a person named Richard M. Nixon'.

He claimed that after an innocent reference to Nixon in a Scientology magazine, two armed secret service agents, acting on Nixon's orders, had threatened staff on duty at the founding church in Washington: 'Hulking over desks, shouting violently, they stated that they daily had to make such calls on "lots of people" to prevent Nixon's name from being used in ways Nixon disliked . . . They said Nixon believed in nothing the Founding Church of Scientology stood for . . .

'We want clean hands in public office in the United States. Let's begin by doggedly denying Nixon the presidency no matter what his Secret Service tries to do to us now . . . He hates us and has used what police force was available to him to say so. So please get busy on it . . .'

Nixon was indeed denied the presidency, although it was possible that the famous televised debates with John F. Kennedy had more to do with it than the HCO Bulletin. But it was becoming evident that the owner of Saint Hill Manor considered he had an important role to play in political and international affairs and it was a responsibility he had no intention of shirking.

An HCO Bulletin in June promulgated the 'Special Zone Plan – The Scientologists Role in Life', in which Hubbard explained how Scientologists could exert influence in politics. 'Don't bother to get elected,' he wrote. 'Get a job on the secretarial staff or the bodyguard.' In this way positioned close to the seat of power, he argued, Scientology would be advantageously situated to transform an organization. 'If we were revolutionaries,' he added, 'this HCO Bulletin would be a *very* dangerous document.'

In August, the 'Special Zone Plan' was absorbed into a new 'Department of Government Affairs' made necessary, Hubbard gravely explained, because of the amount of time senior Scientology executives were having to devote to governmental affairs, as governments around the world disintegrated under the threat of atomic war and Communism. 'The goal of the Department', he wrote 'is to bring government and hostile philosophies or societies into a state of complete compliance with the goals of Scientology. This is done by high-level ability to control and in its absence by a low-level ability to overwhelm. Introvert such agencies. Control such agencies.'

Returning to a familiar theme, Hubbard urged his followers to defend Scientology by attacking its opponents: 'If attacked on some vulnerable point by anyone or anything or any organization, always find or manufacture enough threat against them to cause them to sue for peace . . . Don't ever defend, always attack. Don't ever do nothing. Unexpected attacks in the rear of the enemy's front ranks work best.'

The Department of Government Affairs never existed other than as a 'policy letter',[8] but then much of Hubbard's private world only existed on paper. In HCO Bulletins and Policy Letters replete with the trappings of bureaucratic red tape – colour-coded distribution lists, elaborate references, innumerable abbreviations, etc – Scientology flourished as an international organization of enormous influence waiting in the wings to save the universe from the combined perils of Communism, nuclear weapons and its own folly.

Sitting at an electric typewriter in his study at Saint Hill Manor, often clicking away all night just as in the days when he was writing science fiction, Hubbard demonstrated his extraordinary range as a writer by effortlessly producing sheaves of documents that appeared to have been drafted by committees of bureaucrats and lawyers. Laid out and printed like official government papers, they conferred dry authority on content which, frequently, would not have withstood too close scrutiny. But of course no Scientologist would question the literal truth of anything Hubbard wrote, no matter how improbable – if Ron said it was so, it was so.

Hubbard's blossoming omnipotence was bolstered by the stately fashion in which he now travelled, always first-class, usually accompanied by a faithful courtier and greeted at every destination by an awed welcoming party of admirers. In October and November 1960 he visited South Africa to lecture Scientologists in Cape Town and Johannesburg; in December he flew to Washington DC, spent Christmas and the New Year there, returned to Johannesburg to deliver more lectures in mid-January, and arrived back at Saint Hill Manor towards the end of February 1961.

In March, Hubbard announced the launch of the 'Saint Hill Special Briefing Course' for those auditors who wished to train personally under his auspices. The cost of the 'SHSBC' was £250 per person and the first student to enrol was Reg Sharpe, a retired businessman who had become so enamoured with Scientology that he bought a house in the little village of Saint Hill, adjoining the estate, in order to be close to Ron. For the first couple of weeks there were only two students in the course, but more soon began to arrive from around the world, lured by the promise that 'Ron, personally, would discover and assess with the aid of an E-meter' each student's goal 'for this lifetime'.

Mary Sue, who was the course supervisor, also held out the prospect of material rewards: 'I want you to make money. If any one of you cannot conceive of an auditor driving around in a gold-plated Cadillac or Rolls you had better reorientate yourselves. I like the idea.'9

As the numbers on the Briefing Course increased, accommodation became a problem. The greenhouses where Ron had conducted his pioneering horticultural experiments were demolished to make way for a 'chapel' which in reality was used as a lecture hall. Other buildings went up around the manor without a moment's thought for obtaining planning permission – Hubbard's strongly held opinion was that what he did on his own land was his own business. It was a view the local authority was disinclined to share when someone pointed out what was going on at Saint Hill and Hubbard was eventually prevailed upon to employ an architect and apply for planning approval like everyone else.

The Briefing Course would eventually comprise more than three hundred taped lectures by L. Ron Hubbard, its longevity sustained by 'technical breakthroughs' that followed closely one upon the other, each new technique replacing the last and requiring dedicated Scientologists to trek back to Saint Hill time and time again in order to keep up to date.

When Hubbard was not lecturing he was writing directives covering everything from how to save the world to how to clean his office. No detail was too insignificant to merit his attention: one HCO Policy Letter covering two pages was posted prominently in the garage at Saint Hill explaining how cars should be washed and another was addressed to the Household Section headed 'Flowers, Care Of'. He also dashed off a new potted biography of himself adding further gloss to his already well-burnished career. It was included in a handout headed 'What Is Scientology?':

'For hundreds of years physical scientists have been seeking to apply the exact knowledge they had gained of the physical universe to Man and his problems. Newton, Sir James Jeans, Einstein, have all sought to find the exact laws of human behaviour in order to help Mankind.

'Developed by L. Ron Hubbard, C.E., Ph.D., a nuclear physicist, Scientology has demonstrably achieved this long-sought goal. Doctor Hubbard, educated in advanced physics and higher mathematics and also a student of Sigmund Freud and others, began his present researches thirty years ago at George Washington University. The dramatic result has been Scientology . . .'

The laudable aim of 'helping mankind' sat rather uncomfortably with the requirement for security checks, which were stepped up during 1961. An even more intrusive questionnaire was introduced which appeared to have been designed with perverts and criminals rather than potential trouble-makers in mind. Many of the questions reflected Hubbard's morbid preoccupation with sexual deviation ('Have you ever had intercourse with a member of your family' and 'Have you ever had anything to do with a baby farm?') and a wide range of crimes were also probed ('Have you ever murdered anyone?' and 'Have you ever done any illicit diamond buying?'). In addition Hubbard specifically wanted to know if the individual being checked had ever 'had any unkind thoughts' about himself or Mary Sue. Every check sheet was forwarded to Saint Hill on Hubbard's orders. When combined with the individual folders in which details of auditing sessions were recorded, they made up a comprehensive dossier in which the innermost thoughts of every member of the Church of Scientology were filed.

Three days after Christmas 1961, Hubbard flew to Washington DC to attend a congress and publicize the benefits to be obtained by enrolling in the Saint Hill Briefing Course. He asked Reg Sharpe to accompany him on the trip and Sharpe was very soon made aware of his leader's little foibles. When their aeroplane stopped for re-fuelling at Boston, Hubbard scurried across the passenger terminal and stood with his back pressed against a wall for the duration of the stop, explaining to his bemused companion that there were people 'out to get him'.

In Washington, Sharpe was astonished by the adulation with which Hubbard was received. He lectured for about four hours on each day of the congress to a spellbound audience and had refined his speaking technique to a fine art, shamelessly borrowing the tricks of show business and political conventions. He liked to appear at the back of the hall to the accompaniment of a drum roll and stride through the audience, waving his arms in greeting and shaking hands on the way to the rostrum. His timing, the essence of a good speaker, was faultless and he could hold an entire auditorium in thrall for hours. Like a cabaret artiste doing two spots a night, he got into the habit of changing his clothes during a break, appearing for the second half of his lecture in a silk suit of a different colour, or sometimes a gold lamé jacket. It held the interest of the audience, he explained, and also solved his perspiration problems.

Hubbard's vigorous promotion of Saint Hill as the Mecca of Scientology resulted in hundreds of young Americans making their way to East Grinstead, somewhat to the surprise of the townspeople, who still had very little idea of what was going on. 'Dr Hubbard' had recently adopted a rather lower profile locally: he resigned from his position as the town's Road Safety Organizer, pleading pressure of business, was very rarely seen outside the grounds of Saint Hill Manor and no longer courted publicity from the local newspapers. By and large, the influx of American visitors to the town was welcomed: they were quiet, polite and spent freely. If they were less than forthcoming about what they were doing in the area, that was all right with the locals, who instinctively respected the rights of folk who wanted to 'keep themselves to themselves'.

Members of East Grinstead Urban Council expressed some faint concern inasmuch as Saint Hill Manor was restricted, by planning regulations, to private residential use, but such was Dr Hubbard's reputation that they resolved to do no more than urge him, in confidence, to apply for planning permission regularizing the use of the manor for office and research purposes. He responded by slapping in a planning application to build a seventy-five-room administration centre in the grounds of the manor and circularizing a 'Report to the Community' appealing for support.

In the report, Hubbard revealed to the people of East Grinstead that as a result of his experiments on plants and 'living energies' he was able to reduce the physiological age of an individual by as much as twenty years and increase the average life span by as much as twenty-five per cent. 'We have not announced anything of this to the press,' he confided, 'as we are already overworked in centres of the world for discoveries such as these. But we wanted you as a friend to be aware of this, and consider you have the right to know what is happening here.'

In August, Hubbard turned his attention to the broader arena of international affairs by offering to help President Kennedy narrow the gap in the space race. The young president had committed the United States to landing a man on the moon before the decade was out and, as a loyal American, Hubbard obviously wanted to do what he could to help. On 13 August 1962, he wrote a long letter to the White House to advise Kennedy that Scientology techniques were peculiarly applicable to space flight and that the perception of an astronaut could be increased far beyond human range and stamina to levels hitherto unattained in human beings.

To establish his bona fides, Hubbard claimed to have coached the 'British Olympic team', producing unheard-of results. He added that he had been fending off approaches from the Russians for years, ever since he was offered Pavlov's laboratories in 1938. The first manuscript of his work had been stolen in Miami in 1942, the second in Los Angeles in 1950 and 'only last week' Communist interests had stolen forty hours of tape containing the latest research work from the Scientology headquarters in South Africa.

Although he was convinced that there was a growing library on Scientology in Russia, fortunately the Russians did not yet have the advanced knowledge that would be applicable to the space programme. All the US Government need do, he said, was turn over anyone needing conditioning for space flight and Scientology would do the rest. Each man would need processing for about 250 hours and the cost would only be $25 an hour, with the possibility of a discount for large numbers. 'Man will not successfully get into space without us . . .' he warned. 'We do not wish the United States to lose either the space race or the next war. The deciding factor in that race or that war may very well be lying in your hands at this moment, and may depend on what is done with this letter . . . Courteously, L. Ron Hubbard.'

It seemed that Hubbard seriously expected his offer to receive proper consideration in the Oval Office, for two weeks later he was in Washington discussing with the staff at the Hubbard Communications Office how to handle the expected inflow of astronauts. It was agreed that any dealings with the US Government would be on a cash basis only, that they would reserve the right to reject anyone they considered to be unsuitable and that if Government officials wanted to investigate Scientology techniques they would be told, pleasantly, to 'go up the spout'. If there was a flood of astronauts arriving for processing, Ron would come over from Saint Hill and set up a special operation to handle them.[10]

On the voyage back to England, travelling first-class on the *Queen Elizabeth* with Reg Sharpe, the two men passed their time auditing each other. Hubbard told his friend that in a past life on another planet he had been in charge of a factory making steel humanoids which he sold to thetans, offering hire purchase terms if they could not afford the cash price.

Back at Saint Hill, Hubbard was baffled to discover that the President had not replied to his letter, but everything was made clear to him a few months later when agents of the Food and Drugs Administration staged a raid on the Scientology headquarters in Washington. It was *obvious* to Hubbard that the President had asked the FDA to look into Scientology as a result of his letter and the FDA, wishing to promote its own programmes, had attempted to turn the tables on Scientology.

Chapter 15

Visits to Heaven

'Well, I have been to heaven . . . It was complete with gates, angels and plaster saints – and electronic implantation equipment.' (L. Ron Hubbard, HCO Bulletin 11 May 1963)

* * * * *

The FDA raid on the Church of Scientology on 4 January 1963, was a farce better suited to the Keystone Cops than a federal agency. Two unmarked vans, escorted by motor-cycle police, screeched to a halt outside 1810-12 19th Street, Washington NW, in the middle of the afternoon and as police blockaded both ends of the quiet residential street, FDA agents and US marshals in plain clothes jumped out of the vans and ran into the building. Passers-by might well have assumed they were after terrorists of the most dangerous order. It would then have been something of a surprise when the brave officers began staggering out shortly afterwards with nothing more menacing than piles of books and papers and stacks of boxed E-meters. Such was the haul that two more trucks had to be called in before the afternoon's work was complete, by which time the FDA was able to announce, with an evident sense of triumph, that it had seized more than three tons of literature and equipment.

The feeble justification for these heavy-handed tactics was unveiled when the FDA filed charges accusing the Church of Scientology of having 'false and misleading' labels on its E-meters. As it would have been perfectly feasible to file a similar charge by purchasing a single E-meter from any Scientology office, the raid exposed the Food and Drug Administration to considerable derision and provided the church with a wonderful opportunity to capitalize on its newly martyred status. FDA agents were portrayed as armed thugs bursting into 'confessional and pastoral counselling sessions' and desecrating the sanctity of a church. Scientology press releases described the raid as a 'shocking example of government bureaucracy gone mad' and a 'direct and frightening attack upon the Constitutional rights of freedom of religion'.[1]

On 5 January, L. Ron Hubbard issued a statement from Saint Hill

Manor: 'All I can make of this is that the United States Government . . . has launched an attack upon religion and is seizing and
burning books of philosophy . . . Where will this end? Complete
censorship? A complete ignoring of the First Amendment? Are
churches to be attached and books burned as a normal course of
action?'

There had been no suggestion that the material carted away by the
FDA would be burned, but that did not prevent Hubbard returning
to the theme in a second statement the following day, as well as
making the connection between the FDA raid and his letter to
President Kennedy. He claimed that 'twice in recent years' the White
House had asked for a presentation of Scientology and he had thought
it only courteous to make the same offer to Kennedy, not realizing that
lesser officials were 'imbued with ideas of religious persecution'. He
was still hoping for a conference with the president, he said, slyly
alluding to recent events by adding that he would expect to be given
some guarantee for his 'personal safety'. Hubbard ended on an almost
jocular note: 'As all of my books have been seized for burning, it looks
as though I will have to get busy and write another book.'

In fact, 1963 was one of the few years in which Hubbard did not
produce a single book. Instead, he chose to remain at Saint Hill
issuing increasingly bizarre proclamations. On 13 March – his fifty-
second birthday – he bestowed a general amnesty on his followers, in
the fashion of some middle-eastern potentate: 'Any and all offences of
any kind before this date, discovered or undiscovered, are fully and
completely forgiven. Directed at Saint Hill, on March the thirteenth,
1963, in the 13th year of Dianetics and Scientology. L. Ron
Hubbard.'

The amnesty was followed in May by the foudroyant revelation that
Hubbard had twice visited heaven, 43 trillion and 42 trillion years
earlier. In a four-page HCO Bulletin – dated 11 May AD 13 (meaning
'After Dianetics') – he claimed the first visit had taken place
43,891,832,611,177 years, 344 days, 10 hours, 20 minutes and 40
seconds from 10.02pm Daylight Greenwich Mean Time 9 May 1963.
Nit-pickers might have pointed out that 'Daylight Greenwich Mean
Time' was a term unknown in horology and that, in any case, at
10.02pm on a May evening in Britain it would be dark, but this was a
trifling matter compared with what was to come.

The first surprise was that heaven was not a floating island in the
sky as everyone imagined, but simply a high place in the mountains of
an unnamed planet. Visitors first arrived in a 'town' comprising a
trolley bus, some building fronts, sidewalks, train tracks, a boarding
house, a bistro in a basement and a bank building. Although there
seemed to be people around – in the boarding house, for example,

there was a guest and a landlady in a kimono, reading a newspaper – Hubbard quickly discovered they were only effigies and probably radioactive, since 'contact with them hurts'. However, he was able to report he saw 'no devils or satans' [perhaps because he was supposed to be in heaven].

The bank was the key point of interest in the town. It was an old-fashioned corner building of granite-like material with a revolving door. Inside, to the left of the door, was a counter and directly opposite was a flight of marble stairs leading to the Pearly Gates! 'The gates . . . are well done, well built,' Hubbard wrote. 'An avenue of statues of saints leads up to them. The gate pillars are surmounted by marble angels. The entering grounds are very well kept, laid out like Bush Gardens in Pasadena, so often seen in the movies.'

On his second visit to heaven, a trillion years later, Hubbard noticed marked changes: 'The place is shabby. The vegetation is gone. The pillars are scruffy. The saints have vanished. So have the angels. A sign on one side (the left as you "enter") says "this is Heaven". The right has a sign "Hell" with an arrow and inside the grounds one can see the excavations like archeological diggings with raw terraces, that lead to "Hell". Plain wire fencing encloses the place. There is a sentry box beside and outside the right pillar . . .'

Hubbard's visits to heaven would become something of an embarrassment to Scientologists in future years and they would strive to explain that he had intended his description to be allegory, but Hubbard himself attached a note to the bulletin seeming to deny its contents were allegorical. 'This HCO Bulletin', he stressed, 'is based on over a thousand hours of research auditing . . . It is scientific research and is not in any way based upon the mere opinion of the researcher.'[2]

In August, Hubbard turned his attention to more temporal issues by re-defining Scientology policy towards the media. Typically, he did not mince words. Almost all Scientology's bad publicity, he asserted, could be blamed on the American Medical Association, which wanted to cause maximum harm to the movement in order to protect its private healing monopoly. 'The reporter who comes to you, all smiles and withholds, wanting a story,' he said, 'has an AMA instigated release in his pocket. He is there to trick you into supporting his preconceived story. The story he will write has already been outlined by a sub-editor from old clippings and AMA releases . . .'

Hubbard's sensitivity towards newspapers was understandable, since Scientology was an easy target and wherever it flourished it was attacked by a universally unsympathetic press. In Australia, the church had suffered a great deal of unfavourable publicity, in particular from a Melbourne newspaper, *Truth*, which published a series of hostile features about Scientologists being 'brainwashed' and alienated from their families. The media attacks led to questions in the Parliament of Victoria, allegations of blackmail and extortion, and accusations that Scientology was affecting the 'mental well-being' of undergraduates at Melbourne University. In November 1963, the Victoria government appointed a Board of Inquiry into Scientology.

At Saint Hill Manor, Hubbard at first professed himself to be pleased about the Australian inquiry and even hinted that it had been set up at his instigation. But it soon became evident that the inquiry was basically antagonistic to Scientology and when an invitation arrived from Melbourne from him to appear, he contrived to find compelling reasons to refuse.

In March 1964, the *Saturday Evening Post* published what would be one of the last full-scale media interviews with L. Ron Hubbard, even though he would be pursued by reporters for the rest of his life. It was an unusually objective feature, although little new was revealed except for Hubbard's claim that he had recently been approached by Fidel Castro to train a corps of Cuban Scientologists. The founder of the Church of Scientology appeared willing to discuss any subject except money. He was, he said, independently wealthy and drew only a token salary of $70 a week, Scientology being a 'labour of love'.

Certainly the *Saturday Evening Post* reporter was deeply impressed by Hubbard's lifestyle – the Georgian mansion, the butler who served his afternoon Coca-Cola on a silver tray, the chauffeur polishing the new Pontiac and the Jaguar in the garage, and the broad acres of the estate.[3] But while it might have seemed to a visiting journalist that Hubbard had acquired many of the traditional tastes of an English country gentleman, the reality was very different, as Ken Urquhart, a dedicated young Scientologist who worked as the butler at Saint Hill, explained: 'Neither Ron nor Mary Sue lived the way one might have expected in a house like that. They spent most of their time working; there was very little socializing. They would go to bed very late, usually in the small hours of the morning, and get up in the early afternoon.

'Ron used to audit himself with an E-meter as soon as he got out of bed. When he called down to the kitchen I would take him up a cup of hot chocolate and stay with him while he drank it. He used to sit at a table at the end of his four-poster bed chatting about the news or the weather or the latest goings-on at Saint Hill. I remember he used to talk a lot about his childhood. He seemed to want to give the impression that he was rather upper-class; he liked to use French expressions, for example, although his accent was *dreadful*. He said his mother was a very fine woman. He told me that when she was in hospital desperately ill he got there just in time to tell her that all she had to do was leave her body and go down to the maternity ward and pick up another one. He didn't say what her reaction was.

'When he went to have a bath I'd extricate myself and rush downstairs to cook breakfast for him and Mary Sue. She had a separate bedroom, but usually had breakfast with him – scrambled eggs, sausages, mushrooms and tomatoes. After breakfast he would go into his office and I would rarely see him again until six-thirty when I had to have the table laid for dinner. At six-twenty-five I would go into his office with a jacket for him to wear to table and after dinner they would spend an hour or so watching television with the children and then he and Mary Sue would return to work in their separate offices.

'I really loved working for Ron; I would have done anything for him. To me he was superhuman, a very unusual, very great person who really wanted to help the world. I was less sure about Mary Sue; I never quite knew where I stood with her. She could be very sweet and loving, but also very cold. The first time I had any contact with her was on the first Sunday I was at Saint Hill. She came into the kitchen where I was preparing dinner and did not say a word to me. I thought that was very strange. She was fiercely protective of her children and I liked them a lot. Arthur had a few problems because he was the youngest and the others wouldn't play with him. Diana was heavily into ballet lessons. They were nice.'

Urquhart was a Scot who had been studying music at Trinity College in London when he was introduced to Dianetics. 'It was as if someone had swept the cobwebs out of my mind,' he said. He was working part-time as a waiter when Ron asked him if he would help out at Saint Hill as a butler. 'I wouldn't have done it for anyone else. I used to cook all the meals, sweep the floors, make the beds, rush around all day long, for £12 a week plus room and board. I was perfectly happy, but things changed quite a bit early in 1965 when "ethics" came in. I was assigned a "condition of emergency" because I served him salmon for dinner that was not quite fresh. I was shocked. You had to go through a whole formula, write it up and submit it with an application to be up-graded.'[4]

'Conditions' were an essential part of the new 'ethics technology' devised by Hubbard in the mid-sixties, effectively as a form of social control. It was his first, tentative step towards the creation of a society within Scientology which would ultimately resemble the totalitarian state envisaged by George Orwell in his novel *1984*. Anyone *thought* to be disloyal, or slacking, or breaking the rules of Scientology, was reported to an 'ethics officer' and assigned a 'condition' according to the gravity of the offence. Various penalties were attached to each condition. In a 'condition of liability' for example, the offender was required to wear a dirty grey rag tied around his or her left arm. The worst that could happen was to be declared an 'SP' (suppressive person), which was tantamount to excommunication from the church. SPs were defined by Hubbard as 'fair game' to be pursued, sued and harrassed at every possible opportunity.

'What happened with the development of ethics,' said Cyril Vosper, who worked on the staff at Saint Hill, 'was that zeal expanded at the expense of tolerance and sanity. My feeling was that Mary Sue devised a lot of the really degrading aspects of ethics. I always had great warmth and admiration for Ron - he was a remarkable individual, a constant source of new information and ideas – but I thought Mary Sue was an exceedingly nasty person. She was a bitch.

'Hubbard had this incredible dynamism, a disarming, magnetic and overwhelming personality. I remember being at Saint Hill one Sunday evening and running into him and as we started to talk people gathered round. People had a wonderful feeling with him of being in the presence of a great man.'[5]

In October 1965, the Australian Board of Inquiry into Scientology published its report. Conducted by Kevin A. Anderson QC, the inquiry sat for 160 days, heard evidence from 151 witnesses and then savagely condemned every aspect of Scientology. No one needed to progress beyond the first paragraph to guess at what was to follow:

'There are some features of Scientology which are so ludicrous that there may be a tendency to regard Scientology as silly and its practitioners as harmless cranks. To do so would be gravely to misunderstand the tenor of the Board's conclusions. This Report should be read, it is submitted, with these prefatory observations constantly in mind. Scientology is evil; its techniques evil; its practice a serious threat to the community, medically, morally and socially; and its adherents sadly deluded and often mentally ill.'

In many cases, the report continued, mental derangement and a loss of critical faculties resulted from Scientology processing, which tended to produce subservience amounting almost to mental enslavement. Because of fear, delusion and debilitation, the individual often found it extremely difficult, if not impossible, to escape. Furthermore, the potentiality for misuse of confidence was great and the existence of files containing the most intimate secrets and confessions of thousands of individuals was a constant threat to them and a matter of grave concern.

As for L. Ron Hubbard, the report suggested that his sanity was to be 'gravely doubted'. His writing, abounding in self-glorification and grandiosity, replete with histrionics and hysterical, incontinent outbursts, was the product of a person of unsound mind. His teachings about thetans and past lives were nonsensical; he had a persecution complex; he had a great fear of matters associated with women and a 'prurient and compulsive urge to write in the most disgusting and derogatory way' on such subjects as abortions, intercourse, rape, sadism, perversion and abandonment. His propensity for neologisms was commonplace in the schizophrenic and his compulsion to invent increasingly bizarre theories and experiences was strongly indicative of paranoid schizophrenia with delusions of grandeur. 'Symptoms', the report added, 'common to dictators.'

It continued in similar vein for 173 pages, concluding: 'If there should be detected in this report a note of unrelieved denunciation of Scientology, it is because the evidence has shown its theories to be fantastic and impossible, its principles perverted and ill-founded, and its techniques debased and harmful. Scientology is a delusional belief system, based on fiction and fallacies and propagated by falsehood and deception . . . Its founder, with the merest smattering of knowledge in various sciences, has built upon the scintilla of his learning a crazy and dangerous edifice. The HASI claims to be "the world's largest mental health organization". What it really is however, is the world's largest organization of unqualified persons engaged in the practice of dangerous techniques which masquerade as mental therapy.'[6]

It was not difficult to 'detect' a note of unrelieved denunciation in the Anderson report; indeed, in its intemperate tone, its use of emotive rhetoric and its tendency to exaggerate and distort, it bore a marked similarity to the writings of L. Ron Hubbard. In his determination to undermine Scientology, Anderson completely ignored the fact that thousands of decent, honest, well-meaning people around the world believed themselves to be benefiting from the movement. To condemn the church as 'evil' was to brand its followers as either evil or stupid or both – an undeserved imputation.

Bloodied but unbowed, Hubbard began fighting back against the Anderson report on the day of its publication, beginning with a rebuttal written exclusively for the East Grinstead *Courier*, accusing the Australian inquiry of being an illegal 'kangaroo court' which had refused to allow him to appear in his own defence. Its findings were 'hysterical', he said, and not based on the facts. He compared the inquiry to the heresy trials which had led to witches being burned at the stake in the dark ages.

However, Dr Hubbard – described as 'the son of a Montana cattle baron' – still found it in his heart to be munificent: 'Well, Australia is young. In 1942, as the senior US naval officer in Northern Australia, by a fluke of fate, I helped save them from the Japanese. For the sake of Scientologists there, I will go on helping them . . . Socrates said,

"Philosophy is the greatest of the arts and it ought to be practiced." I intend to keep on writing it and practicing it and helping others as I can.'

For his fellow Scientologists, Hubbard had a slightly different message. What had gone wrong in Australia, he explained, was that he had approved co-operation with an inquiry into *all* mental health services. ('We could have had a ball and put psychiatry on trial for murder, mercy killing, sterilization, torture and sex practices and could have wiped out psychiatry's good name.') Unfortunately, because of bungling somewhere along the line, the inquiry had been narrowed to Scientology only, 'so it was a mess'.

He laid out the procedure to be followed if there were further official inquiries into Scientology. The first step was to identify the antagonists, next investigate them 'for felonies or worse' and then start feeding 'lurid, blood sex crime actual evidence on the attackers' to the press. '*Don't ever* tamely submit to an investigation of us,' he warned. 'Make it rough, rough on attackers all the way.'[7]

Hubbard soon showed he was prepared to take the lead. The storm caused by the Anderson report was not merely restricted to ephemeral headlines: it provoked further and continuing media investigation into Scientology and prodded governments into taking punitive measures against the church. The reaction, sociologist Roy Wallis noted, was comparable to an international moral panic: 'The former conception of the movement as a relatively harmless, if cranky, health and self-improvement cult, was transformed into one which portrayed it as evil, dangerous, a form of hypnosis (with all the overtones of Svengali in the layman's mind), and brainwashing.'[8]

The Australian government was first to act: in December 1965, the State of Victoria passed the Psychological Practices Act which effectively outlawed Scientology and empowered the Attorney General to seize and destroy all Scientology documents and recordings. Then the country playing host to the 'evil Dr Hubbard' could hardly be expected to ignore the Anderson report and on 7 February 1966, Lord Balniel, MP, then chairman of the National Association for Mental Health, stood up in the House of Commons and asked the Minister of Health to initiate an inquiry into Scientology in Britain.

Two days later, Hubbard issued an instruction from Saint Hill Manor: 'Get a detective on that Lord's past to unearth the titbits. They're there.'[9] On 17 February he set up a 'Public Investigation Section' to be staffed by professional private detectives. Its function was to 'help LRH [Hubbard became known in Scientology by his initials] investigate public matters and individuals which seem to impede human liberty' and 'furnish intelligence'. The first private investigator hired to head the section was told to find at least one bad mark ('a murder, an assault, or a rape') on every psychiatrist in Britain, starting with Lord Balniel. Unfortunately for Hubbard, the gallant detective promptly scuttled off and sold his story to a Sunday newspaper, creating more unfavourable publicity for Scientology.[10]

Scientology's 'official' reply to the Anderson report was a forty-eight-page document, bound in black and gold, and titled 'Kangaroo Court. An investigation into the conduct of the Board of Inquiry into Scientology.' It was hardly designed to win the hearts and minds of the average Australian. 'Only a society founded by criminals, organized by criminals and devoted to making people criminals, could come to such a conclusion [about Scientology] . . .' the introduction declared. 'The foundation of Victoria consists of the riff-raff of London's slums – robbers, murderers, prostitutes, fences, thieves – the scourings of Newgate and Bedlam . . . the niceties of truth and fairness, of hearing witnesses and weighing evidence, are not for men whose ancestry is lost in the promiscuity of the prison ships of transportation . . .'

After airing the manifold grievances of the church, 'Kangaroo Court' returned to its initial theme: 'The insane attack on Scientology in the State of Victoria, can best be understood if Victoria is seen for what it is – a very primitive community, somewhat barbaric, with a rudimentary knowledge of the physical sciences.' There followed a defiant quote from L. Ron Hubbard: 'The future of Scientology in Australia is bright and shiny. We will continue to grow and progress. No vested interests or blackhearted politicians, no matter how much power they seem to ally themselves with, can stop our thoughts or our communications . . . We will be here teaching and listening when our opponents' names are merely mis-spelled references in a history book of tyranny.'

Despite his apparent confidence, Hubbard recognized that Scientologists needed a boost to their morale in the face of the concerted attacks from the media following the Anderson report. In February 1966, rumours began to circulate among Scientologists that one of their number had at last achieved the fabled state of being 'clear' (Sonya Bianca's performance at The Shrine in Los Angeles having been long forgotten). To become 'clear' was still the goal of every Scientologist, but it was proving an extraordinarily elusive one. New levels of processing were continually introduced at Saint Hill, each with the promise that it would result in 'clearing', only to be replaced by another level and yet more promises.

Among the students completing the Level VII course in February 1966 was John McMaster, a South African in his mid-thirties who worked on the staff at Saint Hill as director of the Hubbard Guidance Centre. McMaster had been a medical student in Durban when he first came across Scientology in 1959. He had had part of his stomach removed because of cancer and was in more or less continuous pain until his first auditing session, after which the pain disappeared. Totally converted, he arrived at Saint Hill to take the Briefing Course in 1963 and was subsequently invited by Hubbard to join the staff.

After he had graduated as a Level VII auditor, McMaster was sent to Los Angeles by Hubbard to spread the news of the latest 'technology' being taught at Saint Hill. He had only been there a couple of days when he received a cable: 'Congratulations, world's first clear'. He was ordered to return to Saint Hill immediately for a final check on an E-meter by the 'qualifications secretary'. On 8 March he passed the check without a quiver on the needle of the E-meter, proving that he had completely erased the memory bank of his reactive mind. He was clear!

'It's with greatest joy and happiness,' the qualifications secretary advised Hubbard, 'I have to report to you that John McMaster has passed the Clear check and no doubt exists that he has erased his bank completely . . . Thank you for the honour and privilege of checking out the first Clear.'[11]

The excitement this event caused within Scientology was further heightened when the gratifying word was spread that McMaster possessed all the attributes prophesied by Ron sixteen years earlier in *Dianetics, The Modern Science of Mental Health*. Indeed, it was said that the world's first clear was actually *glowing*!

The *Auditor*, the journal of Scientology, trumpeted the joyous event in its next issue and quoted McMaster: 'It is a great privilege to have been able to follow the stepping stones paved in the wake of Time by such a man as L. Ron Hubbard, for although I have worked for it, I could never have realized it without the great gift he has given, not only to me, but all Mankind.' To celebrate the great occasion, Hubbard proclaimed another 'general amnesty'.

On the same day McMaster was checked out as 'clear', a curious advertisement appeared in the personal column of *The Times*: 'I, L. Ron Hubbard, of Saint Hill Manor, East Grinstead, Sussex, having reviewed the damage being done in our society with nuclear physics and psychiatry by persons calling themselves "Doctor" do hereby resign in protest my university degree as a Doctor of philosophy (Ph.D.), anticipating an early public outcry against anyone called Doctor; and although not in any way connected with the bombs of "psychiatrics treatment" or treatment of the sick, and interested only and always in philosophy and the total freedom of the human spirit I wish no association of any kind with these persons and do so publicly declare, and request my friends and the public not to refer to me in any way with this title.'

Next day, the *Daily Mail* rather churlishly pointed out that the title Hubbard had publicly renounced was bogus anyway. Mr Hubbard was not available for comment; his personal assistant, Reg Sharpe, told the newspaper that Ron was abroad on holiday and was not to be disturbed.

Hubbard was not on holiday, he was on his way to Rhodesia, where Prime Minister Ian Smith had recently signed a Unilateral Declaration of Independence in defiance of the British Government. Now that he had no reason to hope that Australia would be the first 'clear' continent, Hubbard had scaled down his ambitions and was looking for a country which would provide a 'safe environment' for Scientology. He chose Rhodesia firstly because he thought he could create a favourable climate by helping to solve the UDI crisis and secondly because he believed he had been Cecil Rhodes in a previous life. He told Reg Sharpe that he hoped to be able to recover gold and diamonds he was convinced Rhodes had buried somewhere in Rhodesia.

On 7 April 1966, the CIA headquarters in the United States received a cable from an agent in Rhodesia: 'Request traces of L. Ron Hubbard, US citizen recently arrived.' The reply confirmed that Headquarters files contained no derogatory information about the subject, but a memo was attached giving excerpts from press reports. It concluded: 'Individuals who have been connected with the organizations headed by Hubbard or who have had contact with him and the organizations, have indicated that Hubbard is a "crackpot" and of "doubtful mental background".'[12]

The 'crackpot' meanwhile had bought a large four-bedroomed house with a swimming-pool in the exclusive Alexander Park suburb of Salisbury and opened negotiations to acquire the Bumi Hills Hotel on Lake Kariba. His plan was to use the hotel as a luxury base from which to spread the influence of Scientology. He believed the Lake Kariba site would attract well-heeled followers who wanted to be instructed in the highest levels of Scientology and were willing to pay around $10,000 for the privilege.

Nothing of this was revealed to the people of Rhodesia, to whom he represented himself as a 'millionaire-financier' interested in pumping money into the crippled economy of the country and stimulating the tourist industry. In an interview in the Rhodesia *Sunday Mail* he said he had left his stately home in Britain on doctor's orders after a third attack of pneumonia. 'I am really supposed to be on vacation,' he explained, 'but I have had so many invitations to invest in businesses here and this country is so starved of finance that I have become intrigued.'

Hubbard was careful to distance himself from what the newspaper called 'the controversial Scientology movement'. It had never really been pushed in Rhodesia, he said, and added: 'I am still an officer of the corporation that administers the movement but it is very largely autonomous now.'[13]

In early May, Hubbard produced, uninvited, a 'tentative constitution' for Rhodesia which he felt would satisfy the demands of the blacks while at the same time maintaining white supremacy. It embodied the principle of one man one vote for a lower house, while real power was vested in an upper house elected by qualified citizens with a good standard of English, knowledge of the constitution and financial standing verified by a bank. Hubbard was apparently convinced that Rhodesia's black population would welcome his ideas, even though it was patently obvious that the qualifications required to cast a vote for the upper house would exclude most blacks.

With his inimitable talent for adopting the appropriate vernacular, Hubbard's proposals were written in suitably constitutional prose, beginning: 'Before God and Man we pledge ourselves, the Government of Rhodesia and each of our officers and men of authority in the Government to this the Constitution of our country . . .'

Copies were despatched to Ian Smith and to Saint Hill Manor in England with instructions to forward the document to the British Prime Minister, Harold Wilson, when Hubbard gave the word. Ian Smith's principal private secretary replied politely to Hubbard on 5 May saying that his suggestions had been passed to a Cabinet sub-committee examining proposals for amending the constitution.

Still as paranoid as ever, Hubbard then wrote to the Minister of Internal Affairs asking if the investigation of his activities and background had been completed and if he could have confirmation that everything was in order. He added a jaunty postscript: 'Why not come over and have a drink and dinner with me one night?'

This provoked a frosty response from the Minister's private secretary: 'My Minister has asked me to thank you for your letter of 5th May 1966 and to say that he has no knowledge of his Ministry carrying out an investigation into your activities. He regrets he is unable to accept your invitation to dinner. Yours faithfully . . .'

Hubbard continued to try and ingratiate himself with the leading political figures in Rhodesia, but with little success. In June, he arranged for John McMaster to visit him from Johannesburg, where he was teaching a clearing course. 'He cabled me and asked me to bring all the clearing course students to Salisbury to take part in a film he wanted to make,' said McMaster. 'I was also to be sure to bring with me two bottles of pink champagne, which was not available in Rhodesia.

'I had no idea why he wanted it but I knew it was important because

I was met by one of Hubbard's assistants at Salisbury airport and the first thing she said to me was, "Have you brought the champagne?" It turned out he wanted to give it to Mrs Smith as a present in order to try and get in with the Prime Minister. Next morning his chauffeur drove him round to Government House and he swaggered up to the front door with a bottle under each arm thinking he was going to take Mrs Smith by storm. But they wouldn't let him past the front door and he came back very upset, really disgruntled.'[14]

Hubbard's high profile as the 'millionaire-financier' who boasted that he could solve the UDI crisis won him few friends among Rhodesia's deeply conservative white society. He often spoke of his willingness to help the government, pointing out that he had been trained in economics and government at Princeton, and seemed surprised that his services were not welcomed. On television, in newspaper interviews and in all his public pronouncements, Hubbard professed support for Ian Smith's government, although in private he thought Smith was a 'nasty bit of work' who was incapable of leadership.[15] Similarly, he publicly espoused sympathy for the plight of the black majorities in both Rhodesia and South Africa, while privately admitting contempt for them. Blacks were so stupid, he told John McMaster, that they did not give a reading on an E-meter.[16]

At the beginning of July, Hubbard was invited to address the Rotary Club in Bulawayo. He delivered a rambling, hectoring speech telling the assembled businessmen how they should run their country, their businesses and their lives and when it was reported in the local newspaper it appeared to be faintly anti-Rhodesian. A couple of days later, Hubbard received a letter from the Department of Immigration informing him that his application for an extension to his Alien's Temporary Residence Permit had been unsuccessful: 'this means that you will be required to leave Rhodesia on or before the 18th July, 1966.'

Hubbard was stunned. Up until that moment he had believed himself to be not just a prominent personality in Rhodesia, but a *popular* one. He asked his friends in the Rhodesian Front party to make representations on his behalf to the Prime Minister, but to no avail. 'Smith ranted and raved at them,' he reported later, 'told them I had been deported from Australia, was wanted in every country in the world, that my business associates had been complaining about me and that I must go.'[17] The Rhodesian Government refused to make any comment on the expulsion order, but Hubbard had few doubts about who was behind it – it was obviously a Communist plot to get him out of the country because he was the man most likely to resolve the UDI crisis.

On 15 July, Hubbard lined up his household staff on the lawn in front of his house on John Plagis Avenue and bade them an emotional farewell for the benefit of Rhodesian television, whose cameras were recording the departure of the American millionaire-financier. At the airport there were more reporters waiting to interview him before he left and one of them warned him to expect a posse from Fleet Street to greet him in London. He was quite cheered by the prospect and began to think that his expulsion might actually increase his status as an international personality.

As Hubbard's plane lifted off the tarmac at Salisbury, frenzied preparations were being made in Britain to give him a hero's welcome on his return. The news that the revered founder of Scientology was being kicked out of Rhodesia had initially been greeted with dismay and disbelief at Saint Hill Manor. 'We were shocked,' said Ken Urquhart, 'no one could understand how such a thing could happen. It was an even bigger surprise for the other orgs because none of them knew he was in Rhodesia. It was supposed to be a big secret. I was by then working as LRH Communicator World-Wide and it was my job to code and de-code the telexes that were going backwards and forwards and between Saint Hill and Rhodesia. He didn't want anyone to know he was away because he thought everyone would start slacking.'

Coaches were laid on to transport every available Scientologist from East Grinstead to Heathrow on the morning of Saturday, 16 July. They took with them hastily prepared 'Welcome Home' banners but neglected to obtain the necessary permission to wave them; airport police politely insisted they should remain unfurled. Some six hundred Scientologists, including Mary Sue and the children, were gathered in the terminal by the time Hubbard's flight landed. They had to wait while he sorted out a problem about his vaccinations with immigration officers and two hours passed before he emerged from Customs, wearing a lightweight suit and sun-hat, looking tired, but smiling broadly. 'I'm glad to be back,' he shouted as police forced a path through his cheering supporters to a yellow Pontiac convertible parked in front of the terminal. He sat on the back, waving presidential style, as the car was slowly driven away.

No one could have asked for a more enthusiastic welcome, although Hubbard was disappointed that Fleet Street had failed to turn out. Only one reporter was at the airport and he only seemed to want to ask about the events in Australia, to which query Hubbard snapped, 'That's past history.'

Pam and Ray Kemp were among the first visitors to Saint Hill after Hubbard's return from Rhodesia. 'He told me everything that had happened,' said Ray Kemp. 'It seems there was a chief of police who was very bullying to the blacks and Ian Smith was very wimpish. Smith couldn't make decisions about anything and would rely on the chief of police to tell him what to do. Ron was at dinner one night with Smith and he warned him that if he continued to be wimpish and not put his foot down the probability was that he would be assassinated. About two days later there was an assassination attempt, although I don't remember whether it was on Smith or the chief of police. The bullet went through his mouth and out the side. Ron somehow got the blame because of what he had said. That was why he was asked to leave.'[18]

Ken Urquhart got a slightly different version: 'He inferred the problem was that he knew what to do about the blacks and he became very popular with them. That's why the government kicked him out. I heard him tell Mary Sue that he had lost £200,000 in investment in Rhodesia.'

Back in the familiar surroundings of Saint Hill Manor, Hubbard had plenty of time to review Scientology's current situation and prospects. It was a far from rosy picture. Apart from the problems in Australia and Rhodesia, trouble was also brewing in the United States, where the Internal Revenue Service was challenging the Church of Scientology's tax-exempt status. In Britain there was another rash of hysterical headlines when the police found a girl wandering the streets of East Grinstead in a distressed condition in the early hours of the morning. It transpired she was a schizophrenic who had been institutionalized before being recruited as a Scientologist.

There were further demands in Parliament for an inquiry into Scientology, to which the Minister of Health tartly replied: 'I do not think any further inquiry is necessary to establish that the activities of this organization are potentially harmful. I have no doubt that Scientology is totaly valueless in promoting health . . .'

Scientology even seemed to be wearing out its welcome in East Grinstead, where the locals were complaining they were being overwhelmed. As if it was not bad enough having strange Americans walking round the streets wearing badges saying 'Don't speak to me, I'm being processed', Scientologists were snapping up all available rented accommodation, crowding the pubs and straining everyone's patience.

'There was a lot of resentment and alarm in the town,' said Alan Larcombe of the East Grinstead *Courier*. 'People felt that Scientology could not be allowed to continue expanding. There was a feeling they were trying to take over – an estate agent, dentist, hairdresser, jeweller's, finance company and a couple of doctors were all Scientology run. People didn't like it. They felt that if you had problems you ought to go and have a chat with your vicar.'

Larcombe paid another visit to Saint Hill Manor and was astonished at the numbers of people who were there. 'It was quite an eye opener. As I pulled up outside the house a bell sounded somewhere and people began pouring out, hundreds and hundreds of them, like wasps leaving a nest. It was an incredible sight. I was completely taken aback by how much the place had grown. I discovered there were so many students there that the sewage system could not cope.'

Hubbard, musing on Scientology's multitude of problems in the autumn of 1966, arrived at a daring and original solution. He kept it a secret, because he loved secrets, although he hinted at what was on his mind in a remark to John McMaster, recently returned from South Africa. 'You know, John,' he said, 'we have got to do something about all this trouble we are having with governments. There's a lot of high-level research still to be done and I want to be able to get on with it without constant interference. Do you realize that 75 per cent of the earth's surface is completely free from the control of any government? That's where we could be free – on the high seas.'[19] McMaster had no idea what he meant and Hubbard did not choose to elaborate.

Soon senior Scientologists were arriving from the United States to take part in a top-secret project under Ron's personal direction. They could sometimes be seen scrambling in and out of a rubber dinghy on the lake or pouring over navigational charts in a classroom. Some evenings they met behind closed doors in the garage and it was said that they spent their time practising tying knots.

By December it was known they were involved in something called the 'Sea Project'. But still no one could imagine what it was.

Chapter 16

Launching the Sea Org

'Hearing of L. Ron Hubbard's plans for further exploration and research into, among other things, past civilizations, many Scientologists wanted to join him and help. They adopted the name "Sea Organization" . . . Free of organizational duties and aided by the first Sea Org members, L. Ron Hubbard now had the time and facilities to confirm in the physical universe some of the events and places he had encountered in his journeys down the track of time . . .' (*Mission Into Time*)

***** *

In 1967, L. Ron Hubbard was fifty-six years old, the father of seven children and a grandfather several times over. With a loyal wife, a home in England and four children still at school, he was at an age when most men put down roots and plan nothing more ambitious than a comfortable retirement. But he was not like most men.

In 1967, L. Ron Hubbard raised a private navy, appointed himself Commodore, donned a dashing uniform of his own design and set forth on an extraordinary odyssey, leading a fleet of ships across the oceans variously pursued by the CIA, the FBI, the international press and a miscellany of suspicious government and maritime agencies. He had begun making secret plans to set up the 'Sea Organization' on his return from Rhodesia in the summer of 1966, shrouding the whole operation with layer upon layer of duplicity. His intention was that the public should believe that he was returning to his former 'profession', that of an explorer, and accordingly, in September 1966, Hubbard announced his resignation as President of the Church of Scientology. This charade was supported by the explanation that the church was sufficiently well established to survive without his leadership. In preparation for his anticipated resignation a special committee had been set up to investigate how much the church owed its founder; it was decided the figure was around $13 million, but Hubbard, in his benevolence, forgave the debt.

Still a member of the Explorers Club, Hubbard applied for permission to carry the club flag on his forthcoming 'Hubbard

Geological Survey Expedition'. Its purpose, he explained, was to conduct a geological survey from Italy, through Greece and Egypt to the Gulf of Aden and down the east coast of Africa: 'Samples of rock types, formations, and soils will be taken in order to draw a picture of an area which has been the scene of the earlier and basic civilizations of the planet and from which some conclusions may possibly be made relating to geological dispositions requisite for civilized growth.'

This highfalutin nonsense sufficiently impressed the Explorers Club for the expedition to be awarded the club flag. [The club could not, however, be said to examine such applications very scrupulously – Hubbard had also been awarded the flag in 1961 for another entirely fictitious venture – the 'Ocean Archeological Expedition', allegedly set up to explore submerged cities in the Caribbean, Mediterranean and adjacent waters.[1]]

On 22 November 1966, the Hubbard Explorational Company Limited was incorporated at Companies House in London. The directors were L. Ron Hubbard, described as expedition supervisor, and Mary Sue Hubbard, the company secretary. The aims of the company were to 'explore oceans, seas, lakes, rivers and waters, lands and buildings in any part of the world and to seek for, survey, examine and test properties of all kinds'.

Hubbard had no more intention of conducting geological surveys than he had of relinquishing control of the Church of Scientology and its handsome income. His real objective was to shake off the fetters on his activities and ambitions imposed by tiresome land-based bureaucracies; his vision was of a domain of his own creation on the freedom of the high seas, connected by sophisticated coded communications to its operations on land. Its purpose would be to propagate Scientology behind a screen of business management courses.

Before the end of 1966, the 'Sea Org' – as it would inevitably become known – had secretly purchased its first ship, the *Enchanter*, a forty-ton sea-going schooner. To further obscure his involvement, Hubbard asked his friend Ray Kemp to be a part owner. Kemp was the man who believed that Hubbard could move clouds with the power of his mind and when he showed up at Saint Hill to sign for the *Enchanter* he swore that Hubbard played a little magical trick on him: 'We'd been sitting talking for hours and it was getting dark when he said, "Well I guess we'd better get this thing signed." I said, "Do you have a pen?" and he said, "Yes, it's over there." I went to pick up the pen on his desk and it disappeared. I thought at first it was the light, but I tried three times to pick up the pen and each time it was not there and I realized he was making it disappear. In the end I said to Ron, "If you'll just leave the bloody pen still for a moment, I'll sign." He could do fun things like that, he was just playing a game.'[2]

Shortly after the purchase of the *Enchanter*, the Hubbard Explorational Company bought an old, rusty North Sea trawler, the 414-ton *Avon River*, moored at Hull, a busy seaport on the north-east coast of England. Hubbard then flew to Tangier in Morocco, where he planned to continue his 'research', leaving his family at Saint Hill Manor. Mary Sue wanted to stay behind because Diana, star pupil at the local dancing school, had been chosen to present a bouquet to Princess Margaret, who was due to open the Genée Theatre in East Grinstead a few weeks later.

Before being driven to the airport, Hubbard scribbled instructions for various members of the 'sea project'. One of them was Virginia Downsborough, a plump and cheerful New Yorker who had been working as an auditor at Saint Hill for nearly three years. Virginia was never entirely sure why she had been honoured with an invitation to join the project, unless it was because she came from a sailing family and knew a little about ships and knots. 'At that time the sea project was just a few of us who would get together in the garage and learn how to tie knots and read a pilot. I bought a little sailing boat and sailed it at weekends, but that was about it. Ron always worked way down the line – he knew what he intended to do, but he never laid it out for us.

'After he had gone I was given a sealed envelope with his initials on. Inside were my orders. I had to go to Hull, get the *Enchanter* ready for sea and sail her to Gibraltar for a refit. Ron gave me a list of things he wanted from Saint Hill, mainly personal possessions and clothes, which I was to bring with me. I left for Hull next day.'

Scientologists were in the habit of following Ron's orders unhesitatingly, no matter how difficult the task, or how ill-equipped they were to carry them out. Virginia Downsborough held a masters degree in education and had run a child development department in a New York school before coming to Saint Hill; nevertheless she set out for Hull without a second thought. 'A lot of things needed to be done before the *Enchanter* was ready to sail,' she recalled, 'so I lived on the *Avon River*, which was moored alongside and was absolutely filthy, for a couple of weeks while the work was being carried out.'

The *Enchanter* sailed in the New Year with a hired skipper and a novice crew of four Scientologists, including Downsborough. In the light of forthcoming Sea Org voyages, it was a comparatively uneventful trip, apart from losing most of the fuel at sea somewhere off the coast of Portugal. After putting in briefly at Oporto, the *Enchanter* arrived safely in Gibraltar, only to discover there was no room in the ways. A message arrived from a Hubbard aide in Tangier saying that Ron was ill and they were to continue to Las Palmas, in the Canary Islands.

'We got the *Enchanter* on the ways in Las Palmas,' said Downsborough, 'and we had not been there very long before Ron turned up.
Bill Robertson – another Scientologist – and myself went to the post
office to post some letters and discovered a telegram there from Ron
saying that he was arriving in Las Palmas almost at that minute and
wanted to be met. We jumped into a taxi and got to the airport just in
time to pick him up as he was coming through Customs. We found
him a hotel in Las Palmas and next day I went back to see if he was all
right, because he did not seem to be too well.

'When I went in to his room there were drugs of all kinds
everywhere. He seemed to be taking about sixty thousand different
pills. I was appalled, particularly after listening to all his tirades
against drugs and the medical profession. There was something very
wrong with him, but I didn't know what it was except that he was in a
state of deep depression; he told me he didn't have any more gains and
he wanted to die. That's what he said: "I want to die."'

It was important for Hubbard to be discovered in this dramatically
debilitated condition at this time, for it would soon be announced to
fellow Scientologists that he had completed 'a research accomplishment of immense magnitude' described, somewhat inscrutably, as the
'Wall of Fire'. This was the OT3 (Operating Thetan Section Three)
material, in which were contained 'the secrets of a disaster which
resulted in the decay of life as we know it in this sector of the galaxy'.[3]
Hubbard, it was said, was the 'first person in millions of years' to map
a precise route through the 'Wall of Fire'. Having done so, his OT
power has been increased to such an extent that he was at grave risk of
accidental injury to his body; indeed, he had broken his back, a knee
and an arm during the course of his research.

Virginia Downsborough did not observe any broken limbs, but
recognized that Ron needed nursing. 'I moved into an adjoining room
in the hotel to take care of him. He refused to eat the hotel food, so I
got a little hotplate and cooked meals for him in the room, simple
things, things that he liked. My main concern was to try and get him
off all the pills he was on and persuade him that there was still plenty
for him to do. He was sleeping a lot and refused to get out of bed.

'I don't know what drugs he was taking – they certainly weren't
making him high – but I knew I had to get him over it. I discussed it
with him and gradually took them away. He didn't carry on about it.
He had brought a great pile of unopened mail with him from Tangier,
a lot of it from Mary Sue, and I got him to start reading her letters.
After about three weeks he decided he would get out of bed and he
started taking little walks and then he got interested in what was
happening on the *Enchanter* and after that he was all right.'

Mary Sue flew in to Las Palmas as soon as Ron was back on his feet and Virginia Downsborough was instructed to find the Hubbards a house. She rented the Villa Estrella, a pretty white-painted hacienda with a red-tiled roof on a rocky promontory facing the sea, about forty-five minutes drive from Las Palmas. 'I cooked dinner for them at the house every evening,' she said. 'Ron used to like to sit up and talk half the night long after Mary Sue had gone to bed. He had this intense ability to communicate and it was fascinating to listen to him. I was intrigued by the concept he presented of himself as being a constant victim of women.

'He talked a lot about Sara Northrup and seemed to want to make sure that I knew he had never married her. I didn't know why it was so important to him; I'd never met Sara and I couldn't have cared less, but he wanted to persuade me that the marriage had never taken place. When he talked about his first wife, the picture he put out of himself was of this poor wounded fellow coming home from the war and being abandoned by his wife and family because he would be a drain on them. He said he had planned every move along the way with Mary Sue to avoid being victimized again.'[4]

When the *Enchanter* came off the ways in the harbour at Las Palmas, Hubbard took her out on extended cruises round the Canary Islands to search for gold he had buried in previous lives. 'He would draw little maps for us,' said Virginia Downsborough, 'and we would be sent off to dig for buried treasure. He told us he was hoping to replace the *Enchanter*'s ballast with solid gold. I thought it was great fun – the best show on earth.'

All these activities were supposed to remain a closely guarded secret and Hubbard insisted on the use of elaborate codes in Sea Org communications. In a despatch to Saint Hill he urged his followers not to feel '007ish and silly' about security and gave an unlikely example of a 'close call' he had had during the war because of a failure of security. It was 1940 and he had been ordered on a secret mission to a hostile foreign country. On a hunch, he did not leave at once and was amazed to receive a letter from Washington addressing him with full rank and title, informing him to wear white cap covers after April 15. Hubbard argued that this was the most terrible breach of security, since the letter would certainly have been forwarded to him and his cover would have been blown with fatal results. 'Had I departed,' he pointed out solemnly, 'that letter, following me, would have sentenced me to death before a firing squad!'[5]

It was a narrow escape that did not bear too much scrutiny. First, Hubbard was not in the US Navy in 1940 and second, mail was not usually forwarded to secret agents working undercover in hostile foreign countries.

While Hubbard was in Las Palmas he developed phobias about

dust and smells which were the cause of frequent explosive temper tantrums. He was always complaining that his clothes smelled of soap or he was being choked by dust that no one else could detect. No matter how frequently the *Enchanter*'s decks were scrubbed, she was never clean enough for the Commodore. Similarly, the routine drive between the harbour and the Villa Estrella became an ordeal for everyone in the car. 'Sometimes I thought we'd never get there,' said Virginia Downsborough. 'Every few miles he would insist on stopping because there was dust in the air conditioner. He would get into such a rage that on occasions I thought he was going to tear the car apart.'

In April 1967, the *Avon River* steamed into the harbour at Las Palmas after a voyage from Hull which the skipper, Captain John Jones, later described as the 'strangest trip of my life'. Apart from the chief engineer, Jones was the only professional seaman on board. 'My crew were sixteen men and four women Scientologists who wouldn't know a trawler from a tramcar,' he told a reporter from the *Daily Mirror* on his return to England.

Captain Jones should perhaps have foreseen the difficulties when he signed on for the voyage and was informed that he would be expected to run the ship according to the rules of *The Org Book*, a sailing manual written by the founder of the Church of Scientology and therefore considered by Scientologists to be infallible gospel. 'I was instructed not to use any electrical equipment, apart from lights, radio and direction finder. We had radar and other advanced equipment which I was not allowed to use. I was told it was all in *The Org Book*, which was to be obeyed without question.'

Following the advice in this esteemed manual, the *Avon River* bumped the dock in Hull as she was getting under way and had barely left the Humber estuary before the Scientologist navigator, using the navigational system advocated by Hubbard, confessed that he was lost. 'I stuck to my watch and sextant,' said Captain Jones, 'so at least *I* knew where we were.'

As the old trawler laboured into the wind-flecked waters of the English Channel, a disagreement arose between the senior Scientologist on board and the Captain about who was in command. By the time the *Avon River* put into Falmouth to re-fuel, both the Captain and the chief engineer were threatening to pack their bags and leave the ship. Frantic telephone calls to East Grinstead eventually led to the protesting Scientologist being ordered to return to Saint Hill and the smoothing of Captain Jones's ruffled feathers. The rest of the trip passed off without incident, although the two seamen remained utterly mystified by their crew and in particular by the hours they spent fiddling with their E-meters.[6]

At Las Palmas, the *Avon River* was hauled up on the slips recently vacated by the *Enchanter* and prepared for a major re-fit. A working party of bright-eyed sea project members had already arrived in the Canaries, among them Amos Jessup, a philosophy major from Connecticut. The son of a senior editor on *Life* magazine, Jessup had gone to Saint Hill in 1966, while he was studying in Oxford, to try and get his young brother out of Scientology and instead had become converted himself. 'I was soon convinced', he said, 'that instead of being some dangerous cult it was an important advance in philosophy.

'I was clear by the spring of '67 and when I heard that LRH was looking for personnel for a communications vessel I immediately volunteered and was sent to Las Palmas. We were all given a "shore story" so that no one would know that we were Scientologists; we were told to say that we were working for the Hubbard Explorational Company on archeological research.

'On the day we arrived, the *Avon River* was being hauled up on the slips. She looked like what she was – an old, worn-out, oil-soaked, rust-flaked steam trawler. Our job was to give her a complete overhaul. We sand-blasted her from stem to stern, painted her, put bunks in what had been the rope locker, converted the liver oil boiling room into additional accommodation, put decks in the cargo holds to make space for offices. LRH designed a number of improvements – a larger rudder and a system of lifts to hoist small boats aboard.'[7]

Hubbard would show up every couple of days to check on the progress of the work, but it was never going ahead fast enough and more sea project members were constantly being flown in to Las Palmas to join the work-force. Hana Eltringham, a former nurse from South Africa, arrived in August. 'At first sight the ship looked terrible, all streaked with rust,' she said. 'You had to climb a long, shaky ladder to get up on to the deck and as I got over the side I could see everything was covered in sand from the sand-blasting and there were people sleeping on the sand, obviously exhausted.

'Nevertheless, it was a tremendous thrill to be there. It was a great honour to be invited to join the sea project; we were an elite, like the Marine Corps. All of us were true and tried Scientologists, highly motivated, and to me it was high adventure.'

After working as a deck hand for a couple of weeks, Hana was promoted to ethics officer. 'My job was to run round making sure the crew weren't goofing. I felt I was responsible for catching errors before he did because he would get very upset – he would literally scream and shout – if something was not being done right. I was mostly scared of him in those days.

'One afternoon I was standing on the deck with a clipboard waiting for him to come on board and I knew something was wrong because I saw his face start to contort when he was still 15 or 20 yards away, walking towards the slips. As he came up to the ship he started shouting, filling his lungs and bellowing "*What are they doing? Why are they doing that?*" and pointing to the side of the ship. He came up the ladder still screaming in a kind of frenzy. I didn't know what was the matter and he told me to look over the side of the ship. I stuck my head over to see what the hell he was screaming about. The painters who were putting white paint on the hull were using old rollers and the paint had a kind of furry coat on it from the rollers. He'd seen that from many yards away. It was extraordinary. I was awed.'[8]

Such incidents inevitably led to the offenders being assigned a 'lower condition', the penalties for which were by then routinely formalized. The least serious was 'emergency' followed by 'liability', in which hapless state the miscreant forfeited pay, was confined to 'org premises' and had to wear the infamous dirty grey rag on one arm. In a condition of 'treason', all uniforms and insignia were removed and the rag was replaced by a black mark on the left cheek. In 'doubt', the offender was fined, barred from the org and could not be communicated with. Lastly came the dreaded 'enemy' – 'May be deprived of property or injured by any means by any Scientologist without any discipline of the Scientologist. May be tricked, sued or lied to or destroyed.'

Even though Hubbard had 'resigned' as president of the Church of Scientology, the flow of edicts continued uninterrupted and he reminded Scientologists of the penalties for lower conditions in a policy letter dictated at the Villa Estrella in Las Palmas. He also found time to record a taped lecture in which he warned of a world-wide conspiracy to destroy Scientology. The resourceful Mary Sue had apparently traced the conspiracy to the very highest levels, to a cabal of international bankers and newspaper barons sufficiently powerful to control many heads of state, among them the British Prime Minister, Harold Wilson.

While Hubbard was fulminating against international conspiracies and bellowing at his amateur work-force as they struggled to prepare the *Avon River* for sea, good news arrived from a 'mission' in Britain (tasks undertaken on Hubbard's behalf were always aggrandized as 'missions'). For many months two senior Scientologists, Joe van Staden and Ron Pook, had been scouring European ports for a big ship, something like a cruise liner, which could be used as the Sea Org's flagship. In September, they reported by telex that they had found, laid up in Aberdeen, just the ship that Ron was looking for. She was the *Royal Scotsman*, a 3280-ton motor vessel built in 1936 and most recently in service as a cattle ferry on the Irish Channel crossing. Despite her age, she was in good condition and could probably be bought, van Staden and Pook thought, for not much more than £60,000. To Hubbard, the money was insignificant; Saint Hill alone was taking in around £40,000 a week in fees. He immediately instructed van Staden and Pool to start negotiating the purchase and to make arrangements for the *Royal Scotsman* to join the other ships in Las Palmas, although *Avon River* was still high and dry on the slips.

It was only natural that the Commodore, who was not the most patient of men, would want his fleet assembled at the earliest opportunity and he was constantly irritated by what he considered to be unnecessary delays in the *Avon River*'s refit. By this time there were thirty-five Scientologists working on the ship from dawn to dusk, sawing, painting, chipping, scrubbing and polishing. The bridge had been completely reconstructed and fitted with new compasses and navigation equipment, all the cabins had been steam cleaned, the fish hold was converted into auditing space with rows of built-in desks, and there was a research office for the Commodore just forward of the bridge.

When at last she was ready for service, the re-launching was rather less than an outstanding success. As the trawler, sprucely white-painted, slid down the ways, it was realized too late that no precautions had been taken to restrain her; she drifted helplessly in the bay until a boat could be found to push her towards a mooring buoy. To compound this embarrassing indignity, the *Enchanter* appeared over the horizon under tow, having broken down while out searching for the treasure buried by the Commodore in previous lives. Two days later, both ships set sail, somewhat uncertainly, for Gibraltar.

The *Royal Scotsman*, meanwhile, had left Aberdeen but had run foul of the Board of Trade, the British agency responsible for the safety of ships registered in the United Kingdom. On 7 November, a solicitor acting for the new owners of the *Royal Scotsman*, had telephoned the Board of Trade in London and asked if the ship could be re-registered as a pleasure yacht and cleared for a voyage to Gibraltar. He was told that such a re-classification would entail considerable modifications – under the Safety of Life at Sea Convention of 1960, the ship would need valid load-line, cargo ship construction, safety equipment and radio certificates.

The Sea Org decided to try another tack: a couple of days later, the *Royal Scotsman* put in to Southampton on the south coast and an attempt was made to clear her with the port authorities as a whaling ship. This sudden transformation not unnaturally aroused suspicions and the authorities responded by slapping a provisional detention order on the ship, preventing her from putting to sea until necessary safety provisions had been complied with.

This news, nervously conveyed to L. Ron Hubbard in Gibraltar, produced a predictable explosion. Hubbard railed at the stupidity of the people who were supposed to be helping him and fumed about the injustice of being prevented from doing what he wanted with his own ship. When he had calmed down, he decided that the only solution was to fly to England with a hand-picked crew, take command of the *Royal Scotsman* and sail her away, protests from the Board of Trade notwithstanding.

Shortly afterwards, a curious party of sailors in blue serge suits, white polo neck sweaters and little tar hats arrived at Gatwick airport on a flight from Gibraltar. They were led by a large, red-faced man wearing a white peaked cap and carrying a letter of authority explaining that they were the delivery crew for a vessel under the seal of the Hubbard Explorational Company. In the customs hall, an officer of HM Customs and Excise glanced briefly at the letter brandished by the red-faced man and casually inquired: 'Is this the same Hubbard who has the place at East Grinstead?' 'Oh yes,' the red-faced man boomed, 'Mr Hubbard is an explorer himself.' Amos Jessup, who was standing directly behind Hubbard, marvelled at his composure.

The improbable sailors boarded a coach waiting outside the airport and were driven straight to Southampton Docks, to the berth occupied by the *Royal Scotsman*. 'Everyone climbed out and stared up at this huge ship,' Jessup recalled. 'I was startled and amazed by the size of it. It was three stories high and 357 feet long. I was assigned to be the bos'n. I didn't know all I should have known about bos'ning and I was rather shocked at the magnitude of what I'd been handed.

'After we got on board, LRH called everyone together and had us sit on the staircase between A deck and B deck. He stood at the bottom of the stairs and said, "This may look like a big and overwhelming thing, but don't let it scare you. I've handled ships bigger than this. She handles like a dream, drives like a Cadillac with big twin screws. There's nothing to it." We were already a can-do kind of group, but everyone felt a bit better after that.'

Over the next few days, there was constant activity at the *Royal Scotsman*'s berth. Every few hours a truck would arrive from Saint Hill loaded with filing cabinets which were humped on board. Taxis disgorged eager Saint Hill volunteers, clutching their bags and the 'billion-year contract' which Hubbard had recently introduced as a condition of service in the Sea Org. Mary Sue and the children arrived and took over the upper-deck accommodation which had been reserved for the Hubbard family.

Diana Hubbard was then fifteen, Quentin thirteen, Suzette a year younger and little Arthur just nine years old. They would have the company of a few other children on the ship and a notice was pinned in the saloon explaining how they were to be treated: 'A tutor will be provided for the children, who will be assigned regular hours of work and play. Anyone who deprives a child of his or her work or play will be assigned to a condition of non-existence. (Penalties for non-existence—Must wear old clothes. May not bathe. Women must not wear make-up or have hair-do's. Men may not shave. No lunch hour . . .?)'

Not everyone joining the crew was a volunteer. John McMaster, whom Hubbard had earlier described as the first Pope of the Church of Scientology, had recently fallen into disfavour, probably because he was beginning to become too influential. Slight and golden-haired, McMaster had been touring the world as an evangelist for Scientology, attracting huge audiences, considerable popularity and the dangerous enmity of L. Ron Hubbard. On a brief return visit to Saint Hill, he was abruptly assigned a lower condition, deprived of all his awards and ordered to re-train from scratch.

He would recall his experiences years later with enormous bitterness, contemptuously referring to Hubbard as 'Fatty': 'All of a sudden I was ordered to appear at Saint Hill Manor at nine o'clock on a Sunday morning with all my clothes. There was a big open truck outside being loaded with files and filing cabinets and I was told to get in the back. I had no idea where I was going. By the time we got to Southampton Docks I was frozen, I could hardly move. This was November, don't forget. They got me on to the poop deck and this big fat body appeared. It was Fatty. "Oh, so you've deigned to come, have you?" he said. "Well I'm here, aren't I?" I said "If you've come to join us, I'll come down and shake your hand," he said. He stepped down, grabbed my hand, realized I was frozen and started screaming and shouting to get me into a warm cabin. I sat in the cabin for about three hours until I had thawed out. I was told that I was going to be a galley hand. By this time I was well used to Hubbard's insanity and there was no way I was going to succumb to it. I wasn't bothered. If they wanted me to clean the heads and scrub the decks, that was fine by me.'[10]

To supplement his inexperienced crew, Hubbard hired a couple of professional seamen, including a chief engineer, but it did not prevent mishaps occurring even before the *Royal Scotsman* had put to sea. One of the recruits was on duty at the gangplank as Quartermaster and failed to notice until it was too late that the ship's rubbing strake had caught on the edge of the dock as the tide ebbed. A small crowd of stevedores watched with undisguised amusement as the crew of the *Royal Scotsman* tried to lever their enormous ship off the dock. It was hopeless: the rubbing strake creaked, splintered and finally broke away from the hull.

Hubbard took the opportunity to parade the entire crew on the dockside to point out what had happened and remind them that as thetans all of them must have had seafaring experience in one or another of their past lives. 'The truth of the matter is that you have all been around a long time,' he stressed. 'Stop pretending you don't know what it is all about, because you *do* know what it is all about.' Amos Jessup said everyone felt better afterwards.

While all this was going on, Hubbard had despatched Hana Eltringham on a top secret mission to re-register the *Royal Scotsman* in Sierra Leone in order to circumvent the attention of the Board of Trade. Hana first flew back to Las Palmas, where she collected a Spanish lawyer who had previously worked for the church, and then together they took a flight to Sierra Leone, a tiny, mosquito-ridden republic on the west coast of Africa. In Freetown, the capital, it took thirty-six hours to complete the paperwork, during which time Hana bought a large Sierra Leonese flag. On 28 November, less than three days after leaving Britain, she was on her way back to Gatwick carrying the ship's new documents. She took a cab from the airport direct to Southampton Docks.

'I arrived back on board at about four o'clock in the afternoon and took the papers straight to LRH, who was having tea in the main dining-room with the ship's officers. He was delighted to see me and very pleased to get the new registration, but as he was reading through the papers his eye caught something and he started to frown. I felt the familiar terror rising. "Did you notice this?" he said, pointing to the name of the ship on the papers. I looked and saw the "s" had been missed out and it was spelled "Royal Scotman". I began to stammer an apology, but he suddenly smiled, grabbed my hand and began pumping it. "Double congratulations," he said. "Now the ship has a new name as well."' He instantly ordered painters to black out the second 's' in the name on the bows, stern, lifeboats and lifebelts.

The following day, the *Royal Scotman* applied for clearance to sail to Brest in north-west France, for repairs. The port authorities in Southampton had no powers to detain a vessel registered in Sierra Leone and the ship sailed at dusk, raising the Sierra Leonese flag and banging into the fenders in the inner harbour on her way out into Southampton Water. It was to be a hair-raising maiden voyage for the Sea Org's flagship, as Hana Eltringham recounted:

'We sailed out of the channel that evening into an awful storm. The engine room was in a very bad condition; the main engines were not running very well and neither were the generators and because the paint was so dirty in the engine room you couldn't follow which were the water lines and which were the fuel lines. Half-way between Southampton and Brest, one of the generators conked out.

'I was on bridge watch as officer of the deck. We were between three to five miles off the north-west tip of France and I could see ahead, on the port side, the buoys marking the rocky coastline going south. But as we came around to try and get into the estuary towards Brest I noticed the the red-flashing buoys were swinging across the bows of the ship and I realized we were caught in a rip tide and were being pushed towards the rocks.

'The ship started to wallow very badly and each time she went over she took longer to recover. Although she had stabilizers, she went from a five degree roll to almost a twenty-five degree roll and on the last roll to port she staggered. We were all hanging on to the bridge and at that moment the old man [Hubbard] began screaming at Bill Robertson, the navigator, "Get us on a course out of here! Get us on a course out of here!" He was really bellowing. The ship started to stagger around, very slowly and painfully. It was scary. I was terrified and I think LRH was too, the way he was screaming and holding on to the bridge and glaring at us.

'Once we had got out of it and were about ten miles off the coast steering south, he took the entire bridge watch into the cabin just behind the bridge and told us that due to what had happened and the ship being at risk and not truly seaworthy he had decided not to go into Brest, even though it would be defying orders. We were going to continue south down to the Mediterranean. The way he was telling us was like he was convincing us it was the right thing to do. He went over and over it, to make sure we understood. Then he entered what had happened in the log book, a two- or three-page entry explaining the reasons for not going into Brest, and we all signed it.

'The following day there was another near catastrophe. We were planning to put into Gibraltar to meet up with the *Avon River*. It was about five or five-thirty in the afternoon and getting dark as we approached the Gibraltar Strait. We were in the northernmost lane entering the Med and we could see there was a storm brewing. The storm came up quickly and the sea was very wild and as we were battling to control the ship the oil lines from the bridge to the engine room lost pressure and the hydraulic steering on the bridge gave way.

'The ship started to drift across the southernmost outgoing lane towards the Moroccan coast. We put our "Not under command" lights on so other ships could see we were drifting and started to work frantically on the back of the poop deck to rig up the emergency steering. It was pouring with rain and very cold. In the middle of all this we were in radio communication with Gibraltar asking for help, for a tug to be sent out to bring us in. They refused. They said that because we had failed to comply with our sailing orders we would not be allowed into any English port. I can remember LRH pleading with them on the radio: "We have wives and children on board, we are at risk." But they would not come to our aid. I was appalled. It was my first major shock.

'We had managed to find all the component parts to hook up the emergency steering on the aft docking bridge and there we were, Ron, Pook and myself, hanging on to the manual steering wheel trying to steer the ship while someone stood holding an umbrella over us, another shone a torch on a little hand compass and someone else talked on a walkie-talkie to the bridge to the person watching the gyro compass. Mary Sue was running backwards and forwards with cups of steaming hot cocoa.

'I could still hear snatches of LRH talking to Gib on the ship-to-shore radio and I remember standing there, holding on to the steering wheel with aching arms and tears streaming down my face, thinking nobody wants us, where can we go? To be refused help by a British port brought home to me the enormity of our situation and my empathy for the old man increased a thousand fold. He was not wanted in England and he had been kicked out of various places around the world. All I could think about was that no one wanted this brilliant man and the treasures he had to offer.'

Denied entry into Gibraltar, the *Royal Scotman* continued into the Mediterranean under her emergency steering and set a course for the little principality of Monaco, where Hubbard hoped he would be more welcome. Food and water was running low and the cook was reduced to serving soup made with seawater by the time the ship hove to off Monte Carlo in early December. She was too big to enter the harbour, but the port authorities agreed to her being re-fuelled and re-provisioned by lighters, and engineers were brought on board to repair the steering. From Monaco, the *Royal Scotman* sailed to Cagliari in Sardinia, where she docked for the first time since leaving Southampton.

If Hubbard had a reason for visiting Sardinia, he kept it to himself. While they were there, he received a cable which brought on another paroxysm of uncontrolled rage and sent everyone around him diving for cover. The *Avon River* had been caught in hurricane-force storms north of the Balearic Islands: much of the deck gear had been swept overboard and the terrified crew was very shaken up. As Hubbard read the cable his face began to twitch. He strode to the chart table, stabbed at it madly with his finger and bellowed, '*What were they doing up there?*'

John O'Keefe, the unhappy Scientologist who had been given command of the *Avon River*, had muddled his instructions and was miles off course when he ran into the storm. He should have been far to the south of the Balearics, heading for a rendezvous with the *Royal Scotman* in Cagliari. Hubbard was still seething when the *Avon River* finally limped into the harbour at Cagliari. He refused to speak to O'Keefe and ordered a Committee of Evidence (a Com-Ev in Scientology-speak) to be convened, which inevitably found O'Keefe guilty of dereliction of duty. He was assigned a lower condition, stripped of his post and given a lowly job in the engine room. O'Keefe, who thought he had done well to save his ship, was devastated.

This humbling ritual cast something of a pall over the Christmas celebrations, after which the Commodore ordered both ships back across the Mediterranean to Valencia in Spain – a five hundred-mile voyage completed without incident, no doubt to the relief of both crews. Tied up alongside in Valencia harbour, O'Keefe sought out his friend Hana Eltringham. 'I was shocked by his condition,' she said. 'He had lost about twenty pounds and looked like a skeleton with hollow eyes and sunken cheeks. It was unbelievable. He told me he was thinking of leaving and I began to think about it too. It was the first time I really questioned what was going on. I mulled it over for about a week, but in the end I couldn't go. I came back to the view that I was a solid Sea Org member and that in order to achieve freedom I had to fight for it, that it wasn't necessarily an easy road and that I would have to overcome obstacles and encounter suppression. It was a critical moment, but I managed to suppress any desire to leave and get away from the insanity.'

No such doubts assailed Stanley Churcher, one of the three professional seamen on the *Royal Scotman*. Hired as the ship's carpenter in Southampton, he was thoroughly sick of his ship-mates by the time they reached Valencia. Placed in a 'condition of doubt' for 'defying an order, encouraging desertion, tolerating mutinous meetings and attempting to suborn the chief engineer', Mr Churcher employed a few choice words to tell the Scientologist officers what he thought of their 'mumbo-jumbo' and was promptly sacked.

Back in England, Churcher told his story to the *People*, one of Britain's saucier Sunday newspapers, who gleefully published it under the headline 'AHOY THERE – It's the craziest cruise on earth' along with pictures of the ship and L. Ron Hubbard, described as the 'boss' of the 'mind-bending cult' of Scientology. Mr Churcher was withering in his disdain. 'There were seven officers of this Scientology lot,' he said, 'who used to swank about in blue and gold-braid uniforms, but I reckon they knew next to nothing about seamanship. Four of them were women. Hubbard called himself the Commodore and had four different types of peaked cap. Hubbard's wife, who had an officer's uniform made for her, seemed to enjoy playing sailors.

'Every day they went below for lectures, but we seamen were never admitted. It was all so blooming mysterious I tried to find out more. I offered to give them seamanship lectures and they were so pleased at these they gave me a free beginner's course in Scientology. I was give a test on their E-meter, a sort of lie detector, and a woman officer asked me a lot of personal questions, including details of my sex life. The oldest student was a woman of seventy-five who told me she was convinced that Mr Hubbard would fix her up with a new body when she died.

'I couldn't make head nor tail of it.'[11]

Chapter 17

In Search of Past Lives

'USIS OFFICER STATES HUBBARD RUNS FLOATING UNIVERSITY OF QUES-
TIONABLE MORAL CHARACTER, NOT ACCREDITED ANY US UNIVERSITIES
AND POOR REPRESENTATIVE FOR US ABROAD . . . FLOATING COLLEGE
PROBABLY PART OF CHARLATAN CULT.' (CIA cable traffic, June/July
1968)

* * * * *

Soon after the *Royal Scotman* docked in Valencia a group of students
flew in from Saint Hill to take a 'clearing course' on board the ship.
One of them was a pretty, dark-eyed New Yorker called Mary Maren:

'I had a friend in dance class in New York who was into Scientology
and he told me about it. They sounded like an interesting group of
people and I thought it would be useful to have this exact scientific
technology at my disposal. I read *Dianetics* and it made a lot of sense
to me.

'By 1967 I was doing the briefing course at Saint Hill and I saw some
people who had come back from this mysterious sea project. One of the
guys was terrified, really scared; I had no idea why he was in such a
state. Two weeks later more came back. They had lost a lot of weight
and looked overwhelmed, as if they had seen some kind of monster in
the sea. Later I discovered that they had been cleaning cattle dung out
of the ship's hold for two weeks, but I didn't know it at the time. I said
to my husband, Artie, I'm never going to join the Sea Org.

'I forgot all that when we all got on a plane to do the clearing course.
It was called the New Year Freedom Flight. I'd never been to Spain
before and it all seemed very exciting. At that time the ship looked
clean, kinda nice. The stateroom I was given was very small and
cramped, but everything looked kinda spiffed up. The atmosphere
was very congenial.

'LRH was on the ship and in a real jolly mood. He used to stay up
late at night on the deck and talk to us into the wee hours about his
whole track adventures, how he was a race-car driver in the Marcab
civilization. The Marcab civilization existed millions of years ago on
another planet; it was similar to planet Earth in the 'fifties, only they

had space travel. Marcabians turned out later not to be good guys so it wasn't a compliment that their civilization was similar to ours. LRH said he was a race driver called the Green Dragon who set a speed record before he was killed in an accident. He came back in another lifetime as the Red Devil and beat his own record, then came back and did it again as the Blue Streak. Finally he realized all he was doing was breaking his own records and it was no game any more.

'People would stand around listening to these stories for hours, very over-awed. At the time it seemed a privilege and honour to share these things, to hear him talking about things that went on millions of years ago like it was yesterday. It was usually entertaining, but I sometimes found it very stressful to take it all in, this powerful, booming outflow, and it was hard to get away. One night I was getting dizzy and dared to ask if I could leave early. I could hear my voice echoing in the cosmos as I said, "If you'll excuse me, I have to go to bed, sir." He said, "OK, sure."'[1]

Talking about his past lives to an adoring, captive audience was one of Hubbard's favourite recreational activities. His stories, no matter how outrageous, were always treated seriously, for everyone on the ship was a dedicated Scientologist committed to the concept of past lives and immortality. It was not in the least improbable to Mary Maren, or any of the others who listened to Hubbard talking on the deck of *Royal Scotman* on those warm Spanish nights, that he had been a Marcabian racing driver.

One of the recurring features of Hubbard's past lives on this planet was a penchant for secreting his worldly goods underground and one of the frustrations of his present life was his inability to find them. He was deeply disappointed that his cruises round the Canary Islands in the *Enchanter* had not resulted in replacing the schooner's ballast with gold bars, but now he had more time, more ships and more personnel at his disposal and in February 1968, he asked for volunteers to accompany him on a special mission on the *Avon River*.

Amos Jessup was among the first to step forward. 'He didn't tell us ahead of time what we were going to do, but it didn't matter to me, I'd have followed him through the gates of Hell if I had to. I was glad to do anything for him because I felt that what he had done to help others was so great an accomplishment he deserved whatever help I could offer. People felt he was a miracle worker, someone who had demonstrated a far higher level of competence than anything we could aspire to. It was as exciting and stimulating as hell to be with him. You had to be on your toes, put out your maximum effort, but it was always very refreshing and therapeutic.'[2]

Hubbard accepted thirty-five volunteers for the mission and for the next few weeks conducted daily training sessions on the deck of the

Avon River, often watched by envious students hanging over the rails of the *Royal Scotman* moored alongside in Valencia harbour. With a stop watch in one hand, the Commodore put the crew through innumerable drills to rescue men overboard, fight fires, handle lines, launch and retrieve small boats and repel boarders – he told them he was worried about piracy in the Mediterranean and wanted to be sure they would not panic if that circumstance arrived.

At the beginning of March the *Avon River* set sail, leaving the *Royal Scotman* seething with speculation about the nature of her mission. She headed east, back across the Mediterranean once again, and anchored in a sheltered bay off Cap Carbonara, on the south-east coast of Sardinia, where Hubbard mustered the crew on the well deck for a briefing. Standing on a hatch cover so that he could be seen, he told them he was on the threshold of achieving an ambition he had cherished for centuries in earlier lives. This was the first lifetime he had been able to build an organization with sufficient resources, money and manpower to tackle the project they were about to undertake. He had accumulated vast wealth in previous lives, he explained, and had buried it in strategic places. The purpose of their present mission was to locate this buried treasure and retrieve it, either with, or without, the co-operation of the authorities.

Several members of the crew were unable to suppress gasps of excitement at this prospect and he smiled broadly before continuing. To the best of his recollection, when he was the Commander of a fleet of war galleys two thousand years ago, there was a temple somewhere on the coast close to where they were anchored. It was called the Temple of Tenet and the high priestess was a charming lady who, he said with a wink, had 'warmed the hearts of sailors'. His intention was to put several parties ashore next morning to search for the ruins of the temple and the secret entrance where he had buried a cache of gold plates and goblets.

'It was an electrifying idea,' said Jessup. 'We all thought it was high adventure. Here was this guy who had cracked through the age-old mystery of the human condition, had dug into, and uncovered, every aspect of human shortcoming, now broaching into a new area, going to sea with a bunch of people in the Mediterranean and digging up buried treasure. It didn't matter to me if it was true or not, what mattered was being able to play a game that LRH had designed. If it was important to him, I would do the best I could.'

The ruins of the Temple of Tenet at first proved difficult to trace, until Hubbard realized that his recollection was based on ancient sailing instructions whereas he had selected the search area using a modern chart. Once this obstacle had been overcome the ruins were soon found, an event which caused a predictable stir on board the

Avon River only marginally spoiled by the discovery that the site was clearly marked as an ancient monument – it might have been more sensible to locate the temple by looking at a guide book.

The fact that the temple was a known ruin also made it rather difficult for the Scientologists to begin sweeping the area with their metal detectors, let alone starting to dig, without arousing the suspicion of the locals. Although one group reported encountering what appeared to be the hidden entrance and a surreptitious probe with a metal detector was positive, Hubbard decided merely to note their findings and move on.

While the search parties wrote up detailed reports of everything they had found, the *Avon River* headed south towards the coast of north Africa, to Tunis, where the ancient civilization of Carthage flourished before the birth of Christ. Hubbard said he knew a Carthaginian priest who had hidden a treasure trove of jewels and gold in a temple which he thought he could find. Moored in the harbour of the Tunisian port of Bizerte, the Commodore briefed his eager search parties by making a clay model of what he could recall of the topography around the temple; they were told to scour the coastline for a 'matching' landscape. He was almost always waiting on the deck when the shore parties returned, impatient to know what they had discovered. Sure enough, they found the site of the temple just as he had described it, but erosion had destroyed the secret tunnel which led to where the treasure was hidden. Hubbard went out to the site, confirmed that they had found the right place and pointed out where the erosion had taken place.

Although they had not yet retrieved any treasure, there was not a man or woman on the mission who was not encouraged by what they had discovered thus far. From Bizerte, the *Avon River* moved along the coast to La Goulette, the outer harbour of Tunis, where an attempt was made to explore the ruins of an underwater city. Their scuba equipment proved unequal to the task and Hubbard mocked up another clay model of yet another temple site, which this time was found to be occupied by a government office building.

While at La Goulette, Joe van Staden, the captain of the *Avon River*, offended the Commodore in some way, was promptly dismissed and replaced by Hana Eltringham. 'I was working in the between decks area,' she recalled, 'when LRH called me over and said, "You're going to be the new Captain." I went completely numb; I was terrified. I can remember sitting at my desk with my head in my hands muttering, "Oh my God, oh my God." As I sat there I suddenly became aware of him standing in the doorway of his cabin beckoning to me. I got up and walked over to him. He had an E-meter in one hand and he thrust the cans at me and said, "Hold these." I stood there in the doorway while he was fiddling with the meter and then he said, "I want you to recall the last time you were Captain."

'Through the confusion and fear I was experiencing, my first thought was that this was ridiculous. Then I started to get vague impressions of a time in some past life when I was the Captain of a ship and there was a storm at sea. He said, "Very good, very good" and asked me to go back earlier and I got a very vivid flash of space ships and space travel. It was very real, not an imaginary thing at all. I told him what I had seen, that I was on some space ship being called urgently to my land base. We were going back as fast as we could when we were blown up in space by some enemy. That was followed by confusion and some spinning motion as if the space ship was disintegrating. He had me go through it again and the effects of the experience subsided a lot. "Good," he said, "very good." That was it.

'I went up on the deck and felt the fear and terror in my stomach just disappear. I suddenly felt very able, very competent to tackle anything that came along. Next morning I had to take the ship from one side of La Goulette harbour to the other for re-fuelling, then pick up a pilot to take us out. I thought he would come out and help. No way. I saw him open the curtains of his cabin for a moment, smile to himself a little bit, then close them. I thought, "The old sod isn't even going to give me a hand."'[3]

A few hours out of La Goulette, on an easterly course towards Sicily, steam began pouring from the hatches over the engine room. Cabbie Runcie, the ship's chief engineer, who was the only 'wog' (the Scientologist's name for a non-Scientologist) on board, appeared on the bridge wiping his hands with an oily rag to announce that a piston ring in the high-pressure cylinder had blown and that they would have to stop for repairs. Runcie was nearly seventy years old, a bald, toothless, taciturn, pipe-smoking Scot who preferred to keep his own counsel and Hubbard was both surprised and irritated by his temerity, particularly as he was a 'wog'. The Commodore ordered Hana to stay on course at the same speed, whereupon Runcie disappeared down the steps to the engine room muttering, 'This is madness, this is stupidity.' It was his only recorded comment on the entire voyage.

Steam was still pouring from the engine hatches when the *Avon River* dropped anchor off the little fishing port of Castellammare on the north coast of Sicily. Thoroughly unconcerned by the banging and swearing from the engine room, Hubbard gathered a small group on the deck and pointed out their next objective – an old watch tower just visible on a high promontory overlooking the harbour. He decreed that the search should take place under cover of darkness and at dusk that evening the search party set out in a rubber dinghy to reconnoitre the watch tower.

They returned several hours later in a state of high excitement, having registered strong readings on a metal detector in one corner of the watch tower. The following night another expedition was mounted, this time armed with shovels. The crew of the *Avon River* waited with nerves on edge, but there was no brass-bound chest in the bottom of the dinghy when it bumped against the side of the ship – the rocky foundations of the watch tower had proved too much for shovels. Hubbard, who appeared quite as disappointed as everyone else, said he did not think it was worth wasting any more time at the site. He promised to send the *Enchanter* back at a later date to find the owner of the land and negotiate its purchase in order to conduct a thorough excavation.

From Sicily, the *Avon River* sailed across the Straits of Messina to the 'toe' of Italy, anchoring off the barren, rocky coastline of Calabria, which had been Hubbard's territory when he was a tax collector at the time of the Roman empire. Not an entirely honest tax collector, however, for he said he had hidden gold in sacred stone shrines along the coast, figuring that they were less likely to be vandalized.

Two small boats were put ashore with search parties, but none of the shrines could be found. The *Avon River* steamed up and down the coast while look-outs swept the shore with binoculars, but still to no avail. Hubbard concluded that the coast had been eroded and the shrines washed into the sea, along with all his hidden gold.

There was, nevertheless, a palpable aura of anticipation building up on board the *Avon River* for everyone knew the climax of the mission was still to come – a visit to a secret space station on the island of Corsica. Hubbard had shown a few favoured members of the crew, including Hana Eltringham, several pages of handwritten and typed notes describing the existence and location of the station in mountainous terrain to the north of the island. It occupied a huge cavern which could only be entered by pressing a specific palm print (the crew had no doubt it was Hubbard's) against a certain rock, which would cause a rock slab blocking the cave to slide away and instantly activate the space station. Inside, there was an enormous mother ship and a fleet of smaller craft, constructed from non-corrosive alloys as yet unknown to earthlings, and everything needed for their operation, including fuel and supplies.

Sadly, the Corsican space station was to remain no more than the subject of thrilling rumours, for towards the end of April an urgent radio message arrived from Mary Sue asking the Commodore to return immediately to Valencia, where there was a 'flap' (the euphemism employed to describe any clash between Scientologists and 'wogs'). Hubbard acquiesced, leaving the crew speculating wildly about what might have happened at the space station. There was strong support for the view that Ron was intending to use the 'mother ship' to escape from earth and continue his work elsewhere, perhaps in a more rewarding environment. The Sea Org, it was hopefully suggested, was perhaps nothing more than a step towards a 'Space Org'.

Such considerations had to be put aside for the time being, for *Avon River* ran into a series of storms as she ploughed towards the Mediterranean coast of Spain. Hubbard's temper worsened with the weather. One dark night, in a gale force wind, Hana became concerned that the ship was being blown too close to the shore and dared to change course without asking the Commodore's permission. As the old trawler turned, she began to buck and wallow. 'She was just coming round nicely', Hana recollected, 'when there was this great bellow from LRH's cabin, which was under the bridge. I heard his feet pounding up the companionway and then the bridge door burst open. He stood there like a madman, with his hair all over the place, glared around and shouted, "What's going on?" I almost leapt at him, grabbed him by both shoulders and told him as clearly as I could what I had done, after which he began to calm down and stopped glaring at everyone like some ferocious beast. It always struck me as odd that a man of his calibre would behave like that; I expected him to be more God-like.'

Hubbard was further displeased, on arriving in Valencia, to discover that the 'flap' had been caused by the port Captain of the *Royal Scotman*, who had consistently refused requests from the Spanish port authorities to move the ship from the dock to a mole in the harbour. The situation had deteriorated to such an extent that the Spaniards were threatening to tow the ship out to sea and deny her re-entry. Hubbard sent a mission ashore to heal the rift and transferred six officers from the *Avon River* to the *Royal Scotman* to report on how the ship was being run.

A few days later, the *Royal Scotman* dragged her anchor in the outer harbour as a storm began to blow up. Hubbard heard what was happening over the radio on the *Avon River*. He grabbed the nearest available officers, jumped into the barge and hurried across to the *Royal Scotman*, running up on to the bridge to take command. The ship was still secured to the harbour wall by wire hawsers which were under enormous pressure; if they snapped, nothing could prevent her being swept on to the rocks. Hubbard managed to slip the hawsers and re-anchor the ship, but not before her rudder had been damaged against the mole.

When the emergency was over, the furious Commodore demanded an 'ethics investigation' to find out who had 'goofed' and meanwhile assigned the entire ship a 'condition of liability'. Since there were so few people he could trust, he appointed Mary Sue to be the new Captain of *Royal Scotman*. Her orders were to take the ship to Burriana, north of Valencia, for repairs and then to cruise up and down the Spanish coast to train the crew. She was to stay at sea until both the crew was sufficiently well trained and the ship sufficiently spruce to qualify for upgrading; until then, the *Royal Scotman* would remain in 'liability'.

So it was that Spanish fishermen working their nets off the coast of Valencia were treated to an unforgettable spectacle over the next few weeks – a large passenger ship cruising offshore with a band of dirty grey tarpaulins knotted around her funnel. Had the fishermen been allowed on board, they would have been even more surprised to see that all the crew, including the diminutive lady Captain, wore grey rags tied to their left arms. It was even said, although perhaps in jest, that Mary Sue's pet corgi, Vixie, was obliged to sport a grey rag tied to her collar.

Hubbard remained on the *Avon River* and sailed south to Alicante, where the students who had been on the *Royal Scotman* were now accommodated in a 'land base', a hotel. His plan to pay them a visit was thwarted by the untimely discovery that the *Avon River* was too big to enter the harbour. For a while he seemed at a loss to know what to do, but after studying a chart he decided that they should go to Marseilles, the second largest city in France and her chief Mediterranean port. As always, no one dared ask why they were going where they were going.

Sailing north, the *Avon River* came across the unhappy *Royal Scotman* apparently anchored for the night, still with her grey rag round the funnel. Hubbard ordered his ship to manoeuvre within hailing distance and bellowed into a bullhorn, 'Well, well, here's a ship in liability that thinks it can anchor for the night, taking it easy.' Mary Sue's voice came drifting back across the water, but the crew of the trawler could not hear what she was saying. 'It might be better training to keep your ship moving at night,' Hubbard boomed, 'or are you scared to keep going in the dark?' Mary Sue's reply remained unintelligible, although it seemed somewhat heated to Hana Eltringham, who was on the bridge with Hubbard.

Friends who were on the 'liability cruise' told Hana later that the conditions on board were appalling. The crew worked to the point of exhaustion, the food was meagre and no one was allowed to wash or change their clothes. Mary Sue enforced the rules rigidly but shared the privations, and was scrupulously fair and popular.

In Marseilles, Hubbard moved into a rented villa on shore while the engine of the *Avon River* was overhauled. A telex was installed in the villa so that he could stay in touch with Saint Hill, from where the news was of increasingly vociferous opposition to Scientology from both press and public. Hubbard was warned that more questions were expected in Parliament about their activities.

At the beginning of June a radio message arrived from Mary Sue to say that the *Royal Scotman* was ready for reassessment. Her husband graciously agreed to up-grade the ship to the next level – 'non-existence' – and gave his permission for her to sail to Marseilles for his inspection, after which he would decide if she could resume operations unhindered by the stigma of a lower condition. The *Royal Scotman* arrived in the harbour at Marseilles looking better than she had at any time since going into service for the Sea Org – she had been painted white from stem to stern, her brasswork was gleaming and the entire crew had been fitted out with smart new uniforms. Hubbard was all smiles, presided over a ceremony to remove all lower conditions and promptly moved back into his cabin on board. A few days later the *Royal Scotman* sailed for Melilla in Spanish Morocco, eight hundred miles distant. No one knew why.

The Commodore's sunny disposition was not to endure. The *Avon River* was stranded in Marseilles harbour by a general strike in France which had paralyzed the country and brought repair work on the ship's engines to a halt. Hubbard began sending messages from the *Royal Scotman* urging Hana Eltringham to somehow get the repair work completed as he needed her urgently. One evening the radio operator told Hana that LRH wanted to speak to her alone; she was to clear the bridge and close the doors. 'I did what I as told,' she said, 'and as I picked up the radio I could hear him sobbing openly. He was weeping with frustration over what was going on on the *Royal Scotman*. He said the new Captain was so incompetent that he had had to take over and he couldn't cope any longer. It shook me like nothing else could. He was my everything. I loved him like a father or a brother, he was part of my family. I really loved him that much I would have done anything for him and there he was weeping over the radio and pleading with me to do everything in my power to get my ship to sea to join him. "I need you to take over as Captain," he said. I was bewildered. I didn't think I was capable of doing it but I knew I would have to try. Part of his brilliance was that he motivated you to do extraordinary things.'

Two days later, when the bridge blocking the harbour was opened in an emergency, the *Avon River* made a dash for the open sea with her engine repairs still incomplete. She got as far as Barcelona before the piston rings blew again. She re-fuelled and limped down to Valencia, where more repairs were undertaken, then a radio message arrived ordering Hana to meet the *Royal Scotman* in Bizerte.

The old trawler arrived at the Tunisian port a few hours before the *Royal Scotman*. John McMaster, who had been away on a promotion tour and had re-joined the *Avon River* in Valencia, watched the arrival of the Sea Org's flagship in Bizerte. 'I'll never forget it,' he said. 'We had been warned over the radio that she was coming and about the time she was due a cruise ship from the Lloyd Tristina Line came in to the river. She was like a beautiful swan, gliding in, coming alongside and docking effortlessly. Perfect! Then our rust bucket chunters in making a huge noise and begins manoeuvring too far out. Someone throws a line from the deck without the faintest hope of reaching the dock and the rope splashes into the water. It was almost twilight and I could hear Fatty's voice coming across the water. He was standing on the bridge screaming: "I've been betrayed, the bastards have betrayed me again!" The Arabs waiting on the dock to take the lines must have wondered what the hell was going on.'[4]

When *Royal Scotman* was eventually moored, Hubbard's first act was to place the *Avon River* in a condition of 'liability' for taking so long to catch up with him. He refused to speak to Hana Eltringham and had no desire to hear how she had risked arrest by slipping out of the strike-bound harbour in Marseilles in order to join him, or how she had sailed more than five hundred miles with steam pouring out of the hatches and the engines threatening to seize up at any moment. 'There was no more talk of me becoming Captain of the *Royal Scotman*,' Hana said.

Beset by traitors and incompetents, Hubbard felt obliged to introduce new punishments for erring Sea Org personnel. Depending on his whim, offenders were either confined in the dark in the chain locker and given food in a bucket, or assigned to chip paint in the bilge tanks for twenty-four or forty-eight hours without a break. A third variation presented itself when Otto Roos, a young Dutchman, dropped one of the bow-lines while the *Royal Scotman* was being moved along the dock. Purple with rage, Hubbard ordered Roos to be thrown overboard.

No one questioned the Commodore's orders. Two crew members promptly grabbed the Dutchman and threw him over the side. There was an enormous splash when he hit the water, a moment of horror when it seemed that he had disappeared and nervous speculation that he might have hit the rubbing strake as he fell. But Roos was a good swimmer and when he climbed back up the gangplank, dripping wet, he was surprised to find the crew still craning anxiously over the rails on the other side of the ship.

'It was not really possible to question what was going on,' explained David Mayo, a New Zealander and a long-time member of the Sea Org, 'because you were never sure who you could really trust. To question anything Hubbard did or said was an offense and you never knew if you would be reported. Most of the crew were afraid that if they expressed any disagreement with what was going on they would be kicked out of Scientology. That was something absolutely untenable to most people, something you never wanted to consider. That was much more terrifying than anything that might happen to you in the Sea Org.

'We tried not to think too hard about his behaviour. It was not rational much of the time, but to even consider such a thing was a discreditable thought and you couldn't allow yourself to have a discreditable thought. One of the questions in a sec-check was, "Have you ever had any unkind thoughts about LRH?" and you could get into very serious trouble if you had. So you tried hard not to.'[5]

On 25 July 1968, while Hubbard was still in Bizerte, the government in Britain finally decided to take action against Scientology. Kenneth Robinson, the Health Minister, stood up in the House of Commons and announced a ban on Scientology students entering the UK. 'The Government is satisfied,' he said, 'having reviewed all the available evidence, that Scientology is socially harmful. It alienates members of families from each other and attributes squalid and disgraceful motives to all who oppose it. Its authoritarian principles and practices are a potential menace to the personality and well-being of those so deluded as to become its followers; above all, its methods can be a serious danger to the health of those who submit to them.'

A few days later, the Home Secretary announced that L. Ron Hubbard was classified as an 'undesirable alien' and would consequently not be allowed back into Britain, a decision that prompted Hubbard to send a telex to Saint Hill complaining that 'England, once the light and hope of the world, has become a police state and can no longer be trusted.'

These developments spurred British newspapers to renewed efforts to find and interview the elusive Mr Hubbard. The *Daily Mail*, which had recently been pleased to publish the numbers of Hubbard's bank accounts in Switzerland, was first to track him down in Bizerte. Hubbard affected an attitude of nonchalant indifference to events in Britain and did his best to charm the *Mail* team. He invited the reporters on board, showed them his sixteen war medals in a framed case behind his desk and politely answered questions for more than two hours.

He claimed he was no longer in control of Scientology, said he was abroad for health reasons and insisted he was still welcome in Britain. 'My name inspires confidence,' he asserted. 'I'm persona grata everywhere. If I wanted to return to Britain, I'd walk in the front gate and the Customs officer would say, "Hullo, Mr Hubbard." That's how it's always been and always will be.'

It was a public relations tour de force; almost the worst thing the newspaper could find to say about him was that he chain-smoked menthol cigarettes and 'fidgeted nervously'.[6] He performed with similar confidence when a British television crew arrived the following day, even when the interviewer asked him, 'Do you ever think you might be quite mad?' Hubbard grinned broadly and replied 'Oh yes! The one man in the world who never believes he's mad is a madman.'

He explained that most of his wealth derived from his years as a writer rather than from Scientology: 'Fifteen million published words and a great many successful movies don't make nothing.' He was in the Mediterranean, he said, studying ancient civilizations and trying to find out why they went into decline.[7]

After the television interview, Hubbard decided not to stay in Bizerte to entertain further media representatives. The *Royal Scotman* rapidly weighed anchor and headed back to sea, leaving late-comers to disconsolately kick their heels in the dust on the Tunisian dockside and wonder what the trip was worth in expenses.

The arrival of the *Royal Scotman* on the Greek island of Corfu two days later aroused little interest locally. Corfu was a popular port of call for cruise liners and a busy harbour, with ships plying in and out all the time. Apart, perhaps, from her Sierra Leonese flag, there was nothing special about the *Royal Scotman*; word went round that she was one of those floating schools that had become popular of late and vague dockside curiosity was satisfied.

Emissaries from the ship paid a visit on the harbourmaster, Marius Kalogeras, and explained that they were representatives of the 'Operation and Transport Corporation Limited', an international business management organization. They would shortly be joined by two other ships and intended, they said, to stay in Corfu for some time while students attended courses on the ships. Their logistic requirements, they pointed out, would result in a considerable injection of funds into the island's economy, not to mention the contribution made by their free-spending students.

The harbourmaster quickly grasped the message, allocated choice berths for the 'OTC' ships in a secluded section of the newly extended quay and promised to provide full facilities. Appraised of this warm welcome, the Commodore began to look upon the island and the Greek people with particular favour, even to the extent of granting an interview to *Ephimeris ton Idisseon*, one of Corfu's daily newspapers, on the subject of the recent coup d'etat in Greece by a clique of military officers known as the 'Colonels'.

The interveiwer's obsequiousness was only surpassed by Hubbard's obvious desire to ingratiate himself, as fawning answer followed fawning question:

'Q.   Mr Hubbard, as the international personality that you are, are
you following the new situation in Greece and what do you think of
the work of the present National Government?

A.   The government is the mirror of the people. Where I go and
wherever the students go, the people continually say how safe they
feel. The decision to form a company to establish its headquarter
offices here shows our confidence in Greece.

Q.   I have been told, Mr Hubbard, that you have read the whole of
the new Greek Constitution from beginning to end. If that's true,
what do you think of it?

A.   Yes, I've read it with much interest. The rights of man have
been given great care in it. I have studied many constitutions, from
the times of unwritten laws which various tribes have followed, and
the present constitution represents the most brilliant tradition of
Greek democracy. Out of all the modern constitutions the new Greek
Constitution is the best . . .'

Hubbard's interpretation of the ruling military junta as a democracy
was somewhat at odds with international opinion, but the interviewer
failed to take issue with it.

By the time the *Avon River* joined the flagship in Corfu, Hubbard
was so enamoured with Greece that he decided to change the names of
all his ships in honour of his new hosts. The *Royal Scotman* became
the *Apollo*, the *Avon River* the *Athena* and the *Enchanter*, which had
been pottering around the Mediterranean on various missions for the
Commodore and frequently breaking down, was re-named the *Diana*.

At the end of August, the first students arrived in Corfu from Saint
Hill, many of them carrying large sums of smuggled cash (the British
government had recently introduced restrictions on the export of
currency and it was causing some cash-flow problems for the Sea Org,
which routinely paid its bills in cash). 'They gave me about £3000 in
high-denomination notes to take out to the ship,' said Mary Maren. 'I
hid it in my boots.'

Smuggling was entirely consistent with the Sea Org's cavalier
disregard for the tedious rules of the 'wog' world. Leon Steinberg, for
example, supercargo on the *Avon River*, was the acknowledged expert
at forging documents of authorization to satisfy the voracious appetite
of maritime bureaucracy, using potato-cuts to replicate the essential
rubber stamp. They were almost always accepted, to the huge
enjoyment of the Scientologists, who called them 'Steinidocuments'.[8]

The course being offered in Corfu was for advanced Scientologists
to train as 'operating thetans' at Level VIII, the highest that could be
attained at that time. To become a Class VIII auditor was the
ambition of every self-respecting Scientologist, although none of them
was prepared for the new autocracy that had developed within the Sea

Org. 'The atmosphere was very unfriendly when we arrived,' said Mary Maren. 'One of our group was a bit drunk and he was grabbed by one of the officers who really roughed him up, yelling at him, "This is a ship of the Sea Org and it's run by L. Ron Hubbard . . ." I knew it was not going to be like Valencia and I didn't like it.'

Students were outfitted with a sparse uniform of green overalls, brown belt and brown sandals and were humiliated at every opportunity. 'We were told we were lower than cockroaches and didn't even have the right to audit Mary Sue's dog,' said Maren. The working day began at six o'clock every morning and ended at eleven o'clock at night after a ninety-minute lecture delivered by Hubbard in the forward dining-room on B Deck. 'We were always terrified of falling asleep. LRH would be carried away dramatizing different topics and we'd be pinching each other to stay awake. We were terrorized; it was continuous stress and duress.'

The course had not been going long before Hubbard decided that too many mistakes were being made during auditing and he announced that in future those responsible for errors would be thrown overboard. Everyone laughed at Ron's joke.

Next morning, at the regular muster on the aft well deck, two names were called out. As the students stepped forward, Sea Org officers grabbed them by their arms and legs and threw them over the side of the ship while the rest of the group looked on in amazement and horror. Hubbard, Mary Sue and their sixteen-year-old daughter Diana, all in uniform, watched the ceremony from the promenade deck. The two 'overboards' swam round the ship, climbed stone steps on to the quayside and squelched back up the ship's gangplank, gasping for breath. At the top, they were required to salute and ask for permission to return on board.

'Overboarding' was thereafter a daily ritual. The names of those who were to be thrown overboard were posted on the orders of the day and when the master-at-arms walked through the ship at six o'clock every morning banging on cabin doors and shouting 'Muster on the well deck, muster on the well deck!' everyone knew what was going to happen. 'Anyone to be thrown overboard would be called to the front,' said Ken Urquhart, 'and the chaplain would make some incantation about water washing away sins and then they would be picked up and tossed over. People accepted it because we all had a tremendous belief that what Ron was doing would benefit the world. He was our leader and knew best.'[9]

'I thought it was terrible, inhumane and barbaric,' said Hana Eltringham. 'Some of the people on the course were middle-aged women. Julia Salmon, the continental head of the LA org, was fifty-five years old and in poor health and she was thrown overboard.

She hit the water sobbing and screaming. LRH enjoyed it, without a doubt. Sometimes I heard him making jokes about it. Those were the moments when I came closest to asking myself what I was doing there. But I always justified it by telling myself that he must know what he was doing and that it was all for the greater good.'

Diana Hubbard also appeared to enjoy the ceremony and often ordered overboards. 'I remember coming out on deck one day when I was chief officer,' said Amos Jessup, 'and finding my whole division of four or five people being thrown overboard. I didn't know anything about it and said, "What the hell's going on here?" Then I noticed Diana looking down at me from the deck above and I thought, "Jesus Christ!"'

Of the four Hubbard children on the ship, only Diana had so far been appointed an officer in the Sea Org. She was a 'lieutenant commander' at the age of sixteen and wore a uniform with a mini-skirt and a peaked hat, habitually perched on the back of her head in order not to muss her long auburn hair. Quentin, who was 14, was supposed to be an auditor but could summon up little interest compared to his teenage passion for aeroplanes: he was often to be seen walking along the deck with both arms outstretched, wheeling and diving in some imaginary dogfight, lips vibrating to simulate appropriate engine noises. Suzette and Arthur, who were thirteen and ten respectively, seemed perfectly content to make the best of their strange lives and enjoy the influence their name bestowed.

Diana was perhaps the least liked of the Hubbard children, certainly as far as John McMaster was concerned. McMaster, still working as a galley hand, was overboarded five times on the *Apollo* and nursed a deep resentment against Hubbard and his officious daughter. 'The last time someone called down and said, "John, you're wanted on the poop deck, the Commodore wants to give you a special award." I had some misgivings, but I went up anyway and when I stepped on to the poop deck I realized it was all a nasty little trick. The whole crew was marshalled there and up on the promenade deck there was Fatty and the royal family and all the upstart lieutenants. Hubbard was leaning over the railings with a sorrowful, I've-been-betrayed-again look on his face.

'I began to seethe. I was made to stand immediately below the "royal family" and Diana comes down and stands in front of me and reads out a list of my crimes, things like trying to take over and undermining this and that. It was all lies. I was so mad I nearly picked her up and threw *her* overboard. Then she chants, "We cast your sins and errors to the waves and hope you will arise a better thetan."

'I nearly said, "Go and fetch that fat bastard up there! *He's* the dishonest one! Throw *him* overboard." I should have done; I wish I had, it would have broken the spell they were all under. I was grabbed by these four big thugs and flung over and I started laughing and laughing. I thought, "Jesus, I'm going to get off this floating insanity even if I have to swim to Yugoslavia."' [10] He left the ship several months later.

It was predictable that a 'school ship' which tossed its students overboard every morning would attract a certain amount of attention. Corfiot dock workers could hardly believe their eyes when the first people went over the side of *Apollo*, although they soon treated the whole business as a huge joke and regularly gathered to watch the fun. But interest was also stirred in other quarters.

The Nomarch (mayor) of Corfu asked Major John Forte, the honorary British vice-consul on the island, what he knew about this strange ship. Forte, a retired army officer who had made his home on Corfu, knew a lot. He had reported the arrival of the *Royal Scotman* in Corfu to the Foreign Office in London, correctly deducing that it was, in his words, the 'sinister Scientology ship'. Subsequently he had been instructed to deliver a letter to Hubbard to inform him that he had been declared persona non grata in Britain. It had proved to be far from easy.

'I was met at the gangway', the major reported, 'by a small boy aged about twelve with a very intent but far off expression on his face who politely but firmly inquired my business. I asked where I could find the Captain. In all seriousness, the lad insisted, "*I* am the Captain." Apparently the children take it in turns to act the role of different officers on the ship and are indoctrinated into actually believing they really are the character they happen to be portraying. After an interesting conversation with the lad, I was whisked away by one of the staff to the dirty and evil-smelling bowels of the ship where I was introduced to an outsize female character known as "supercargo", who looked as if she might have been a wardress in a Dickensian reformatory in a bygone age. "Supercargo" signed a receipt for the letter and promised to get it delivered to Hubbard who was alleged to be away cruising on the *Avon River*. About a month later, the letter, which had been crudely opened and resealed, was returned to me with a note from "supercargo" saying that Hubbard could not be traced, his whereabouts being unknown.' [11]

Hubbard was on board all of this time, lying low and waiting for an appropriate moment to step ashore. While the rumours built up about the 'mystery ship' in the harbour, local traders unashamedly welcomed the estimated $50,000 the Sea Org was spending in Corfu every month and on 16 November, Hubbard was invited to a reception in his honour at the Achilleon Palace, a lavish casino on the island. It was the first time he had left the ship since its arrival in August and he was accorded a standing ovation as he entered the palace.

Much gratified, Hubbard returned the hospitality by inviting local dignitaries to a re-naming ceremony on board the *Apollo*. All the Sea Org officers paraded on the quayside in their best uniforms and Diana Hubbard, her hat on straight for once, climbed a rostrum and broke a bottle of champagne against the ship's stern, proclaiming, 'I christen thee yacht *"Apollo"*.' As the new gold name on the stern was unveiled, Hubbard joined his daughter on the rostrum and said, 'I wish to thank you very much because you are here and because you have honoured us with your presence, O Citizens of Corfu . . .'

Behind these cordial scenes, problems were fermenting. The Greek Government had instituted inquiries about Scientology through its Embassy in London. Security agents acting for the Colonels had been instructed to check out the ship, but were assured by the harbourmaster that the Scientologists were harmless people who abided by the law and gave no trouble. 'I have seen people being tossed into the sea,' he admitted, 'but they have told me this is part of their training course.' Major Forte complained that he was besieged by people objecting to Scientologists being 'harboured' on the island and Corfu's leading daily newspaper, *Telegrafos*, published a highly critical feature about Scientology which really raised Corfiot suspicions with a passing mention of 'black magic'.

By January 1969, Corfu traders were so alarmed by the prospect of action being taken against the Scientologists that a delegation sent a telegram to Prime Minister Papadopoulos submitting its 'warmest plea' for 'Professor Hubbard's Philosophy School' to be allowed to remain in Corfu. The Secretary General of the Ministry of Merchant Marine replied that there was 'never any objection' to the *Apollo* remaining in Corfu.

Hubbard, meanwhile, was promising to lavish further largesse on the island. In a typically magniloquent manifesto headed 'Corfu Social and Economic Survey' he envisaged building hotels, roads, factories, schools, a new harbour, three golf courses, seven yacht marinas and various resort facilities, as well as establishing a Greek University of Philosophy funded by Operation and Transport Corporation. The headline on the front of *Ephimeris ton Idisseon* next day was 'CORFU WILL KNOW BETTER DAYS OF AFFLUENCE'.

Deputy Prime Minister Patakos hastily issued a statement emphasizing that 'no permission had yet been granted to the Scientologists to become established on Greek soil'. Hubbard responded by announcing that his Scientology School in Corfu would open 'within two or three weeks'.

By this time Major Forte was convinced that Hubbard's intention was to take over partial control of the island and establish the world headquarters of Scientology and he was lobbying assiduously against allowing him a foothold. Hubbard, on the other hand, was convinced as usual that there was a conspiracy and that Forte was an agent of British intelligence working a 'black propaganda' section. He would later allege that the major had spread vicious rumours about black magic rites being held on board the *Apollo* and Scientologists poisoning wells and casting spells on local cattle.[12] In reality, decisions were being made at a level far above that of an insignificant honorary vice-consul; the Greek Minister for Foreign Affairs had lodged an official request with the UK and Australian Governments for information regarding the status of Scientology in their countries.

On 6 March, Hubbard's opponents received unexpected support from the US Sixth Fleet when a task force arrived off Corfu and a detachment of Marines set up sentry posts around the berths occupied by the Sea Org ships apparently in order to prevent US Navy personnel from coming into contact with Scientologists. 'Somehow it seemed', said Major Forte 'that this was a carefully planned operation designed to bring forcibly home to the authorities the grave danger of contamination by this undesirable cult.'

Unlikely as this theory was, less than two weeks later the Nomarch of Corfu ordered Hubbard and his ships to leave Greece within twenty-four hours. 'The old man almost had a heart attack when he got the news,' said Kathy Cariotaki, a Sea Org member who was on the bridge with Hubbard at the time. 'He went absolutely grey with shock.'[13]

At five o'clock on the afternoon of 19 March 1969, with the harbour sealed by police, the *Apollo* slipped her lines and sailed out into the Aegean Sea.

Major John Forte watched her leave from the waterfront and realized he was standing next to one of the island's notorious Lotharios. He commiserated with him on the departure of so many pretty young girls. 'As a matter of fact I'm not sorry they're gone,' the man replied. 'They were a lot of cockteasers. When it came to the point they all tell you they are only allowed to have sexual relations with fellow Scientologists.'

Forte laughed. It was, he thought, an intriguing aspect of the philosophy of the Church of Scientology.

Chapter 18

Messengers of God

'It is possible that Commodore Hubbard and his wife . . . are philanthropists of some kind and/or eccentrics, but if one does not accept this as an explanation, there has to be some other gimmick involved in this operation. What this gimmick might be is unknown here, although people in Casablanca have speculated variously from smuggling to drug traffic to a far-out religious cult.' (Cable from US Consul General, Casablanca, to Washington, 26 September 1969)

* * * * *

At the time of her ignominious departure from Corfu, the *Apollo* informed the port authorities that she would be making for Venice, information which was doubtless passed to the CIA and to the Foreign Office in London, since both the United States and the United Kingdom were anxious to keep track of the wily Commodore of the Sea Org. But once the ship was out of sight of the Greek mainland, Hubbard ordered a change of course. The *Apollo* turned west towards Sardinia, where she was rapidly re-fuelled and re-provisioned before heading for the Strait of Gibraltar and sailing out of the Mediterranean.

For the next three years, the *Apollo* patrolled the eastern Atlantic, aimlessly sailing from port to port at the Commodore's caprice and rarely stopping anywhere for longer than six weeks. She ventured out into the Atlantic as far as the Azores and once put in to Dakar, the capital of Senegal, but most of the time she criss-crossed a diamond shaped patch of ocean bordered by Casablanca, Madeira, Lisbon and the Canaries, with no objective other than to stay on the move.

'LRH said we had to keep moving because there were so many people after him,' explained Ken Urquhart, who was by then the Commodore's personal communicator. 'If they caught up with him they would cause him so much trouble that he would be unable to continue his work, Scientology would not get into the world and there would be social and economic chaos, if not a nuclear holocaust.'[1]

US intelligence services were mystified by what Hubbard was up to and cables arriving in Washington began speculating on a variety of illicit activities ranging from white slavery to drug-running. In September 1969, while the *Apollo* was in Casablanca, the local US consul cabled Washington with an account of a visit to the ship. All concerned, he noted, have been 'perplexed by the vagueness of the replies' to simple questions about the ship's activities. The consul had picked up a brochure which was no more forthcoming, explaining that trainees on board were learning 'the art and the culture of navigation, the theory of which, when applied, demonstrates a very useful practice at sea'.

Since the ship was registered in Panama, the Panamanian consul tried his luck, but with no better results. He found the ship 'in a very bad state of repair' and believed that 'the lives of the crew had been in jeopardy' while the vessel was at sea. 'The Panamanian consul has tried unsuccessfully to meet Commodore Hubbard, who has taken a suite at the El Mansour Hotel and has instructed the hotel personnel to refuse all telephone calls.'[2]

In frequent communiqués from the ship to his faithful disciples, Hubbard expounded on the enemy forces ranged against Scientology and elaborated on the 'international conspiracy' theory of which he had always been enamoured. Out in the Atlantic, cruising on his flagship, the Commodore's pre-occupatioon with Communist conspiracies developed into a fixation about something called the 'Tenyaka Memorial' – a name he gave to the mysterious agency he claimed was co-ordinating the attacks on Scientology. His hunt for the Tenyaka Memorial was the subject of a rambling thirty-one-page monologue, dated 2 November 1969 and headed 'Covert Operations', in which he said that he and Mary Sue had 'just discovered' that members of the World Federation of Mental Health were working for British and US intelligence agencies. 'These bastards who are in charge of security in these Western countries,' he wrote, 'ought to be simply electric shocked to death. I'm not kidding. Because these same guys . . . have meetings with the Russians every year.' Later the Commodore decided that the Tenyaka Memorial was run by a Nazi underground movement intent on world domination.[3]

Both Hubbard and Mary Sue, who rejoiced in the titles of 'Deputy Commodore', 'Commodore Staff Guardian' (CSG) and 'Controller', peppered their memoranda with military terminology and intelligence jargon. Mary Sue ran the powerful Guardian's office, which was Scientology's intelligence bureau. In a 'Guardian Order' dated 16 December 1969, she warned that the 'enemy' was infiltrating double agents into the church and urged the use of 'any and all means' to detect infiltration. One of the 'operating targets' was to assemble full data by investigation for use 'in case of attack'.[4] 'Smersh' even figured in one of Hubbard's 'flag orders', which defined Scientology's second zone of action thus: 'To invade the territory of Smersh, run it better, make tons of money in it, to purify the mental health field.'[5]

The need for security was made very real to those Scientologists who were flown out to join the ship at its various ports of call. They were briefed and repeatedly drilled on their 'shore stories' – that they were employees of Operation and Transport Corporation, a business management company. They were warned not to use Scientology-speak on shore, to deny any link between OTC and Scientology and, in particular, to feign ignorance of L. Ron Hubbard.

All outgoing private mail had to be left, unsealed, with the master-at-arms and every letter was read by an ethics officer to check for possible breaches of security. Approved mail was shipped in bulk to Copenhagen for posting. Lest curiosity prompted enemies ashore to sift through the ship's garbage for incriminating paperwork, all papers were bundled up and dumped at sea. And on the rare occasions when 'wogs' were allowed on board, the crew carried out a 'clean ship drill', which involved hiding any Scientology materials from view and turning all the pictures of L. Ron Hubbard to the wall.

Hubbard's persistent reiteration that Scientology was beset by dark forces, seeking to destroy anything that helped mankind, fostered a siege mentality among the crew of the *Apollo* and provided spurious justification for the harsh conditions on board. Throughout the Sea Org, the need for dedication, vigilance and sacrifice was constantly stressed and it generated fierce loyalty which was blind to logic or literal truth. The 'shore story', which everyone knew was a pack of lies, was a regrettable necessity if the world was to be saved by Scientology.

It was also a regrettable necessity to prevent anyone from 'blowing the org'. Although all the passports were locked in a safe, attempts to jump ship were not unknown. Whenever it happened, Sea Org personnel were rushed ashore to stake out the relevant local consulate, where the fugitive was likely to try and obtain a new passport. If they were too late, a 'dead agent caper' was activated. The runaway was accused of being a thief or a trouble-maker in order to discredit whatever story he was telling in the Consulate; in the parlance of wartime spies, he would be neutralized and considered a 'dead agent'.[6]

Despite the continuing restrictions on personal liberty, life on board improved somewhat after the *Apollo* left the Mediterranean. The 'heavy ethics' were eased – there was no more overboarding, for example – and the Commodore's demeanour was markedly sunnier. 'He'd often take a stroll along the promenade deck and stop to talk to people,' said Urquhart. 'He normally wore a white silk shirt with a gold lanyard, a cravat and naval cap with lots of scrambled egg on the peak and you could always see him in the centre of the crowd that gathered round him whenever he stopped to talk. But there was still a lot of tension on board and the very real possibility that somebody would make a mistake that would cause a flap. Someone might upset a harbourmaster, or say the wrong thing in answer to a question, or let slip something about Scientology. Some shit was going to hit the fan every day, you could count on it.'

No attempt was made on board ship to maintain the myth that Hubbard was no longer in charge of Scientology. Between forty and fifty feet of telex messages arrived every day from Scientology offices around the world and he received weekly reports detailing every org's statistics and income. Money was, without question, one of the Commodore's primary interests, although he liked to profess a lofty disregard for such matters as financial gain. Loyal members of the Sea Org, who were paid $10 a week, believed the Commodore drew less than they did, because that is what he told them. The reality was that Hubbard was receiving $15,000 a week from church funds through the Hubbard Explorational Company and that huge sums of money were being creamed from 'desk-drawer' corporations and salted away in secret bank accounts in Switzerland and Liechtenstein. When one of these accounts had to be closed in 1970, $1 million in cash was transferred on board the *Apollo*.[7]

There was also a considerable disparity between the way the Hubbards lived on the ship and the conditions endured by everyone else. Most of the crew lived in cramped, smelly, roach-infested dormitories fitted with bunks in three tiers that left little room for personal possessions. Hubbard and Mary Sue each had their own state-rooms in addition to a suite on the promenade deck comprising an auditing-room, office, an elegant saloon and a wood-panelled dining-room, all off-limits to students and crew. Hubbard had a personal steward, as did Mary Sue and the Hubbard children, who all had their own cabins. Meals for the Commodore and his family were cooked in a separate galley by their personal chef, using ingredients brought by couriers from the United States.

When Mike Goldstein, an anthropology major from the University of Colorado, was sent out to join the Sea Org, he was pressed into service as a courier. 'I was briefed in Los Angeles and drilled on my shore story. It was all made to seem very mysterious and cloak and dagger. It was scary. I was warned to follow my instructions to the letter and given a box to take out with me to the ship. I was to say it contained company papers of the Operation and Transport Corporation. Going through the security control in Los Angeles airport, the box set the buzzer off. I nearly died. They opened it up and discovered it contained Hubbard's underpants, tied in a bag with metal clips.

'When I got to New York I found I was expected to courier something else - fourteen boxes which had to be maintained at a certain temperature. No one would tell me what was in them, only that it was vital they arrived intact at the ship. In London I had to change planes. Transferring from one terminal to another with these fourteen boxes was murder. I arrived in Madrid and was taken by Sea Org members to an apartment, where the boxes were put in refrigeration. Next day I caught a plane for Casablanca, only to discover the ship had moved on further south to Safi. By then I was completely paranoid about the boxes, terrified that the heat would get to whatever was in them. I got them wrapped up and found a bus to take me to Safi, where I finally arrived at the ship and handed over the boxes. I was wondering what the hell was in them, but I didn't find out until later. I was carrying fourteen boxes of frozen shrimps for the Hubbard family.'[8]

Like all Scientologists, it had been Goldstein's long-time ambition to meet L. Ron Hubbard and when he first got to the ship he used to contrive excuses to walk past Hubbard's research room on the promenade deck just so that he could catch a glimpse of the great man at work. He was amazed at the amount of paperwork that Hubbard seemed to get through, although many of his preconceptions about the Sea Org were soon shattered. 'I had been told that Flag [the *Apollo*] was perfection and that everyone was super-efficient. But then I was appointed Flag Banking Officer and handed a real dog's breakfast: the ship's finances were in a mess. There were drawers full of money everywhere and more than a million dollars in the safe, but no proper accounts. We paid for everything in cash and were working with three different currencies – Spanish, Portuguese and Moroccan – and it seemed that if anyone wanted money for something they just asked for it. I decided it had to be done by the book and told everyone they would have to account for what they had already spent before they could have any more. The ship was a different world, you have to understand. It was supposed to run Scientology for the whole planet, but it was a world unto itself.'

It was also a world entirely of Hubbard's creation and he added to it, at around this time, a bizarre new element – an elite unit made up of children and eventually known as the Commodore's Messenger Organization. The CMO was staffed by the offspring of committed Scientologists and its original, apparently innocuous, function was simply to serve the Commodore by relaying his verbal orders to crew and students on board the *Apollo*. But the messengers, mainly pubescent girls, soon recognized and enjoyed their power as teenage clones of the Commodore. In their cute little dark blue uniforms and gold lanyards, they were trained to deliver Hubbard's orders using his exact words and tone of voice; if he was in a temper and bellowing abuse, the messenger would scuttle off and pipe the same abuse at the offender. No one dared take issue with whatever a messenger said; no one dared disobey her orders. Vested with the authority of the Commodore they came to be widely feared little monsters.

From 1970 onwards, messengers attended Hubbard day and night, working on six-hour watches around the clock. When he was asleep, two messenger sat outside his state-room waiting for the buzzer that would signal he was awake. Throughout his waking hours, they sat outside his office waiting for his call. When he took a stroll on the deck, they followed him, one carrying his cigarettes, the other an ashtray to catch the ash as it fell. Every minute öf the Commodore's existence had to be recorded in the 'Messenger Log' which noted when he woke, ate, slept, worked and the details of every message he had required to be run.

It was, of course, the greatest possible honour to be selected as a messenger and it was perhaps understandable that the girls would vie with each other to curry favour with the Commodore and dream up ways of pleasing him, by springing forward to light his cigarette, perhaps, or reverently dusting the individual sheets of his writing paper, particularly since they were awarded extra points for little acts of thoughtfulness.

Doreen Smith was just twelve years old, a skinny kid with long blond hair, big eyes and smeared make-up, inexpertly applied, when she arrived in the Azores in September 1970, to join the crew of the *Apollo*. Born into Scientology, she had wanted to be a messenger for as long as she could recall. 'I remember sitting on my luggage on the dockside and looking up at the ship. She was the biggest ship in the port, painted all white, with these huge gold letters, Apollo, and she made a real awesome impression on me. We had to wait on the dock to be cleared by the medical officer. I spotted LRH, or thought I did, standing with his hand on the shoulder of a young girl in a shiny blue short-sleeved pullover with a gold lanyard. He gave her a little shove and she went running down deck after deck to the gangway, skidding to a stop at the bottom to welcome us on board on behalf of the Commodore. It was the first time I'd seen a messenger.'[9]

Two days later, Doreen received a nasty taste of life at sea. Weather reports indicated that a hurricane was heading straight for the Azores. It was too dangerous for a ship the size of the *Apollo* to remain in the harbour and there was no time to sail out of reach. Hubbard took the ship to sea and sailed up and down in the lee of the island, changing course as the wind changed direction. 'It was a very impressive feat of seamanship,' said Hana Eltringham. 'I was on the bridge for almost all the time and I was petrified. Day didn't look much different from night, the wind was howling continually and you could hardly see the bow of the ship because of breaking waves and spray. LRH sat at the radar for thirty-six hours without a break, except to go to the bathroom. He was very calm throughout, constantly reassuring everyone it was going to be all right.'[10]

When the hurricane had passed, Doreen was put to work washing dishes in the galley while she trained first as an 'able seaman', then as a 'page', before she could qualify to join the CMO. She had to appear before a board of fourteen-year-old messengers, win its approval and run sample messages before she was accepted. The most exciting moment of her life was when she was taken ashore in Morocco to buy her uniform – dark blue stretch pants and a blue tunic. 'I was thrilled to death,' she said. 'It was what I had wanted from day one. LRH was my hero. We'd always had his picture hanging on the wall at home and we listened to his tapes all the time. I was his greatest fan.'

Hubbard so much enjoyed the company of his pretty young messengers that it inevitably put a strain on his relationship with his wife and children. It was obvious to Mary Sue, as it was to everyone on board, that the Commodore favoured his messengers above his own children, for whom he seemed to have little time or consideration. Diana, the eldest, had inherited her father's self-confidence and was least affected by his lack of regard. Then eighteen she was one of the Commodore's Staff Aides, who formed the senior management body directly under Hubbard. She was engaged to another Sea Org officer and had a reputation on board for being cold and authoritarian, although she was much admired by the messengers for her long auburn hair, her beauty and her status; they called her 'Princess Diana'.

None of the children had had a proper education since leaving England in 1967. On the bridge, Diana could handle the ship with brisk efficiency, but she read nothing more demanding than romantic novels and in conversation she rivalled Mrs Malaprop. Her latest malapropisms were the source of much secret merriment among her fellow officers.

Her brother, Quentin, was seventeen in January 1971 and was deeply unhappy. He was working as an auditor, but all his life he had longed to be a pilot and frequently pleaded with his father to be allowed to leave the ship to take flying lessons. Quiet and introverted, Quentin was furtively described as 'swishy' because no one wanted to say out loud what everyone suspected – that he was homosexual. Hubbard's loathing of homosexuals was well documented in his voluminous writings and there was not a Scientologist alive who would risk suggesting to him that his son's sexuality was in doubt.

Suzette and Arthur were less troubled by the sacrifice of their childhood. Suzette was fifteen, a cheerful, uncomplicated teenager with a great sense of fun and none of her older sister's drive or ambition. Moved from post to post around the ship, she performed tolerably well and displayed no executive aspirations. All the children had to stand watch along with the rest of the crew and Suzette could always be relied upon to be on duty on time. Not so her twelve-year-old brother, Arthur, who often refused to get out of bed when he was supposed to be on night watch. If the watchkeeper going off duty tried to rouse him, he would threaten to make a noise and wake his father. Anyone who woke Hubbard was in serious trouble and it was often less troublesome to do Arthur's duty than chance waking the slumbering Commodore.

Arthur was commonly described as a 'holy terror' and rampaged through the ship at will, playing practical jokes, like throwing buckets of water into occupied toilet cubicles, without fear of retribution. Yet there were moments when even the irrepressible Arthur experienced a sense of loss. Doreen Smith and Arthur were the same age and the firmest of friends. 'He'd often say to me that he wished his father had more time for him,' Doreen said. 'I suppose, at one time or another, we all wished we had more ordinary lives.'

Arthur's special responsibility on board ship was to look after his father's motor-cycles, in particular a huge Harley Davidson that had been given to Hubbard by the Toronto org. One afternoon, the Commodore told Doreen to make sure Arthur had cleaned the Harley Davidson properly by wiping a tissue over the mudguards and petrol tank and bringing it back to show him. She returned with a black smudge on the tissue. Hubbard was incensed. 'You go and assign Arthur liability,' he roared at Doreen, 'he's not doing his duty.'

Doreen was relieved that Arthur didn't seem to be too worried by his father's reaction, or by the need to tie a grey rag round his arm, but it was not the end of the matter. Mary Sue, who was fiercely protective of her children, felt it was Doreen's fault that Arthur had been assigned liability. Later that afternoon, she grabbed her by the arm and starting shaking her. 'You little fiend,' she hissed, sinking her nails into the girl's arm, 'you're destroying my family.'

The messengers were nothing if not loyal to each other. While Doreen was still sobbing, one of them ran to tell the Commodore what had happened. As Doreen got back to her post outside Hubbard's office, she saw Mary Sue going in and heard him roar, 'Close the fucking door!' Through the engraved glass, she could see Mary Sue's silhouette standing to attention in front of the desk while the Commodore ranted. Doreen could not make out everything he said, but she distinctly heard him bellow at the top of his lungs, 'Nobody manhandles my messengers, is that clear?' Mary Sue mumbled her agreement. 'Yes *what?*' he bellowed. 'Yes *sir!*' she replied smartly.

Outside, the messengers were trying hard not to put their ears to the keyhole, but they heard enough to be *thrilled*.

A few months later, Diana upset her father in some way. Hubbard reeled off a long reprimand to the messenger on duty, adding at the end of it: 'OK, go and spit in Diana's face.' The messenger was a little dark-eyed girl called Jill Goodman, thirteen years old. She ran along the deck to Diana's office, burst in, spat in her face with unerring accuracy and began shouting her message as Diana let out a scream of fury. Mary Sue, who was in an adjoining office, burst in as her daughter was wiping the spittle from her face. She grabbed Jill round the throat as if she was going to strangle her and also began screeching. Jill started crying and when Mary Sue let her go, she immediately rushed off to tell the Commodore. Another acrimonious husband and wife row followed, which ended with Mary Sue throwing her shoes at the luckless messenger Hubbard despatched to chastise her further.

The Commodore was soon embroiled in another domestic drama of a different, and totally unexpected, nature. He received word from Los Angeles that his daughter Alexis was trying to make contact with him. Now twenty-one years old, Alexis lived with her mother and stepfather, Miles Hollister, on the Hawaiian island of Maui. Although her mother rarely spoke about her father – Sara was still frightened of her first husband and looked back on her divorce as a lucky escape from his clutches – Alexis had read enough about L. Ron Hubbard to begin to think of him as a rather romantic figure and she was naturally curious to meet him. In 1970, on a visit to England, she called at Saint Hill Manor in the hope of seeing him and was disappointed to discover he was not there. A year later, while she was home from college for the summer vacation, she wrote to him care of the Church of Scientology in Los Angeles.

Hubbard acted swiftly when he heard about Alexis' inquiries. He scribbled a note to her and dispatched detailed instructions to Jane Kember who was running the Guardian's Office at Saint Hill, about how the matter was to be handled. The messengers had got into the habit of standing beside the Commodore when he was writing at this desk and whipping away each sheet of paper as he reached the bottom of the page. Doreen Smith was on duty when the Commodore was writing to Alexis and she was shocked by what she was surreptitiously reading as his hand flew over the page. He ended his instructions to Kember with a little homily, 'Decency is not a subject well understood.'

When Alexis returned to college in the United States she learned that there was a man staying in the local motel who had been asking to see her. She invited him to her dorm, where he introduced himself as

L. Ron Hubbard's agent and said he had a statement to read to her. While Alexis sat stunned, the man read out a statement in which Hubbard categorically denied he was her father:

'Your mother was with me as a secretary in Savannah in late 1948 . . . In July 1949 I was in Elizabeth, New Jersey, writing a movie. She turned up destitute and pregnant.' Hubbard implied that Alexis's father was Jack Parsons, but out of the kindness of his heart he had taken her mother in to see her through 'her trouble'. Later he said he came up from Palm Springs, California, where he was living, and found Alexis abandoned; she was just a toddler, a 'cute little thing', and so he had taken her along on his wanderings for a couple of years.

Hubbard told Alexis that her mother had been a Nazi spy during the Second World War and suggested that the divorce action was a spurious ploy on her part to win control of Scientology – 'They [Sara and Miles Hollister] obtained considerable newspaper publicity, none of it true, and employed the highest priced divorce attorney in the US to sue me for divorce and get the foundation in Los Angeles in settlement. This proved a puzzle since where there is no legal marriage, there can't be any divorce.'

When the agent had finished reading, he asked Alexis if she had any questions. She asked in a small voice if she could see the statement. He refused. Mustering what composure she could, she said that what she had heard was self-explanatory and asked him to leave. Alexis made no further attempts to see her father.[11]

At around this time, another young woman began causing problems for the Commodore. Susan Meister, a twenty-three-year-old from Colorado, had joined the crew of the *Apollo* in February 1971, having been introduced to Scientology by friends while she was working in San Francisco. When she arrived on the ship she was a typically eager and optimistic convert and wrote home frequently, urging her family to 'get into' Scientology. 'I just had an auditing session,' she wrote on 5 May. 'I feel great, great, *great* and my life is expanding, *expanding* and it's *all Scientology*. Hurry up! Hurry, hurry. Be a friend to yourselves – get into this stuff *now*. It's more precious than gold, it's the best thing that's ever ever ever ever come along. Love, Susan.'

By the time of her next letter, on 15 June, the Commodore's conspiracy theories had clearly made an impression. 'I can't tell you exactly where we are. We have enemies who . . . do not wish to see us succeed in restoring *freedom* and *self-determination* to this planet's people. If these people were to find out where we were located they would attempt to destroy us . . .'

Ten days later, when the *Apollo* was docked in the Moroccan port of

Safi, Susan Meister locked herself in a cabin, put a .22. target revolver to her forehead and pulled the trigger. She was found at 7.35 pm lying across a bunk, wearing the dress her mother had sent her for her birthday, with her arms crossed and the revolver on her chest. A suicide note was on the floor.

Local police were called, but the death of an American citizen inevitably alerted US consular officials and exposed the *Apollo* to the kind of attention that Hubbard had been trying to avoid for years. Following the Commodore's oft-repeated doctrine, the Sea Org went on to the attack. Susan Meister, who had seemed a rather quiet and reserved young woman to her friends, was portrayed as an unstable former drug addict who had made previous attempts at suicide; Peter Warren, the *Apollo*'s port Captain, hinted that compromising photographs of her had been found.

These smear tactics were soon extended to embrace William Galbraith, the US vice-consul in Casablanca, who had driven to Safi to make inquiries into the incident. On 13 July, he had lunch with Warren and Joni Chiriasi, another member of the crew, at the Sidi Bouzid restaurant in Safi before being taken to look round the ship. Afterwards, Warren and Chiriasi both signed affidavits accusing Galbraith of threatening the ship – 'He said that if the ship became an embarrassment to the United States, Nixon would order the CIA to sink or sabotage it.' Galbraith also allegedly referred to the Church of Scientology as a 'bunch of kooks' and speculated that the ship was being used as a brothel or a casino or for drug-trafficking.

Next day, Norman Starkey, captain of the *Apollo*, forwarded copies of the affidavits to the Senate Foreign Relations Committee in Washington, with a covering letter complaining that Galbraith had threatened 'to murder the vessel's company of 380 men, women and children, many of whom are Americans'. Letters were also sent to John Mitchell, the Attorney General, and to the Secret Service, all with copies to President Nixon, who was yet to be engulfed by Watergate.

A few days later, Susan Meister's father arrived in Casablanca to investigate his daughter's death but found it impossible to make headway with the disinterested Moroccan authorities, who were somewhat more concerned with a recent attempted coup d'état than a lone American making inquiries about his daughter. Meister, who refused to believe that Susan had committed suicide, could not even discover where her body was being kept and in desperation he turned to L. Ron Hubbard for help.

He later wrote a dispiriting account of his visit to the ship, escorted by Peter Warren: 'Passing the guarded gates into the port compound, we had our first look at Hubbard's ship *Apollo*. It appeared to be old and as we boarded it, the girls manning the deck gave us a hand salute. All were dressed in work-type clothing of civilian origin. Most appeared to be young. Upon boarding, we were shown the stern of the ship, which was used as a reading-room, with several people sitting in chairs reading books. The mention of Susan seemed to meet with disapproval from those on board . . . we were shown where Susan's quarters were in the stern of the ship below decks where it appeared fifty or so people were sleeping on shelf-type bunks. Susan's letter had mentioned she shared a cabin all the way forward with one other person. Next we were shown the cabin next to the pilot house on the bridge where the alleged suicide had taken place . . . We were not allowed to see any more of the ship. I requested an interview with Hubbard as he was then on board. Warren said he would ask. He returned in about half an hour and said Hubbard had declined to see me.'

After his return to America, Meister discovered to his anger and astonishment that his daughter had been buried even before he arrived in Morocco. He arranged to have the body exhumed and returned to the United States, but before the remains of Susan Meister were put to rest, a final dirty trick was played: Meister's local health authority in Colorado received an anonymous letter warning of a cholera epidemic in Morocco that had so far caused two or three hundred deaths. 'It's been brought to my attention,' wrote the poison pen, 'that the daughter of one George Meister died in Morocco, either by accident or cholera, probably the latter.'[12]

At the beginning of 1972, Hubbard fell ill, suddenly and inexplicably, with a sickness that defied diagnosis and presented a bewildering range of symptoms. Towards the end of January, the Commodore sent a pathetic note to Jim Dincalci, the ship's medical officer: 'Jim, I don't think I'm going to make it.'

Dincalci, who had been appointed medical officer on the strength of six months' experience as a nurse before joining Scientology, was unsure what to do. He had been deeply shocked when he first arrived on the ship in 1970 to realize that Hubbard became ill just like ordinary mortals, since he clearly remembered reading in the first Dianetics book that it was possible to cure most ailments with the power of the mind. In his first week as medical officer, Hubbard began complaining of feeling unwell and Dincalci was very surprised when a doctor was called. He prescribed a course of pain-killers and antibiotics, but Dincalci naturally did not bother to collect the pills because he was convinced that Ron would not need them.

'I thought', he said, 'that as an operating thetan he would have total control of his body and of any pain. When he discovered I hadn't got him the pain-killers, he flew off the handle and started screaming at me.'[13]

Fearful of making another mistake, Dincalci sought advice about the Commodore's illness from Otto Roos, who was one of the senior 'technical' Scientologists on board. Roos ventured the view that the problem stemmed from some incident in his past which had not been properly audited. The only way to find it would be to comb through all the folders in which Ron's auditing sessions were recorded.

Hubbard gave his approval to this course of action, adding a note to Otto Roos: 'I'm delighted that somebody is finally going to take responsibility for my auditing.' Roos began calling in the folders from Saint Hill and from all the Scientology branches in the United States where Hubbard had been audited. There were hundreds of them, dating back to 1948; Roos calculated they would make a stack eight feet high. He began working through the folders, discovering, to his disquiet, numerous 'discreditable reads' – moments when the E-meter revealed that Hubbard had something to hide.

Towards the end of March, while Roos was still poring over the folders, a messenger arrived at his cabin saying that the Commodore wanted to see all the folders. Roos was dumbfounded: it was an inviolable rule of Scientology that no one, no matter who he was, was allowed to see his own folder. He told the messenger it was out of the question. A few minutes later, the door burst open and two hefty members of the crew barged in, picked up the filing cabinets and staggered out with them.

Two days passed before a messenger told Roos he was wanted by the Commodore. From the moment the Dutchman entered Hubbard's office, it was apparent the Commodore had made a dramatic recovery. Hubbard leapt up from his desk with a roar and struck out at Roos with his fist, following up with a furious kick. He was shouting so wildly that Roos was unable to make out what he was saying apart from that it was something to do with the 'discreditable reads'. Mary Sue was sitting in the office with a long face watching what was going on. When Hubbard had calmed down a little he turned to her and asked her, as his auditor, if he had ever had 'discreditable reads'. Mary Sue's expression did not alter. 'No sir,' she said, 'you never had such reads.'

Roos could see folders scattered across Hubbard's desk, open at the pages where he had noted the 'reads' that Mary Sue denied existed. He said nothing. Hubbard paced the room, fretting that Roos had 'undoubtedly told this all over the ship' and that everyone was talking and laughing about it. In fact, Roos had informed no one, although it did not prevent him from being put under 'cabin arrest'.

After he had been dismissed, Mary Sue kept running down to his cabin with different folders, trying to explain away the 'discreditable reads'. He had been using outdated technology, she said, and 'should have known about it'. Later Diana Hubbard also stopped by, pushed opened Roos's door, screamed, 'I hate you! I hate you!' and stalked off.[14]

The *Apollo* was docked in Tangier throughout this drama and Mary Sue was busy supervising the decoration and furnishing of a split-level modern house, the Villa Laura, on a hillside in the suburbs of Tangier. The Hubbards planned to move ashore while the ship was put into dry dock for a re-fit and Mary Sue was looking forward to it.

Hubbard was still dreaming of finding a friendly little country where Scientology would be allowed to prosper (not to say take over control) and he had begun casting covetous eyes on Morocco, at whose Atlantic ports he had been calling regularly ever since leaving the Mediterranean. The Moroccan monarchy was going through a period of crisis and Hubbard felt that King Hassan would welcome the help that Scientology could offer in identifying potential traitors within his midst and be suitably grateful thereafter.

Some months previously, the Sea Org had set up a land base in a small huddle of office buildings on the airport road outside Tangier. The erection of a sign on the road announcing, in English, French and Arabic, the arrival of 'Operation and Transport Corporation Limited, International Business Management' immediately attracted the attention of Howard D. Jones, the local American consul general. He became even more interested a few days later when, at a party in Tangier, he met a nervous American girl who admitted working for OTC but would say nothing about it. 'I am here with a Panamanian corporation,' she said, 'but that is all I can tell you.'

Nothing could have been more calculated to prompt the consul to make further inquiries. He soon made the connections between OTC, the 'mystery ship' *Apollo* and L. Ron Hubbard, the founder of Scientology, but he discovered very little more, to judge by a frustrated cable he despatched to Washington on 26 April 1972: 'Little is known of the operations of Operation and Transport Company here, and its officers are elusive about what it does. However, we presume that the Scientologists aboard the *Apollo* and in Tangier do whatever it is that Scientologists do elsewhere.

'There have been rumours in town that *Apollo* is involved in drug or white slave traffic. However, we doubt these reports . . . The stories about white slave traffic undoubtedly stem from the fact that included among the crew of the *Apollo* are a large number of strikingly beautiful young ladies. However, we are skeptical that a vessel that stands out like a sore thumb, in which considerable interest is bound to be generated, and with a crew numbering in hundreds, would be a reasonable vehicle for smuggling or white slaving.'[15]

The US consul, although he had no way of knowing it, was looking in the wrong direction. Very little was happening on the ship that would have been of interest to Washington, but a great deal was happening ashore. The Operation and Transport Corporation was relentlessly trying to make inroads into Moroccan bureaucracy, undeterred by numerous setbacks. It acquired an inauspicious foothold with a government contract to train post office administrators on the assurance that Scientology techniques would accelerate their training, but the pilot project soon foundered. 'We took half the students,' said Amos Jessup, 'while the other half were trained in the traditional way. We spent a month trying to teach them certain study techniques but they got so anxious that the others were forging ahead learning post office techniques that they walked out.'

Jessup, who spoke French, led OTC's next assault – on the Moroccan army. He and Peter Warren made friends with a colonel in Rabat and demonstrated the E-meter to him. 'He was properly amazed by it,' said Jessup, 'and arranged for us to give a presentation to a general who was said to be a friend of the Minister of Defence and the right hand man of the King. We were taken to this gigantic, luxurious house, where we did a few drills. The general said he was very interested and would get back to us. We waited in a little apartment in Rabat the Sea Org had rented to us, but didn't hear anything so went back to the ship. Shortly afterwards, the general led an unsuccessful coup and committed suicide. We realized then that he wouldn't have passed word about the E-meter to the King.'

Another OTC mission was having more success with the Moroccan secret police and started a training course for senior policemen and intelligence agents, showing them how to use the E-meter to detect political subversives. The *Apollo*, meanwhile, sailed for Lisbon for her re-fit and Mary Sue and Ron moved into the Villa Laura in Tangier. Hubbard seemed strangely depressed; Doreen Smith reported that he often talked about 'dropping his body', which was Scientology-speak for dying.

Loyal wife that she was, Mary Sue took it upon herself to deal with one of the sources of her husband's troubles – his estranged son, Nibs. After 'blowing the org' in 1959, fortune had not smiled on Nibs. He had drifted from job to job, finding it ever more difficult to support his wife and six children, and as the realization dawned that he would never be allowed back into Scientology, he became an even more prominent critic of his father and his father's 'church'. When the church was locked in litigation with the Internal Revenue Service, Nibs testified on behalf of the IRS.

In September 1972, Mary Sue orchestrated a campaign to 'handle' Nibs, instituting a search through all the Sea Org files and instructing the Guardian's office to do the same. She told an aide that Nibs' 'big button' was money and that it was time to start hunting through the old files to dig up former complaints about him.[16]

The church never revealed what it found out about the Founder's son, but on 7 November Nibs recorded a video-taped interview with a church official retracting his IRS testimony and all allegations he had previously made against father. They were made 'vengefully', he explained, at a time when he was undergoing a great deal of personal and emotional stress: 'What I have been doing is a whole lot of lying, a whole lot of damage to a lot of people that I value highly.

'I happen to love my father, blood is thicker than water, and basically it may sound silly to some people but it means a great deal to me that blood is thicker than water and another thing, as a matter of interest too, would be I made some pretty awful statements about the Sea Org and none of these are true. I've no personal knowledge of any wrong doing or illegal acts or brutality or anything else against people by the Sea Org or any member of the Scientology organization.'

At the Villa Laura in Tangier, Hubbard had little time to reflect on this filial declaration of love. Indeed, it was more likely he was reflecting on the curious inevitability with which his plans were ending in tears. The OTC training course for Moroccan secret policeman was breaking up in disarray under the stress of internecine intrigue between pro-monarchy and anti-monarchy factions and the fear of what the E-meter would reveal. 'It was a crazy set up,' said Jessup, 'you couldn't tell who was on which side.'

It was possible that the Sea Org might have stayed to try and unravel this complication, had not word arrived from Paris that the Church of Scientology in France was about to be indicted for fraud. There was a suggestion that French lawyers would be seeking Hubbard's extradition from Morocco to face charges in Paris.

The Commodore decided it was time to go. There was a ferry leaving Tangier for Lisbon in forty-eight hours: Hubbard ordered everyone to be on it, with all the OTC's movable property and every scrap of paper that could not be shredded. For the next two days, convoys of cars, trucks and motor-cycles could be observed, day and night, scurrying back and forth from OTC 'land bases' in Morocco to the port in Tangier.

When the Lisbon-bound ferry sailed from Tangier on 3 December 1972, nothing remained of the Church of Scientology in Morocco. Hubbard left behind only a pile of shredded paper, a flurry of wild rumours and a scattering of befuddled US consular officials.

Chapter 19

Atlantic Crossing

'REVIEW OF AVAILABLE INFO REGARDING OVERSEAS ACTIVITIES CHURCH OF SCIENTOLOGY REVEALS ONLY THAT ITS FOUNDER L. RON HUBBARD IS ECCENTRIC MILLIONAIRE WHO HAS BEEN EXPELLED FROM RESIDENCE IN SEVERAL COUNTRIES BECAUSE OF HIS ODD ACTIVITIES AND BEHAVIOUR. HE IS OWNER OF SEVERAL SHIPS WHOSE APPEARANCE IN PORTS IN VARIOUS PARTS OF WORLD HAVE STIMULATED QUERIES . . . FROM OTHER GOVERNMENTS ASKING INFO RE VESSELS MISSION AND CREW. RESPONSES INDICATE WE KNOW VERY LITTLE . . .' (Outgoing signal from CIA headquarters, 16 October 1975)

* * * * *

Hubbard did not join the exodus on the Lisbon-bound ferry from Tangier; he was driven from Villa Laura to the airport, where there was a direct flight leaving for Lisbon that afternoon. Sea Org personnel were waiting to meeting him in the Portuguese capital and they hurried him through the airport to a waiting car which headed downtown to the Lisbon Sheraton. The Commodore then sat fretting in his hotel suite for several hours while lawyers in Paris, Lisbon and New York assessed the risk of his extradition to face fraud charges in France. Ordinarily, he would have avoided such legal imbroglio by sailing away from it in his flagship, but the *Apollo* was in dry dock and thus provided no sanctuary.

With Hubbard in the hotel were Ken Urquhart, Jim Dincalci and Paul Preston, a former Green Beret recently appointed as the Commodore's bodyguard. Urquhart said that Hubbard was 'fairly relaxed' and gave them a little briefing on the need to maintain 'safe spaces'.[1] Dincalci disagreed: 'He was very nervous and afraid of what might happen. I could see he was shredding. After two or three hours there was a telephone call from the port Captain. When he put the phone down he said, "This is really serious. I've got to get out of here *now*".'[2]

Urquhart was sent out to book seats on the first available flight to the United States and collect some cash. It was agreed that Preston would travel with Hubbard and Dincalci would 'shadow' them so that he could inform the ship immediately if there were any problems. The loyal Urquhart returned with three Lisbon-Chicago tickets on a flight leaving early next morning. Although he had booked them through to Chicago, the flight stopped in New York and he suggested they got off there in case there was a 'welcoming party' waiting at Chicago's O'Hare airport. He also had a briefcase stuffed with banknotes in different currencies – escudos, marks, francs, pounds, dollars and Moroccan dirhams, about $100,000 in total; it was the best he could do, he told Ron.

The flight left next morning after only a short delay, with Dincalci sitting several rows away from Hubbard and Preston. At J.F. Kennedy airport in New York, Dincalci stood behind them in the Customs queue and looked on in horror as a Customs officer told Hubbard to open his briefcase. Having looked inside he promptly invited Hubbard to step into an interview room.

'As they took him away I thought, oh God, that's it, now everyone will know L. Ron Hubbard is back in America,' said Dincalci. 'He came out about fifteen minutes later looking like a zombie. He'd had to give them a lot of information about the money. We got into a taxi outside and I said, "Where are we going?" He said, "I can't think." He was literally in shock. We drove into Manhattan and he pointed to a hotel, it was a Howard Johnson's or something like that, and said, "We'll stay there."'

The three of them checked in using false names: Hubbard was Lawrence Harris, Preston was Don Shannon and Dincalci was Frank Morris. Dincalci then went across the street to a deli and bought lunch. Back in the hotel, he asked the Commodore if he should return to the ship, but Hubbard did not seem to understand the question. Next day, he sent Dincalci out to buy clothes for all of them and to look for a place to live; the question of Dincalci returning to the ship was never mentioned again.

Dincalci soon found a suitable apartment in Queens, in a fifteen-storey building with its own heated swimming-pool called 'The Executive'. It was in a safe, upper middle-class residential area close to Forest Hills and convenient to the subway. For the first few weeks, Hubbard did nothing but watch television all day long, switching from channel to channel, absorbed by everything from soap operas to rock music shows.

The America to which Hubbard had returned after an absence of nearly a decade had changed beyond his recognition, particularly when viewed through a colour television screen. It was a country obsessed with the unfolding revelations of Watergate, haunted by a war incomprehensibly lost in Vietnam and beset by crises, not least in confidence. The Commodore of the Sea Org knew little of the black crisis, the urban crisis, the drugs crisis, the energy crisis or any of the events that were branded into the American conscience by place names such as Kent State, Attica and Chappaquiddick.

While Preston stayed in the apartment to look after Hubbard, Dincalci went out every day to the United Nations building to research international extradition laws. A few days before Christmas 1972, he returned to the apartment and told Ron he was in the clear; he had established beyond doubt that the United States would not extradite its own citizens. Hubbard began making plans to travel, to visit the org in Los Angeles. He even thought about throwing a party, but within a couple of days a message arrived from the Guardian's Office in California telling him he was still not safe and to stay undercover. It was a cheerless Christmas.

The Guardian's Office was the conduit for communications with the Commodore and the strictest security prevailed to prevent his whereabouts being discovered. Preston picked up and delivered the mail every other day at a post office box in New Jersey. Everything was in code and no personal mail of any kind was forwarded. Telephone calls were similarly coded, using the page numbers of the *American Heritage Dictionary*—345/16 was the sixteenth word from the top on page 345. Preston would go to a payphone well away from the apartment, call the Guardian's Office in Los Angeles and reel off the numbers. If there was an incoming message he used a small tape machine to record it and transcribed it when he got back to the apartment.

When they were out and about in New York, both Dincalci and Preston went to inordinate lengths to ensure they were not being tailed, frequently back-tracking and crossing from an uptown to a downtown train. Travelling on the subway, they would choose a stop at random, hold open the doors as they were beginning to close and leap out at the last moment.

Inside the apartment, a routine was soon established. Dincalci got up early and went out to do the day's food shopping and buy the paperback books that the Commodore read voraciously. 'I soon got to know what he liked,' said Dincalci. 'It was all blood and thunder escapist stuff. I'd choose them by the cover – the more lurid the cover, the more he liked them.' Hubbard woke at about ten or eleven o'clock; the television was turned on immediately and stayed on for the remainder of the day, even if he was reading or writing.

While Dincalci was out running errands for the Commodore, Preston stayed in the apartment to prepare breakfast and lunch. Dincalci cooked dinner when he got back in the evening. For the first two months it was always fishsticks, breaded chicken, steaks or hamburgers, until Hubbard tired of the diet and encouraged Dincalci to try other dishes.

After dinner Hubbard had a single tot of brandy and sometimes talked into the night. 'He'd jump around from subject to subject,' said Dincalci. 'One minute he'd be talking about how an angel had given him this sector of the universe to look after and next minute he'd be talking about the camera he wanted me to buy for him next day. I used to watch him talking; sometimes his eyes would roll up into his head for a couple of minutes and he'd be kinda gone. One of the things that upset him was that he'd never gotten back the money that he had stashed away in previous lives. There was some inside the statue of a horse in Italy which he had hidden in the sixteenth century. He was a writer and had written *The Prince*. "That son-of-a-bitch Machiavelli stole it from me," he said. He talked a lot about his childhood and all the horses he had ridden when he was little, how he would get on them before he could walk. I didn't get the impression that it was a happy childhood, not at all. There was a lot of bitterness there about his parents. He said, over and over, he had graduated from George Washington University. "They say I didn't," he used to complain, "but I did." He said that he was editor of the University paper for four years and that would prove it.

'He said that when Pearl Harbor was bombed he was on some island in the Pacific and he was the senior person in charge because everyone else had been killed. He was controlling all the traffic through the island until a bomb exploded right by him at the airport and he was sent home, the first US casualty of World War Two. He had a big fatty tumour, a lymphoma, on the top of his head which he said had slivers of shrapnel in it. We had it X-rayed once and had the film enlarged fifty times to find the shrapnel, but there was nothing there. When he came back from the war his first wife didn't go to see him, even though he was wounded. He had nothing good to say about her. His second wife, whom he never really married, was a spy who had been sent by the Nazis to spy on him during the war.

'Most nights I'd give him a massage before he went to bed and he always said he felt better for it. In my mind I never questioned anything he said except once when he was talking about out-of-the-body experiences and how beautiful it was to sit on a cloud. I was always running about New York looking at things for him and I thought if he was such hot shit, why did I have to go and look? Why couldn't he go out of his body and take a look himself?'

In February, Hubbard began to get jittery about the security in the Executive building and Dincalci was asked to look for somewhere with a 'lower profile'. He found a large apartment in a scruffier neighbourhood of Queens – a nondescript second-floor walk-up in the middle of a block on Codwise Place – owned by a Cuban family who lived on the first floor of the house. Dincalci paid three months' rent in advance, in cash, and said his brother and his uncle would be moving in immediately.

Soon after the move, Hubbard decided to go out for a walk. Dincalci was concerned that the preparations the Commodore was making to pass unnoticed in the street would almost certainly mark him out for attention. 'His hair had grown very long, almost down to his shoulders and he looked pretty unkempt. He insisted on wearing this big hat with the brim turned up. It made him look like Bozo the clown. If he had walked into any org they would have kicked him out.' After being cosseted by central heating for three months, Hubbard stepped out into a freezing February day, immediately got a chill in his tooth and attracted a retinue of jeering street kids. It discouraged him from venturing out again by himself.

His aching teeth appeared to trigger other complaints and Dincalci was driven to distraction trying to nurse an intractable and irritable elderly patient who was at first reluctant to consult either doctor or dentist. When one of Hubbard's rotten teeth dropped out, Dincalci painstakingly ground all his food. Eventually Hubbard agreed to seek professional medical help. On visits to a chiropractor in Greenwich Village he always wore a wig as a disguise and on one occasion Dincalci and Preston took the be-wigged Commodore to a local Chinese restaurant for his favourite dish, egg foo yong. It was their only social outing.

On the recommendation of an allergist, Hubbard began a regular course of injections, administered by Dincalci, which seemed to help him. As his health improved, he started taking more interest in the affairs of the Church of Scientology, even writing bulletins with some of his old enthusiasm. 'He wrote tremendously fast by hand,' said Dincalci. 'It was like automatic writing you get in the occult. He'd have a glazed look, as if he was kinda gone, his eyes would roll up and the corners of his mouth would turn down and he'd start this frenzied writing. I've never seen anyone write so fast.'

Now sixty-two, Hubbard was also beginning to ponder his place in posterity. The Church of Scientology had been swift to make use of the recently enacted Freedom of Information Act, which had revealed that government agencies held a daunting amount of material about Scientology and its founder in their files, much of it less than flattering. Hubbard, who had never been fettered by convention or strict observance of the law, conceived a simple, but startlingly audacious, plan to improve his own image and that of his church for the benefit of future generations of Scientologists. All that needed to be done, he decided, was to infiltrate the agencies concerned, steal the revelant files and either destroy or launder any damaging information they contained. To a man who had founded both a church and a private navy this was a perfectly feasible scheme. The operation was given the code name Snow White – two words that would figure ever more prominently over the next few months in the communications between the Guardian's Office in Los Angeles and the Commodore's hiding place in Queens, New York.

In September 1973, Hubbard got word from the Guardian's Office that the threat of extradition had diminished and it was safe for him to return to the ship and, coincidentally, to his wife and children. He left next day, with Paul Preston, on a Boeing 747 bound for Lisbon, leaving Dincalci behind to pack up all their belongings and close the apartment at Codwise Place.

No one on the ship knew where Hubbard had been for the previous ten months, nor that he was returning, but his arrival back on board was predictably cause for celebration.

'When he came back on board he looked better than I had ever seen him look,' said Hana Eltringham. 'He was bright and bouncy, busting out all over. He had lost weight and could hardly contain his happiness at being back.'[3]

If there was an emotional reunion with Mary Sue and the children, it was not widely observed. Instead, Hubbard gathered the crew on A Deck to explain that he had been away touring the orgs in the United States, raising quite a laugh when he said that he had walked into some of them without being recognized. Preston, sitting at the back of the room, knew it was a lie but obviously said nothing; he had once driven Hubbard past the New York org but all the Commodore had said was that he thought it needed a bigger sign.

While Hubbard had been away, his accommodation on the *Apollo* had been extended and improved and his research room had been totally encased in lead, insulated from contact with the hull, to make it sound-proof. A working party had spent three months crawling through the ventilation shafts and scrubbing them with toothbrushes in order that he would no longer be troubled by his well-known allergy to dust. In the previous few weeks the ship had been cleaned from stem to stern and every deck subjected to a 'white glove inspection'. Any ledge or flat surface that produced a smudge on the fingers of a white cotton glove resulted in the entire area being cleaned again.

The Commodore soon had the ship on the move and there were many light hearts on board when the *Apollo* weighed anchor and set sail, after almost a year in dock in Lisbon. She headed north along the Atlantic coast of the Iberian peninsula, stopping for a few days at the historic cities of Oporto and Corunna, then turning south again to Setubal and Cadiz. At the beginning of December, she returned to Tenerife in the Canary Islands, one of her regular ports of call before the Lisbon re-fit.

Hubbard wanted to spend some time ashore in Tenerife taking photographs, and his cars and motor-cycles were unloaded on to the dock. He had at his disposal a big black Ford station wagon, a 1962 yellow Pontiac Bonneville convertible and a Land Rover, but as often as not he chose to make his forays ashore astride his monstrous Harley Davidson, on which no doubt he cut a particular dash.

One afternoon, snaking round the switchback curves up in the volcanic mountains of Tenerife, Hubbard skidded on a patch of loose gravel, lost control and fell off, smashing several cameras that were on straps round his neck. Although in considerable pain, he managed to get back on the bike and ride it down to the port. He let it drop on the quayside and staggered up the gangway of the *Apollo* with his trousers torn and the mangled cameras still around his neck. Jim Dincalci, back on board as medical officer, was summoned immediately. Only too well aware that he was not qualified to deal with broken bones or possible internal injuries, he suggested that the Commodore should be taken to a hospital for a check-up. Hubbard refused adamantly, but huffily agreed to be examined by a local doctor. He prescribed rest and pain-killers, to be taken two at a time as required.

After the doctor had left the ship, Dincalci, who still clung to the remnants of a conviction that an operating thetan had no need for anything as mundane as a pain-killer, offered the Commodore a single pill and a glass of water.

'Why only one?' Hubbard snapped, his eyes bulging with anger. Dincalci hastily produced a second pill, but Hubbard's temper gave way. He leapt up from his chair and began pacing the room in a fury, shouting unintelligible abuse at the fools in his midst who cared nothing for the fact that he was dying. Suddenly he turned on Dincalci. 'It's *you*,' he roared. '*You're* trying to kill me.'

Dincalci was shattered by the accusation. 'I felt I had rapport with him, I felt like a son to him. It was like having my father say I was trying to kill him. No, it was worse. Here was the man who was trying to save the universe saying I was trying to kill him. I was crushed. I felt I had lost everything; what little self-esteem I had was gone in that moment.'

Dincalci very quickly found himself chipping paint and the ticklish task of nursing the Commodore was handed over to Kima Douglas, a strikingly attractive artist from South Africa who had had two years' nursing experience in the labour ward of the British hospital in Bulawayo. 'I think he had broken an arm and several ribs,' she said. 'He certainly had massive black bruises everywhere. We strapped up his arm and strapped his ribs, but he couldn't lie down so he slept in a chair as best he could. He must have been in agony. He screamed and hollered and yelled. It was absolutely ungodly; six weeks of pure hell.

'He was revolting to be with – a sick, crotchety, pissed-off old man, extremely antagonistic to everything and everyone. His wife was often in tears and he'd scream at her at the top of his lungs, "Get out of here!" Nothing was right. He'd throw his food across the room with his good arm; I'd often see plates splat against the bulkhead. When things got really bad, I'd go and make him English scrambled eggs, well salted and peppered, and toast and butter and take it up to him. I even fed him once.

'He absolutely refused to see another doctor. He said they were all tools and would only make him worse. The truth was that he was terrified of doctors and that's why everyone had to be put through such hell.'[4]

She could not help but recall how he had changed in the months since she first joined the ship. 'My expectation of L. Ron Hubbard was that he would be a psychic person who could look at me and see every evil thing I had ever done in my whole life. I was still searching for something, although I didn't know what, and the thought of someone being able to look into my head both terrified and excited me. I'd been indoctrinated with all the things he could do. There were wild stories that if an atomic bomb was about to go off in Nevada, Ron could defuse it with the power of his mind. At that time everyone was talking about atomic warfare and I truly believed he had come to save the planet. As I walked up the gangway to the ship, he stepped out of his office wearing a white uniform and his Commodore's hat with two messengers close behind him. I was introduced to him and he shook my hand and was very charming. He seemed to be a jovial, happy, golden man. I felt I had arrived.'

Kima called on her unlovable patient every two days, but the burden of day-to-day care fell on the messengers. 'Before the motor-cycle accident he was a very nice, friendly person,' said Jill Goodman [who was thirteen years old when she became a messenger]. 'Afterwards, he was a complete pain in the ass. It was like having a sick, crotchety grandfather. You never knew what he was going to be like when you went in there.'[5]

'He didn't get out of that red velvet chair for three months,' said Doreen Smith. 'He'd sleep for about forty-five minutes at a time, then be awake for hours, screaming and shouting. It was impossible to get him comfortable. None of us got any sleep. I was better with a cushion, someone else was better with a footstool, someone else with cotton padding, so every time he woke up we all had to be in there, fussing around him while he was screaming at us that we were all "stupid fucking shitheads" . . . he was out of control and even the toughies were in tears at times. The red chair to us became a symbol of the worst a human being can be – all we wanted to do was chop it up in little pieces and throw it overboard.'[6]

While Hubbard was still fuming in his red velvet chair, still ascribing sinister motives to every mishap and imagined slight, he issued an edict that would introduce another Orwellian feature to life on board the *Apollo*. Convinced that his orders were not being carried out with sufficient diligence, he established a new disciplinary unit called the Rehabilitation Project Force. Anyone found to have a CI (a 'counter-intention' to his orders or wishes) was to be assigned to the RPF, along with all trouble-makers and back-sliders. 'I was shocked when I heard about it,' said Hana Eltringham. 'To me it was like setting up a penal colony within our midst.'

Since it was only necessary to incur the Commodore's disfavour to be assigned to the RPF, its numbers swelled rapidly. RPF inmates wore black boiler suits, were segregated from the rest of the crew and slept in an unventilated cargo hold on filthy mattresses that were due to be thrown out before the Commodore decided they would be suitable for his new unit. Seven hours' sleep were permitted, but there was no leisure time during the day and discipline was harsh. Meal breaks were brief and the RPF was obliged to eat whatever food was left from the crew meal.

'Things took a real downhill turn around that time,' said Gerry Armstrong, who was then the ship's port captain. 'He became much more paranoid and belligerent. He was convinced there were evil people on board with hidden evil intentions and he wanted to get them all in the RPF. The RPF was used as an incredible daily threat over everyone. If he could smell something coming from the vents, whoever was the current vents engineer would be assigned to the RPF. If the cook burned his food – RPF. If a messenger complained about someone – RPF.

'His actions definitely became more bizarre after the motor-cycle accident. You could hear him throughout the ship screaming, shouting, ranting and raving day after day. He was always claiming that the cooks were trying to poison him and he began to smell odours everywhere. His clothes had to be washed in pure water thirteen times, using thirteen different buckets of clean water to rinse a shirt so he wouldn't smell detergent on it.

'At that time no one would have dared to think that the emperor had no clothes. He controlled our thoughts to such an extent that you couldn't think of leaving without thinking there was something wrong with you.'[7]

To the relief of the entire crew, the Commodore was more or less recovered from his accident by the time of his sixty-third birthday in March 1974 and the ship resumed its aimless wandering, this time on a triangular course bettween Portugal, Madeira and the Canaries. But a subtle and bizarre change had taken place in the pecking order on board: after the Commodore and his wife, the most powerful people

on the ship were now little girls dressed in hot pants and halter tops –
the new uniform of the Commodore's faithful band of messengers.

While Hubbard had been suffering so vociferously, the messengers
had assumed many extra little tasks on his behalf. They washed and
combed his hair, helped him dress and undress, massaged his back,
mixed his special night-time vitamin drink and smeared on his fleshy
features the cream he mistakenly believed kept him looking youthful.
When he recovered, the messengers continued with these duties and
constantly competed with each other to find further little ways of
pleasing the Commodore.

The ritual of his ablutions, as devised by the messengers, set the
tone for Hubbard's increasingly baroque lifestyle. 'At first I was
surprised at all the things we had to do,' said Tanya Burden, who had
joined the ship in Madeira as a trainee messenger at the age of
fourteen. 'But then I thought this man has studied for fifty years to
help the world and has done so much for mankind, why should he
have to do anything for himself? When he woke up he would yell
"Messenger" and two of us would go into his room straight away. He
would usually be lying in his bunk in his underwear with one arm
outstretched, waiting for us to pull him up to a sitting position. While
one of us put a robe round his shoulders, the other one would give him
a cigarette, a Kool non-filter, light it and stand ready with an ashtray.
I would run into the bathroom to make sure his toothbrush, soap and
razor were all laid out in a set fashion and I prepared his bath, checked
the shampoo, towel and the temperature of the water.

'When he went into the bathroom we would lay out his clothes,
powder his socks and shoes and fold everything ready to get him
dressed. Everything had to be right because if it wasn't he would yell
at us and we didn't want to upset him. The last thing we wanted to do
was upset him. When he came out of the shower, he would be in his
underwear. Two of us held his pants off the floor as he stepped into
them. He didn't like his trouser legs to touch the floor, God forbid
that should happen. We pulled up his pants and buckled his belt,
although he zipped them. We put on his shirt, buttoned it up, put his
Kools in his shirt pocket, tied his cravat and combed his hair. All this
time he'd be standing there watching us run around him. Then we'd
follow him out on to the deck carrying anything he might need – cloak,
hat, binoculars, ashtray, spare cigarettes, anything he could possibly
think of wanting. We felt it was an honor and a privilege to do
anything for him.'[8]

The messengers were all potential high school cheerleaders in
appearance – pretty blondes with even white teeth and red lips, pert
little breasts straining against knotted halter tops, bare midriffs, tight
hot pants, long tanned legs, bobbysox and platformed-soled sandals.

They had devised the uniform themselves, with the Commodore's approval, and it gave them maximum opportunity to flaunt their pubescent assets to advantage.

While male members of the crew competed avidly to deflower the messengers, Hubbard himself never once exhibited any sexual interest in them. 'He never tried anything with me,' said Tanya, 'and as far as I know he never did with any of the other girls. He didn't sleep with Mary Sue; we thought perhaps he was impotent. I think he got his thrills by just having us around.'

'I once asked him why he chose young girls as messengers,' said Doreen Smith. 'He said it was an idea he had picked up from Nazi Germany. He said Hitler was a madman, but nevertheless a genius in his own right and the Nazi Youth was one of the smartest ideas he ever had. With young people you had a blank slate and you could write anything you wanted on it and it would be your writing. That was his idea, to take young people and mould them into little Hubbards. He said he had girls because women were more loyal than men.'

The more the messengers did for the Commodore, the more he came to think of them as the only members of the crew he could trust. At nights, when they were undressing him and going through the elaborate business of getting him ready for bed, he liked to talk to them, sharing confidences and telling them about his adventures. They would sit on the carpet at the end of his bed listening to his stories, wide-eyed, for hours. The special status they enjoyed did nothing for their characters. 'We became', Jill Goodman admitted, 'poisonous little wenches. We had power and we were untouchable.' It was not in the least unusual for a fourteen-year-old messenger to march up to a senior executive on the ship and scream: 'You fucking asshole, you're going to the RPF. That'll teach you to fuck up.' It was unthinkable to answer back; it would have been like answering back to Hubbard. 'A sort of *Lord of the Flies* syndrome" began working with the messengers,' said Rebecca Goldstein, who had been recruited into Scientology by her brother, Amos Jessup. 'They were so drunk with their own power that they became extremely vengeful, nasty and dishonest. They were a very exclusive, dangerous little group.'

In May 1974, Hubbard did a very curious thing which perhaps indicated that he was losing his facility to distinguish, even in his own mind, between fact and fiction: he applied to the US Navy for the war medals he had always claimed he had been awarded but knew he had never won.

On 28 May, the ship's liaison office in New York wrote to the Navy Department enclosing an authorization from Hubbard to obtain his medals and asking for them to be forwarded as soon as possible. The letter provided some helpful background data on Mr Hubbard, quoted from one of his spurious 'official' biographies: 'He served in the South Pacific and in 1942 was relieved by fifteen officers of rank and was rushed home to take part in the 1942 battle against German submarines as Commanding Officer of a Corvette serving in the North Atlantic. In 1943 he was made Commodore of corvette squadrons and in 1944 he worked with amphibious forces.' There followed a list of seventeen medals awarded to Mr Hubbard, including the Purple Heart and the Navy Commendation Medal, many of them with bronze stars.

On 18 June, the Navy Department replied, enclosing the four routine medals awarded to former Lieutenant Lafayette R. Hubbard, US Naval Reserve, and noting, 'The records in this Bureau fail to establish Mr Hubbard's entitlement to the other medals and awards listed in your request.'[9]

The Commodore apparently had no difficulty circumventing this little problem: he quickly put into circulation an eight-by-ten colour photograph of twenty-one medals and palms he had won during the war. Some were missing, he explained to the crew. He had actually won twenty-eight medals, but the remainder were awarded to him in secret because naval command were embarrassed that he had sunk a couple of subs in their own 'back yard'.

In the summer, the Commodore turned his attention from his own image to that of his ship. He was taken with an idea to improve the *Apollo*'s public relations by staging free concerts and dance performances for the local residents at her regular ports of call. After hours of watching television in Queens, he considered himself an expert on popular music and modern dance and believed he had made important 'discoveries' about the nature of rock music and the need for a strong heavy beat. He often demonstrated his theories to a mystified Jim Dincalci. On the ship, he was able to put his ideas into practice with his own band, the 'Apollo Stars', made up of volunteers from the crew chosen at auditions conducted by the Commodore with all the confidence and aplomb of a man who had spent a lifetime in show business.

Ken Urquhart, who probably knew more about music than anyone on board, resolutely refused to become involved. 'My favourite composer was Mozart, not the horrible, raucous noise they were making. They practiced on the deck most afternoons, playing music made up by LRH with a very primitive, animal beat. There was no way I was going to go near them.' Mike Goldstein, who had played drums in a semi-professional group while he was at university, volunteered to play with the Apollo Stars in order to get out of the RPF. 'LRH had said anyone in the RPF who was accepted for the band or the dance troupe would be let out. I volunteered because I thought anything was better than running around in a black boiler suit. I was wrong. The band was terrible, awful; it was the most embarrassing thing I have ever done.'

Hubbard's idea was that the Apollo Stars would be playing on the aft well deck each time the ship entered a harbour and that bookings for both the band and dance troupe would be arranged in advance at every port of call. Since he would be making appearances himself, he had a new uniform designed with a suitably theatrical flair. It featured a powder blue kepi with a lavishly gold-braided peak and a cloak in the same hue, lined with scarlet silk. He looked, Urquhart reported, 'most peculiar'.

Quentin Hubbard, now twenty, began rehearsing with the dance troupe and enjoyed it so much he made the mistake of telling his father he would like to be a dancer. 'Oh no you wouldn't,' Hubbard replied. 'I have other plans for you.' There was no further discussion and Quentin was no longer allowed to perform. Not long afterwards, he made a feeble attempt at suicide while the ship was docked at Funchal in Madeira.

'He'd gone missing ashore for a while,' said his friend Doreen Smith, 'and while people were out looking for him he just walked back on board. I went to see him in his cabin to make sure he was OK and found him lying on his bunk. He smiled at me and I said, "Hi, how are you feeling?" He said, "Not so good, my stomach's real upset." Then he said, "Doreen, I've done the most awful thing. I've taken a whole lot of pills." I said, "Oh shit. Get out of the bunk and don't go to sleep." I began walking him around the cabin and said, "You know I'm going to have to tell your Dad, don't you?" He nodded and said, "I know. He'll know what to do."'

Doreen ran to the Commodore's cabin and said 'Quentin's taken some pills.' Hubbard did not need it spelled out. He told Doreen to fetch some mustard from the galley and mixed it into a drink which he made Quentin gulp down. The boy vomited repeatedly and was taken to the sick bay to recover. His father sent down a message that as soon Quentin was well enough to leave the sick bay, he was to be assigned to the RPF. Mary Sue, who had a reputation for protecting her children against the excesses of the ship's regime, was powerless to intervene. She was supposed to be responsible for welfare on board – indeed, she had won a special dispensation from the Commodore to allow married couples in the RPF to spend one night together a week – but knew her husband was in a towering rage over Quentin and there was nothing she could do.

Rebecca Goldstein was among the inmates of the RPF when Quentin arrived. 'It was real tough for him,' she said. 'He was very delicate and refined, not at all self-important, very unlike his father. He had hardly any facial or body hair and it was very hard to say whether he had started shaving. There were rumours that he'd attempted suicide before. He cringed from his father, he was completely overwhelmed by him.'

The valiant attempts of the Apollo Stars and its associated dance troupe to win the hearts and minds of the Spanish and the Portuguese people did not meet with overwhelming success, although the political climate did not help. There had been a military coup in Portugal earlier in the year and the subsequent unease tended to make the Portuguese nervous of mysterious foreign ships calling at its ports for no apparent reason. The *Apollo* had also managed to upset the Spaniards by mistakenly attempting to enter a major naval base at El Firol.

The ship's real problem, however, was that its 'shore story' was wearing thin. Portuguese and Spanish port authorities were still being told that the *Apollo* was owned by a highly successful business consultancy firm, but all they could see was an old, rust-streaked ship, often festooned with ragged laundry and crewed by young people in tattered, ill-assorted uniforms. It was little wonder that suspicions mounted about its activities and rumours took hold that the ship was operated by the CIA.

Jim Dincalci, who had been put ashore to run a port office in Funchal, Madeira, became alarmed by the rumours. 'It seemed to be common knowledge in Madeira that the ship was not what it was supposed to be and most people seemed to think it was a CIA spy ship. I had made friends on the island and had contacts in local Communist cells. The word was that the Communists were out to get the ship next time she arrived in Madeira. I sent telexes to LRH warning him what was happening and advising him not come to Madeira until things had calmed down. I was absolutely shocked to see the ship come into the harbor.'

The *Apollo* arrived in Funchal on 7 October and moored in her usual berth. Emissaries were sent ashore to advertize a 'rock festival' to be held at the weekend, featuring the Apollo Stars. Late on the afternoon of Wednesday, 9 October, while Mary Sue and several members of the crew were ashore, a small crowd of young men began to gather on the quayside. By the way they were glowering and gesticulating at the ship, it was obvious to those on board that this was not a social call. Soon the crowd, which was growing all the time, began chanting 'C-I-A, C-I-A, C-I-A.'

Nervous Scientologists lining the rails of the ship tried chanting 'CIA' back at the crowd, but it did nothing to lower the tension. Then the first stone clanged against the *Apollo*'s hull and a bottle smashed on the fore deck. More stones and bottles followed as the crowd's anger spread. The crew scattered to take shelter and began picking up the stones from the deck and throwing them back into the crowd. In a matter of moments it became a pitched battle.

Hubbard, who was watching what was going on from the bridge, got out a bullhorn and boomed 'Communista, Communista' at the crowd. Then he began taking photographs of the stone-throwers with a flash unit, further inflaming their tempers. Several of the crew were hit by flying stones, including Kima Douglas, whose jaw was broken by a large lump of rock that hit her full in the face. On the quayside, one of the crowd opened his trousers, waggled his penis and took a direct hit with a well-aimed stone from the ship.

With stones and sticks and bottles flying in all directions, there was total confusion on board the *Apollo*. Some crew members would later describe the Commodore as being perfectly cool through the whole incident, others said he appeared to be terrified. Whatever his state, no one was taking charge and everyone was screaming orders. In one part of the ship someone was trying to get together a party to repel boarders; in another, the sea hoses were being run out and trained on the crowd in an attempt to persuade them to disperse.

Any remaining vestige of control among the rabble-rousers vanished when the ship turned its hoses on them. On the quayside there were several motor-cycles belonging to members of the crew and two of the ship's cars – a Mini and a Fiat. All the motor-cycles were hurled into the harbour, then both cars were pushed over the edge of the quay, hitting the water with an enomous splash and quickly disappearing under the surface. Meanwhile, others in the crowd slipped the *Apollo*'s mooring-lines from the bollards and she began to drift away from the quayside.

At this point, the Portuguese authorities belatedly appeared on the scene to restore order. Armed militia were put on board to provide protection, a pilot assisted with anchoring the ship in the harbour and a launch rescued those members of the crew who had been stranded ashore, including Mary Sue. The police demanded the film that Hubbard had been taking during the riot and the Commodore, mighty pleased with himself, dutifully handed over two rolls of unexposed film from cameras he had not been using. It was nightfall before the decks had been cleared of the broken glass and rubble.

Since it rather appeared as if the people of Madeira were no longer interested in a rock concert featuring the Apollo Stars, the ship sailed next day, leaving information with the harbour authorities in Funchal that she was heading for the Cape Verde Islands, 1500 miles to the south. She departed on a purposeful southerly course until she was

out of sight. She then turned west, equally purposefully, prompting
the crew to speculate with mounting excitement that the Commodore
had decided to return to the United States.

For the next six days, in glorious weather, the *Apollo* sailed due west
across a glassy ocean, followed by sporting dolphins and whales. On
16 October, she put into St George, on the northern tip of Bermuda,
to re-fuel and Hubbard announced to the crew that their next port of
call would be Charleston, South Carolina. There was an enormous
cheer at this news: many of the crew were US citizens and some of
them had not been home for years.

Eight miles off Charleston, a coded radio message from the
Guardian's Office warned the Commodore that the FBI were waiting
on the dock to meet the ship. Hubbard's instinct was to go ashore and
brazen it out; Mary Sue was terrified at the prospect and convinced
that her husband would be immediately arrested. A furious argument
followed. 'Everyone could hear them screaming at each other for
about two hours,' said Hana Eltringham. 'She was adamant that we
should not go ashore. She said he would be indicted ten or fifteen
times and it would be the end of him and she wasn't going have it.'

For once, Mary Sue won. Hubbard called his senior aides together
on the promenade deck and said there was to be a change of plans. He
was going send a signal to Charleston to say that the ship was heading
north to pick up spare parts in Halifax, Nova Scotia. Then they were
going to sail south, to the Caribbean.

The *Apollo* docked at Freeport in the Bahamas two days later, while
FBI agents waited patiently in Halifax, Nova Scotia. It did not take
them long to find out what had happened, however, and the ship was
doggedly tracked as she meandered from island to island around the
Caribbean for the next twelve months. If no one in Washington could
make out what L. Ron Hubbard was up to, it was hardly surprising,
because L. Ron Hubbard did not know himself.

It seemed the Commodore was simply enjoying a Caribbean respite
while he decided on his next move. He had a set of tropical uniforms
made for himself in white silk and the messengers were also kitted out
in tight white uniforms, with mirrored sunglasses – an innovation
suggested by the Commodore which gave them an appropriately
sinister appearance. At most ports of call, the Apollo Stars trundled
ashore to perform for apathetic audiences with nothing better to do
than sit in the sun at a free concert and wonder where the musicians
had come from. The Commodore took up photography again and
attempted to ingratiate himself with local politicians by offering to
take their portraits. He photographed the Prime Minister and members of the opposition in Curaçao and spent some time at a convent
taking pictures of nuns. He was very pleased with the result and sent a

framed enlargement, and a cheque for $1000, to the convent to thank the nuns for their co-operation.

He could well afford it, as Kima Douglas knew better than anyone. 'While we were in the Bahamas, a story came out that the Swiss were going to change the tax laws in some way that would affect the money we held there. The old man went crazy. I heard him screaming and yelling and ran upstairs to find what was wrong. He was pacing up and down and shouting at the top of his voice, "Do you know what they're doing? Everything's gone. Gone! Gone! We're going to lose everything."' When he had calmed down a little, Kima suggested that perhaps the money should be moved. Three hours later, she was on a plane to Zurich, with two other Scientologists, carrying handwritten instructions from Hubbard authorizing the transfer of all his assets to a bank in Liechtenstein.

When they arrived, they were taken down into the vault of the bank and shown the money. Kima Douglas, who thought she could no longer be surprised by anything in Scientology, was awestruck. 'Everyone's eyes widened. There was a stack, about four feet high and three feet wide, of dollars, marks and Swiss francs in high-denomination notes. I couldn't begin to guess how much was there, but it was certainly more than the three of us could carry.'

It took nearly two weeks to make arrangements to move the cash to a bank in Liechtenstein and then the serial numbers – the first and last note of each bundle – had to be noted. When the mission returned to the Bahamas, Kima had to describe to the Commodore the exact size of the various piles of money. 'He was very pleased,' she said. 'He thought he'd outdone the Swiss.'

Hubbard's mood, as always, remained mercurial and very much subject to his notorious phobias. He discovered that the unfortunate Hana Eltringham possessed a particularly acute sense of smell and employed her as a 'sniffer dog' to root out the source of the smells that plagued him. 'Whenever he complained of bad smells,' she said, 'I would be called out of my office by a messenger to go to his quarters and crawl around on my hands and knees to try and locate where the smell was coming from. I would trace it to one corner, then we would rip off the wall cladding and very often find something like mildew.'

It was in the interests of every member of the crew to bend over backwards to keep the Commodore sweet, none more so than Kathy Cariotaki, head of the ship's 'household unit', a position which, because of its proximity to the Commodore, almost guaranteed an extended assignment in the RPF. But Kathy had won considerable praise for extracting an apology of sorts from the Greek government after the Corfu débâcle and she used her innate diplomatic skills to good advantage while running the 'household unit'.

'If a cycle started up when he began claiming things tasted funny, you had to be ready to handle it. If a dish didn't taste right, he'd start hollering and yelling that we were starving him and everyone would be under the gun. My solution was to have two back-up meals prepared at dinner every night so that there was always something else to put in front of him quickly.

'Mary Sue was a diet addict, she was always trying this diet or that diet. One day she sent orders down to the galley about what she wanted to eat that evening according to her latest diet. When the meal was served I'd usually listen to see if there was going to be an upset, but this night everything seemed fine so I went into my office. Then a messenger came round and said the Commodore wanted to see me on A Deck lounge. By the time I got there he was hollering at the top of his lungs. I couldn't understand what in the world he was saying until he brought it down several decibels and shouted that the cooks were starving Mary Sue. He'd given her his dinner and I saw that she was shovelling it down like it was the end of the world. She gave me a look which said, "Don't open your mouth."

'Their relationship was very strange. I got them to celebrate their wedding anniversary, organized a special dinner with candles and made sure she had a present for him and he had one for her. Mary Sue was close to the children, but he wasn't – he hardly ever saw them. Diana was married by then and ate with her husband, while the younger children ate with the crew. I initiated Sunday dinners for the whole family and took every opportunity to get them together at birthdays and anniversaries, otherwise they hardly ever saw each other.'[10]

When the Commodore went ashore on photo-shoots, Kathy Cariotaki acted as his driver and always checked the route the day before. In Kingston, Jamaica, Hubbard decided he wanted to take some pictures in the slum areas. At his insistence, Kathy had hired an old Pontiac convertible which was bright red and inevitably attracted attention, much of it overtly hostile. Hubbard, sitting on the back of the car, seemed oblivious to the atmosphere and continued shooting pictures while a group of black youths jeered and cat-called at the 'whiteys'. At one point a boy on a bicycle rode up behind the car and made a loud whooping noise; Hubbard turned round and whooped back so fiercely that the boy fell off his bicycle. Kathy sensed that the Commodore did not appreciate the danger, but back on the ship he banged on Mary Sue's door and said, 'Guess what, honey? I almost caused a riot this afternoon.'

In St Vincent, in the spring of 1975, the ship was prepared to receive a surprise visitor from Bremerton, Washington – the Commodore's father. Harry Ross Hubbard was eighty-eight years old and very frail, but determined to make peace with his estranged son. The old gentlemen arrived on the quayside in a taxi and the Commodore went down the gangway to meet him – the first time anyone had ever seen him leave the ship to welcome a visitor.

The crew had been ordered to conceal all evidence of Scientology from the Commodore's father, but he was too old and confused to care about such things. He sat talking with his son for hours and wandered amiably about the ship evincing very little curiosity about what was going on. With a plentiful supply of beer and a couple of fishing trips, he was content. When he got back home to Bremerton, he told Marnie, his sister-in-law, that he had had 'a wonderful trip'.[11] He died a few months later.

The *Apollo* had not been in the Caribbean for long before she again began to arouse suspicions at her various ports of call. She cruised from the Bahamas to the West Indies to the Leeward and Windward Islands, the Netherlands Antilles and back again and rumours of illicit or clandestine activity followed her as tenaciously as the seagulls. In Trinidad, a weekly tabloid newspaper speculated that the ship was connected to the CIA and suggested that the crew was somehow linked with the horrific Sharon Tate murders in Los Angeles. As the American Embassy drily cabled to Washington: 'The controversial yacht *Apollo* seems to have worn out its welcome in Trinidad.'[12]

To those on board ship, it was obvious that a conspiracy was at work. The Captain, Bill Robertson, explained that Secretary of State Henry Kissinger, who was 'one of the top SMERSH guys', had been bringing pressure to bear and threatening to cut foreign aid to any island that welcomed the *Apollo*.[13] It made perfect sense to a Scientologist.

Courses were still being held on the ship for senior Scientologists and in June 1975, one of the new students was Pam Kemp, Hubbard's old friend from Saint Hill days. She was shocked to see how much he had aged. 'I saw this figure coming on board in a big hat and red-lined Navy Cloak and I thought if I'm not mistaken that's LRH, although he was very slow and old looking. I went up to him and said, "Hi, Ron." He looked through me like he didn't know who I was. I thought maybe he was a little deaf so I went around another way and as he was coming towards me I said, "Hi, Ron. How are you?" He didn't recognize me, didn't know who I was. I thought, how weird. Later I discovered he probably didn't see me properly because he needed glasses, but would never wear them.'[14]

Not long afterwards, Hubbard suffered a minor stroke while the ship was in harbour in Curaçao. He was rushed to the local hospital, kept in intensive care for two days and then transferred to a private room, where he stayed for three weeks, with messengers on duty day and night outside his door. 'To keep him in the hospital,' said Kima Douglas, 'we had to bring food from the ship. He wouldn't touch the hospital food, so we ferried every meal out in hot and cold boxes, ten miles each way.' When he had recovered sufficiently to leave hospital, he moved into a cabana bungalow in the grounds of the Curaçao Hilton to convalesce.

While he was there, he despatched an aide, Mark Schecter, to the United States on a top secret mission. Schecter carried a suitcase full of money. His orders were to hand it over to another Scientologist, Frankie Freedman, who had found a motel for rent in Daytona Beach, Florida.

Although only a handful of people were aware of it, the Sea Org's seafaring days were over.

Chapter 20

Running Aground

'I don't think I will ever regret making my discoveries public. My sole purpose was to serve and give man the knowledge I had . . . I've never looked to quarrel with anybody.' (First statement to the press by L. Ron Hubbard for five years, read by Diana Hubbard at a reception in Quebec, to launch a new edition of *Dianetics* 28 April 1976.)

* * * * *

Frankie Freedman, a former pit boss in a Las Vegas casino and a Scientologist of ten years' standing, knew the Sea Org was going ashore because he had been scouring South Carolina, Georgia and Florida for a property with a security perimeter which could be used as a staging-post until a permanent land base was established. His 'shore story' was that he was a representative of a phoney corporation—Southern Land Sales and Development—which was looking to lease properties for church-organized retreats. 'LRH knew that if we went into town and said we were Scientologists,' said Freedman, 'we'd be out on our asses.'[1]

Early in August 1975, Freedman found a run-down motel, the Neptune, on the shore at Daytona Beach in Florida. He contacted the owner, presented his Southern Land Development business card, and offered to rent the entire motel for three months. They agreed on a figure of $50,000. Two days later, Mark Schecter arrived with the money in a suitcase.

In his cabana at the Hilton in Curaçao, Hubbard summoned the faithful Dincalci, who was once more restored to favour, and told him: 'We're going to leave the ship. Get some money, go to Daytona Beach and find me a place close to the Neptune motel. They have those condomiums all over the place – pick up one of them.' Dincalci remembered being rather touched by Hubbard's mis-pronunciation of condominium which seemed to emphasize how long the Commodore had been absent from his own country.[2]

On board the *Apollo*, it was by this time common knowledge that the Commodore was planning to return to the United States. Sea Org officers were already making plans to get the crew ashore in small groups through the international airports at Miami, Washington DC and New York so as not to alert federal agencies to what was happening. Non US-citizens were provided with return tickets and told to enter the United States as tourists. The ship was to be left at Freeport in the Bahamas with a skeleton crew until she could be sold.

Hubbard, meanwhile, slipped out of Curaçao on a direct flight to Orlando, Florida, accompanied by Mary Sue and Kima Douglas. They were driven to Daytona Beach, where Jim Dincalci had rented adjoining suites in a modern seafront hotel a couple of hundred yards down the road from the Neptune motel. Within a few days, the first Sea Org personnel began moving into the Neptune. None of them was supposed to know the Commodore was living just down the road.

'We all used to pretend not to know where he was,' said David Mayo, 'although it was pretty obvious. We could see his hotel from the balcony of the motel, but everyone was told to stay away, not even go in there for a drink, because there were SPs [suppressive persons] there. Nobody believed that; it was too outlandish. Then he used to visit us every day and he would arrive in a gold Cadillac which we had seen leave the hotel a few minutes earlier. It would turn in the opposite direction, go round the block and then come in the motel as if it had come from somewhere else.'[3]

Hubbard seemed in good spirits in Daytona and his health was much improved. 'He was really happy, was eating well and didn't curse so much,' said Dincalci. 'I guess it was the first time he'd been able to put himself out and about. There were things to do and people to see. He went out and bought some cars for the org – a couple of Matadors and a Chevy station wagon – and he enjoyed doing that; he liked wheeling and dealing. He liked the fact that he could see the org from where we were, but that no one knew we were there. Sometimes Sea Org people would take a swim from the beach right in front of our hotel and that meant he wouldn't go out until late in the evening. When he visited the org in his flash gold Cadillac, everyone would be out saluting him. He always arrived from an inland direction and said he'd driven half a day to get there.'

Holidaymakers at Daytona Beach observed the comings and going at the Neptune motel without much curiosity and the Scientologists were not around long enough to make their presence felt, for in October a perfect location was found for a permanent land base, on the other side of the Florida panhandle.

Clearwater was a quiet retirement resort, just north of St Petersburg, which liked to refer to itself as 'sparkling Clearwater'. It was a sobriquet derived more from its location, straddling a peninsula between Tampa Bay and the Gulf of Mexico, than from the nature of its social life: more than a third of Clearwater's 100,000 residents were over the age of sixty-five and so there was a leisurely, faintly antiquated, ambience about the place. Shuffleboard was the most popular afternoon recreation, after snoozing in the shade of trees draped with Spanish moss, and it was still possible to enjoy that rare delight, a real chocolate malt, at Brown Bros luncheonette.

Change was not a welcome phenomenon in a place like Clearwater, yet the town had suffered, to a certain extent, from the urban blight that had afflicted so many American cities in the 'sixties and 'seventies. Downtown residents had moved out to the suburbs, stores migrated to the shopping malls and tourists favoured the new hotels in the beach areas across the causeway. The centre of Clearwater was fast becoming an empty shell, epitomized by the fading grandeur of the town's major landmark, the eleven-storey Fort Harrison Hotel. With its chandeliered lobby overlooking a kidney-shaped swimming pool and its tier upon tier of forlornly empty rooms, the Fort Harrison marked the passing of an era and it was a surprise to no one that it was up for sale.

Its purchase, in October 1975, by Southern Land Sales and Development Corporation, occasioned no more than passing interest, although the attorney acting for the owners confessed that it was 'one of the strangest transactions' he had ever been involved in.[4] Not only did Southern Land pay the $2.3 million purchase price in cash, the corporation was so secretive it would not even admit to having a telephone number. A few days later, Southern Land also bought the old Bank of Clearwater building, not far from the Fort Harrison, for $550,000, also in cash.

Reporters on the two local newspapers, the *Clearwater Sun* and the *St Petersburg Times*, naturally began making routine inquiries about Southern Land's intentions and were surprised to discover there were no records anywhere of a Southern Land Sales and Development Corporation. Then a middle-aged man wearing, it was reported, a 'green jump-suit', arrived in Clearwater and announced that an organization called United Churches of Florida had leased both buildings for ecumenical meetings and seminars. This failed to clear up the mystery, because there were no records of United Churches, either.

Although Hubbard had not yet seen his latest real estate acquisitions, he had little doubt, from the detailed reports he had been receiving at Daytona Beach, that Clearwater would be an ideal headquarters for Scientology and a base from which the church could grow and prosper. He considered moving into the penthouse at the Fort Harrison – there was a drive-in garage on the ground floor and direct elevator access to the upper floors – but decided it would be safer to stay out of town. Frankie Freedman found four empty apartments in a condominium complex called King Arthur's Court in Dunedin, a small town on the coast about five miles north of Clearwater. Hubbard and Mary Sue, accompanied by a discreet entourage of messengers and aides, moved in on 5 December 1975. That location, too, was supposed to remain a closely-guarded secret.

There were a number of compelling reasons why Hubbard wanted to stay in hiding and continue the charade, for public consumption, that he had no influence or responsibilities in Scientology. One of them was that he had no desire, at the age of sixty-four, to risk going to prison.

Operation Snow White, the impudent plan to launder public records that he had dreamed up three years earlier, was progressing rapidly and with a degree of success that few would have believed possible. By the beginning of 1975, the Guardian's Office had infiltrated agents into the Internal Revenue Service, the US Coast Guard and the Drug Enforcement Agency. By May, Gerald Wolfe, a Scientologist working at the IRS in Washington as a clerk-typist, had stolen more than thirty thousand pages of documents relating to the Church of Scientology and the Hubbards. He was known to the Guardian's Office by the code-name, 'Silver'.

Within the hierarchy of the Church of Scientology, ultimate responsibility for the activities of Operation Snow White rested with Mary Sue Hubbard, the controller, but it was inconceivable that she was acting on her own initiative or not discussing progress with her husband. And although the amateur agents had discovered it was ridiculously easy to infiltrate, bug and burgle US government offices, the risks were considerable, both to the agents themselves and their church superiors. Hubbard was not too worried about who would take the rap if Operation Snow White was exposed, as long as it was not him.

A few days before he moved to Dunedin, he approved a Guardian's Office proposal to infiltrate agents into the US Attorney's offices in Washington DC and Los Angeles with the specific task of providing an early warning of any legal moves against him. In its usual clumsy prose, the Guardian's Office defined the first priority of 'Program LRH Security' as 'Maintain an alerting Early Warning System throughout the GO N/W [Guardian's Office network] so that any situation concerning govts or courts by reason of suits is known in adequate time to take defensive actions to suddenly raise the level on LRH personal security very high.'[5]

Confident that the Guardian's Office would protect him, Hubbard planned to insinuate himself into Clearwater society by posing as a photographer with an interest in taking scenic pictures for the tourist industry. 'Taking pictures of "beautiful CW" is the local button,' he

wrote in a letter to Henning Heldt, a deputy guardian. 'My portrait of
the mayor will hang in city hall never fear.'

The mayor of Clearwater, Gabriel Cazares, had more important
things on his mind than having his portrait taken. Like many of the
good citizens of Clearwater, he was concerned by the sudden influx of
strangely incommunicative young people. They were busily scrubbing
and cleaning the Fort Harrison Hotel and the old bank building, wore
a form of uniform and appeared to be guarded. 'I am discomfited,' the
perplexed mayor finally announced, 'by the increasing visibility of
security personnel, armed with billy clubs and mace, employed by the
United Churches of Florida. I am unable to understand why this
degree of security is required by a religious organization.'

For his discomfiture, the mayor was instantly placed on Scientology's 'enemies list'. He would have been even more discomfited had he
seen a directive issued in December outlining plans to take control of
'key points in the Clearwater area'. The aim of 'Project Power' was to
'establish the indispensibility of United Churches' in the community
and the means of achieving the objective involved classic Hubbardian
strategy:

'The overall plan is to locate opinion leaders – then, their enemies,
the dirt, scandal, vested interest, crime of the enemies (with overt data
as much as possible). Then turn this over to UC [United Churches]
who will approach the opinion leader and get his agreement to look
into a specific subject (which will lead to the enemies' crimes). UC
then "discovers" the scandal, etc, and turns it over to the opinion
leader for his use. Ops [operations] can be done as a follow up to
remove or restrain the enemy.'[6]

Before United Churches' cover was blown, Hubbard made a foray
into Clearwater to direct the taping of a radio show in which three
local ministers had been invited to participate. The Commodore had
abandoned his gold-embossed naval whites in favour of a beret and
khaki fatigues and in this freakish outfit, topped by headphones, he
bustled about, twiddling knobs, adjusting microphones and directing
where everybody should stand. 'They introduced him to me as Mr
Hubbard,' said the Reverend R. L. Wicker, of Clearwater's Calvary
Temple of God. 'But that didn't mean anything to me. They said he
was an engineer.'

In January, the Guardian's Office discovered that local newspapers
were moving closer to discovering the real identity of United Churches. Silver reported that a Bette Orsini of the *St Petersburg Times*
was asking questions about the tax-exempt status of the Church of
Scientology. And June Byrne, a Scientologist who had got a job as a
clerk in the news room at the *Clearwater Sun,* told the GO that
reporter Mark Sableman seemed to be making a connection between

United Churches and Scientology. He had been checking the registration plates of cars used by United Churches officials and had
discovered one was licensed in the name of 'R. Hubbard'.

On 28 January 1976, the 'Reverend' Arthur J Maren, a striking
figure with an Old Testament beard, arrived in Clearwater from Los
Angeles to announce at a news conference that the Church of
Scientology were the owners of the Fort Harrison Hotel and the Bank
of Clearwater building. Its involvement had not previously been
revealed only out of an altruistic desire to avoid overshadowing the
work of its subsidiary organization, United Churches. On 5 February,
five hundred citizens attended an open day at the Fort Harrison Hotel
to view the renovation work that had already been completed. Maren
reassured those present that there was nothing to fear from Scientology. 'Scientologists are people who don't drink or violate laws,' he
said. 'They are friendly and want to contribute.' Next day, the Church
of Scientology filed a $1 million lawsuit against Mayor Gabriel
Cazares, accusing him of libel, slander and violation of the church's
civil rights.

Hubbard thought it was unlikely that his own security in King
Arthur's Court had been compromised, since his location was known
to so few people and all of them were well-trained and fanatically
loyal. But there was a kind of perfidious inevitability that he would
eventually be wrong-footed, as had happened so often in his singular
career. This time it was no one's fault but his own. He decided he
needed a new wardrobe for his new life on shore. His usual habit was
to order what he wanted from a tailor in Savile Row, via his secretary
at Saint Hill Manor, but on this occasion he was impatient and
decided to call in a local tailor from Tarpon Springs, the next town up
Route 19A, north of Dunedin. The tailor turned out to be a
science-fiction fan and while he was measuring his new client they got
talking about science fiction. Hubbard let slip his identity and the
tailor was delighted to be able to shake the hand of the great L. Ron
Hubbard, whose sci-fi stories he had for so long admired. Back in
Tarpon Springs, he told his wife, 'You'll never guess who I was just
measuring for a suit . . .' News travelled fast thereabouts and it was
not long before a reporter began knocking on the doors of King
Arthur's Court in Dunedin.

Hubbard bolted. 'We're leaving right *now*,' he shouted at Kima
Douglas, then head of the household unit. 'What do you want to take
with you?' Kima, who was accustomed to handling crises, suggested
her husband, Mike. Hubbard agreed he could be their driver. 'He was
more agitated than I had seen him for years,' Kima recalled. 'We did
not have time to do anything but pack a small bag.' Hubbard had five
suitcases already stowed in the trunk of his gold Cadillac and they

swept out of King Arthur's Court as the sun was setting in the gulf. With Mike Douglas at the wheel, Kima on the front seat beside him and Hubbard cowering in the back to avoid being seen, they headed across the Florida panhandle on Route 4 in the direction of Orlando.

It was a journey that Kima Douglas would never forget: 'Somewhere near Orlando we stopped at a hotel, I think it was a Great Western, and checked in under false names. LRH was supposed to be my father. We got adjoining rooms and then LRH sent Mike out to telephone Mary Sue from a payphone to find out what had happened. When he came back, he said he had not been able to get through because she had moved her office. The old man just broke down and wept; tears poured out of his eyes. We didn't know what the hell was happening. He started to wail, "Don't you see? If she's moved her office it means that someone's been there. The whole thing's broken down. Don't you understand?" It looked like he was going to have a heart attack right there, so Mike went out to the payphone again to try and get some more information. When he got back he said everything was OK. Mary Sue had moved her office from one apartment to another because she thought she would be more comfortable.'

Early next morning Hubbard apprised his travelling companions that they were going to drive the 1200 miles to New York, but they were going to ditch the Cadillac because it was too noticeable. He gave Douglas $5000 to go out and buy another car; Douglas returned an hour later with a second-hand Chevrolet hatchback, big enough for their suitcases and suitably nondescript. They left immediately.

'We were on the road for three or four days,' said Kima. 'It was a horrendous trip. He sat in the back smoking cigarettes like mad and every time he saw a police car he'd scream, "There they are, they're after us!" We had to keep turning off the highways and freeways, stopping continually, to avoid police cars. We went through some real hokey places. One time he got out of the car and started beating the roof with frustration. I said to him very quietly, "Get back in the car, sir. Everything's all right."

'He kept saying we had to get to New York, we had to get to New York, but as we were driving through New Jersey I could see he was getting more and more affected by the pollution. He was hyperventilating, panting for breath. It was scary, really scary. We headed for Queens, where he had stayed before, and an aeroplane went overhead throwing out all kinds of shit. I pointed to it and said, "Sir, I'm not going to do this to you. There's no way you're going to stay here." By then he was like a child and mumbled something about do whatever you want. I said we should turn round and go back to Washington DC. He just said, "Do whatever you have to do."'[7]

Mike Douglas swung the wheel on the Chevrolet and turned back in the direction from which they had just come, south along the New Jersey turnpike, across the Delaware river into Maryland as far as the outskirts of Washington DC. They found rooms for the night in a hotel just off the Capital Beltway. Next morning, Kima drove downtown to look for more permanent accommodation. She found a comfortable brownstone on Q Street in Georgetown, only nine or ten blocks from the Washington org, and signed a $1300-a-month rental agreement.

Within a few days of moving into the brownstone, Hubbard had recovered his composure. Telex communications were set up and the usual retinue of messengers and aides moved in, including Jim Dincalci, who drove up from Florida towing a U-Haul trailer loaded with the Commodore's personal possessions and private papers. Daily reports began arriving from Mary Sue, many of them detailing the activities of Operation Snow White. 'It was strange to think', said Kima, 'that while we were lying low in Washington, other Scientologists were going through the files in government buildings not far from where we were living.'

In the bustling streets of Georgetown, Hubbard felt safe to go out and about, although he grew a beard and took to wearing a curious assortment of old clothes in the fond belief that he would merge into the cosmopolitan atmosphere. 'He bought clothes from Salvation Army stores, real grungy stuff,' said Alan Vos, one of the aides who had moved into the Q Street brownstone. 'It was strange because on the ship he had had all these phobias about dust and smells and how his clothes had to be washed, but that all vanished when we were living together in Washington.

'He used to go out walking and sit in the sidewalk cafés on Connecticut Avenue. The Scientology office was just a couple of blocks away and he was often handed flyers by people recruiting for Scientology; he thought it was very funny. One day he got talking to a woman in a restaurant about Scientology and he suggested she should go round to the org on S Street. I heard later that when she got there they asked who had sent her and she pointed to LRH's picture on the wall and said, "That man over there." They went crazy and started an investigation on her, thinking she was some kind of government plant.

'It seemed to me that LRH was happy in Washington, happy to be getting out, mixing with other people, going to the movies. On the ship he had no idea what was happening in the world. He thought about moving his headquarters to Washington and looked at a property – there was a hotel for sale on Dupont Circle – but Mary Sue talked him out of it. She didn't like Washington and convinced him it was too dangerous. That's the kind of thing she used to do – play on his fears and psychoses about violence and police.'[8]

Hubbard spent quite a bit of time researching in the library of Congress, reading up on black magic and the occult, and most days he took a walk in Rock Creek Park, where he believed that FBI agents were trained. He bought a trick camera with a lens that looked sideways and amused himself by taking pictures of trainee agents for future reference. Kima Douglas thought he was mad to take the risk.

Coincidentally, Rock Creek Park was also the chosen venue for a fake hit-and-run accident which the Guardian's Office set up in an attempt to end the political career of the troublesome mayor of Clearwater. Gabriel Cazares by then figured prominently on the Church of Scientology's hit-list and the Guardian's Office had been trying to dig up some dirt on him for weeks. Scientologists had gone back to his home town of Alpine, Texas, trawled through public records, nosed around the courthouse and even checked the head-stones in the local graveyard, without success. But then it was disclosed that Cazares would be attending the national mayors' conference in Washington from 13-17 March and the Guardian's Office made hasty plans to give him a welcome.

A Scientologist posing as a Washington reporter sought an inter-view with Cazares and introduced him to a friend, Sharon Thomas, who offered to show the mayor the sights of Washington. Miss Thomas was, of course, working for the Guardian's Office. Driving with the mayor through scenic Rock Creek Park, she temporarily lost control of her car and ran into a pedestrian, who crumpled dram-atically. To the mayor's horror, Miss Thomas accelerated away without stopping, leaving the injured man lying on the road.

A Guardian's Office memo the following day discussed ways of using the accident to discredit Cazares and concluded: 'I should think the mayor's political days are at an end.' Curiously Cazares was also on the Commodore's mind. On the very same day, Hubbard scrawled a note to the GO: 'Cazares – is there still some possibility the Cubans in Miami might get the idea he is pro-Castro?'

The 'victim' of the hit-and-run accident was a young man called Michael Meisner, a Scientologist since 1970. Meisner was the key figure in Operation Snow White: he was 'running' all the GO agents who had been infiltrated into government agencies in Washington, had personally taken part in several burglaries at the Department of Justice and organized the copying of tens of thousands of secret government files. For almost eighteen months, GO agents had been sneaking in and out of government buildings without hindrance, but on the evening of 11 June 1976, things started to go wrong when the FBI discovered Meisner and Silver in the US Courthouse Library at the foot of Capitol Hill. They were waiting for cleaners to vacate an office from which they were going to steal files, but they told the FBI

agents they were doing legal research. They presented fake identification documents and were allowed to leave.

Next day, in the brownstone on Q Street, an agitated Hubbard
showed Kima Douglas a telex from Mary Sue and asked, 'What am I
going to do about this?' 'The essence of the report,' said Kima, 'was
that they had caught the man who had been getting all this great
information for us from the tax files.' Although no arrests had yet been
made, Hubbard surmised, correctly, that there was trouble in store.
His instinct, once again, was to flee.

A bolthole had been established on the other side of the country in
anticipation of just this eventuality. On the following morning, Kima
Douglas checked in at National Airport with her elderly "father", for a
flight to Los Angeles. Travelling under false names, they sat together
in the first-class cabin and watched an adventure movie, featuring a
spectacular hang-glider rescue, which the old man very much enjoyed.
At LAX, they were met by a limousine and driven to Overland
Avenue in Culver City, where Gerry Armstrong had rented four
adjoining apartments. Back at the brownstone on Q Street in Georgetown, the occupants were toiling in and out of the house, loading
boxes into two U-Haul trailers parked outside. They would leave that
night for the long drive across the continent to Los Angeles.

Overland Avenue was a wide tree-lined street with low-rise apartment blocks on one side and the usual American suburban parade of
shopping plazas, filling stations and used-car lots on the other. It was
middle-class and anonymous, the kind of place where people could
come and go for months without ever being noticed by their neighbours. Armstrong had already set up a telex link before the Commodore arrived. Special decoder equipment was installed to provide
direct secure communications with Clearwater and the Guardian's
Office in Los Angeles, code-named Beta. Overland Avenue's code
name was Alpha.

Among early telex messages to arrive at Alpha was the news that
Gerald Wolfe, agent Silver, had been arrested at his desk at the IRS
building in Washington and a warrant had been issued for the arrest of
Michael Meisner,who was missing from his home. Hubbard was not
surprised by Meisner's disappearance – he was staying at Beta, where
he was being provided with a new appearance and identity. Mary
Sue's plan was that he should 'lose himself' in some large city.

Mary Sue soon joined her husband at Overland Avenue to discuss
the situation and some pressing family problems. She persuaded him
that they would be able to resume family life in safety if they could
find a remote ranch somewhere in southern California, but the truth
was that the family had already disintegrated under the stress of
constantly being 'on the run'. Diana's marriage was in trouble,

Quentin was supposed to be working for the org in Clearwater but was constantly absent, reckless Suzette was dating 'wogs' and Arthur had dropped out of the California Institute of the Arts after gentle Jim Dincalci had pulled strings to get him a place. 'I took his portfolio along,' said Dincalci, 'made up a story about him and gave him a false hyphenated name to disguise who he was. He was accepted on the strength of his portfolio and his mother and father were very happy with it, but he didn't last long.'

Not unreasonably, Mary Sue longed for some kind of stability and missions were despatched to find a property for the family, although Hubbard insisted that there had to be enough space to accommodate his messengers and his ever-changing court of loyal aides. The Commodore could not countenance life without a bevy of nubile messengers at his beck and call.

Kima Douglas went to look over a beautiful farm with its own beach not far from Santa Barbara and pleaded with him to buy it, but he said it was too expensive at $4 million. Then a mission scouring the Palm Springs area reported back on a promising property in the desert at La Quinta, on the east side of the San Jacinto Mountains, which was on the market for $1.3 million. Hubbard drove down to look at it in his new red Cadillac Eldorado convertible, wearing a jaunty little cap pulled down over his straggling long hair, which had at last turned grey. It was not a car that guaranteed him a low profile, but he had insisted on having it. He swept in through the high gates of the Olive Tree Ranch at La Quinta, took a quick look round, professed himself satisfied and returned immediately to Los Angeles.

La Quinta was about twenty minutes' drive from Palm Springs and was a quiet little community of cheap low-roofed houses that simmered on a flat patch of sun-scorched earth between the mountains. Olive Tree Ranch occupied the land behind the seedy La Quinta Country Club and perversely grew dates and citrus fruit rather than olives. The main house was a sprawling white adobe hacienda with a red-tiled roof built around a courtyard. There was a swimming-pool with an island in the middle sporting a single, surprising, palm tree and two other smaller houses, one called Rifle and the other The Palms.

As soon as the purchase papers had been signed, a working party from the Los Angeles RPF moved in to begin renovations and improvements. Hubbard had decided he would live in Rifle and wanted the house painted white throughout, with white tiles on the floor and all white furniture. Telex machines were installed in the main house, but it was intended that the ranch would be insulated as much as possible from the Church of Scientology. Everyone living and working there was given a cover name, warned not to use Scientology words or bring Scientology books on to the property.

The Hubbards moved in at the beginning of October 1976 and began to enjoy a new life of tranquillity on their ranch in the desert. The messengers noticed a change in the Commodore; he was much more relaxed than formerly and usually in good spirits. But on the morning of Wednesday, 17 November, as Doreen Smith was running across the Rifle to begin her watch, she could hear him shouting at the top of his voice: 'That stupid fucking kid! That stupid fucking kid! Look what he's done to me! Stupid fucking . . .' As she got closer, she could hear another unearthly, chilling noise. It was Mary Sue keening, barely drawing breath, but emitting a terrible endless scream.

When she entered the house, the messenger she was relieving was in tears. She sobbed out the awful news: 'Quentin's killed himself.'

Quentin had been found in Las Vegas at 0832 hours on 28 October, slumped over the steering-wheel of a white Pontiac parked off Sunset Road alongside the perimeter fence of McCarran Airport at the end of the north-south runway. All the car windows were rolled up and a white vacuum cleaner tube led from the passenger's vent window to the exhaust tail pipe. Tissue papers had been stuffed into the window opening around the tube and the car's engine was still running.

Officer Bruns of the Las Vegas Metropolitan Police Department was first on the scene. He wrenched open both the car doors and ascertained that the young man inside was still alive, though unconscious, probably because the tube had fallen off the tail pipe. He carried no identification of any kind and there were no licence plates on the car. There was nothing in the car but a Grundig portable radio, a black tote bag containing miscellaneous clothing and an open, partly consumed, bottle of tequila. 'The vehicle appeared as though the subject might have been sleeping in it,' the police report noted. 'The subject himself was very unkempt, his clothing was dirty, and would be possibly described as a vagrant type subject. A white male, appeared in his mid to late 20s. The subject was transported to Southern Nevada Memorial Hospital via Mercy Ambulance . . .'[9]

As no one knew who he was, Quentin was admitted to hospital as 'John Doe'. The only identifying marks that the hospital could record were his red hair and red moustache. He never regained consciousness and died at 2115 on 12 November. The police records listed him as a 'possible suicide'.

On Monday, 15 November, the Las Vegas coroner's office began making attempts to establish 'John Doe's' idenity. His car, which had been impounded, was re-checked and a Florida Highway Patrol smog sticker was found, along with a vehicle identification number. A telex to the Florida department of motor vehicles came up with the information that the vehicle was registered to a Quentin Hubbard of 210 South Fort Harrison Avenue, Clearwater. Descriptions of the car and the dead man were telexed to Clearwater police department with a request that the information be checked.

At 8.40 pm that same day, a man called Dick Weigand telephoned the deputy coroner from Los Angeles airport, said he was leaving for Las Vegas in five minutes and hoped to be able to identify John Doe. They agreed to meet at ten o'clock that night at the Medical Examiner Facility on Pinto Lane. Weigand was a senior Guardian's Office agent. He arrived at Pinto Lane five minutes late and explained that he had been contacted by a Kathy O'Gorman, who lived at the same address in Clearwater as Quentin Hubbard. However, he said he had only seen Quentin a couple of times and could not be sure of making a positive identification. Weigand viewed the body twice, stared into Quentin's white face, with his unmistakable red hair and moustache, then shook his head and said he was not sure. He could give no more help and he did not even know the telephone number of Kathy O'Gorman in Clearwater. Weigand disappeared into the garish Las Vegas night and immediately put a call through to the Guardian's Office to give them the bad news: it was Quentin, all right.

Mary Sue screamed for ten minutes when she heard the news. 'It was horrendous,' said Kima Douglas. 'It kept on going. I couldn't believe she could get that much air in her lungs. The only time I had ever really seen her cry before was when Vixie, her Corgi, died and I had to give it mouth-to-mouth resuscitation to try and revive it. The old man didn't cry or get emotional. He was furious – really angry that Quentin had done it.'

That same morning, a detective from Clearwater police department telephoned Las Vegas to say that 210 South Fort Harrison Avenue was the address of the US headquarters of the Church of Scientology, but that the church's public affairs officer, one Kathy O'Gorman, had refused to give him any information about Quentin Hubbard. The detective said that the Clearwater police had had 'many problems' with the church; as far as he knew, the founder, L. Ron Hubbard, lived on a yacht in the bay.

The Guardian's Office, meanwhile, had moved swiftly to 'handle' the situation. Its local representative in Las Vegas was a pit boss at the Sands Hotel by the name of Ed Walters. 'I had been working as a covert operator for about eight years,' he said. 'I had secretly tape-recorded a psychiatrist and got him to talk about lobotomies to try and discredit him and I had bugged the meetings of Clark County Mental Health Association, things like that. I worked on anything that org conceived to be a threat to the Hubbards.

'When they found out Quentin was here, I was told to get hold of all his medical files. There was apparently evidence that he had had a homosexual encounter shortly before he was found and they didn't want anything like that to get out. There was a girl Scientologist working in the hospital in a very secure position and she got all the reports on Quentin and gave them to me and I handed them over to the Guardian's Office.'[10]

On the morning of Thursday, 18 November, Arthur Maren arrived at the coroner's office in Las Vegas and introduced himself as director of public affairs for the Church of Scientology. He said he would be able to make a positive identification of the body and at 11.25 he confirmed that John Doe was, indeed, Geoffrey Quentin McCaully Hubbard, aged twenty-two. Maren said that Quentin's parents were not in the United States, but were away on a trip round the world.

Maren went backwards and forwards to the coroner's office over the next few days providing information designed to deter any further investigation into Quentin's death. He even persuaded the coroner to describe the cause of death as 'undetermined' in a press release. Quentin was said to have been on vacation and in Las Vegas to check out enrolment requirements for a flying school.

On Monday, 22 November, a young woman called Mary Rezzonico turned up with an authorization signed by L. Ron Hubbard and Mary Sue Hubbard for the release of their son's remains and his personal effects. Rezzonico said she had personally obtained the signatures over the weekend at 'an unspecified location in Ireland'.

Quentin was cremated next day at Palm Crematory in Las Vegas. 'I knew he had homosexual problems,' said Ed Walters, 'but he was a good kid. He was just a young, soft boy, not the ruthless, hard-nosed type. He had wanted to get out of Scientology for some time, but you don't just leave something like Scientology. You quit and then instantly become an enemy. He knew his father violently attacked anyone who betrayed him and he knew that the Guardian's Office would be after him as a traitor. He had grown up in Scientology and would have been tremendously afraid of the world out there, full of wogs and evil people. I guess he just couldn't handle it.'

'He was just a miserable, miserable boy,' said Kima Douglas. 'He was a little kid out of his depth who knew he could never compete with his father.'

A final macabre chapter was still to be enacted. Quentin had chosen to die at the end of an airport runway, watching the aircraft he had longed to fly landing and taking off. It was thus resolved that his ashes should be scattered from a light aircraft over the Pacific. Frank Gerbode, a Scientologist in Palo Alto, had his own aeroplane.

'The Guardian's Office telephoned and asked me to help with a special project,' Gerbode said. 'I was to fly my plane out over the

Pacific with a couple of GO people who were going to scatter Quentin's ashes. I wasn't supposed to tell anybody, of course. It turned out to be a gruesome business. It's not easy to throw particulate matter out of a light aircraft and the ashes blew back into the plane. I was taking little bits of Quentin Hubbard out of the upholstery for months afterwards.'[11]

Chapter 21

Making Movies

'The crime committed by these defendants is of a breadth and scope previously unheard of. No building, office, desk or file was safe from their snooping and prying. No individual or organization was free from their despicable conspiratorial minds. The tools of their trade were miniature transmitters, lock picks, secret codes, forged credentials, and any other device they found necessary to carry out their conspiratorial schemes. It is interesting to note that the founder of their organization, unindicted co-conspirator L. Ron Hubbard, wrote in his dictionary entitled *Modern Management Technology Defined* that, "Truth is what is true for you." Thus, with the founder's blessings, they could wantonly commit perjury as long as it was in the interests of Scientology.' (Government sentencing memorandum on Mary Sue Hubbard, et al, October 1978)

* * * * *

At Olive Tree Ranch, everything changed after Quentin's death. The Commodore's all-too-brief bonhomie disappeared and he reverted to the familiar bellowing, foul-mouthed tyrant, plagued by phobias, surrounded by fools and besieged by enemies.

When he was in the throes of a tantrum, he often looked deranged, with his long, unkempt hair, glaring eyes and flecks of saliva around his mouth. But no one would risk even *thinking* such a thing, lest it show up during auditing. There was a particularly feared phenomenon on the E-meter called a 'rock slam', when the needle wavered violently, apparently indicating a discreditable thought. 'Rock slams' almost inevitably led to long periods of incarceration in an RPF, by then a feature of most of the major orgs.

For those Scientologists who had only ever seen the dozen official pictures of L. Ron Hubbard, seeing him for the first time at La Quinta was something of a shock, as Anne Rosenblum discovered when she arrived to start training as a messenger: 'The first night I was there I didn't talk to LRH since he was busy, but I saw him. He had long reddish-gray hair down past his shoulders, rotting teeth and a really fat gut. He didn't look anything like his pictures. The next day I met him. He was doing exercises in his courtyard and called me over. I was nervous meeting him. I was really surprised that I didn't feel this "electric something or another" that I was told happens when you are around him.'

Anne had been told that both Mary Sue's pet dogs were 'clear' and that they would bark at anyone who had committed 'overts' (crimes) about the Hubbards. She was dismayed when she walked into Rifle for the first time and one of the dogs came tearing out of Mary Sue's room, barking furiously at her. 'I started walking around wondering what deep, dark terrible overts I had committed on LRH or Mary Sue in this life or past lives.'[1]

Because their loyalty was unquestioned, the messengers knew more about what was going on in Scientology than anyone other than Hubbard and Mary Sue. They knew all about Operation Snow White, for example, because the Hubbards often discussed its Machiavellian twists and turns over dinner. They were also privy to the family's intimate secrets. One afternoon, while Hubbard was away from his office, Doreen Smith came across a pile of letters Quentin had written to his father. She was surprised: she knew the Commodore had not replied to any of them because all his mail went out via the messengers.

'Out of curiosity, I pulled the letters out and read a couple,' she confessed. 'It sounded like Quentin had gone crazy. He was talking about people coming from outer space and what we were going to do about it and how he knew the Marcabs were coming every five thousand years to check on our development. It seemed like he had taken his father's space odyssey stories and plumped them in his own reality. It was real loony tune stuff.' She told no one about this except, of course, all the other messengers.

Doreen was close to the younger Hubbard children and was shocked by Quentin's letters. She was even more shocked by what happened when the Commodore fell out with his youngest daughter, Suzette. 'She was dating another Scientologist but for some reason the Commodore didn't approve of him and so he sent a messenger with $5000 in cash to buy him off. The messenger was told to threaten the guy that he would be declared SP if he didn't take the money and sign an agreement to stop seeing Suzette.

'But the agreement also made it look as if the guy was blackmailing Hubbard and threatening to take her away. That's what Hubbard told Suzette was happening. I was in his office when he called her in and showed her the agreement, shouting things like, "I told you so." Suzette might have seen through it, but she was a toughie. She started dating wogs and then, when she was being audited – auditing is like a confessional – she would describe everything she had done on the date in great detail, knowing that her father would read her folder. It was her way of getting back at him. The only form of communication she could have with her father was through her auditor.

'He went purple with rage when he read her folder with all that stuff in it and her saying things like, "If my father doesn't like what I'm doing, I don't give a damn." When he had finished reading it, he threw it across the room and then threw a yellow legal pad at me and told me to take down a letter. He started dictating a letter disinheriting Suzette and I began to cry. In the end I said, "I can't do this." I put down the pad and let him have it. "Quentin's dead," I said, "and now you're tearing your family apart. You can't do this to your family and to Mary Sue. If you want to send this letter, write it yourself." Then I excused myself from the watch and ran out. Afterwards, I discovered he tore up the letter. He never did disinherit Suzette.' (Doreen was a particular favourite with the Commodore and one of the few people at Olive Tree Ranch who would have dared suggest he might have made a mistake. He called her 'Do', had a little engraved dog-tag made for her and in rare moments of amiability he would give her an affectionate pat her on the head and say, 'That's my Do.')

Arthur, the youngest of the Hubbard children, was in rather better favour with his father, although he made a pest of himself with everyone else at Olive Tree Ranch by riding his motor-cycle around the property at breakneck speed. 'He was a brat,' said Jim Dincalci. 'All the time.' His talent as an artist was being employed to paint a series of watercolours illustrating incidents in his father's early life, which were to be used in a glossy, coffee-table tome published by the church under the title, *What Is Scientology?*

There were pictures of little Ron riding on his grandfather's cattle ranch, sitting by a campfire with the Pikuni Indians, journeying 'throughout Asia' at the age of fourteen, as a university student attending one of the first nuclear physics courses and supporting himself as an essayist and technical writer (the caption somehow failed to mention his science fiction). Two paintings showed him crippled and blinded in a naval hospital after the war and a third depicted him miraculously restored to health by the power of mind. Arthur's pictures were unremarkable art, but fascinating inasmuch as they illustrated most of the significant lies told by his father about his life before Scientology.

In the early part of 1977, Hubbard became enthused by a project called the 'Purification Rundown' which he believed would rid the world of drug addiction. His debut as an authority on the subject was marked by the issue of a bulletin in which he warned about the effects of LSD and listed its characteristics, as if after months of research. 'All the information came from one person who had taken LSD once.' said Jim Dincalci. 'That was how he did his research.'[2]

At Hubbard's request, Dincalci put together the elements of the Purification Rundown, a regimen of exercise, diet and vitamins designed to rid the body of toxic substances. Dincalci never thought of it as much more than a simple plan for healthier living, but in the grand arena of the Commodore's fantasies it was transformed into a sensational discovery, the instant solution to the international drugs crisis, the salvation of the world's youth, a beacon of hope for drug addicts everywhere.

Strenuous attempts were made to provide scientific evidence to back up the vivifying claims made for the Purification Rundown and Hubbard was so carried away by his own brilliance that he soon began to dream of a suitable award for his contribution to humanity – a Nobel Prize, for example. He issued a written order to Laurel Sullivan, his personal public relations officer, allocating 'unlimited funds' to a project aimed at getting him a Nobel Prize and inquiries were immediately instituted to see if there were any Scientology connections, or strings that could be pulled, with members of the Nobel nominating committee.

Poor Mary Sue, meanwhile, was floundering in the aftermath of Operation Snow White. The real problem was what do with Michael Meisner, who was growing restive as a fugitive and disenchanted with the efforts of his superiors to resolve his quandary. At one point Mary Sue had considered trying to make him the scapegoat, suggesting he had organized the burglaries in a fit of jealous pique because his wife was doing better as a Scientologist than he was. Another Guardian's Officer suggestion was that the authorities should be told that Meisner was trying to blackmail the church.

After eight months on the run, moving from one secret address to another, Meisner threatened to 'blow'. He was immediately placed under guard. The fugitive had become a captive. On 20 June 1977, while being held at an apartment in Glendale, he gave his guards the slip, changed buses twice to avoid pursuit and went into a bowling alley, from where he telephoned the FBI. He said he wanted to give himself up.

Two days later, the Guardian's Office received a letter from Meisner, postmarked San Francisco, saying that he was lying low for a while to think things over. This information was passed to Mary Sue, who responded: 'I frankly would not waste Bur 1 [Bureau One, the GO investigative division] resources looking for him, but would instead utilize resources to figure out a way to defuse him should he turn traitor.'[3] It was too late. Meisner was already in Washington describing to dumbfounded FBI agents the scope and success of Operation Snow White.

At six o'clock on the morning of 8 July 1977, 134 FBI agents armed with search warrants and sledgehammers, simultaneously broke into the offices of the Church of Scientology in Washington and Los Angeles and carted away 48,149 documents. They would reveal an astonishing espionage system which spanned the United States and penetrated some of the highest offices in the land.

Hubbard's reaction to the raid was true to form: he immediately assumed the Guardian's Office had been penetrated by suppressives. It was clear to him he could now trust no one but the messengers. He also realized that the documents seized by the FBI would inevitably implicate Mary Sue in Operation Snow White and he was acutely aware of the need to put some distance between himself and his wife.

On 15 July, in the middle of the night, a Dodge station wagon pulled out through the high gates of Olive Tree Ranch. To ensure it was not followed, the car showed no lights until it reached Highway 111, the main road between Indio and Palm Springs. Hubbard was slouched on the back seat of the car, grasping his midriff and complaining of stomach pains. With him were three messengers, Diane Reisdorf, Claire Rousseau and one of the few male messengers, Pat Broeker. They headed north on Interstate 5, turning east at Sacramento, across the Sierra Nevada and the state line, through Reno to Sparks, a city of low-rent houses, casinos and motels, situated on the Truckee River. The sun was just rising when they checked into a motel under false names. Their story was that Pat and Claire were married, Diane was their cousin and Hubbard their elderly uncle.

While Hubbard stayed in his room at the motel, Pat went out to look for an apartment. He quickly found somewhere suitably anonymous, paid cash and equipped it with everything they would need for an indefinite stay. The four of them moved in a few days later.

For the remainder of 1977, Hubbard stayed in hiding at Sparks. He cut off all direct communications with the Guardian's Office and his family and relied on his three messengers to maintain secret links with the Church hierarchy. It was not long before they began to run out of money and elaborate arrangements were made for the transfer of cash from Clearwater. Pat Broeker met the DCO/CMO/CW (Deputy Commanding Officer, Commodore's Messenger Organization, Clearwater) at Los Angeles airport where they exchanged identical suitcases. Broeker collected a case containing one million dollars in hundred-dollar bills and returned to Sparks, frequently doubling back to ensure he was not being followed. To further launder the money, the bills were broken down into lower denomination notes in local casinos.

For a man whose activities were under intense investigation by the FBI, Hubbard seemed remarkably insouciant. Most mornings he took a long walk, then spent the rest of the day writing film scripts. He had an idea for a feature film called *Revolt in the Stars*, a dramatization of high-level Scientology training about events which happened seventy-five million years ago when an evil ruler by the name of Xenu massacred the populations of seventy-six planets, transported their frozen spirits back to earth and exploded them in volcanoes. He also wanted to make films that could be used for recruiting and instruction within the church and the more he thought about the idea of being a film director, the more he liked it. He was sixty-six years old and had only ever shot home movies, but he did not consider his age or lack of experience to be any kind of drawback.

A few days after Christmas 1977, word arrived at Sparks that the Commodore was unlikely to be indicted as a result of the FBI raid and he decided it was safe to move back to La Quinta. There was just one problem. He suspected that Mary Sue was still under FBI surveillance, so if he returned to Olive Tree Ranch, she would have to move out.

Hubbard arrived back at the ranch on the morning of 2 January 1978 to the ritual rapturous welcome from his followers. He spent a number of hours with Mary Sue behind the closed doors of his study. No one knew what passed between them, but Mary Sue left the ranch that evening at the wheel of her BMW. Next day, Doreen Smith was sent to Los Angeles to help her look for a house.

With the Commodore's return, security was stepped up. Guards with walkie-talkies patrolled the property day and night and were drilled on how to deal with process servers. If a visitor asked for Mr Hubbard, they were to deny all knowledge of him; if someone tried to press papers on them, they were to kick them away. In a real emergency, a button on every walkie-talkie would set off alarms all around the property. At the back of Rifle, a tan-coloured Dodge Dart with a souped-up engine and a full tank of petrol was kept ready for a getaway at all times.

Behind the security screen, the Commodore was directing the setting up of a full-scale film unit. More property was purchased around La Quinta – a ten-acre ranch, code-named Munro, became a barracks for the film unit personnel and a studio was built in a huge barn on the Silver Sand Ranch, a 140-acre grapefruit farm. Lights, dollies, cameras and a vast range of technical equipment were all moved into the new studio. Hubbard took to wearing a cowboy hat, suspenders and a bandana, which he imagined gave him an artistic mien appropriate to a film director.

The Cine Org was to cut its teeth making simple promotional films illustrating various situations in which Scientology could be used beneficially. Hubbard wrote all the scripts and knew exactly what he wanted, but found it infuriatingly difficult to transfer his vision on to celluloid. Surrounded by an army of enthusiastic amateurs running around desperate to please, nothing seemed to go right. If the actors remembered their lines, the lighting was botched; if the lighting was all right, the sound failed; if the sound was satisfactory, the sets fell down . . . The Commodore's temper worsened day by day.

An appeal had gone out to Scientology branches around the world for volunteers with acting and film-making experience to help Ron in a special project. Among the first to arrive was a middle-aged couple from Las Vegas whose show business experience extended to four performances of their own dance and comedy act at the Sahara Showcase. Adelle and Ernie Hartwell were champion ballroom dancers who had taken a few Scientology courses and had been led to believe that joining the Cine Org would give them their big break.

They were disillusioned from the moment of their arrival. 'I was absolutely shocked', said Ernie, 'to see every one running around in shorts, ragged clothes, dirty and unkempt. They put us in a little three-room shack on the edge of the ranch. We go inside and what a mess! The place was over-run with bugs and insects.'

'The main thing I disliked,' said Adelle, 'was that when we first got there we were programmed on the lies we had to tell. If we ran into one of our friends, we had to tell a lie to them and tell them we were just there for a vacation . . . We were schooled on how to get away from process servers, FBI agents, any government officials or any policeman who wanted anything to do with Hubbard.'

Adelle's introduction to the Commodore was unforgettable. She was working in the wardrobe department when she heard a barrage of abuse from behind a screen: 'You dirty goddam sons of bitches, you're so goddam stupid. Fuck you, you cock-suckers . . .' It seemed to go on for several minutes. 'I had something in my hand and it fell to the floor,' she recalled. 'I said, "Who in the world is that?" They said it was the Boss – we weren't allowed to use the name Hubbard for security reasons. "You mean the leader of the church speaks like *that*?" I asked. "Oh yes," was the reply. "he doesn't believe in keeping anything back."'

Adelle Hartwell was supposed to be a make-up assistant on a movie called *The Unfathomable Man*, which chronicled Hubbard's view of mankind from the beginning of time to the present day. She soon learned that Hubbard was a director who liked plenty of gore, and gallons of fake blood had to be prepared in advance of every day's shooting. 'Did he ever like those films to be bloody,' she said. 'It was enough to make you sick.

'We'd be shooting a scene and all of a sudden he'd yell, "Stop! Make it more gory." We'd go running out on the set with all this Karo Syrup and food colouring and we'd just dump it all over the actors. Then we'd film some more and he'd stop it again and say, "It's still not gory enough," and we'd throw some more blood on them.'[4]

On one occasion, when filming a bombing raid on an FBI office – a scene Hubbard very much enjoyed – he ordered so much blood to be poured over the unhappy actors that their clothes became glued to their bodies and had to be cut off by wardrobe assistants.

When the Cine Org was shooting in the studio, all the sets had to be cleaned and scrubbed with special soap every morning before Hubbard arrived and the messengers would go round with white gloves to ensure that it had been done properly. Hubbard had a director's chair that no one else was allowed to sit in and as he was walking around the set a messenger would follow close behind him, ready to put the chair underneath him if he chose to sit down. One unfortunate girl got the positioning wrong by a few inches and as the Commodore sat down he missed the chair and sprawled on the floor. No one laughed: it was not wise to laugh at the Commodore. The girl was immediately despatched to the RPF.

Despite the somewhat desperate desire on everyone's part that the Cine Org should succeed, its films were in no danger of winning Oscars. One of the fundamental problems was that the scripts, although no one would admit it, were as amateurish as everything else. Narratives tended to begin, 'From the beginning of history, Man has searched for truth . . .' and many of the roles were wooden stereotypes or ludicrous caricatures reflecting Hubbard's multitude of prejudices. One film, titled *The Problems of Life*, featured a perplexed young couple searching for a meaning to their lives. They first consulted a psychiatrist, predictably portrayed as a demented sadist, then sought advice from a scientist, who was shown madly scribbling theorems on a blackboard as if completely insane. Finally they approached a beaming Scientologist and concluded they were at last in the right place. Subtlety was not one of Hubbard's more obvious talents as a scriptwriter.

'The trouble was that he wanted to make movies that would take over Hollywood,' said Kima Douglas, 'but they were terrible, really terrible. The crew would have to do scenes over and over again before he was satisfied. Occasionally the day would end up with a "Fine, well done everybody", but more often there were tantrums and he'd storm off the set screaming that it had better be right tomorrow.'[5]

Gerry Armstrong was put in charge of set building. 'It was all hokey, worse than high school,' he said. 'When we were shooting films he was the most abusive I have ever seen him, screaming and yelling all the time. People were running around terrified. He'd cover up his own incompetence by attacking everyone else. The guy had poor eyesight and he was running the cameras, so the shots were often out of focus and he'd scream at the cameraman, "You can't frame a shot!" Or he'd hear a hum on the microphone and start yelling, "Sound! Sound! You fucking idiots! Get off the set!"[6]

Faithful Jim Dincalci was by this time convinced that Hubbard was unbalanced and he asked to be relieved of his post on the Commodore's staff. He was immediately ostracized. 'For two months Hubbard would not even acknowledge my existence. He would not say hello or even nod at me. On the set in the morning he would say hello to everyone and deliberately skip me.' Dincalci was also less inclined to believe the Commodore's stories of his past life adventures: 'A friend of mine, Brian Livingstone, told me one time that Hubbard had finished [reading] a book and passed it on to him to read. He started reading it that night and next day he heard Hubbard talking about a lifetime where he had done these various things and Brian had just read about *the same things in the book*!'

Hubbard knew little of what was happening to Mary Sue during this period because the messengers censored her letters in order to avoid upsetting the Commodore. If Mary Sue sent bad news, the messengers cut out the offending passages with a razor blade, believing it to be their duty to keep such problems 'off his lines'. But they naturally read all Mary Sue's communications themselves and were certainly not above gossip. On one occasion she wrote to ask, plaintively, why Ron spent so much time with 'his people' and so little time with her. 'I understand you're trying to save the world,' she wrote, 'but I need some time, too.' The contents of that letter were soon common knowledge all round Olive Tree Ranch.

In truth, Mary Sue had much to complain about, because she had no doubt that she was going to have to take the rap for Operation Snow White. 'Hubbard abandoned her', said Ken Urquhart, 'and made it quite clear within the org that he had abandoned her. It's the one thing I find hard to forgive – that he was prepared to allow his wife to go to jail for crimes he was equally guilty of. After the FBI raid I was put to work making up reports to show that he did not know what was going on. In other words, I was to cover his ass. He was privy to almost all of it and was as guilty as Mary Sue.'[7]

On 15 August 1978, a federal grand jury in Washington indicted nine Scientologists on twenty-eight counts of conspiring to steal government documents, theft of government documents, burglarizing government offices, intercepting government communications, harbouring a fugitive, making false declarations before a grand jury and conspiring to obstruct justice. Heading the list of those indicted was Mary Sue Hubbard. She faced a maximum penalty, if convicted, of 175 years in prison and a fine of $40,000. On 29 August, all nine defendants were arraigned in the federal courthouse at the foot of Capitol Hill and pleaded not guilty.

A few days later, Hubbard collapsed while he was filming on location in the desert. 'The temperature was somewhere between 118 and 122 degrees,' said Kima Douglas. 'I had been watching the old man out there wheezing and struggling for breath, with flecks around his mouth. It was crazy; I knew he wouldn't be able to take it much longer. We always had a motor home at the location – he'd have his lunch in it and sometimes have a lie-down while the set was being prepared. This particular day he came back to the motor home and said he didn't feel well. His pulse was extremely erratic and his blood pressure was way up. I thought he was going to die and said that we ought to get him to hospital. He gripped my arm and said, "This time, *no!*"'

Hubbard was taken back to Olive Tree Ranch, apparently slipping in and out of a coma. At one point he muttered to Kima, 'If I die, bury me in the date field.' A Scientologist doctor, Gene Denk, was summoned from Los Angeles and driven to the ranch blindfolded but he seemed unsure what was wrong with the Commodore. Hubbard had always said that he only got ill because his enemies were pushing bad energy on him; it was just something saviours had to put up with, he would explain with a shrug. Auditing was the way to exorcize bad energy.

David Mayo, the senior case supervisor in Clearwater, did not know where he was going or what he had to do. All he was told was that an urgent, top-secret telex had arrived at the CMO instructing him to be on the next flight to Los Angeles. He was given twenty minutes to get to the airport and didn't even have time to say goodbye to his wife. No one was to know that he had gone. It was nightfall when he arrived at Los Angeles airport. He was met by a Scientologist he vaguely recognized and hurried out to a waiting car, which swept out of the airport complex and up on to Los Angeles' bewildering network of freeways. Neither of the men in the car would tell Mayo where they were taking him. Somewhere on the outskirts of the city they stopped at a parking lot and switched cars. Half an hour later, in another parking lot, Mayo was bundled into a third car and this time he was blindfolded. He asked what was going on and the driver replied: 'We're taking you to LRH. He's sick. Keep the blindfold on until we arrive.'

Mayo was dismayed when he was at last ushered into the Commodore's room at Rifle. 'He was obviously very ill, lying on his back almost in a coma. He could talk a little, but very slowly and quietly. There was medical equipment all round him, including an electric pulse machine to re-start his heart. Denk told me he thought LRH was close to death. He would have moved him into a hospital but he thought the ride in the ambulance might finish him off. I was given his PC folders and told to solve the problem. I started looking through the folders that night and began auditing him next day.'[8]

Hubbard slowly recovered, proving the wondrous efficacy of auditing to everyone at Olive Tree Ranch except, perhaps, the Commodore's auditor. Mayo was deeply disturbed by what he learned during his daily auditing sessions with Hubbard: 'He revealed things about himself and his past which absolutely contradicted what we had been told about him. He wasn't taking any great risk because I was a loyal and trusted subject and had a duty to keep such things confidential.

'It wasn't just what I discovered about his past. I didn't care where he was born or what he had done in the war, it didn't mean a thing to me. I wasn't a loyal Scientologist because he had an illustrious war record. What worried me was when I saw things he did and heard statements he made that showed his intentions were different from what they appeared to be. When I was with him messengers often arrived with suitcases full of money, wads of hundred-dollar bills. Yet he had always said and written that he had never received a penny from Scientology. He would ask to see it, the messenger would open the case and he'd gloat over it for a bit before it was put away in a safe in his bedroom. He didn't really spend much, so I guess it was getaway money. I didn't mind the idea of him having money or being rich. I thought he had done tremendous wonders and should be well paid for it. But why did have to lie about it?

'I slowly began to realize that he wasn't acting in the public good or for the benefit of mankind. It might have started out like that, but it was no longer so. One day we were talking about the price of gold, or something like that, and he said to me, very emphatically, that he was obsessed by an insatiable lust for power and money. I'll never forget it. Those were his exact words, "an insatiable lust for power and money".'

By the middle of October, the Commodore was back on his feet, back making movies. Mayo was ordered to be an actor and was appalled by Hubbard's behaviour on the set. 'He walked around with an electric bullhorn yelling orders through it even if the person was only a few feet away. The crew were in a constant state of fear. He'd say he wanted a certain set built and describe it. Everyone would work in a frenzied state to get it done, often through the night, not stopping for meals and praying it would be right and that they would not get into trouble. When he arrived to begin shooting he invariably decided he didn't like it. It had been altered; he wanted it blue, not green. Some of the crew would be sent to the RPF and others would be running around trying to find some blue paint. Then he'd want to know why it was blue and not yellow.

'When I was trying to be an actor I'd have to do the same line over and over again. It was never right. It was too loud, too quiet, too intense, not intense enough. Then he'd scream, "Why aren't you doing it *enthusiastically*?" He'd end up stamping off, screaming that it was all impossible and that no one would do what he said. One of the main reasons why he got sick, I think, was that he had so many failures and so much frustration and upset over the movies. Everyone was tip-toeing around waiting for explosions.

'One incident was quite dramatic and revelatory. During a period when things had got very, very bad, some of the crew tried to lighten things up by making a little video recording intended as a joke. It was a humorous skit on an incident that had happened a couple of days earlier. They thought it would amuse him and sent him the video tape. I was standing outside his office waiting to see him when he played it. There was a tremendous explosion. He started yelling and screaming and messengers began running in and out. He was literally *shouting* at the television. He didn't think it was funny at all. He thought he was being held up to ridicule and that the crew were mocking him and he was furious. Messengers were sent to find the names of everyone involved and they were all sent to the RPF. Then he thought that there were people who were not directly involved but might know about it and he wanted their names and they were sent to the RPF as well.'

Cine Org members assigned to the RPF were sent to work on quarter pay – $4.00 a week – at a recently acquired property about forty miles from La Quinta which was to be the Commodore's 'summer headquarters'. Gilman Hot Springs was a faded resort straddling Route 79 between Riverside and Palm Springs. Its 550 acres boasted a yellowing golf course, a decrepit motel, the Massacre Canyon Inn, and a collection of miscellaneous buildings in various states of disrepair, one of them a house satirically named 'Bonnie View'. The entire property had been purchased for $2.7 million cash and local people were told it was going to be used by members of an organization called the 'Scottish Highland Quietude Club'.

Hubbard had not seen the place but declared an ultimate intention to move into Bonnie View and the RPF was toiling to prepare the house for him, ripping out the vents, tiling the floors, painting and decorating and vainly attempting to create a dust-free and odourless habitat. It was honest labour much preferable to the stress and hysteria prevalent in the Cine Org, which by then employed around 150 people.

Like almost every episode in Hubbard's life, the Cine Org ended in sudden collapse and farce. The Hartwells, the stage-struck ballroom dancers who thought they were breaking into show business, had disentangled themselves by the end of 1978 and returned to Las Vegas, poorer but wiser. Ernie Hartwell did not particularly want to stir up any trouble but he thought that the church was trying to entice Dell back and break up his marriage. He was a straight-talking Navy veteran who worked in a casino and was not the kind of guy to be cowed by 'kids running around in sailor suits', which was his favourite description of Scientologists. He began threatening to go to the FBI and the newspapers and telling everything he knew. Actually he did not know much, other than the best-kept secret in Scientology – the whereabouts of L. Ron Hubbard.

Ed Walters, the agent who had 'handled' Quentin's suicide, was ordered to 'handle' Hartwell. 'I'll never forget sitting in the local Guardian's Office the day I brought Ernie in,' said Walters. 'These two young kids who've never met Hubbard are sitting there and they obviously think that Hartwell's a liar. One of them says, "You don't know what you're talking about. You say you actually met Ron Hubbard . . ." Ernie says, "Yeah, I was with him down in the desert." "Well, if you met him," says the GO guy, "how would you describe him?" I knew that what he meant was how did Hubbard look, but Ernie says, "How would I describe him? I'd describe him as fucking nuts."

'My heart was pumping. No one talks like that about LRH. The GO people were stunned. To them it proved that Ernie was a liar. I said, "Well, Ernie, you don't really *mean* that he's nuts, do you?" He says, "Yeah!" So I asked him to give me an example, hoping to tone it down a bit. "Are you kidding?" He says. "One day we get there and he's playing director with all these kids following him around. He starts screaming at the wall, he says there's supposed to be shelves there and why aren't there shelves there. So one of his people turns to me and says put some shelves there. So I say OK, I need a hammer, nails and wood. Then this fucking kid just says to me make it go right."

'To tell someone "Make it go right" was typical Scientology-speak. I knew then that he was telling the truth.'[9]

Walters liked Ernie Hartwell and tried, over the next couple of days, to dissuade him from carrying out his threats. 'Next thing that happens,' he said, 'was that the GO sent some people to tell me to stay out of it. They were going to handle Hartwell. They were not going to allow Hubbard to be exposed by this man and they insinuated they would destroy him if they had to. Ernie was just a troubled old guy off the street who should never have been in Scientology in the first place. How could they think of destroying someone like that? Something just went off inside me.'

Walters began telephoning his closest friends in Scientology, among them Art Maren, to tell them he was thinking of getting out. Maren rushed to Las Vegas and begged Ed to re-consider. It dawned on Walters, with a sense of deep shock, that his friend Artie was *frightened*. Next day Walters went to the FBI.

Alarm bells were already ringing at Olive Tree Ranch, where someone had been seen taking photographs of the property. Hubbard reacted as he always reacted in a crisis: he fled.

The chosen getaway vehicle was a white customized Dodge Ram van with darkened windows, fitted out inside with a bed, CB radio and the latest stereo system. Hubbard had had it made so that he could sleep on long journeys by road, but it served the purpose for which it was now needed – to get him out of Olive Tree Ranch unseen.

Kima and Mike Douglas were again chosen to go with him. They left at nightfall, with the Commodore in his usual state of paranoid hysteria. 'As we drove up into the San Jacinto Mountains,' said Kima, 'he was lying on the bed in the back, alternately urging Mike to drive faster and complaining that he was feeling sick. We were already tearing round these hairpin bends as fast as we could, but he kept repeating, "We've got to get out of here. Go faster, Go faster."'

They checked into an isolated motel up in the mountains and Hubbard stayed in his room while the Douglas's went out every day looking for a place where they could set up yet another secret base for the Commodore. They eventually found several adjoining apartments for rent in new building just off the main street in Hemet, a small town on the west side of the mountains. Hubbard moved in at the end of March 1979, along with a slimmed-down staff of messengers and aides.

In many ways, Hemet was an ideal place to hide. It was a sleepy little farming town, surrounded by orange groves and unremarkable in every way except perhaps for its resemblance to a Rockwell painting. Its main street signs reflected quiet respectability, small-town values and quintessential Americana: Sun-up Milk Drive-In; Dollar Saver; Smile Jesus Loves You; Hemet Retirement Home; Happy Birthday Doug & Laura; Virgin Mortuary; Hemet Motel Pets Welcome; Gun Shop; Church of the Open Bible . . . The Commodore's new base was behind Lee's Acupuncture Clinic, adjacent to a Pick 'n' Save supermarket and a drive-in McDonald's.

In this amiable suburban setting, an extraordinary security cordon was tightened around the man whose name was not now allowed to be mentioned. Within Scientology, Hubbard's new location was known only as 'X'. The summer headquarters at Gilman Hot Springs was only fourteen miles distant, to the north, but no one was allowed to travel directly between the two places. Mike Douglas, one of the few people with authority to make regular journeys between Hemet and Gilman, clocked up 120 miles each time.

Inside the apartments behind the acupuncture clinic, a skilful alarm system was devised, with buzzers and red lights everywhere. All the staff were drilled regularly so they knew what to do if strangers arrived at the door – they had to deny all knowledge of L. Ron Hubbard, of course, but they also had to try and act normally while the Commodore was being hustled out through a back escape route to a getaway car that would always be ready in a garage opening on to a different street.

Once all the security precautions were in place, Hubbard relaxed and settled down to enjoy life in Hemet. Although he occasionally threw his food across the room when he believed the cook was trying to poison him, by and large he was better tempered than he had been when he was trying to make movies. He usually got up about midday, audited himself for an hour and then dealt with whatever correspondence the messengers had decided he should see. In the afternoons he devoted several hours to taping lectures and mixing suitable background music, and in the evenings he watched television and reminisced to a small, but always attentive, audience.

'I believed the stories he told were true for him,' said Kima Douglas. 'He was a good story-teller and it was nice to listen to him. He told us once how he was Tamburlaine's wife and how he had wept when Tamburlaine was routed in his last great battle. Another time he was on a disabled spaceship that landed here before life began and realized the potential and brought seeds back from another planet to fertilize planet earth. I didn't see why that couldn't be true.'

David Mayo recalled sitting on the floor with a couple of messengers while the Commodore played hill-billy songs on his guitar and talked about the time he had earned his living as a troubadour in the Blue Mountains. 'I think he made up the songs as he went along,' said Mayo. 'Afterwards, everyone clapped.'

After several weeks at Hemet, Hubbard began venturing out into the town in a variety of extraordinary disguises. He had a baseball cap with false hair sewn into it, plastic padding to change the shape of his face and stage make-up to alter the colour of his eyebrows and sideburns. 'He always thought he looked wonderful,' said Kima, 'but he usually looked like a funny old man. I always thought it would have been safer to dress him up like a nonentity, but he would never have it. He always wanted to wear his hat at an angle, kind of jaunty, display a bit of panache. He was fun like that. He'd walk down the main street, always followed by a couple of messengers, little girls in white shorts or tight, tight jeans and he thought he looked like one of the locals, but he never did.'

Hubbard knew so little about contemporary America that he considered shopping malls to be a wondrous innovation and he would spend hours wandering around them, buying plastic trinkets. Although he never spent much when he was out shopping, he was investing huge sums in stocks, precious stones and gold. Michael Douglas had been appointed the Commodore's 'finance officer' and was managing an enormous portfolio of stocks running into millions of dollars. There were bags of gold coins and diamonds stuffed in two safes at the Hemet apartments and more jewels were lodged in the vaults of a local bank.

Through the summer months of 1979, Hubbard followed closely the progress of the battery of lawyers which was fighting to prevent Mary Sue and her co-defendants from being brought to trial. In the intimacy of the Hemet hideaway, he made no secret of his intention to sever all his connections with his wife. He frequently asserted that he had never known anything about what Mary Sue was doing and whined about the fact that she was getting him into trouble. Everyone knew it was a lie.

David Mayo was sent to see Mary Sue at her house off Mulholland Drive in Los Angeles, to suggest that she might consider a divorce. 'She was really offended and very upset,' said Mayo. 'I thought she was going to blow my head off. I went back several times later to make sure that she wasn't going to rat on him. That's what he was really worried about, that she would reveal during the case that she was only relaying his orders. She had covered up for him so much, and there had been so many opportunities for her to betray him, that she couldn't believe he would think that. She kept saying to me, "What is he worried about?" I thought to myself, "My God, I can't tell her."'

Hubbard, still not convinced that he could trust his wife, decided to risk meeting her himself at Gilman Hot Springs. At summer head-quarters, no one was supposed to know that the Commodore was visiting, although it was not hard to guess since a working party was assigned to spend two days scrubbing 'Bonnie View' and polishing all surfaces by hand. Mary Sue was told to go to a hotel in Riverside and wait to be picked up by Kima Douglas, who drove her on a roundabout route to Gilman, checking all the time that they were not being followed. Hubbard arrived on the bed in the back of the Dodge Ram, which drove through the gates of the resort at high speed. Waiting guards immediately put a chain across the entrance. No messengers were present during the meeting, so no one knew what was discussed and no one saw either the Commodore or his wife leave the property.

Mary Sue never betrayed her husband, but then she had never intended to. The trial was scheduled for 24 September in Washington, but the government prosecutors and defence attorneys were still bargaining at that date and a stay was granted. On 8 October, in an unusual legal manoeuvre, an agreement was reached that the nine defendants would plead guilty to one count each if the government presented a written statement of its case, thereby avoiding a lengthy trial.

On 26 October, US District Judge Charles R. Richey accordingly found the nine Scientologists guilty on one count each of the indictment. Mary Sue and two others were fined the maximum of $10,000 and jailed for five years. The remaining defendants received similar fines and prison sentences of between one and four years. Sentencing Mary Sue, the judge told her: 'We have a precious system of government in the United States . . . For anyone to use those laws, or to seek under the guise of those laws, to destroy the very foundation of the government is totally wrong and cannot be condoned by any responsible citizen.' All the defendants indicated an intention to appeal on the grounds that the evidence against them had been obtained illegally.

Scientology lawyers were still hoping to prevent the damning documents seized in the FBI raids, currently under seal, from being released. But on 23 November, the day after Thanksgiving, the appellate court ordered the seal to be lifted and began releasing the documents, much to the delight of newspapers and television stations throughout the United States. At last they were able to report the astonishing details of Operation Snow White and give the public a peek into the strange and secretive world of the Church of Scientology.

Exposed and vilified in headlines across the nation, Hubbard became morose, suspicious and fearful once again for his safety. Kima and Mike Douglas had finally asked themselves what they were doing at Hemet and had 'blown the org'. The departure of two such long-standing and trusted aides made the Commodore nervous about the loyalty of everyone around him, except for Pat Broeker, the messenger who had accompanied him to Sparks, Nevada, and his new wife Annie, also a messenger. The Broekers were flattered and pleased to become the Commodore's closest confidantes.

Hubbard's grip on reality, always tenuous, slipped further. He issued orders for plans to be prepared for a new house somewhere near Hemet. It was to be, an aide reported, in 'a non-black area, dust-free, defensible, with no surrounding higher areas and built on bedrock'. It was also to be surrounded by a high wall with 'openings for gun emplacements'.[10]

At the end of February 1980, a few days before his sixty-ninth birthday, Hubbard disappeared with Annie and Pat Broeker.

He was never seen again.

Chapter 22

Missing, Presumed Dead

'I would say that 99 per cent of what my father has written about his own life is false.' (Ron DeWolf, formerly L. Ron Hubbard Junior, May 1982)

* * * * *

For nearly six years, no one knew where L. Ron Hubbard was hiding or whether he was dead or alive. He was hunted high and low by television and newspaper reporters, federal investigators and law officers: none of them unearthed a single clue to his whereabouts. Mary Sue, his loyal and loving wife for more than twenty-five years, did not know where her husband was, neither did their children. The Commodore had effectively vanished.

After Hubbard skipped from Hemet with the Broekers, the apartments were closed. Once all the papers and personal effects had been packed and moved out, a working party cleaned each apartment with an alcohol solution to remove fingerprints, carefully wiping down all the walls, fixtures, door knobs, shelves, windows and mirrors. Pat Broeker, acting on Ron's orders, supervised the operation.

Broeker also directed, apparently at the behest of the absent Commodore, a massive corporate reorganization of the Church of Scientology, ostensibly designed to further shield Hubbard from legal liabilities and to ensure that the income flowing to him from the church, then running at about $1 million a week, could never be traced.[1] He was assisted by his friend and fellow messenger David Miscavige, a ruthless and ambitious nineteen-year-old who had learned management technique at the Commodore's knee, as a cameraman in the Cine Org. Miscavige was small, slight and asthmatic, but his lack of stature did not prevent him from adopting Hubbard's principle that the way to get things done was to browbeat subordinates by bellowing and threatening. His strutting figure became widely feared at Gilman Hot Springs and at the former Cedars of Lebanon Hospital in Los Angeles, recently purchased by the church for its new headquarters.

Many long-serving senior Scientologists were purged during the re-structuring and none had redress to Hubbard, for the messengers controlled his communication lines. Apart from the Broekers, Miscavige was said to be the only other Scientologist privy to the Commodore's location, although most of the staff at Gilman knew that Ron could not be far away because it only took Pat Broeker four or five hours to make the round trip from Gilman to Ron's hide-out.

During this upheaval, no one could be sure if it was really Hubbard who was issuing the orders or, indeed, if it was his ultimate intention that the messengers should take over control. In letters to those who had formerly been close to him, he gave no hint that he was juggling with the massive and complex structure of Scientology. 'Dearest Do,' he wrote to Doreen Smith in June 1980, 'life is a bit dull for me . . . I'll have to get up and get my wits to work to find something advantageous to do, so this is just a hello really. I hope you and the others are well and doing well . . .'[2]

David Mayo also received a number of letters from Hubbard and began to worry about his state of mind. 'In the first paragraph of one letter he said something like, "You might think I've gone crazy, but I'm still OK, just believe what I say is true." I remember thinking, God, whatever's coming must be pretty weird. It was real demented stuff, berating psychiatrists and claiming they were the root of all evil, not just on this planet but since time immemorial. He had it figured out that back in the beginning of the universe, psychiatrists created evil on a particular star system. When I read it I thought my God, he *is* crazy! He can exhort me not to think he's crazy, but this letter belies it.'[3]

In May 1981, when the purge was well under way and the messengers were consolidating their power, Miscavige moved to oust Mary Sue as Controller. He first chipped away at her position by making it known among her friends that Ron wanted her out. Then, at a stormy meeting in Mary Sue's office, Miscavige told the Commodore's wife that she was an embarrassment to the church, that she was certain to lose the appeal against her prison sentence and that it was important for the public image of the church that she be disciplined. Mary Sue lost her temper, screamed and raged at the upstart messenger and at one point threw an ashtray at him. But Miscavige stood his ground in the full knowledge that Mary Sue's position was hopeless. Without being able to count on her husband's support, she had no alternative but to step down. Afterwards she wrote bitter letters of complaint to Ron, but she suspected they were never delivered.[4] Miscavige would later complete his humiliation of the Hubbard family by having Arthur and Suzette ejected from Gilman Hot Springs as 'security risks' and appointing Suzette as his personal maid at the Cedars complex.[5]

Mary Sue's resignation as Controller was not announced until September, when the church issued a press release piously justifying the 'shake-up' as a reaction to the indictments resulting from Operation Snow White and admitting that the Guardian's Office 'went adrift' by engaging in a battle with the federal government.

In April 1982, David Mayo received another long letter from the Commodore in which he said he did not expect to live much longer – a few months at the least, a few years at the most. Until he was able to pick up a new body, grow to adulthood and resume his rightful position as the head of Scientology, Hubbard was assigning responsibility for safeguarding the 'purity' of the technology to his friend Mayo. David Mayo believes that Miscavige and his cohorts interpreted this news as a threat to their position and began making plans to remove him.

Meanwhile, yet another enemy stepped into the arena to do battle with the church. A commission had been set up in Clearwater to investigage Scientology and its star witness was to be none other than L. Ron Hubbard Junior, who had recently changed his name to DeWolf in order to further disassociate himself from his father. Pink-faced and bespectacled, Nibs told the commission that his father was a habitual liar, paranoid, schizophrenic and megalomaniac who had fabricated most of his qualifications and written *Dianetics* off the top of his head without doing any research.

Worse was to come. In July, Nibs gave an interview to the Santa Rosa *News-Herald* in which he portrayed his father as a wife-beater who had experimented in black magic and fed him and his sister bubble gum spiked with phenobarbitol. 'He had one of those insane things, expecially during the '30s, of trying to invoke the devil for power and practices. My mother told me about him trying out all kinds of various incantations, drugs and hypnosis . . . He used to beat her up quite often. He had a violent, volcano-type temper, and he smacked her around quite a bit. I remember in 1946 or 1947 when he was beating up my mother one night, I had a .22 rifle and I sat on the stairway with him in my sights and I *almost* blew his head off.'

It was not quite the pre-publication publicity St Martin's Press might have wished to launch *Battlefield Earth: A Saga of the Year 3000*, L. Ron Hubbard's first science-fiction book for more than thirty years. It was evident that the Commodore, wherever he was, had been busy, for the eight hundred-page *Battlefield Earth* was trumpeted not only as the longest science-fiction book ever written but merely the prelude to *Mission Earth*, an epic work of more than one million words due to be published in ten separate volumes over the next four years.

Battlefield Earth was the story of how Jonnie Goodboy Tyler, one of the few surviving human beings still on earth, turned the tables on

the huge, shambling, hairy aliens who had taken control of the planet.
Many science-fiction buffs did not feel the work matched the pace and
excitement of Hubbard's earlier fiction. Indeed, his agent, Forrie
Ackerman, wondered if it had really been written by Ron and took the
trouble to have the dedication on his personal copy ('To 4E, my
favourite monster and long-time friend') verified by a handwriting
expert. Hubbard's fellow sci-fi writer, A.E. van Vogt, whose endorsement of the book as a 'masterpiece' appeared prominently on the
cover, later confessed that he had been daunted by its size and had not
actually bothered to read it.[6] Hubbard always sent van Vogt and his
wife a Christmas card and that year he included a note boasting that it
had only taken him a month to write *Battlefield Earth*.

If Hubbard had lost his touch as a fiction writer, he was still
perfectly capable of adding, even at this late stage in his life, further
embellishments to his early career. 'I had, myself, somewhat of a
science background,' he wrote in the introduction, 'had done some
pioneer work in rockets and liquid gases, but I was studying the
branches of man's past knowledge at that time . . . For a while, before
and after World War Two, I was in rather steady association with the
new era of scientists, the boys who built the bomb . . .'

It was essential for Hubbard's reputation that *Battlefield Earth*
became a bestseller. The Church of Scientology guaranteed to buy
50,000 hardback copies, mounted a massive publicity campaign to
support the book and instructed Scientologists throughout the United
States to go out and buy at least two or three copies each. *Battlefield
Earth* duly made its debut on the major bestseller lists. Those
Scientologists who were beginning their prison sentences at around
that time no doubt found sufficient leisure hours in their cells to enjoy
their leader's latest œuvre. Mary Sue's second in command, Jane
Kember, was driven to prison by her friend Virginia Downsborough.
'It was pathetic really,' said Downsborough, 'even when she was
actually on her way to prison Jane still thought that Ron was going to
surface and fix everything. All she had done was what he had told her
to and she couldn't believe that he would betray her. It was
incredible.'[7]

Attorneys acting for Mary Sue had appealed, unsuccessfully, to the
Supreme Court to have her conviction overturned and in January
1983 a US district judge in Washington rejected her request to be sent
to a half-way house instead of prison. Mary Sue, who was then
fifty-one, sobbed in the courtroom and said she wanted to 'sincerely
and publicly apologize', but Judge Norma H. Johnson was unsympathetic, describing the offences as not only serious but heinous.
'Because of your leadership role,' she said, 'I find your degree of
culpability was great.' Mary Sue reported next day to the Federal

Correctional Institution in Lexington, Kentucky, to begin serving a four-year term.

Meanwhile, Mary Sue's stepson had filed a petition in Riverside, California, for the trusteeship of his father's estate, claiming that Hubbard was either dead or mentally incompetent. Nibs, who was then working as the manager of an apartment block in Carson City, Nevada, and taking home $650 a month, estimated the estate was worth $100 million, which was an indication of how little anyone knew of how much the Commodore was making out of the Church of Scientology – during 1982 alone, Hubbard raked in at least $40 million from various Scientology corporations.[8]

The petition claimed Hubbard 'has lived a life characterized by severe mental illness . . . consistent failure . . . and the use of false and fraudulent, oftentime criminal means, to cover up these failures and to acquire wealth, fame and power in order to destroy his perceived "enemies".' DeWolf further alleged that the church leaders were stealing millions of dollars' worth of gems and cash from his father's estate.[9] Attorneys acting on Mary Sue's behalf filed a counter-petition asserting that Nibs was 'simply trying to get his hands on his Dad's money'.

This intriguing litigation generated a flurry of media speculation about the fate of the founder of Scientology, but the question of whether Hubbard was dead or alive was quickly settled when the church produced a signed declaration with the Commodore's finger-prints on every page, authenticated by independent experts. Hubbard described his son's allegations as malicious, false and ill-founded. 'With respect to Ronald DeWolf,' he wrote, 'I consider him neither a friend nor a family member in the true sense of the word. Although biologically he is my son, his hostility and animosity to me are apparent and have been for years . . . I am not a missing person. I am in seclusion for my own choosing. My privacy is important to me, and I do not wish it or my affairs invaded in the manner permitted by this action. As Thoreau secluded himself by Walden Pond, so I have chosen to do in my own fashion.'

The court accepted the documents as proof that Hubbard was still alive and dismissed DeWolf's suit, but in his determination to blacken Hubbard's name, Nibs had clearly inherited something of his father's perseverance. He surfaced again in the June 1983 issue of *Penthouse* magazine, making even more sensational allegations – that Hubbard had been involved in black magic since the age of sixteen, believed himself to be Satan, wanted to become the most powerful being in the universe, smuggled gold and drugs, was a sadist and a KGB agent. He had bought Saint Hill Manor, Nibs claimed, with money obtained from the Russians. 'Black magic is the inner core of Scientology,' Nibs stressed, 'and it is probably the only part of Scientology that really works. Also, you've got to realize that my father did not worship Satan. He thought he *was* Satan.'

It was wild stuff, perhaps a little too wild. Just like his father, Nibs lacked subtlety. Had he been more restrained, the interview might have made an impact. Instead, it simply strained the reader's credulity to such an extent that it was hard to decide who was the most deranged – L. Ron Hubbard Senior or L. Ron Hubbard Junior. In November 1983, an optimistic letter from Ron was distributed to Scientologists around the world to tell them how well everything was going. He described himself as 'ecstatic' with the state of management and confident that their legal problems were behind them. 'Those who were harassing Scientology in the past', he wrote, 'are beginning to present a panorama of coattails.' He explained that he had been working on very advanced research for the last two years which was 'opening the sky to heights not previously envisioned' and concluded, 'So I wanted to say hello and to tell you the results of an overview of the game and, boy, does that future look good . . . Love, Ron.'

Ron did not bother to mention how Mary Sue was making out at the Federal Correctional Institution in Kentucky, neither did he comment on the time-bomb ticking away under the church in the slight form of his disenchanted archivist and biographer Gerry Armstrong, who had taken thousands of documents with him when he left Scientology – documents that *proved* the founder of Scientology was a charlatan and a liar.

For many months church attorneys had been trying to force Armstrong to return the material, having initially succeeded in having the documents placed under court seal. In May 1984, the issue went to trial at Los Angeles Superior Court before Judge Paul G. Breckenridge. A procession of witnesses trooped into the courtroom to tell their dismal stories about life in Scientology, at the end of which the judge refused to order the return of the documents and delivered a damning verdict on Scientology: 'The organization clearly is schizophrenic and paranoid, and this bizarre combination seems to be a reflection of its founder. The evidence portrays a man who has been virtually a pathological liar when it comes to his history, background and achievements. The writings and documents in evidence additionally reflect his egoism, greed, avarice, lust for power, and vindictiveness and aggressiveness against persons perceived by him to be disloyal or hostile.

'At the same time it appears that he is charismatic and highly capable of motivating, organizing, controlling, manipulating and inspiring his adherents. He has been referred to during the trial as a "genius", a "revered person", a man who was "viewed by his followers in awe". Obviously, he is and has been a very complex person and that complexity is further reflected in his alter ego, the Church of Scientology . . . He has, of course, chosen to go into seclusion, but . . . seclusion has its light and dark side too. It adds to his mystique, and yet shields him from accountability and subpoena or service of summons.'

The judge then turned to Mary Sue, who had been released after serving a year of her prison sentence and had given evidence during the hearing: 'On the one hand she certainly appeared to be a pathetic individual. She was forced from her post as Controller, convicted and imprisoned as a felon, and deserted by her husband. On the other hand her credibility leaves much to be desired. She struck the familiar pose of not seeing, hearing, or knowing any evil . . .'

The Church of Scientology immediately appealed against the decision of the court, ensuring that the documents remained under seal and unavailable to hordes of waiting newspapermen, at least for the time being.

Three weeks later, a judge in the High Court in London joined in the attack by memorably branding Scientology as 'immoral, socially obnoxious, corrupt, sinister and dangerous' and describing the behaviour of Hubbard and his aides as 'grimly reminiscent of the ranting and bullying of Hitler and his henchmen'.

Mr Justice Latey had been hearing a case involving a custody dispute over the children of a practising Scientologist and his wife, who had broken away from the cult. Awarding custody to the mother, the judge gave Scientology short shrift: 'It is corrupt because it is based on lies and deceit and had as its real objective money and power for Mr Hubbard, his wife and those close to him at the top. It is sinister because it indulges in infamous practices both to its adherents who do not toe the line unquestioningly and to those outside who criticize or oppose it. It is dangerous because it is out to capture people, especially children and impressionably young people, and indoctrinate and brainwash them so that they become the unquestioning captives and tools of the cult, withdrawn from ordinary thought, living and relationship with others.' As to the Hubbards, the judge considered the evidence clear and conclusive: 'Mr Hubbard is a charlatan and worse, as are his wife Mary Sue Hubbard and the clique at the top, privy to the cult's activities.'

Following the teaching of L. Ron Hubbard, most Scientologists assumed that such attacks were orchestrated and engineered by their multitude of enemies. In 1985, when CBS's '60 minutes' investigated Scientology and presenter Mike Wallace quoted the 'schizophrenic and paranoid' decision of Judge Breckenridge, the Reverend Heber Jentzsch, president of the Church of Scientology, had a ready, if incomprehensible, reply: 'I traced back where that came from, this whole schizophrenic paranoia concept that he has. It came from Interpol. At that time, the president of Interpol was a former SS officer, Paul Dickopf. And to find that Judge Breckenridge quoted a Nazi SS officer as the authority on Scientology, I find unconscionable . . .'

On 19 January 1986, Scientologists around the world received their last message from L. Ron Hubbard. In Flag Order number 3879, headed 'The Sea Org and The Future', he announced that he was promoting himself to the rank of Admiral. Alongside the procla- mation, in a Scientology magazine, was a colour photograph of the grey-haired Commodore in his Sea Org peaked cap. He was grinning broadly, with a definite twinkle in his eyes. He had never looked more like Puck.

Creston, population 270, elevation 1110 feet, straddles a dusty road junction twenty miles north of the old mission town of San Luis Obispo in California. On the main streeet, which at most times of the day is deserted, there may be found the Loading Chute Steak Dining-Room, Creston Realty, a post office with a flagpole and two phone booths outside and a ramshackle wooden building with peeling red paint and a slipped sign proclaiming it to be the Long Branch general store. Rusting automobile hulks sprouting weeds, flea-bitten tethered horses and satellite dishes are a common feature in the gardens of the unassuming houses thereabouts.

On O'Donovan Road, which runs south off the main street, there is a small library, a school, the Creston Community Church Bible Classroom and the meeting hall of Creston Women's Club. Attached to the front of the meeting hall is a notice board offering for sale a horse, a pick-up and a '69 sedan, both these last 'needing work'. It is evident that the good people of Creston have yet to share the affluence to be seen displayed so ostentatiously elsewhere in California.

But further along O'Donovan Road, the rural landscape is clearly manicured by money. Rolling hills of green velvet are stitched with white picket fences and the houses stand well back from the road behind meadows sprinkled with wild daisies and studded with twisted oak trees. Four miles out of the town there is a graded track off to the right and a metal sign indicates it is a private road leading to the Emmanuel Conference Centre. This track winds up the hillside along the edge of the Whispering Winds Ranch, a 160-acre spread which, according to local gossip, was once owned by the actor Robert Mitchum. The gates to the ranch may be found after about 400 yards and the track then forks to a small cedarwood house on the right, continuing on the left up the hill to the Camp Emmanuel ecumenical retreat. It is a quiet place, a perfect place to hide.

In the summer of 1983 the ranch was bought by a young couple who called themselves Lisa and Mike Mitchell. The San Luis Obispo real estate agent involved in the sale guessed by his accent that Mitchell was from New York. He walked into the office straight off the street and said he wanted to buy a large, secluded ranch where he could breed Akitas, a rare Japanese dog. The realtor took Mitchell out to look at Whispering Winds, which was on the market for $700,000. He examined the ranch house with great care, even climbing up into the roof, where he seemed disconcerted by the insulation. 'I'll have to get that out of there,' he told the agent, explaining that his wife was allergic to fibreglass. Nevertheless, he liked the property and said he would buy it. Money was no problem – he had just come into an inheritance worth several million dollars. Good as his word, Mitchell paid the full price in cash, with thirty cashier's cheques drawn on several California banks.[10]

The Mitchells moved into the ranch shortly afterwards, along with their elderly father. They kept very much to themselves, avoiding all contact with their neighbours. Maxine Kuehl and Shirley Terry, who ran Camp Emmanuel, rarely spoke to either of them and knew nothing of the old man except that his name was Jack. Robert Whaley, a retired marketing executive from New York who lived in the cedar house overlooking Whispering Winds, similarly saw little of them, although he was intrigued by what was going on.

It seemed to Whaley that his new neighbours had more money than sense. The three-level ranch house was gutted and re-modelled not once, but several times. A lake in front of the house was widened and deepened and stocked with bass and catfish. A race-horse track, with an observation tower and viewing stands, was built to one side of the house and never used. Miles of white picket fence went up, either following the contours of the land or running absolutely straight. One section of fence was torn down three or four times, apparently because it was not straight enough. Thoroughbred horses, buffalo and llamas were soon grazing in the fenced paddocks, and swans and geese graced the lake.

'I was amazed how much they were spending on the place,' said Whaley. 'There was absolutely no regard for expense. When they were having new irrigation lines installed, they put in a twelve-inch pipe, big enough for a town. None of them was very friendly, but I once asked Mitchell who was doing all the planning and he said his wife's father, Jack, was handling most of it as he used to be a civil engineer.'[11]

While the renovations were under way, Jack lived in a $150,000 Bluebird motor home parked on the property, but he could often be seen pottering around in baggy blue pants and a yellow straw hat, taking photographs. He was overweight, and with his white hair and white beard, reminded Whaley of Kentucky Chicken's Colonel Sanders. Once Whaley walked across to Whispering Winds to see if he could borrow a tool and surprised the old man in the stable. Jack was busy filing a piece of metal and was evidently not pleased to see his neighbour: he glared suspiciously at Whaley for a second, then scurried off into a workshop without a word, locking the door behind him.

The incident did not bother Whaley overmuch; he preferred to keep to himself anyway. He used to work in the magazine business in New York and was accustomed to oddball characters. Before the war, he had been a marketing executive for science-fiction pulps and had known most of the leading writers, although there was nothing about the old man with a beard that struck a chord.

One other thing he thought was rather odd about the folk across the way was that they rarely had visitors, except at night. He would often see headlights coming up the track late and turning through the gates of Whispering Winds. Usually it was just one car, but on the evening of 24 January 1986 there seemed to be cars coming and going all night . . .

The telephone was already ringing when Irene Reis, co-owner of the Reis Chapel in San Luis Obispo, arrived for work on the morning of Saturday 25 January. A voice at the other end of the line identified himself as Earle Cooley, an attorney, and asked if they did cremations. Mrs Reis replied that they did, although the crematory was usually closed at weekends. Special arrangements could be made if necessary. Cooley then asked if a body could be collected from the Whispering Winds Ranch on the O'Donovan Road in Creston. Irene's husband, Gene, drove the hearse out to Creston, not imagining it was anything but a routine job.

Cooley accompanied the body back to San Luis Obispo. At the Reis Chapel, a tasteful white adobe building with a red pantile roof on Nipomo Street, he asked Mrs Reis if arrangements could be made for an 'immediate cremation'. He presented a death certificate signed by a Gene Denk of Los Angeles certifying the cause of death as cerebral haemorrhage and a certificate of religious belief forbidding an autopsy. It was not until Mrs Reis looked at the documents that she realized the body lying in her chapel was that of L. Ron Hubbard.

Mrs Reis knew enough about Hubbard to insist on informing the San Luis Obispo Country sheriff-coroner. Deputy coroner Don Hines arrived at the Reis Chapel within a few minutes. No one had had any idea that Hubbard was in the vicinity and Hines wanted to make sure that everything was done by the book – it was not every day that a 'notorious recluse' turned up in San Luis Obispo. Hines said that no cremation could take place until an independent pathologist had examined the body. He also ordered the body to be photographed and fingerprinted to ensure positive identifications. (Later the fingerprints were revealed to match those on file at the FBI and the Department of Justice.) It was three-thirty in the afternoon before Hines was satisfied and agreed to release the body for cremation. On the following day, the ashes of L. Ron Hubbard were scattered on the Pacific from a small boat.

The news of the death of the founder of Scientology was broken to 1800 of his followers hastily gathered in the Hollywood Palladium on the afternoon of Monday, 27 January. David Miscavige made the announcement that Ron had moved on to his next level of research, a level beyond the imagination and in a state exterior to the body: 'Thus, at 2000 hours, Friday 24 January 1986, L. Ron Hubbard discarded the body he had used in this lifetime for seventy-four years, ten months and eleven days. The body he had used to facilitate his existence in this universe had ceased to be useful and in fact had become an impediment to the work he now must do outside its confines. The being we knew as L. Ron Hubbard still exists. Although you may feel grief, understand that he did not, and does not now. He has simply moved on to his next step. LRH in fact used this lifetime and body we knew to accomplish what no man has ever accomplished – he unlocked the mysteries of life and gave us the tools so we could free ourselves and our fellow men . . .'

At a press conference later that day, it was revealed that Hubbard had made a will on the day before his death leaving the bulk of his fortune, 'tens of millions of dollars', to the church. Generous provision had been made, it was said, for his wife and 'certain of his children'. Nibs, predictably, got nothing. Nor did Alexis, the daugher he denied was his.

There are those who still believe that Hubbard died years earlier and that his death was covered up by the messengers while they consolidated their control over the church.

There are those who still believe that Hubbard will soon be entering another body, or might even have done so already, prior to resuming his position as the head of Scientology.

There are those who still believe that, for all his faults, Hubbard made a significant contribution to helping his fellow men.

And there are those who now believe, sadly, that they were the unwitting victims of one of the most successful and colourful confidence tricksters of the twentieth century.

Notes

Chapter One

1 *Oregon Journal*, 22 Apr 1943
2 *Mission Into Time*, published by the Church of Scientology, 1973
3 Letter to author, 25 May 1986
4 1938 biography of L. R. Hubbard by Arthur J. Burks, president American Fiction Guild
5 Interview Andrew Richardson, Helena, Montana
6 Harry Ross Hubbard navy record
7 *Facts About L. Ron Hubbard – Things You Should Know*, Flag Divisional Directive, 8 Mar 1974
8 *Mission Into Time*
9 Letter to author, 4 Mar 1986/US Govt Memorandum, 16 Nov 1966
10 Letter to author, 1 Feb 1986

Chapter Two

1 *Facts About L. Ron Hubbard*
2 *What Is Scientology?* 1978
3 *Ibid*
4 LRH in *Scientology – A New Slant On Life*
5 *Facts About L. Ron Hubbard*
6 Letter to author fm Montana Historical Society, 24 Mar 1986
7 Interview Gorham Roberts, Helena, Apr 1986
8 Interview Mrs Margaret Roberts, Helena, Apr 1986
9 H. R. Hubbard navy record

Chapter Three

1 Deck log, *USS Gold Star*
2 L. R. Hubbard Service Record Book, US Marine Corps
3 *Ibid*
4 Unidentified newspaper clipping
5 Letter fm H. R. Hubbard to Dean of South Eastern University, 1930
6 Certified airman's file, Federal Aviation Administration, 12 May 1986

7 *Ibid*
8 L. R. Hubbard Service Record Book, US Marine Corps
9 *Preble County News*, 21 July 1983, (reprint of original article)
10 *Adventure*, 1 October 1935
11 The *Hatchet*, 24 May 1932
12 Letter fm Oceanographic Office, Department of Navy, 22 June 1970
13 Letter to author fm University of Michigan, 23 Apr 1986
14 Letter to author fm Director of Archives, *The New York Times*, 14 April 1986
15 Report fm Clifford Kaye, US Geological Survey, 22 June 1970
16 Letter fm Dept of Natural Resources, San Juan, 10 Oct 1979
17 Letter fm Dr Meyerhoff, 11 Feb 1980
18 *Adventure*, 1 October 1935

Chapter Four

1 Letter to author fm Mrs Catherine Gillespie, Dec 1986
2 Certified airman's file
3 *Ibid*
4 Interview Mrs Roberts
5 Gruber, Frank, *The Pulp Jungle*, 1967
6 Certified airman's file
7 *Adventure*, 10 October 1935
8 Interview Robert Macdonald Ford, Olympia, Washington, 1 Sept 1986
9 *Facts About L. Ron Hubbard*
10 L. Ron Hubbard autobiographical notes, 1974
11 *Rocky Mountain News*, 20 February 1983
12 *A Brief Biography of L. Ron Hubbard*, 1963
13 Interview Ford

Chapter Five

1 Williamson, Jack, *Child of Wonder*, 1985

2 Asimov, Isaac, *In Memory Yet Green*, 1979
3 *Ron the Writer* Public Affairs Dept, Author Services Inc, 1982
4 *The John W. Campbell Letters, Vol I*, 1985
5 *Ron the Writer*
6 *Mission Into Time*
7 *Ibid*
8 The *Aberee*, December 1961
9 Interview Ford
10 *The John W. Campbell Letters*
11 Letter fm H. Latane Lewis II, 14 February 1938
12 Sprague de Camp, L., *Elron of the City of Brass (Fantastic*, August 1975) & *Science Fiction Handbook*, 1953
13 Asimov, op-cit.
14 Aldiss, Brian, *Trillion Year Spree*, 1986
15 *Fantastic*, August 1975
16 FBI Files on L. R. Hubbard
17 Interview Mrs Roberts
18 Letter to author fm *National Geographic*, 3 Mar 1986
19 Interview Ford

Chapter Six

1 Memorandum fm Hubbard to Magnuson, 21 July 1941
2 Memorandum for Asst Hydrographer, 22 October 1941
3 Despatch fm US Naval Attaché, Melbourne, 14 February 1942
4 Memorandum fm CO *USS YP-422*, 12 September 1942
5 Moulton testimony in Church of Scientology *v.* Armstrong, 21 May 1984
6 *USS PC-815* Action Report, 24 May 1943
7 Memorandum fm Commander NW Sea Frontier, 8 June 1943
8 Record of proceedings, Board of Investigation, *USS PC -815*, 30 June 1943
9 Letter of admonition from Commander, Fleet Operational Training Command, Pacific, 15 July 1943
10 Report on the Fitness of Officers, 29 May – 7 July 1943

11 Letter fm L.R. Hubbard Junior, 26 January 1973
12 L. Ron Hubbard autobiographical notes, 1972
13 *Ron The Writer*
14 *Rocky Mountain News*, 20 February 1983
15 Deck log *USS Algol*, National Archives
16 Foreword to *Godbody* by Theodore Sturgeon, 1986
17 Asimov *op.cit*
18 Williamson *op. cit*
19 Hubbard, L.R., *My Philosphy*, 1965

Chapter Seven

1 L. R. Hubbard Claim No 7017422, Veterans Administration archives
2 Rogers, Alva, *Darkhouse*, 1962
3 Symonds, John, *The Great Beast*, 1971
4 Letter fm L. Sprague de Camp to Symonds, 5 August 1952
5 Interview Nieson Himmel, Los Angeles, 14 August 1986
6 Letter to author fm Jack Williamson, 1 November 1986
7 Rogers, *op. cit.*
8 *Ibid*
9 Interview Himmel
10 Grant, Kenneth, *The Magical Revival*, 1972
11 Interview Himmel
12 Symonds, *op.cit.*
13 Rogers, *op.cit.*
14 Parsons file, OTO archives, New York
15 Crowley, Aleister, *The Book of the Law*
16 Grant, *op.cit.*
17 Parsons *v.* Hubbard and Northrup, Case No 101634, Circuit Court, Dade County, Florida
18 *Book of Babalon*, OTO archives, New York
19 *Ibid*
20 Parsons, John, 'Magical Record', OTO archives, New York
21 Symonds, *op.cit.*
22 Letter to author fm Mrs Catherine Gillespie, November 1986
23 Hubbard file, VA archives
24 L. R. Hubbard navy record
25 OTO archives, New York

26 *Ibid*
27 Grant, *op.cit.*
28 Parsons *v.* Hubbard and Northrup
29 Hubbard file, VA archives
30 *Pasadena Star News*, 21 June 1952 and 5 July 1952

Chapter Eight

1 Report of Physical Examination, VA File, 19 September 1946
2 Transcript Church of Scientology *v.* Armstrong
3 Hubbard file, VA archives
4 Interview Merwin, Los Angeles, August 1986
5 *The John W. Campbell Letters, Vol I*
6 Interview Mrs Roberts
7 Interview Ford
8 Interview Forrest Ackerman, Hollywood, 30 July 1986
9 Hubbard file, VA archives
10 *Ibid*
11 *Shangri-La*, LASFAS club organ, No 6, May-June 1948
12 Interview Arthur Jean Cox, Los Angeles, 18 August 1986
13 Interview A. E. van Vogt, Los Angeles, 22 July 1986
14 FBI memo, 13 April 1967
15 L. R. Hubbard navy record

Chapter Nine

1 Wollheim, Donald, *The Universe Makers*, 1972
2 *Los Angeles Times*, 27 August 1978
3 Winter, Joseph A. *A Doctor's Report on Dianetics*, 1951
4 *Explorers Journal*, Winter/Spring 1950
5 Hubbard autobiographical notes, 1972
6 Asimov, *op. cit.* 7 *op. cit.*
7 Williamson, *op. cit.*
8 *Fantastic*, August 1975
9 Interview Jack Horner, Santa Monica, 24 July 1986
10 Interview Ackerman
11 *Scientific American*, Jan 1951
12 *New Republic,* 14 August 1950
13 *LOOK,* 5 December 1950
14 *The New York Times*, 6 August 1950
15 *Newsweek*, No 36, August 1950
16 *Parade*, 29 October 1950

17 *Los Angeles Daily News* 6 September 1950

Chapter Ten

1 Interview Cox and letter to Martin Gardner, 30 April 1952
2 Interview Ackerman
3 Evans, Christopher, *Cults of Unreason*, 1973
4 Interview A. E. van Vogt
5 Interviews Barbara Kaye, Los Angeles, 28 July – 5 August 1986
6 Interview Perry Chapdelaine, Nashville, 25 April 1986
7 Winter, *op. cit.*
8 Letter to B. Kaye fm Hubbard, 21 Oct 1951
9 US Govt memo to director FBI fm SAC Newark, 21 March 1951
10 Interview Horner
11 Van Vogt, A.E., *Dianetics and the Professions*, 1953
12 Maloney, John W., *A Factual Report on Dianetics*, February 1952
13 Interview Richard de Mille, Santa Barbara, 25 July 1986
14 US Govt memo to Director FBI fm SAC Chicago, 27 April 1951
15 Letter in FBI files, 10 Mar 1951
16 US Govt memo 62-116151-70, 7 Mar 1951
17 Airgram to Legal Attaché, Havana, 27 April 1951
18 Divorce complaint No. D 414498, 23 April 1951, Los Angeles Superior Court
19 Interview Caryl Warner, Hollywood, August 1986

Chapter Eleven

1 Interview de Mille
2 Diane Lewis research report, Wichita January 1987
3 *Wichita Eagle-Beacon*, 26 Mar 1983
4 FBI memo, 15 May 1951
5 Interviews Kaye
6 FBI file, 14 May 1951
7 Interview de Mille
8 Case No A36594, District Court of Sedgwick County, Kansas
9 O'Brien, Helen, *Dianetics in Limbo*, 1966
10 Telephone interviews with Helen O'Brien, Los Angeles, August 1986

11 Interview Chapdelaine
12 Hubbard file, VA archives
13 Purcell, Don, *Dianetics Today*, January 1954
14 Interview Moore, Wichita, November 1986
15 US Govt memos, 1 Oct 1951 and 16 Oct 1951
16 FBI Dn file 100-6136
17 Purcell, *op. cit.*
18 Hubbard Dianetic Foundation Inc in Bankruptcy, No 379-B-2, District Court of Kansas
19 Non-attributable interviews in Los Angeles, August 1986, and Haywards Heath, Sussex, May 1986

Chapter Twelve

1 *What Is Scientology?*
2 Ability No. 81, 1959
3 Hubbard L. Ron, *"Have You Lived Before This Life?"* 1968
4 Anderson, Kevin V. *Report of the Board of Inquiry Into Scientology*, Australia, 1965
5 Wilson, Bryan, *Religious Sects*, 1970
6 Interview Carmen D'Alessio, London Jan 1986
7 Interviews O'Brien
8 Interview Fred Stansfield, Burbank, July 1986
9 Evidence of L. Ron Hubbard Jr. at Clearwater hearings, May 1982
10 Bankruptcy file 23747, Federal Records Center, Philadelphia
11 Letter fm Hoover to Senator Homer Ferguson, 2 Mar 1953
12 Interview Ray Kemp, Palomar, Ca, Aug 1986
13 Interview Horner
14 Interview Galusha, Denver, Colorado, Mar 1986

Chapter Thirteen

1 FBI memo, 11 October 1957
2 FBI memo, 27 February 1957
3 HCO Technical Bulletin, Vol II, 1955
4 Interview Cyril Vosper, London, December 1985
5 Inteview Pam Kemp, Palomar, Ca, Aug 1986
6 Founding Church of Scientology v. US Court of Claims No. 221-61

7 Anderson, *op. cit.*
8 FBI Airtel, 7 August 1958
9 Interview Vosper
10 Interview Kemp

Chapter Fourteen

1 Interview Alan Larcombe, East Grinstead, November 1985
2 *Garden News*, 18 December 1959
3 Atack, *Hubbard through the looking glass*
4 Interview Joan Vidal, London, January 1986
5 Interview Mrs Roberts
6 Atack, *Hubbard through the looking glass*
7 Letter fm Mary Sue Hubbard to Marilyn Routsong, 4 February 1960
8 Interview George Hay, London, March 1987
9 HCO News Letter, 7 May 1962
10 Minutes of special staff meeting, HCO Washington, 29 August 1952

Chapter Fifteen

1 The Findings on the US Food and Drug Agency 1968
2 Anderson, *op. cit.*
3 *Saturday Evening Post*, 21 March 1964
4 Interview Ken Urquhart, Maclean, Va, Apr 1986
5 Interview Vosper
6 Anderson, *op. cit*
7 Wallis, Roy *The Road To Total Freedom*, London 1976
8 Foster, Sir John, *Enquiry into the Practice & Effects of Scientology*, London, 1971
9 Secretarial Executive Director, Office of LRH, 9 Feb 1966
10 The *People*, 20 Mar 1966
11 *Saxon Hamilton Journal*, Summer 1985
12 CIA files obtained via FOI
13 Rhodesia *Sunday Mail*, 22 May 1966
14 Interview McMaster, London, Mar 1986
15 CIA memo, 22 Aug 1966
16 Interview McMaster
17 CIA memo
18 Interview Kemp
19 Interview McMaster

Chapter Sixteen

1 Letter from assistant secretary, Explorers Club, 8 December 1966
2 Interview Kemp
3 *Mission Into Time*
4 Interview Virginia Downsborough, Santa Barbara, Ca, August 1986
5 Despatch fm LRH, 22 Apr 1967
6 Evans, Christopher, *Cults of Unreason*, London 1973
7 Interview Amos Jessup, San Diego, July 1986
8 Interview Hana Eltringham, Los Angeles, Mar 1986
9 HCO Policy Letter, 26 Sept 1967
10 Interview McMaster
11 The *People*, 21 February 1968

Chapter Seventeen

1 Interview Mary Maren, Los Angeles, August 1986
2 Interview Jessup
3 Interview Eltringham
4 Interview McMaster
5 Interview David Mayo, Palo Alto, August 1986
6 *Daily Mail*, 6 August 1968
7 Malko, George, *Scientology: The New Religion*, New York, 1970
8 Interview Jessup
9 Interview Urquhart
10 Interview McMaster
11 Forte, John, *The Commodore and the Colonels*, Corfu Tourist Publications and Enterprises, 1981
12 Letter fm Mary Sue Hubbard to Sir John Foster, 6 November 1969
13 Interview Kathy Cariotaki, San Diego, July 1986

Chapter Eighteen

1 Interview Urquhart
2 *Los Angeles Times*, 29 August 1970
3 The *Guardian*, 12 February 1980
4 Guardian Order, 16 December 1969
5 Flag Order of 1890, 26 March 1969
6 Affidavit of Gerald Armstrong, 19 March 1986
7 Testimony, Armstrong *v.* Church of Scientology
8 Interview Michael Goldstein, Denver, Co, March 1986

9 Interview Doreen Gillham, Malibu, August 1986
10 Interview Eltringham
11 Letter fm Sara Hollister; testimony Armstrong *v.* Church of Scientology
12 Jon Atack archives
13 Interview Jim Dincalci, Berkeley, Ca. August 1986
14 The O. J. Roos Story, 7 September 1984
15 *Los Angeles Times*, 29 August 1978
16 Letter fm Mary Sue Hubbard to Jane Kember, 2 September 1972

Chapter Nineteen

1 Interview Urquhart
2 Interview Dincalci
3 Interview Eltringham
4 Interview Kima Douglas, Oakland, California, Sept 1986
5 Interview Jill Goodman, New York, Mar 1986
6 Interview Gillham
7 Interview Gerald Armstrong, Boston, Feb 1986
8 Interview Tanya Burden, Boston, Feb 1986
9 L. R. Hubbard navy record
10 Interview Kathy Cariotaki, San Diego, July 1986
11 Interview Mrs Roberts
12 *Los Angeles Times*, 29 August 1978
13 Capt. Bill Robertson Debrief Transcript, May 1982
14 Interview Kemp

Chapter Twenty

1 Interview Frankie Freedman, Sherman Oaks, Ca, Aug 1986
2 Interview Dincalci
3 Interview Mayo
4 *Clearwater Sun*, 5 Dec 1975
5 GO order 261175, 26 Nov 1975
6 *St Petersburg Times*, 9 Jan 1980
7 Interview Douglas
8 Interview Alan Vos, Maclean, Va, March 1986
9 Officer's Report, D.R. No 76-57596, Las Vegas Metropolitan Police Department
10 Interview Ed Walters, Las Vegas, Aug 1986

11 Interview Dr Frank Gerbode, Palo
   Alto, Aug 1986

Chapter Twenty-One

1 Affidavit of Anne Rosenblum
2 Interview Dincalci
3 Lamont, Stewart, *Religion Inc*,
   London, 1986
4 Affidavits of Adelle & Ernest
   Hartwell *St Petersburg Times*, 9 Jan
   1980
5 Interview Douglas
6 Interview Armstrong
7 Interview Urquhart
8 Interview Mayo
9 Interview Walters
10 John Atack archives

Chapter Twenty-Two

1 *Forbes*, 27 October 1986
2 Interview Gillham
3 Interview Mayo
4 Testimony, Church of Scientology *v.*
   Armstrong
5 Newsletter of Center for Personal
   Achievement, 13 February 1984
6 Interview van Vogt
7 Interview Downsborough
8 *Forbes*, 27 October 1986
9 Case No. 47150, re the Estate of L.
   Ron Hubbard, Superior Court for the
   County of Riverside
10 San Luis Obispo Telegram-Tribune,
   30 January 1986
11 Interview Robert Whaley, Creston,
   August 1986

Bibliography

ALDISS, BRIAN, *Billion Year Spree* (Weidenfeld & Nicholson, London, 1973)

ANDERSON, KEVIN V., *Report of the Board of Inquiry into Scientology* (Government Printer, Melbourne, 1965)

ASIMOV, ISAAC, *In Memory Yet Green* (Doubleday, New York, 1979)

ATACK, JON, *Hubbard through the Looking Glass: Scientology Exposed* (Unpublished manuscript)

BECKSTEAD, GORDON, (ed) *Prologue to Survival* (Psychological Research Foundation, Phoenix, Arizona, 1952)

BRADDESDON, WALTER, *Scientology for the Millions* (Sherbourne, Los Angeles, 1969)

BURRELL, MAURICE, *Scientology: What it is and what it does* (Lakeland, London, 1970)

CHAPEDELAINE, PERRY ET AL, *The John W. Campbell Letters, Volume 1* (AC Projects, Franklin, Tennessee, 1985)

COHEN, DAVID, *Masters of the Occult* (Dodd Mead, 1971)

COLBERT, JOHN, An Evaluation of Dianetic Theory (Thesis for MSc in Education, City College, New York, 1951)

COOPER, PAULETTE, *The Scandal of Scientology* (Tower, New York, 1971)

DALTON, DAVID R., *Two Disparate Philosophies* (Regency, London, 1973)

DE CAMP, L. SPRAGUE, *Spirits, Stars and Spells* (Publisher not known, 1966)

DE MILLE, RICHARD, *Introduction to Scientology* (Scientology Council, Sequioa University, California, 1953)

ELLWOOD, ROBERT S., *Religious and Spiritual Groups in Modern America* (Prentice Hall, New Jersey, 1973)

EVANS, CHRISTOPHER, *Cults of Unreason* (Harrap, London, 1973)

FISCHER, HARVEY JAY, *Dianetic Therapy: An Experimental Evaluation* (Unpublished PhD dissertation, School of Education, New York University, 1953)

FOSTER, SIR JOHN, *Enquiry into the Practice and Effects of Scientology* (HMSO, London, 1971)

GARDNER, MARTIN, *Fads and Fallacies in the Name of Science* (Dover Publications, New York, 1957)

GARRISON, OMAR V., *Hidden Story of Scientology* (Arlington Books, London, 1957)

GOODSTONE, TONY (ED), *The Pulps: Fifty Years of American Pop Culture* (Chelsea House, New York, 1970)

GRANT, KENNETH, *The Magical Revival* (Muller, London, 1972)

GRUBER, FRANK, *The Pulp Jungle* (Sherbourne Press, Los Angeles, 1967)

HORNER, JACK, *Dianology: A Better Bridge to Personal Creative Freedom* (The Association of International Dianologists, California, 1970)

– *Summary of Scientology* (HASI, London, 1956)

HUBBARD, L. RON, *Dianetics: The Modern Science of Mental Health* (Hermitage House, New York, 1950)

– *Science of Survival* (Hubbard Dianetic Foundation, Wichita, 1950)

– *Scientology 8-8008* (Publications Organisation World-Wide, 1953)

– *The Story of Dianetics and Scientology* (Hubbard Communications Office, London 1958)

– *Scientology – A New Slant on Life* (AOH DK Publications, Denmark, 1965)

– *Dianetics: The Evolution of a Science* (Publications Organisation World-Wide, 1968)

- *The Organisation Executive Course* (Scientology Publications Organisation, Denmark, 1970)
- *Mission Into Time* (American St Hill Organisation, Los Angeles, 1973)
- *Volunteer Ministers Handbook* (Church of Scientology, California, 1976)
- *What Is Scientology?* (Church of Scientology, California, 1978)
- *Notes on the Lectures of L. Ron Hubbard* (Hubbard Communications Office, East Grinstead, 1982)
- *The Dynamics of Life* (new Era Publications, Denmark, 1983)
- *Battlefield Earth* (NE Publications, Tonbridge, Kent, 1982)

KAUFMAN, ROBERT, *Inside Scientology* (Olympia Press, London, 1972)

KING, FRANCIS, *Ritual Magic in England* (Neville Spearman, London, 1968)
- *Magical World of Aleister Crowley* (Neville Spearman, London, 1970)

KOTZE, G. P. C. ET AL, *Report of the Commission of Enquiry into Scientology* (Government Printer, Pretoria, South Africa, 1973)

LAMONT, STEWART, *Religion Inc* (Harrap, London, 1986)

LEE, JOHN A., *Sectarian Healers and Hypnotherapy* (Queens Press, Toronto, 1970)

LIFTON, ROBERT, *Thought Reform and Psychology of Totalism* (1961)

MALKO, GEORGE, *Scientology: The Now Religion* (Dell, New York, 1970)

MARTIN, WALTER, *The Kingdom of the Cults* (Bethany House, Minneapolis, 1984)

O'BRIEN, HELEN, *Dianetics in Limbo* (Whitmore, Philadelphia, 1966)

POWLES, SIR GUY RICHARDSON and DUMBLETON, E.V., *Report of the Commission of Inquiry into the Hubbard Scientology Organisation in New Zealand* (Government Printer, Wellington, 1969)

REYNOLDS, QUENTIN, *Fiction Factory* (Random House, New York, 1955)

ROGERS, ALVA, *Requiem for Astounding* (Advent Publishing, Chicago, 1964)

SARGANT, WILLIAM, *Battle for the Mind* (Pan Books, London, 1959)

SHAPIRO, DAVID, *Neurotic Styles* (Basic Books, New York, 1965)

SHARPE, REG, *This is Life* (Publications Organisation World-Wide, 1966)

SYMONDS, JOHN, *The Great Beast* (MacDonald, London, 1971)

VAN VOGT A. E., *Reflections* (Fictioneer Books, Lakemont, Georgia, 1975)

VOSPER, CYRIL, *The Mind Benders* (Neville, Spearman, London, 1971)

WALLIS, ROY, *The Road to Total Freedom* (Heinemann, London, 1976)

WILLIAMSON, JACK, *Wonder's Child: My Life in Science-Fiction* (Blue Jay Books, 1984)

WILSON, BRYAN R., *Religious Sects* (Weidenfeld & Nicholson, London, 1970)

WINTER, JOSEPH A., *A Doctor's Report of Dianetics: Theory and Therapy* (Julian Press, New York, 1951)

WOLLHEIM, DONALD, *The Universe Makers* (Victor Gollancz, London, 1972)

ZARETSKY, IRVING, and LEONE, MARK (EDS) *Religious Movements in Contemporary America* (Princeton University Press, 1974)

Index